CRITICAL SURVEY OF POETRY

African American Poets

Editor

Rosemary M. Canfield Reisman
Charleston Southern University

SALEM PRESS
A Division of EBSCO Publishing, Ipswich, Massachusetts

Cover photo:
Maya Angelou (©Daniel Coston/Retna Ltd./Corbis)

ISBN: 978-1-42983-645-6

CONTENTS

CONTRIBUTORS

Karley K. Adney
*University of Wisconsin,
Marathon County*

Paula C. Barnes
Hampton University

Cynthia S. Becerra
Humphreys College

Lindsay Christopher
University of Denver

Anita Price Davis
Converse College

Desiree Dreeuws
Sunland, California

Jack Ewing
Boise, Idaho

Thomas R. Feller
Nashville, Tennessee

Scott Giantvalley
*California State University,
Dominguez Hills*

Vincent F. A. Golphin
The Writing Company

Nelson Hathcock
Saint Xavier University

Sarah Hilbert
Pasadena, California

KaaVonia Hinton
Old Dominion University

Mary Hurd
*East Tennessee State
University*

Tracy Irons-Georges
Glendale, California

Maura Ives
Texas A&M University

Philip K. Jason
*United States Naval
Academy*

Rebecca Kuzins
Pasadena, California

William T. Lawlor
*University of Wisconsin-
Stevens Point*

Michael Loudon
Eastern Illinois University

Charmaine Allmon Mosby
Western Kentucky University

Allene Phy-Olsen
Austin Peay State University

Honora Rankine-Galloway
*University of Southern
Denmark*

Danny Robinson
Bloomsburg University

Alexa L. Sandmann
University of Toledo

John C. Shields
Illinois State University

Judith K. Taylor
*Northern Kentucky
University*

Betty Taylor-Thompson
Texas Southern University

Edward E. Waldron
Yankton College

Craig Werner
University of Wisconsin

Patricia A. R. Williams
Amherst College

Cynthia Wong
Western Illinois University

Gay Pitman Zieger
Santa Fe College

AFRICAN AMERICAN POETRY

The struggle for freedom—social, psychological, and aesthetic—is the distinguishing attribute of African American poetry from its origins during slavery through its pluralistic flowering in the twentieth century. Although the impact of the struggle has only intermittently been simple or direct, it has remained a constant presence, both for writers concentrating directly on the continuing oppression of the black community and for those forging highly individualistic poetic voices not primarily concerned with racial issues.

Generally, two basic "voices" characterize the African American poetic sensibility. First, black poets attempting to survive in a literary market dominated by white publishers and audiences have felt the need to demonstrate their ability to match the accomplishments of white poets in traditional forms. From the couplets of Phillis Wheatley through the sonnets of Claude McKay to the modernist montages of Robert Hayden to the rap and hip-hop stylings of Queen Latifah, Public Enemy, Ice-T, Mos Def, Tupac Shakur, and KRS-One, African American poets have mastered the full range of voices associated with the evolving poetic mainstream. Second, black poets have been equally concerned with forging distinctive voices reflecting both their individual sensibilities and the specifically African American cultural tradition.

This dual focus within the African American sensibility reflects the presence of what W. E. B. Du Bois identified as a "double-consciousness" that forces the black writer to perceive himself or herself as both an "American" and a "Negro." The greatest African American poets—Langston Hughes, Sterling A. Brown, Gwendolyn Brooks, Robert Hayden, Amiri Baraka, Maya Angelou, Rita Dove, Yusef Komunyakaa, and Kevin Powell—draw on this tension as a source of both formal and thematic power, helping them to construct a poetry that is at once unmistakably black and universally resonant.

CAGED EAGLES

From the beginning, African American poets have continually adjusted to and rebelled against the fact of double consciousness. To be sure, the rebellion and adjustment have varied in form with changing social circumstances. Nevertheless, Baraka's statement in his poetic drama *Bloodrites* (pr. 1970) that the aware black artist has always been concerned with helping his or her community attain "Identity, Purpose, Direction" seems accurate. Over a period of time, the precise emphasis has shifted among the terms, but the specific direction and purpose inevitably reflect the individual's or the era's conception of identity. To some extent, this raises the issue of whether the emphasis in "African American" belongs on "African" or on "American." Some poets, such as Baraka during his nationalist period, emphasize the African heritage and tend toward assertive and frequently separatist visions of purpose and direction. Others, such as Jean

Toomer in his late period, emphasize some version of the "American" ideal and embrace a variety of strategies for the purpose of reaching a truly integrated society.

Wheatley, the first important African American poet, was forced to confront this tension between African and American identities. As an "American" poet of the eighteenth century—before the political entity known as the United States was formed—her writing imitated the styles and themes of British masters such as John Milton, John Dryden, and Alexander Pope. Brought to America at age six, she experienced only a mild form of slavery in Philadelphia, because her owners, Thomas and Susannah Wheatley, felt deep affection for her and respected her gifts as a writer. Unlike other Wheatley servants, Phillis, treated more as a stepdaughter than as a servant, was exempted from routine duties and had a private room, books, and writing materials. At the same time, her career was hobbled by the blatant discrimination heaped on all "African" people. For example, in 1772, Susannah Wheatley sought patrons to help publish the then eighteen-year-old Phillis's first collection of twenty-eight poems. Colonial whites rejected the proposal because Phillis was a slave, forcing her to seek a publisher in London.

Although her poem "On Being Brought from Africa to America" views slavery as a "mercy," because it led her from "pagan" darkness to Christian light, she was never accepted as a poet on her own merits. However, in England, whose antislavery movement was stronger than that of the colonies, people of wealth and stature, such as the countess of Huntingdon and the earl of Dartmouth, embraced the poet. Lady Huntingdon, to whom Wheatley's first volume, *Poems on Various Subjects, Religious and Moral* (1773), was dedicated, financed the publication and put Phillis's picture on the frontispiece. Wheatley's work was advertised as the product of a "sable muse," and she was presented as a curiosity; the racism of the times made it impossible for her to be accepted as a poet who was as accomplished as her white contemporaries. That sentiment was made clear by Thomas Jefferson in his *Notes on the State of Virginia* (1777): "Religion indeed has produced a Phyllis Whately [sic] but it could not produce a poet. The compositions published under her name are below the dignity of criticism." Those sentiments are counterbalanced by a contemporary, Jupiter Hammon, also a slave poet, who in "An Address to Miss Phillis Whealy [sic]" praised her talent and influence as part of God's providence:

> While thousands tossed by the sea,
>   And others settled down,
> God's tender mercy set thee free,
>   From dangers that come down.

Other early writers, such as George Moses Horton and Frances Watkins Harper, shared a common purpose in their antislavery poetry but rarely escaped the confines of religious and political themes acceptable to the abolitionist journals that published their work. The pressures on the African American poet became even more oppressive during the post-Reconstruction era as the South "reconquered" black people, in part by establishing control over the literary image of slavery. "Plantation Tradition" portrayed contented slaves and benevolent masters living in pastoral harmony. Paul Laurence Dunbar attained wide popularity in the late nineteenth and early twentieth centuries, but only by acquiescing partially in the white audience's stereotypical preconceptions concerning the proper style (slave dialect) and tones (humor or pathos) for poetry dealing with black characters.

A VOICE OF THEIR OWN

Spearheading the first open poetic rebellion against imposed stereotypes, James Weldon Johnson, a close friend of Dunbar, mildly rejected Dunbar's dialect poetry in his preface to *The Book of American Negro Poetry* (1922), which issued a call for "a form that will express the racial spirit by symbols from within rather than by symbols from without." He explained:

> The newer Negro poets discard dialect; much of the subject matter which went into the making of traditional dialect poetry, 'possums, watermelons, etc., they have discarded altogether, at least, as poetical material. This tendency will, no doubt, be regretted by the majority of white readers; and indeed, it would be a distinct loss if the American Negro poets threw away this quaint and musical folk-speech as a medium of expression. And yet, after all, these poets are working through a problem not realized by the reader, and perhaps, by many of these poets themselves not realized consciously. They are trying to break away, not from the Negro dialect itself, but the limitations on the Negro dialect imposed by the fixing effects of long convention.
>
> The Negro in the United States has achieved or been placed in a certain artistic niche. When he is thought of artistically, it is as a happy-go-lucky, singing, shuffling, banjo-picking being or as a more or less pathetic figure. The African American poet realizes that there are phases of Negro life in the United States which cannot be treated in the dialect either adequately or artistically. Take, for example, the phases rising out of life in Harlem, that most wonderful Negro city in the world. I do not deny that a Negro in a log cabin is more picturesque than a Negro in a Harlem flat, but the Negro is here, and he is part of a group growing everywhere in the country, a group whose ideals are becoming increasingly more vital than those of the traditionally artistic group, even if its members are less picturesque.

HARLEM RENAISSANCE

This call was heeded by the poets of the Harlem Renaissance, who took advantage of the development of large black population centers in the North during the Great Northern Migration of blacks from the rural South to the urban North during the 1910's and 1920's. Where earlier poets lived either among largely illiterate slave populations or in white communities, the New Negroes—as Alain Locke, one of the first major black critics, labeled the writers of the movement—seized the opportunity to establish a sense of identity for a sizable black audience. Locke viewed the work of poets such as Claude McKay, Countée Cullen, and Jean Toomer as a clear indication that blacks were preparing for a full entry into the American cultural mainstream.

The support given Harlem Renaissance writers by such white artists and patrons as Carl Van Vechten and Nancy Cunard, however, considerably complicated the era's achievement. On one hand, it appeared to herald the merging predicted by Locke. On the other, it pressured individual black writers to validate the exoticism frequently associated with black life by the white onlookers. Cullen's "Heritage," with its well-known refrain "What is Africa to me?," reflects the sometimes arbitrarily enforced consciousness of Africa that pervades the decade. African American artists confronted with white statements such as Eugene O'Neill's "All God's Chillun Got Wings" could not help remaining acutely aware that they, like Wheatley 150 years earlier, were cast more as primitive curiosities than as sophisticated artists. However, an expansion in the American literary canon and evolution in African American literature could not be denied. It was celebrated in the March, 1925, issue of Van Vechten's literary journal, *Survey Graphic*, guest-edited by Locke, who was then a Howard University philosophy professor.

The first flowering of Harlem as an artistic center came to an end with the Great Depression of the 1930's, which redirected African American creative energies toward political concerns. The end of prosperity brought a return of hard times to the African American community and put an end to the relatively easy access to print for aspiring black writers.

THE 1930'S

If the Harlem Renaissance was largely concerned with questions of identity, the writing in Hughes's *A New Song* (1938) and Brown's *Southern Road* (1932) reflects a new concern with the purpose and direction of both black artists and black masses. Hughes had earlier addressed the caution in an essay, "The Negro Artist and the Racial Mountain," published in the June 23, 1926, issue of *The Nation*:

> The Negro artist works against an undertow of sharp criticism from his own group and unintentional bribes from the whites. But in spite of the Nordicized Negro intelligentsia and the desires of some white editors we have an honest American Negro literature already with us. . . . I am ashamed for the black poet who says, "I want to be a poet, not a Negro poet," as though his own racial world were not as interesting as any other world. An artist must be free to choose what he does, certainly, but he must also never be afraid to do what he might choose.

Whereas many of the Harlem Renaissance writers had accepted Du Bois's vision of a "talented tenth" who would lead the community out of cultural bondage, the 1930's writers revitalized the African American tradition that perceived the source of power—

poetic and political—in traditions of the "folk" community. Margaret Walker's "For My People" expresses the ideal community "pulsing in our spirits and our blood." This emphasis sometimes coincided or overlapped with the proletarian and leftist orientation that dominated African American fiction of the period. Again external events, this time World War II and the "sell-out" of blacks by the American Communist Party, brought an end to an artistic era.

THE POSTWAR ERA

The post-World War II period of African American poetry is more difficult to define in clear-cut terms. Many new poets became active, especially during the 1960's and 1970's, while poets such as Hughes and Brown, who had begun their careers earlier, continued as active forces. Nevertheless, it is generally accurate to refer to the period from the late 1940's through the early 1960's as one of universalism and integration, and that of the mid-1960's through the mid-1970's as one of self-assertion and separatism.

The return of prosperity, landmark court decisions, and the decline of legal segregation in the face of nonviolent protest movements created the feeling during the early postwar period that African American culture might finally be admitted into the American mainstream on an equal footing. Poets such as Brooks, who became the first black person to win the Pulitzer Prize in poetry—for *Annie Allen* (1949)—and Hayden, who later became the first black Library of Congress poet, wrote poetry that was designed to communicate to all readers, regardless of their racial backgrounds and experiences. Neither poet abandoned black materials or traditions, but neither presented a surface texture that would present difficulties for an attentive white reader. Brooks's poem "Mentors" typifies the dominant style of the "universalist" period. It can be read with equal validity as a meditation on death, a comment on the influence of artistic predecessors, a commitment to remember the suffering of the slave community, and a character study of a soldier returning home from war.

The universalist period also marked the first major assertion of modernism in black poetry. Although both Hughes and Toomer had earlier used modernist devices, neither was perceived as part of the mainstream of experimental writing, another manifestation of the critical ignorance that has haunted black poets since Wheatley. Hayden and Melvin B. Tolson adopted the radical prosody of T. S. Eliot and Ezra Pound, while Baraka, Bob Kaufman, and Ted Joans joined white poets in New York and San Francisco in forging a multiplicity of postmodernist styles, many of them rooted in African American culture, especially jazz.

THE BLACK ARTS MOVEMENT

As in the 1920's, however, the association of black poets with their white counterparts during the 1950's and 1960's generated mixed results. Again, numerous black writers believed that they were accepted primarily as exotics and that the reception of their work was racially biased. With the development of a strong Black Nationalist political movement, exemplified by Malcolm X (who was to become the subject of more poems by African American writers than any other individual), many of the universalist poets turned their attention to a poetry that would directly address the African American community's concerns in a specifically black voice. LeRoi Jones changed his name to Amiri Baraka and placed the term "Black Arts" in the forefront as an indicator of a new cultural aesthetic in the poem "Black Dada Nihilismus." Brooks announced her conversion to a pan-Africanist philosophy, and community arts movements sprang up in cities throughout the United States.

A major movement of young black poets, variously referred to as the New Black Renaissance or the Black Arts movement, rejected involvement with Euro-American culture and sought to create a new black aesthetic that would provide a specifically black identity, purpose, and direction. Poets such as Haki R. Madhubuti (Don L. Lee), Sonia Sanchez, Nikki Giovanni, and Etheridge Knight perceived their work primarily in relation to a black audience, publishing with black houses such as Broadside Press of Detroit and Third World Press of Chicago. Most poets of the Black Arts movement remained active after the relative decline of the Black Nationalist impulse in the late 1970's and 1980's, but, with such notable exceptions as Madhubuti, their tone generally became more subdued. They have been joined in prominence by a group of poets, many of whom also began writing in the 1960's, who have strong affinities with the modernist wing of the universalist period. If Madhubuti, Knight, and Giovanni are largely populist and political in sensibility, poets such as Michael S. Harper, Ai, and Jay Wright are more academic and aesthetic in orientation. Although their sensibilities differ markedly, all the poets asserted the strength of both the African American tradition and the individual voice.

A new pluralism began to emerge, testifying to the persistence of several basic values in the African American sensibility: survival, literacy, and freedom. The publication of the anthology *Black Fire* (1968), coedited by Baraka and Larry Neal, signaled the emergence of the new age. The shift in goals, simply put, was from the uplift of the black community to the transformation of American society. The collection made it clear that African American artists had moved beyond cultural navel gazing. The poets now defined themselves as a Third World people engaged in a global struggle. Neal's essay "The Black Arts Movement" became the period's manifesto:

National and international affairs demand that we appraise the world in terms of our own interests. It is clear that the question of human survival is at the core of contemporary experience. The black artist must address himself to this reality in the strongest terms possible. Consequently, the Black Arts Movement is an ethical movement. Ethical, that is, from the viewpoint of the oppressed. And much of the oppression confronting the Third World and black America is directly traceable to the Euro-American cultural sensibility. This sensibility, antihuman in nature, has, until recently, dominated the psyches of most black artists and intellectuals. It must be destroyed before the black creative artist can have a meaningful role in the transformation of society.

Even highly idiosyncratic poets, such as Toomer in "Blue Meridian" and Ishmael Reed in his "neo-hoo-doo" poems, endorsed those basic values, all of which originated in the experience of slavery. In his book *From Behind the Veil: A Study of Afro-American Narrative* (1979), Robert B. Stepto identifies the central heroic figure of the African American tradition as the "articulate survivor," who completes a symbolic ascent from slavery to a limited freedom, and the "articulate kinsman," who completes a symbolic immersion into his cultural roots. The articulate survivor must attain "literacy" as defined by the dominant white society; the articulate kinsman must attain "tribal literacy" as defined by the black community.

In the 1960's and 1970's, the American Civil Rights and subsequent Black Power movements breathed life into human rights struggles throughout the world. Poets in other parts of the African world began to be heard in the United States during the 1970's, which gave evidence that black bids for survival, literacy, and freedom were indeed universal. Derek Walcott of St. Lucia, South African Dennis Brutus, and Nigeria's Wole Soyinka were among the most important voices.

Walcott, like McKay a Jamaican, showed a reverence for the native Caribbean cultures. Another theme in his early work was outrage at the injustices of colonial rule. Beginning with *The Gulf, and Other Poems* (1969), the poet begins to grapple with ideological and political questions. The strength of the reflection grows in *Sea Grapes* (1976) and comes to full potency in *The Star-Apple Kingdom* (1979).

Brutus's first volume of poems, *Sirens, Knuckles, Boots* (1963), was published while he was doing an eighteen-month stretch on Robben Island, apartheid South Africa's most infamous jail. The equivalent of Alcatraz, it was considered escape-proof because of the water that separated its inmates from the mainland. After release in 1965, Brutus was exiled to London. The poet joined the Northwestern University English faculty in 1970. Three years later, *A Simple Lust* detailed for American audiences the horror of South African prisons and apartheid's injustices. The collection was also influenced by medieval European sensibilities and images. In the first poem of the collection, Brutus speaks in the voice of a troubadour who fights for his beloved against social injustice and betrayal. Even though outwardly European, the poem reverberates the sense of the heroic found in many American-born black writers' works.

Like these Caribbean and South African counterparts, American poets of African descent made reference to, but transformed, European influences. Maya Angelou's "Still I Rise" and Mari Evans's "Vive Noir!" convey the drama of knighthood's quests against an unjust society through plain language and images drawn from black environments. The works also toss aside traditional notions of grammar, spelling, and punctuation as a means to emphasize the rejection of conventional European sensibilities. Evans, for example, sick of the language of oppressors as much as the slums of inner cities, asserts she is

> weary
> of exhausted lands
> sagging privies
> saying yessuh yessah
> yesSIR
> in an assortment
> of geographical dialects

The Black Arts movement faded in the mid-1970's, without changing the world or stabilizing the growth it gave to African American consciousness. New Orleans poet Kalamu ya Salaam, in an essay in *The Oxford Companion to African American Literature* (1997), traced the beginning of the swan song to 1974:

> As the movement reeled from the combination of external and internal disruption, commercialization and capitalist co-option delivered the coup de grace. President Richard Nixon's strategy of pushing Black capitalism as a response to Black Power epitomized mainstream co-option. As major film, record, book and magazine publishers identified the most salable artists, the Black Arts movement's already fragile independent economic base was totally undermined.

1970's-1990's

As in the 1930's, after the Harlem Renaissance subsided most of the independent publications, public forums, and other outlets for African American cultural expression had evaporated. Lotus Press and Broadside Press in Detroit and Third World Press in Chicago would continue to create outlets for excellent literature. White-owned book companies and magazines shifted focus to the movements for women's equality and against the Vietnam War. That set the stage for the emergence of Audre Lorde, Lucille Clifton, and Yusef Komunyakaa.

Lorde's *The Black Unicorn* (1978) used African symbols and myths to explore the dimensions within her existence. Adrienne Rich acknowledged the volume as a kind of declaration of independence: "Refusing to be circumscribed by any single identity, Audre Lorde writes as a Black woman, a mother, a daughter, a Lesbian, a feminist, a visionary." In an interview with editor Claudia Tate in *Black Women Writers at Work* (1983), Lorde averred the Black Arts movement's stress on representation of the global experience of blacks and the oppressed. Tossing aside previous notions that true African American art is political at its core, she sketched a vision of poetry as a reflection of the personal:

Black men have come to believe to their detriment that you have no validity unless you're "global," as opposed to personal. Yet our *real power* comes from the personal; our real insights about living come from the deep knowledge within us that arises from our feelings. Our thoughts are shaped by our tutoring. We were tutored to function in a structure that already existed but that does not function for our good. Our feelings are our most genuine path to knowledge. Men have been taught to deal only with what they understand. This is what they respect. They know that somewhere feeling and knowledge are important, so they keep women around to do their feeling for them, like ants do aphids.

The African American poets who rose in prominence during the 1980's employed stylistic traditions that stretched back to Hughes and other Harlem Renaissance writers. The themes of survival and freedom remained pronounced in their works. The major difference was that, instead of grappling with outside forces, they confronted their nightmares.

Komunyakaa took on Vietnam. The Bogalusa, Louisiana, native won a Bronze Star for his service during the war as a writer and editor of the military newspaper *The Southern Cross*. His poem "Facing It," which reflects on a visit to the Vietnam Veterans Memorial in Washington, D.C., exposes the war as a personal bad dream: "My clouded reflection eyes me like a bird of prey, the profile of the night slanted against the morning." The poet becomes the black granite slab and the archetype of the tens of thousands of visitors. As the poem unfolds, it becomes clear that the conflict is a ghost that will haunt every American for generations.

In September, 1994, the largest gathering of black poets since the end of the Black Arts period was held in Harrisonburg, Virginia, at James Madison University. Thirty of the top black poets since the 1960's—old voices such as Baraka, Madhubuti, Sanchez, Giovanni, and Evans, and new voices such as E. Ethelbert Miller and Toi Derricotte—came together with more than 250 scholars, reporters, and critics. According to a report in *The Washington Post* (October 1), the one subject none of the writers wanted to discuss was what qualities set African American poetry apart from the mainstream. The reporter said that the poets "hate the question, because it reminds them of days when black poetry was relegated to the 'Negro' section of anthologies." However, each of these poets was living with the deep awareness that African American poets were still not equal members of an elitist literary establishment.

Literacy, frequently illegal under the slave codes, both increases the chance of survival and makes freedom meaningful. Tribal literacy protects the individual's racial identity against submersion in a society perceived as inhumane and corrupt. "The literature of an oppressed people is the conscience of man," wrote Lance Jeffers in an essay printed in the January, 1971, issue of the journal *Black Scholar*:

Nowhere is this seen with more intense clarity than the literature of Afroamerica. An essential element of Afroamerican literature is that the literature as a whole—not the work of occasional authors—is a movement against concrete wickedness. The cry for freedom and the protest against injustice are a cry for the birth of the New Man, a testament to the Unknown World (glory) to be discovered, to be created by man.

To a large extent, black poets writing in traditional forms established their literacy as part of a survival strategy in the white literary world. Those concerned with developing black forms demonstrate their respect for, and kinship with, the culturally literate African American community.

JUST PLAIN FOLKS

Against this complex of values and pressures, folk traditions have assumed a central importance in the development of the African American sensibility. Embodying the "tribal" wisdom concerning survival tactics and the meaning of freedom, they provide both formal and thematic inspiration for many black poets. African American poets have become extremely adept at manipulating various masks. Originating with the trickster figures of African folklore and African American heroes such as Brer Rabbit, these masks provide survival strategies based on intellectual, rather than physical, strength.

Existing in a situation during slavery in which open rebellion could easily result in death, the slave community capitalized on the intimate knowledge of white psychology encouraged by the need to anticipate the master's wishes. The white community, conditioned not to see or take into account black needs and desires, possessed no equivalent knowledge of black psychology. Lacking knowledge, whites typically turned to comfortable stereotypes—the loyal mammy, the singing darkie, the tragic mulatto, the black beast—for their interpretation of black behavior. The observant slave found it both easy and rewarding to manipulate white perceptions of reality by appearing to correspond to a stereotypical role while quietly maneuvering for either personal or community gain. The nature of the mask, which exploits a phenomenon of double consciousness by controlling the discrepancy between black and white perspectives, is such that the true goal must always remain hidden from the white viewer, who must always feel that he is making the "real" decisions. Brer Rabbit asks not to be thrown in the briar patch; he will be allowed to escape, however, only if Brer Bear, the symbolic white man, believes that Brer Rabbit's mask is his true face.

This folk tradition of masking adds a specifically African American dimension to the standard poetic manipulation of persona. African American poets frequently adopt personas that, when viewed by white audiences, seem transparent incarnations of familiar stereotypes. Dunbar's dialect poetry and Hughes's Harlem street poems, for example, have been both accepted and dismissed by white readers as straightforward, realistic portraits of black life. An awareness of the complex ironies inherent in the African American folk traditions on which each drew, however, uncovers increasingly complex levels of awareness in their work. Dunbar's melodious dialect songs of plantation life contrast sharply with his complaint against a world that forced him to sing "a jingle in a broken tongue." Similarly, his classic poem "We Wear the Mask" expresses the anguish of a people forced to adopt evasive presentations of self in a nation theoretically committed to pluralism and self-fulfillment. Less agonized than Dunbar, Hughes manipulates the surfaces of his poems, offering and refusing stereotypical images with dazzling speed. "Dream Boogie" first connects the image of the "dream deferred" with the marching feet of an army of the dispossessed, only to resume the mask of the smiling darkie in the sardonic concluding lines:

> What did I say?
> Sure,
> I'm happy!
> Take it away!
> Hey, pop!
> Re-bop!! Mop!
> Y-e-a-h!

The critical record gives strong evidence that Hughes is frequently taken at "face" value. His mask serves to affirm the existence of a black self in control of the rhythm of experience, as well as to satirize the limitations of the white perception.

Throughout the history of African American poetry, poets choosing to address the black political experience without intricate masks have been plagued by the assumption that their relevance was limited by their concentration on racial subject matter. Particularly in the twentieth century, a new stereotype—that of the "angry black" writer—has developed. The conditions of black life frequently do, in fact, generate anger and protest. African American poets, from Wheatley through Alberry Whitman in the late nineteenth century to Cullen and Giovanni, frequently protest against the oppression of blacks. McKay's sonnet "If We Must Die" embodies the basic impulse of this tradition, concluding with the exhortation, "Like men we'll face the murderous, cowardly pack,/ Pressed to the wall, dying, but fighting back!" Far from being limited by its origins in the African American experience, such poetry embraces a universal human drive for freedom. Winston Churchill quoted lines from the poem (ironically written partially in response to British exploitation of McKay's native Jamaica) during the early days of World War II. The stereotype of the angry black, while based on a limited reality, becomes oppressive at precisely the point that it is confused with or substituted for the full human complexity of the individual poet. Giovanni, at times one of the angriest poets of the Black Arts movement, pinpoints the problem in her poem "Nikki-Rosa":

> I really hope no white person ever has cause to write about me because they never understand Black love is Black wealth and they'll probably talk about my hard childhood and never understand that all the while I was quite happy.

The drive for freedom transcends any single tone or mode. While frequently connected with the protest against specific conditions limiting social, psychological, or artistic freedom, the impulse modifies a wide range of poetic voices. At one extreme, explicitly political poems such as Baraka's "Black Art" call for "Poems that shoot/ guns." Even Baraka's less assertive poems, such as "For Hettie" or the more recent "Three Modes of History and Culture," seek to envision a world free from oppression. At another extreme, the drive for freedom lends emotional power to "apolitical" poems such as Dunbar's "Sympathy," with its refrain, "I know why the caged bird sings." Although the poem does not explicitly address racial issues, the intense feeling of entrapment certainly reflects Dunbar's position as a black poet subject to the stereotypes of white society. Similar in theme, but more direct in confronting racial pressures, Cullen's sonnet "Yet Do I Marvel," a masterpiece of irony, accepts the apparent injustices of creation, concluding: "Yet do I marvel at this curious thing/ To make a poet black, and bid him sing." Hughes's "Mother to Son" and "I, Too," with their determination to keep moving, reflect a more optimistic vision. Despite the hardships of life in a country that forces even the "beautiful" black man to "eat in the kitchen," Hughes's characters struggle successfully against despair. Significantly, many of Hughes's poems are very popular in the Third World. "I, Too," for example, has become a kind of anthem in Latin America, which honors Hughes as a major poet in the Walt Whitman tradition.

Whereas Hughes and Walker frequently treat freedom optimistically, Brown's "Memphis Blues" provides a stark warning of the ultimate destruction awaiting a society that fails to live up to its ideals. McKay's sonnet "America," with its echoes of Percy Bysshe Shelley's "Ozymandias," strikes a similar note, envisioning the nation's "priceless treasures sinking in the sand." Perhaps Hayden best embodies the basic impulse in his brilliant "Runagate Runagate," which employs a complex modernist voice to celebrate the mutually nourishing relationship between the anonymous fugitive slaves and the heroic figure of Harriet Tubman, who articulates and perpetuates their drive for freedom. Blending the voices of slavemasters, runaway slaves, the spirituals, and American mythology, Hayden weaves a tapestry that culminates in the insistent refrain, "Mean mean mean to be free."

Hayden's use of the anonymous voice of the runaway slave with the voice of the spirituals underscores both the drive for freedom and the nature of the individual hero who embodies the aspirations of the entire community. It exemplifies the importance of folk traditions as formal points of reference for the African American poetic sensibility.

MUSIC AND MESSAGE

Poets seeking to assert a specifically black voice within the context of the Euro-American mainstream repeatedly turn to the rhythms and imagery of folk forms such as spirituals and sermons. During the twentieth century, the blues and jazz assumed equal importance. As Stephen Henderson observes in *Understanding the New Black Poetry*

(1973), these folk traditions provide both thematic and formal inspiration. Hayden's "Homage to the Empress of the Blues," Brown's "Ma Rainey," Brooks's "Queen of the Blues," and poems addressed to John Coltrane by Harper ("Dear John, Dear Coltrane," "A Love Supreme"), Madhubuti ("Don't Cry, Scream"), and Sanchez ("A Coltrane Poem") are only a few of countless African American poems invoking black musicians as cultural heroes. Bluesmen such as Robert Johnson (who wrote such haunting lyrics as "Crossroads," "Stones in My Passageway," and "If I Had Possession over Judgement Day") and singers such as Bessie Smith frequently assume the stature of folk heroes themselves. At their best they can legitimately be seen as true poets working with the vast reservoir of imagery inherent in African American folk life. Du Bois endorsed the idea by montaging passages of African American music with selections of Euro-American poetry at the start of each chapter of *The Souls of Black Folk* (1903). Similarly, Johnson's poem "O Black and Unknown Bards" credits the anonymous composers of the spirituals with a cultural achievement equivalent to that of Ludwig van Beethoven and Richard Wagner.

These folk and musical traditions have suggested a great range of poetic forms to African American poets. Johnson echoed the rhythms of black preaching in his powerful volume *God's Trombones: Seven Negro Sermons in Verse* (1927), which includes such classic "sermons" as "The Creation" and "Go Down Death—A Funeral Sermon." Hughes and Brown used their intricate knowledge of black musical forms in structuring their poetry. Early in his career, Hughes was content simply to imitate the structure of the blues stanza in poems such as "Suicide." As he matured, however, he developed more subtle strategies for capturing the blues impact in "The Weary Blues," which establishes a dramatic frame for several blues stanzas, and "Song for Billie." The latter mimics the subtle shifts in emphasis of the blues line by altering the order of prepositions in the stanza:

> What can purge my heart
>   of the song
>   and the sadness?
> What can purge my heart
>   But the song
>   of the sadness?
> What can purge my heart
>   of the sadness
>   of the song?

The persona moves from a stance of distance to one of identification and acceptance of the blues feeling. In merging emotionally with the singer, he provides a paradigm for the ideal relationship between artist and audience in the African American tradition.

Brown's blues poem "Ma Rainey" incorporates this call-and-response aspect of the blues experience into its frame story. Ma Rainey attains heroic stature because her voice and vision echo those of the audience that gathers from throughout the Mississippi Delta to hear its experience authenticated. Brown's attempt to forge a voice that combines call and response points to what may be the central formal quest of African American poetry. Such an ideal voice seeks to inspire the community by providing a strong sense of identity, purpose, and direction. Simultaneously, it validates the individual experience of the poet by providing a sense of social connection in the face of what Ralph Ellison refers to as the "brutal experience" underlying the blues impulse. Both Ellison and Hughes, two of the most profound critics of the blues as a literary form, emphasize the mixture of tragic and comic worldviews in the blues. Hughes's definition of the blues attitude as "laughing to keep from crying" accurately reflects the emotional complexity of much blues poetry.

Like the blues, jazz plays a significant formal role in African American poetry. Poets frequently attempt to capture jazz rhythms in their prosody. Ambiguous stress patterns and intricate internal rhyme schemes make Brooks's "We Real Cool" and "The Blackstone Rangers" two of the most successful poems in this mode. Brown's "Cabaret" and Hughes's "Jazzonia" employ jazz rhythms to describe jazz performances. On occasion, poets such as Joans ("Jazz Must Be a Woman") and Baraka ("Africa Africa Africa") create "poems" that, like jazz charts, sketch a basic rhythmic or imagistic structure that provides a basis for improvisation during oral performance. Jazz may be most important to African American poetry, however, because of its implicit cultural pluralism. In his critical volume *Shadow and Act* (1964), Ellison suggests a profound affinity between the aesthetics of African American music and European American modernism: "At least as early as T. S. Eliot's creation of a new aesthetic for poetry through the artful juxtapositioning of earlier styles, Louis Armstrong, way down the river in New Orleans, was working out a similar technique for jazz." As Ellison suggests, jazz provides an indigenous source for an African American modernism incorporating voices from diverse cultural and intellectual sources. In effect, this enables the African American poet to transform the burden of double consciousness, as manifested in the traditions of masking and ironic voicing, into sources of aesthetic power.

Many of the masterworks of African American poetry, such as Hughes's "Montage for a Dream Deferred," Brooks's "In the Mecca," Hayden's "Middle Passage," and Jay Wright's "Dimensions of History," accomplish precisely this transformation. Choosing from the techniques and perceptions of both European American and African American traditions, these works incorporate the dreams and realities of the American tradition in all its diversity. Aware of the anguish resulting from external denial of self and heritage, the African American tradition recognizes the potential inherent in all fully lived experience. Hughes's vision of individuals living out a multiplicity of dreams within the American Dream testifies to his profound respect and love for the dispossessed.

The blend of the spoken word, politics, and music in the 1970's laid the foundations for rap music to become a major art form for social criticism. From Gil Scott-Heron's "The Revolution Will Not Be Televised" to Public Enemy's "Fight the Power," the rhymed critiques of life in America move beyond racial icons to indict anyone who turns away from the plight of the oppressed as the enemy. There is debate outside the community as to whether rappers are poets or song stylists. Even some successful African American writers look on the rap and hip-hop as clever wordplay, but lacking the discipline of traditional poetry. Nevertheless, anthologies edited by up-and-coming African American poets such as Kevin Powell and Clarence Gilyard suggest that the works of some of these artists deserve to be added to the American canon.

In 2008, when voters of all races chose an African American to be president of the United States, it could no longer be claimed that racism continued to block the achievement of the American democratic ideal. Though the people of the United States still had their flaws, and though economic and social injustices still existed, it was now evident that the dreams expressed more than sixty years before by one of America's greatest poets, the late Margaret Walker, could at last come true: A new world was being born, a world for the lovers of freedom, a world that would be large enough for everyone.

BIBLIOGRAPHY

Brown, Sterling. *Afro-Blue: Improvisations in African American Poetry and Culture.* Urbana: University of Illinois Press, 2003. A study of the influence of the blues tradition on African American speech, poetry, and thought, noting the three distinct types of blues poetics, as explained in chapters on Sterling A. Brown, Langston Hughes, and Jayne Cortez. Notes and index.

Chapman, Abraham, and Gwendolyn Brooks, eds. *Black Voices: Anthology of African-American Literature.* New York: Signet Classics, 2001. A reissue of a classic anthology. The book, first produced in two volumes in the late 1960's and early 1970's, was the first great collection of black writing. It pulls together poetry, fiction, autobiography and literary criticism, with informative, concise author biographies.

Harper, Michael S., and Anthony Walton, eds. *The Vintage Book of African American Poetry.* New York: Vintage, 2000. This anthology contains the works of fifty-two poets, presented chronologically, and includes not only those who are famous but also some who are undeservedly neglected. Brief but insightful introduction by the editors. Biographical headnotes.

Lee, Valerie, ed. *The Prentice Hall Anthology of African American Women's Literature.* Upper Saddle River, N.J.: Pearson Prentice Hall, 2006. A comprehensive collection, beginning with works written during the colonial and antebellum period and ending with the twenty-first century. A final section is devoted to feminist and womanist criticism. Map. Bibliography.

Liggins Hill, Patricia et al., eds. *The Riverside Anthology of the African American Literary Tradition.* New York: Houghton Mifflin, 1998. Contains 550 selections, ranging from African proverbs, folktales, and chants to works by contemporary authors such as Rita Dove.

Miller, E. Ethelbert. *Beyond the Frontier: African American Poetry for the Twenty-first Century*. Baltimore: Black Classic Press, 2002. An unusual collection of poems, relating the experiences of African Americans as people who are indeed pioneers, whether they are struggling for social justice or discovering that the secret of survival is the capacity to love. More than one hundred poets are included. Compact disc available.

Powell, Kevin, ed. *Step into a World: A Global Anthology of the New Black Literature*. New York: John Wiley & Sons, 2000. The broadest collection of hip-hop generation writers available. Includes fiction writers, poets, journalists, and commentators, as well as established authors such as Junot Diaz, Edwidge Danticat, Danyel Smith, and Paul Beatty.

Rampersad, Arnold, and Hilary Herbold, eds. *The Oxford Anthology of African-American Poetry*. New York: Oxford University Press, 2005. Poems from different time periods, written in a wide variety of styles, are grouped thematically, though alphabetized within each of the fifteen sections. The result is a unique vision of the African American poetic tradition. Biographies and index.

Schwarz, A. B. Christa. *Gay Voices of the Harlem Renaissance*. Bloomington: Indiana University Press, 2003. Schwarz examines the work of four leading writers from the Harlem Renaissance—Countée Cullen, Langston Hughes, Claude McKay, and Richard Bruce Nugent—and their sexually nonconformist or gay literary voices.

Thomas, Lorenzo. *Extraordinary Measures: Afrocentric Modernism and Twentieth-Century American Poetry*. Tuscaloosa: University of Alabama Press, 2000. A critical reappraisal of the development of African American poetry during the twentieth century, noting in particular the influence of literary movements such as modernism and the effects of radical changes in American society.

Craig Werner; Vincent F. A. Golphin
Updated by Rosemary M. Canfield Reisman

HARLEM RENAISSANCE

The Harlem Renaissance, also known as the New Negro movement and dating from approximately 1919 to 1935, is recognized as one of the most important and productive periods in the history of American literature, art, and culture. From the movement came some of the finest music, literature, and art of the twentieth century.

At the end of World War I, black veterans returning to their southern homelands found little change. Despite having served their country, they were afforded no special recognition for their sacrifices and were faced with the same poor living conditions and threats of lynchings and public humiliation that existed before the war. Meanwhile, urban areas in the North and West had profited somewhat from the war with an upswing in new industries. In addition, the decline in immigration from Europe had created a severe labor shortage, which opened up employment opportunities.

In search of economic stability, better lives, and better education for their children, African Americans left the South for industrial centers such as Pittsburgh and Detroit and for cities such as Chicago and New York City. The greatest number of African Americans went to New York City, which had always been a cultural mecca and already had a large black population in Harlem. Harlem's boundaries had been greatly expanded in 1910 when African American real estate agents and church groups had bought large tracts of land, so housing was available to the black migrants, though they faced greatly inflated rental charges. This influx brought problems. Established residents did not embrace the change, seeing the newcomers as interlopers who would try to take their jobs. Eventually, the wide variety of people from different backgrounds provided opportunities for cultural growth and diversity.

Harlem had already been a center for political activism, where silent marches—and some louder ones—protesting injustice had taken place. Marcus Garvey, charismatic leader of the Back to Africa movement, had his headquarters there, and both the National Urban League and the National Association for the Advancement of Colored People (NAACP) had offices there. The National Urban League's *Opportunity: A Journal of Negro Life*, a periodical designed to stimulate pride in past racial achievements and hope for the future, and the NAACP's *Crisis*, edited by historian, journalist, and social critic W. E. B. Du Bois, both provided avenues for sharing ideas. Many writers had come to Harlem intending to turn the lives of migrants into novels and short stories. Alone, these writers might not have created the Renaissance community. However, two very influential leaders—Alain Locke, philosopher, writer, and educator, and Charles Johnson, the director of research for the Urban League—orchestrated a plan for turning the area into a literary haven, calling out to promising writers from other states and offering prize incentives for the best work. Both felt that unfortunate stereotypes could be changed by showing what African Americans were capable of in literature, art, and music. With white publishers beginning to open their doors to black authors, the stage was set: Harlem became a vibrant site of artistic experimentation.

The migrants from the South had brought with them the music of New Orleans and St. Louis, and jazz and blues clubs opened in Harlem. These clubs attracted both blacks and whites and were excellent places to meet and plan strategies, talk over works in progress, display art, drink, and listen to musicians such as Bessie Smith, Louis Armstrong, Billie Holiday, Cab Calloway, and Duke Ellington. One of the most noted venues, the Cotton Club, practiced its own kind of discrimination. Its entertainers had to be light-skinned. Thus, Josephine Baker, whose act featured a banana skirt, had to go to Europe to achieve fame.

The art world exploded with new experimental expression, brighter colors, and freer forms. The colors became bolder, more alive, and more apt to attract attention and elicit discussion; paintings were everywhere. Artists and art lovers met at coffeehouses, where they shared and generated new ideas.

Writers, in particular, benefited from the camaraderie. They tried out ideas and established salons, often under the auspices of white benefactors, where they read and critiqued one another's works. It became known that the African American was in "vogue," a term that distressed some intellectuals because it implied a temporary condition. It was true that some white patrons simply liked the exotic feel of being associated with another race. One unkind rumor suggested that Zora Neale Hurston was paid to attend white parties and act like an African American. Writers gave talks, took part in symposiums, and generally enjoyed the star status. In addition, theaters began employing black actors and producing works by black playwrights. By the mid-1920's, Harlem had indeed become the epicenter for change and freedom. For more than a decade thereafter, it was abuzz with excitement and seriousness of purpose. Locke felt that the urban setting helped African Americans appreciate the great variety of perspectives and ambitions among them, as Harlem was home to business professionals, preachers, outcasts, students, and criminals, as well as those involved in the arts.

In March, 1924, the National Urban League hosted a dinner to honor the emerging array of talented black writers. Du Bois urged Harlem writers to attend and meet with white writers and publishers. This gathering had a huge impact. White-run publishing companies were now more eager to solicit manuscripts from black authors.

In 1925, Locke and Johnson were asked to edit a black artisans edition of *Survey Graphic*, a national magazine devoted to social issues and cultural affairs. The issue, "Harlem: Mecca of the New Negro," became a landmark in the Black Arts movement. It featured works by Countée Cullen (1903-1946), Langston Hughes (1902-1967), Du Bois (1868-1963), James Weldon Johnson (1871-1938), and Jean Toomer (1894-1967). Encouraged, Locke expanded the introduction and used the magazine as the basis for an anthology that included works by Claude McKay (1889-1948), Hurston (1891-1960), and Jessie R. Fauset (1882-1961). The anthology, *The New Negro: An In-*

terpretation (1925), gave Locke the reputation of being the architect, or, as he preferred to be called, the "midwife" of the Harlem Renaissance.

Locke hoped that greater exposure would demonstrate that African Americans had cultural awareness and self-confidence and in no way were of lesser intelligence or creativity than whites. He hoped to dispel the stereotypes in literature of Uncle Tom or Uncle Remus—no more grinning mammies or faithful family retainers willing to sacrifice themselves to preserve the status of their white employers and no more stock figures, African Americans shuffling to do service, or acting dumb to entertain. The New Negro movement aimed to set those stereotypes to rest. The New Negro spoke his mind, had confidence, and fought back. Mainly, Locke hoped that the image of the humble, self-effacing, always accommodating African American would fade, to be replaced by a self-assertive, independent individual who resisted domination. Arts and letters, Locke believed, could serve to raise racial consciousness.

THE WRITERS AND THEIR WORKS

The poetry of the Harlem Renaissance was the most celebrated, coming from the minds of sensitive, culturally aware, honest, and skilled poets who, by virtue of the genre, had to make each word count. Sometimes those words cut deeply, though not without reason. They opened eyes to outrages and called for action. There were no dominant themes in the poetry, though much of it explored Harlem and race in the United States. Some works protested racial injustice, but most avoided overt protests or propaganda, focusing instead on the psychological and social impact of race. At the time, writers were more interested in acquainting the white public with the lives of African Americans. They wanted to demonstrate these individuals' great capacity for deep thoughts, for grappling with problems, and for seeking truth, justice, and beauty.

This period of artistic and cultural blossoming was sometimes fraught with problems, mainly among those African Americans who were concerned with their public image now that works by black writers were receiving wider white readership. The purpose of writing and the obligations of writers came into question. Poets in particular seemed to divide into three groups: those who wanted to pattern their works after the great masters, thinking it made little sense to try to improve upon perfection; those who wanted to write in the language of the people, to stick with the vernacular of the common man and woman; and those who favored telling the truth about African American life, the delights as well as the horrors.

Many African American poets modeled their works on literary classics, especially favoring allusions that required readers to work toward understanding. Some writers were accused of catering to the white taste for seedy tales of degradation. They presented African American life as it was lived by a portion of the community: scam artists, gamblers, heavy drinkers, and carousers. Hughes was criticized for writing of the "low downs," the ordinary people. Hurston used black dialect to convey the essence of her characters and was told that she was bringing the race down.

Du Bois had high expectations and rules for writers, saying that they had a social re-sponsibility to present African Americans in their best light and that their works should be "uplifting." He thought that all writing should be propaganda. He found the new real-ism too gritty. However, the new writers felt the constraints too limiting. They wanted their literary talent to discredit the stereotypes. Mainly they wanted to counteract the postcard images of happy darkies in the cotton fields grinning instead of tending to the wounds, invisible to the public, created by the sharp briars of the plant. They wanted the balance of a bookie or a pimp, acting as some real people act. The concept of creating works that were spiritually uplifting went against the artistic ideal of showing life as it is, and some writers would not yield to pressure from the intellectuals.

COUNTÉE CULLEN

Poet Countée Cullen liked traditional verse forms such as the sonnet because his mainstream education exposed him to the literature he loved. He became known as the black John Keats. His works appeared structured, even gentle, but his words conveyed the system of discrimination so prevalent in those days. In "For a Lady I Know," he slaps at white womanhood, while undoubtedly delighting service workers. He says, "She even thinks that up in heaven/ Her class lies late and snores// While poor black cherubs rise at seven/ to do celestial chores." In "Incident," the subject is far more pain-ful. He tells of riding in a public conveyance in Baltimore when he was a boy, just eight, and smiling at another boy who had been staring at him. In response, the child stuck out his tongue and called him "nigger." The last stanza captures the impact of the incident: "I saw the whole of Baltimore/ From May until December;/ Of all the things that happened there/ That's all that I remember."

CLAUDE MCKAY

In 1922, Claude McKay broke the color barrier when a white-owned firm published his poetry collection *Harlem Shadows* to high acclaim. The title poem speaks of the old Harlem, with its "girls who pass to bend and barter at desire's call." However, he speaks of these prostitutes affectionately, calling them lasses, "little dark girls . . . in slippered feet" who work from dusk to dawn, brought down by poverty to use their "timid little feet of clay, the sacred brown feet." His work has been credited with being the forerun-ner in the shift in African American poetry to modernism and to the New Negro movement.

McKay wrote a strong protest poem that called for African Americans, if cornered by the oppressor, to die with dignity. In "If We Must Die," he urges African Americans, without identifying race, not to allow themselves to be "hunted and penned" like hogs, but to stand nobly like men. Though "pressed to the wall," dying, they should fight back so that even in death they will be honored by the cowards who outnumber them. In

"America," McKay wrote with great affection for his native country, saying that "Although she feeds me bread of bitterness/ And sinks into my throat her tiger's tooth," he must "confess" that he loves "this cultured hell that tests" his youth. Her "vigor" and "bigness" give him the strength to stand up against any hatred.

LANGSTON HUGHES

The most widely known and respected poet of the period was Langston Hughes. His early works reflected the music of African Americans, the soul, and the jazz. In 1925, while busing tables in the District of Columbia, Hughes slipped a famous poet a few of his works. Headlines the next day announced the discovery of a new poet. One of the poems was "The Weary Blues," which became the title of his first collection, published in 1926 when he was twenty-four years old. The individual poems—"The Weary Blues," "Dream Variations," "The Negro Speaks of Rivers," "A Black Pierrot," "Water Front Streets," "Shadows in the Sun," and "Our Land"—come together like an opus. Hughes used the free-style rhythms of blues and jazz, music that reached into the souls of black people. His "The Weary Blues" conveyed weariness with such lines as "Droning a drowsy syncopated tune/ Rocking back and forth to a mellow croon/ I heard a Negro play" and "He did a lazy sway . . ./ . . ./ With his ebony hands on each ivory key/ He made that poor piano moan with melody/ O Blues!" and "Swaying to and fro on his rickety stool/ He played that sad raggy tune. . . ." The use of alliteration in "droning/drowsy" and the long slow sadness of such words as "mellow," "croon," "lazy," "sway," and "crooned that tune" spoke of exhaustion, physical but also almost certainly emotional.

Hughes was most adept at including what was not exactly a threat; but definitely an expression of a limit to the tolerance of those who are asked to wait for the right time to realize their hopes. In "Harlem," he asks:

> What happens to a dream deferred?
>   Does it dry up
> like a raisin in the sun?
> Or fester like a sore—
> And then run?
> Does it stink like rotten meat?
> Or crust and sugar over—
> like a syrupy sweet?
>
>   Maybe it just sags
> like a heavy load.
>
> *Or does it explode?*

The setting aside of that one line in italics tells the whole story, serving as a warning that perhaps a kind of violence is inevitable.

In another work, "I, Too, Am America," Hughes relates a veiled threat: A young man is always expected to eat in the kitchen when his employers have company. He says that he attempts to ignore the slight, knowing that the good food will nourish his body and help him to grow strong, and that one day he will already be at the dining room table when the company arrives and no one will dare send him off to the kitchen, not only because he has become strong and could resist them but also because they will realize that he is beautiful and will be ashamed. His title and last line, "I, too, am America," say it all.

JAMES WELDON JOHNSON

James Weldon Johnson hoped his poems would afford greater appreciation of preachers and lead to a reassessment of African Americans. His *God's Trombones: Seven Negro Sermons in Verse* (1927) was made up of an opening prayer and sermons often given by preachers. He used a scholarly style to show whites that religion is important to blacks and that black preachers are social and intellectual leaders in the community. In a powerful retelling of the Creation as it appears in the Bible, he has God walking out into a great black emptiness, his smile bringing on the light. God rolls the light in his hands to make first the sun and then the moon and stars. He throws the world between the sun and the moon and then walks on it to make hills and valleys. There follow all the lakes and flowers, until he realizes he is lonely. So he scoops up some clay from the bed of a river and makes a man.

A BLACK AWAKENING

While courted by wealthy whites and invited to parties, most of the black poets stayed true to their form and did not let their messages be toned down. Not fearful of losing their popularity, they portrayed life as it was and kept their patronage. In poetry, African Americans found a way to further the oral tradition and the stories told through hymns and folk music. No longer necessary were the seemingly innocuous lyrics of such works as "follow the drinking gourd" (look to the Big Dipper for the escape route to the North) or musical maps to the Underground Railroad. Now poets could speak truth and reflect the reality of black life. They produced some remarkable works that went beyond the horrors that African Americans experienced and to the heart of all who have suffered, felt lost and afraid, and been hurt by life circumstances or unfairness.

The Harlem Renaissance was called a period of great cultural, artistic, and literary achievement, but it was also a time of awakening, when blacks, seeing chances for better lives, took them; when pride in being black became a factor; and when celebrations and recognition of black artists gave the general populace good feelings. Many of the stars of the Harlem Renaissance were either homosexual or bisexual, but for the most part, their sexual proclivities remained hidden, lest publishers or readers wane. The silent awareness among them fostered a strong bond that helped to unite them in their writings on particular themes. They could allude to their sexual feelings without letting the public in on their secrets. Works required much reading between the lines.

The Harlem Renaissance changed the way African Americans were perceived by others and how they viewed themselves. It produced poetry and fiction that will endure because these works went beyond skin tone to the hearts of humanity and to the human condition that weathers external changes.

BIBLIOGRAPHY

Chapman, Abraham. "The Harlem Renaissance in Literary History." *CLA Journal* 11, no. 1 (September, 1967): 38-58. A personal accounting of Chapman's dismay at the scant attention paid to the Renaissance and its writers.

_____, ed. *Black Voices: An Anthology of African American Literature.* New York: New American Library, 1968. The introduction to Chapman's classic collection still stands as one of the most comprehensive statements regarding the long history of blacks in literature.

Gates, Henry Louis, Jr., and Evelyn Brooks Higginbotham, eds. *Harlem Renaissance Lives, from the African American National Biography.* New York: Oxford University Press, 2009. This is a compendium of the main features of the Harlem Renaissance, its germination, and the major artists, writers, and musicians involved. The introduction by Cary D. Wintz is especially valuable.

Lewis, David Levering. *When Harlem Was in Vogue.* New York: Alfred Knopf, 1981. This remains the standard work on the Harlem Renaissance. It reads as a narrative, involving the reader in the day-to-day details while covering all the salient points.

Major, Clarence, ed. *The Garden Thrives: Twentieth Century African-American Poetry.* New York: Harper Perennial, 1996. A good collection of the major poems, with commentary and an introduction by a leading authority in black literature.

Gay Pitman Zieger

MAYA ANGELOU
Marguerite Annie Johnson

Born: St. Louis, Missouri; April 4, 1928

OTHER LITERARY FORMS

In addition to being a poet, Maya Angelou (AN-juh-lew) is an essayist, playwright, screenwriter, and the author of children's books and other pieces of short fiction. Along with two volumes of her autobiography, her collection of essays *Even the Stars Look Lonesome* (1997) was on *The New York Times* best-seller list for ten consecutive weeks. Her two-act drama *The Least of These* was produced in Los Angeles in 1966. With her screenplay *Georgia, Georgia* she became, in 1972, the first African American woman to have an original screenplay produced. In 1974 she adapted Sophocles' *Aias* (early 440's B.C.E.; *Ajax*, 1729) for the modern stage. Her children's book *My Painted House, My Friendly Chicken, and Me* was published in 1994. Her works have been translated into at least ten languages.

ACHIEVEMENTS

Maya Angelou's work has garnered many prestigious awards. For her writing of the revue *Cabaret for Freedom*, which she and Godfrey Cambridge produced, directed, and performed in 1960 for the purpose of raising money for Martin Luther King, Jr.'s Southern Christian Leadership Conference (SCLC), she was named northern coordinator for the SCLC in 1959. She later worked with civil rights leader

Malcolm X. Other honors include a nomination for a National Book Award (1970) for *I Know Why the Caged Bird Sings* (1969), a Pulitzer Prize nomination (1972) for *Just Give Me a Cool Drink of Water 'fore I Diiie*, Antoinette Perry ("Tony") Award nominations (1973 and 1977), a Golden Eagle Award for documentary (1977), a Matrix Award from Women in Communications (1983), the North Carolina Award in Literature (1987), the Langston Hughes Award (1991), the Horatio Alger Award (1992), the Spingarn Medal (1993), a Grammy Award for Best Spoken Word or Non-Traditional Album (1994), the National Medal of Arts (2000), and the prestigious Order of Kilimanjaro Award from the National Association for the Advancement of Colored People (2001). She was named Woman of the Year in Communications and one of the one hundred most influential women by *Ladies' Home Journal* (1976), Distinguished Woman of North Carolina (1992), and Woman of the Year by *Essence* magazine (1992). She also received a Yale University fellowship (1970) and a Rockefeller Foundation scholarship in Italy (1975).

A high school graduate, Angelou has received honorary degrees from Smith College (1975), Mills College (1975), Lawrence University (1976), and Wake Forest University (1977). She was appointed Reynolds Professor of American Studies at Wake Forest University in Winston-Salem, North Carolina, in 1981. She read the poem she had composed in honor of the inauguration of President Bill Clinton at the inaugural ceremonies in January, 1993; only one poet before her, Robert Frost, had been invited to read at an inauguration ceremony. In all, she has received more than thirty honorary degrees.

Although many titles have been assigned to Angelou, one is especially significant to her: the modern female African American Marcel Proust. Angelou is known for addressing the world through the medium of her own life. The first volume of her autobiography made her the first African American woman to appear on nonfiction best-seller lists; four volumes followed the first.

BIOGRAPHY

Born Marguerite Annie Johnson, re-christened Maya, and taking the professional name Angelou (an adaptation of the name of her first husband, Tosh Angelos), Maya Angelou studied music and dance with Martha Graham, Pearl Primus, and Ann Halprin. Her early career was as an actress and singer, to which she quickly added the roles of civil rights worker (as the northern coordinator for the SCLC, 1959-1960), editor (as associate editor for the *Arab Observer*, 1961-1962), educator (beginning with the School of Music and Drama at the University of Ghana's Institute of African Studies, 1963-1966), and finally writer—first as a reporter for the *Ghanaian Times* (1963-1965). During the late 1960's and 1970's, she taught at many colleges and universities in California and Kansas, accepting the post of Reynolds Professor at Wake Forest University in 1981. Since then she has also been a sought-after speaker.

She has told much of her own life's story in her five-volume autobiography. Undoubtedly, Angelou's legacy will be her writings: Although the best-selling *I Know Why the Caged Bird Sings* was censored, her excellent work as an author in all genres has kept her story before the world. Angelou's early years have been burned into the minds of numerous readers. An image from this work centers on three-year-old Marguerite and four-year-old Bailey Johnson aboard a train, alone, traveling from California to their grandmother's home in Stamps, Arkansas, after the breakup of their parents' marriage. The two children wore their names and their destination attached to their clothes. This locomotive quest for family is both a factual part of and an apt metaphor for the life of the world-famous poet. Her first feeling of being truly at home, she has said, came in Africa, after she accompanied her second husband to Egypt and then traveled to Ghana.

A second image from Angelou's childhood involves the seven-year-old's rape by her mother's boyfriend. When no legal punishment followed, the rapist was murdered, possibly by the victim's uncles. Guilt following this incident drove Angelou inward, and she began reading the great works of literature. Reading her way through the Stamps library, she fell in love with William Shakespeare and Paul Laurence Dunbar, among others. The child of a fractured nuclear family came to see herself as a child of the fractured human family.

By age thirteen, Angelou had grown closer to her mother; at sixteen she became a mother herself. To earn a living for herself and her son, Guy, she became a waitress, a singer, and a dancer. These and other occupations were followed by acting, directing, producing, and the hosting of television specials. She loved to dance, but when her knees began to suffer in her early twenties, she devoted her attention to her other love: writing. She began supporting herself through her writing in 1968. Her family came to include "sister friends" and "brother friends," as her troubled brother Bailey became lost in the worlds of substance abuse and prison. She married, but she has refused to attach a number to her marriages, as that might, she says, suggest frivolity, and she insists that she was never frivolous about marriage. To "brother friend" James Baldwin she gives much credit for her becoming an autobiographer. She assisted "brother friends" Martin Luther King, Jr., and Malcolm X in their work and pursued her own work to better the entire human family.

The hope that Angelou found so significant in the 1960's is reflected in the poem she composed for Clinton's presidential inauguration. The dream of King is evident in the words written and delivered by Angelou "on the pulse of [that] morning."

ANALYSIS

Asked in 1983 what she hoped to achieve as a writer, Maya Angelou answered, "to remind us that we are more alike [than un-alike], especially since I've grown up in racial turbulence and unfairness." Two 1990's poems reflect the dichotomy of her declaration: "Human Family" celebrates family likeness, and "Son to Mother" denounces wrongs inflicted by various branches of the human family. Angelou in her poetry dissects and resurrects humankind: She condemns its shamefulness and rejoices in its possibilities and its glories.

STILL RISING

"Some poets sing/ their melodies," writes Angelou in "Artful Pose," published in 1975, "tendering my nights/ sweetly." Angelou, in contrast, chooses to write "of lovers false" "and hateful wrath/ quickly." She adds the word "quickly" to balance and countermand "sweetly." Her style as she speaks to live audiences and to readers, whether her tone is optimistic or pessimistic, reveals a sense of "gusto." In 1982 she offered this bit of self-analysis:

> If you enter a room of hostile strangers with gusto, there are few who can contain, preserve their hostility. . . . [I]t speaks immediately to the gusto in other people.

European American audiences applaud her and purchase her work even as she berates them: "You may write me down in history/ With your bitter, twisted lies," she says in the opening lines of one of her most famous poems, "Still I Rise."

"I'll play possum and close my eyes/ To your greater sins and my lesser lies," she writes in a jump-rope rhythm in "Bump d'Bump." "That way I share my nation's prize," she continues. "Call me a name from an ugly south/ Like liver lips and satchel mouth"; gusto, anger, and a challenge to humankind are integral ingredients of Angelou's poetry.

In "Man Bigot" Angelou writes,

> The man who is a bigot
> is the worst thing God has got
> except his match, his woman,
> who really is Ms. Begot.

Angelou is not unwilling to amuse as she challenges her audience. She did not leave the entertainment field behind when she turned to verse. Other entertaining and uplifting elements of her poetry are sass and the celebration of womanhood. "Men themselves have wondered/ What they see in me," says the speaker of "A Phenomenal Woman." A part of her mystery, she says, is in "the fire in my eyes," "the joy in my feet," and

> The grace of my style.
> I'm a woman
> Phenomenally.
> Phenomenal woman,
> That's me.

SASS AND ANGER

Sass is an element in 1978's "Still I Rise," but anger consistently tempers its speaker's joy. "Does my sassiness upset you?" and "Does my haughtiness offend you?" she asks her European American readers. "Out of the huts of history's shame/ I rise," says her African American speaker. In "Miss Scarlett, Mr. Rhett, and Other Latter-Day Saints," Angelou writes,

> Animated by the human sacrifice
> (Golgotha in black-face)
> Priests glow purely white on the
> bas-relief of a plantation shrine.

In "Slave Coffle" (1983) she speaks as a slave to whom "all the earth is horror," as the speaker realizes "Before the dawning,/ bright as grinning demons" that "life was gone."

Although Angelou has told interviewers that she has mellowed since writing her first volume of poetry, her verse remains harsh to the reader's mind and ear. Shame and ignorance recur as significant themes. Pride, however, is at least as significant.

PRIDE IN ANCESTORS

In 1975, Angelou declared "Song for the Old Ones" her favorite poem. Her celebration of those who kept her race alive remained a favorite theme. Her 1990 volume of poetry, *I Shall Not Be Moved*, has as its title the chorus to the poem "Our Grandmothers." Her sense of pride in these old ones and her sense of kinship with them is evident in the words she gives one of these grandmothers. To those who hurled ribbons of invective into the wind of history,

> She said, But my description cannot
> fit your tongue, for
> I have a certain way of being in this world,
> and I shall not, I shall not be moved.

In "Old Folks Laugh" (1990), she writes that old folks' laughter frees the world. The freedom that the grandmothers offer their children in "Our Grandmothers" is the freedom to be fully human: They tell them, "When you learn, teach. When you get, give."

"I laugh until I start to crying,/ When I think about my folks," says the speaker of "When I Think About Myself." Angelou's poetry shows that the stories of her people continued to fill and to break her heart. The title of the volume containing "Song for the Old Ones," *Oh Pray My Wings Are Gonna Fit Me Well*, seems, as does the title of her 1990 volume, *I Shall Not Be Moved*, to derive from her wish to be worthy of and to emulate the old ones.

That Angelou gives the final position in the 1990 volume to the poem dedicated to other, less great, old ones is significant, as is the idea of that poem: "When great souls die," she says in the final stanza,

> Our senses, restored, never
> to be the same, whisper to us.
> They existed. They existed.
> We can be. Be and be
> better. For they existed.

Unbelievable cruelty has given rise to unbelievable valor. Angelou cannot and will not forget the history of human cruelty as she feels that human beings must learn from their shared history. She continues to show human beings what they must learn that they can be better.

GUILT AND RESPONSIBILITY

Crucial to her overall idea is the shared guilt and responsibility of all history's survivors. In "I Almost Remember" (1975), the speaker recalls smiling and even laughing, but now

> Open night news-eyed I watch
> channels of hunger
> written on children's faces
> bursting bellies balloon
> in the air of my day room.

The speaker's garden, television, and day room suggest the luxuries and the guilt of one of the "haves" as she/he witnesses the suffering of the "have-nots" on the "channels of hunger." Similarly, "Harlem Hopscotch," with a seemingly different tone and a hopscotch rhythm, shows children singing of "good things for the ones that's got." "Everybody for hisself," they continue. The pain of both the television viewer and the children reflects the suffering as well as the scarring of the human psyche.

"Take Time Out" challenges the acceptance of the status quo, challenging the attitude of all human players of life's game:

> Use a minute
> feel some sorrow
> for the folks
> who think tomorrow
> is a place that they
> can call up
> on the phone.

The speaker of this poem asks that kindness be shown for the folk who thought that blindness was an illness that affected eyes alone. "We'd better see," says the speaker,

> what all our
> fearing and our
> jeering and our
> crying and
> our lying
> brought about.

Society is responsible for its children and for its own and its children's attitudes. As she shows in "Faces,"

> the brown caramel days of youth
> Reject the sun-sucked tit of
> childhood mornings.
> Poke a muzzle of war in the trust frozen eyes
> of a favored doll.

This is what humanity has wrought and what it must not accept. Humankind must be rendered both human and kind, the poet seems to say.

NEW DREAMS

Angelou calls repeatedly on the human race to spare itself from suffering. "There's one thing that I cry for I believe enough to die for/ That is every man's responsibility to man," says the speaker of "On Working White Liberals." "Dare us new dreams, Columbus," says the speaker of "A Georgia Song" (1983). In "America" (1975) Angelou speaks of America's promise that "has never been mined": "Her proud declarations/ are leaves in the wind." The United States, says the speaker, "entraps her children/ with legends untrue." This country of such high promise—the promise that all are equally entitled to life, liberty, and the pursuit of happiness—has not yet been discovered. Its citizens are led by their poet laureate to see that it is high time that the discovery be made.

OTHER MAJOR WORKS

SHORT FICTION: "Steady Going Up," 1972; "The Reunion," 1983.

PLAYS: *Cabaret for Freedom*, pr. 1960 (with Godfrey Cambridge; musical); *The Least of These*, pr. 1966; *Encounters*, pr. 1973; *Ajax*, pr. 1974 (adaptation of Sophocles' play); *And Still I Rise*, pr. 1976; *King*, pr. 1990 (musical; lyrics with Alistair Beaton, book by Lonne Elder III; music by Richard Blackford).

SCREENPLAYS: *Georgia, Georgia*, 1972; *All Day Long*, 1974.

TELEPLAYS: *Black, Blues, Black*, 1968 (10 episodes); *The Inheritors*, 1976; *The Legacy*, 1976; *I Know Why the Caged Bird Sings*, 1979 (with Leonora Thuna and Ralph B. Woolsey); *Sister, Sister*, 1982; *Brewster Place*, 1990.

NONFICTION: *I Know Why the Caged Bird Sings*, 1969; *Gather Together in My Name*, 1974; *Singin' and Swingin' and Gettin' Merry Like Christmas*, 1976; *The Heart of a Woman*, 1981; *All God's Children Need Traveling Shoes*, 1986; *Wouldn't Take Nothing for My Journey Now*, 1993; *Even the Stars Look Lonesome*, 1997; *A Song Flung Up to Heaven*, 2002; *Hallelujah! The Welcome Table: A Lifetime of Memories with Recipes*, 2004.

CHILDREN'S LITERATURE: *Mrs. Flowers: A Moment of Friendship*, 1986 (illustrated by Etienne Delessert); *Soul Looks Back in Wonder*, 1993; *My Painted House, My Friendly Chicken, and Me*, 1994; *Kofi and His Magic*, 1996; *Angelina of Italy*, 2004; *Izak of Lapland*, 2004; *Mikale of Hawaii*, 2004; *Renie Marie of France*, 2004.

MISCELLANEOUS: *Letter to My Daughter*, 2008.

BIBLIOGRAPHY

Angelou, Maya. Interviews. *Conversations with Maya Angelou*. Edited by Jeffrey M. Elliott. Jackson: University Press of Mississippi, 1989. Part of the University Press of Mississippi's ongoing Literary Conversations series, this work is a collection of more than thirty interviews with Angelou, accompanied by a chronology of her life. Provides a multifaceted perspective on the creative issues that have informed Angelou's work as an autobiographer and a poet.

Bloom, Harold, ed. *Maya Angelou*. New York: Bloom's Literary Criticism, 2008. Collection of essays providing criticism of Angelou's works, including her poetry.

Egan, Jill. *Maya Angelou: A Creative and Courageous Voice*. Pleasantville, N.Y.: Gareth Stevens, 2009. A biography of Angelou that sheds light on the thoughts and ideals that are expressed in her actions and her writings.

Gillespie, Marcia Ann, Rosa Johnson Butler, and Richard A. Long. *Maya Angelou: A Glorious Celebration*. Foreword by Oprah Winfrey. New York: Doubleday, 2008. A personal, illustrated biography of Angelou created by long-time friends Gillespie and Long and niece Butler. Contains more than 150 photographs, portraits, and letters.

Hagen, Lynn B. *Heart of a Woman, Mind of a Writer, and Soul of a Poet: A Critical Analysis of the Writings of Maya Angelou*. Lanham, Md.: University Press of America, 1996. This critical volume surveys Angelou's entire opus. Chapters include "Wit and Wisdom/Mirth and Mischief," "Abstracts in Ethics," and "Overview."

Lisandrelli, Elaine Slivinski. *Maya Angelou: More than a Poet*. Springfield, N.J.: Enslow, 1996. Lisandrelli discusses the flamboyance of Angelou, comparing her to the earlier African American author Zora Neale Hurston. Their hard work, optimism, perseverance, and belief in themselves are extolled.

Lupton, Mary Jane. *Maya Angelou: A Critical Companion*. Westport, Conn.: Greenwood Press, 1998. While focusing mainly on the autobiographies, Lupton's study is still useful as a balanced assessment of Angelou's writings. The volume also contains an excellent bibliography, particularly of Angelou's autobiographical works.

Pettit, Jayne. *Maya Angelou: Journey of the Heart*. New York: Lodestar Books, 1996.

Includes bibliographical references and an index. Traces Angelou's journey from childhood through her life as entertainer, activist, writer, and university professor.

Williams, Mary E., ed. *Readings on Maya Angelou.* San Diego, Calif.: Greenhaven Press, 1997. This collection of essays by literary scholars and noted faculty offers diverse voices and approaches to Angelou's literary canon.

Judith K. Taylor

AMIRI BARAKA
Everett LeRoi Jones

Born: Newark, New Jersey; October 7, 1934
Also known as: LeRoi Jones

PRINCIPAL POETRY

Spring and Soforth, 1960
Preface to a Twenty Volume Suicide Note, 1961
The Dead Lecturer, 1964
Black Art, 1966
A Poem for Black Hearts, 1967
Black Magic: Sabotage, Target Study, Black Art—Collected Poetry, 1961-1967,
     1969
In Our Terribleness: Some Elements and Meaning in Black Style, 1970 (with Fundi
     [Billy Abernathy])
It's Nation Time, 1970
Spirit Reach, 1972
Afrikan Revolution, 1973
Hard Facts, 1975
AM/TRAK, 1979
Selected Poetry of Amiri Baraka/LeRoi Jones, 1979
Reggae or Not!, 1981
Transbluesency: The Selected Poems of Amiri Baraka/LeRoi Jones, 1995
Wise, Why's, Y's, 1995
Funk Lore: New Poems, 1984-1995, 1996
Somebody Blew Up America, and Other Poems, 2003
Un Poco Low Coup, 2004
Mixed Blood: Number One, 2005

OTHER LITERARY FORMS

Amiri Baraka (buh-RAH-kuh) is a protean literary figure, equally well known for his poetry, drama, and essays. In addition, he has written short stories and experimental fiction. Baraka's early plays, notably *Dutchman* (pr., pb. 1964), *The Slave* (pr., pb. 1964), and *The Toilet* (pr., pb. 1964), were produced under his given name, LeRoi Jones, and derive from his period of involvement with the New York City avant-garde. Baraka's critical and political prose has appeared in many collections, and throughout his career, he has been active as an anthologist of African American literature.

Amiri Baraka
(Library of Congress)

ACHIEVEMENTS
Amiri Baraka has been the recipient of many awards and honors. He won the Longview Best Essay of the Year (1961) for his essay "Cuba Libre," the Obie Award for Best American Play of 1964 for *Dutchman*, the American Book Award from the Before Columbus Foundation for *Confirmation: An Anthology of African-American Women* (1984), a PEN-Faulkner Award (1989), the Langston Hughes Award (1989), the Lifetime Achievement Award from the Before Columbus Foundation (1989), Italy's Ferroni Award and Foreign Poet Award (1993), and the Playwright's Award from the Black Drama Festival of Winston-Salem, North Carolina, in 1997. He received fellowships and grants from the John Whitney Foundation, the Guggenheim Foundation, and the National Endowment for the Arts, the Rockefeller Foundation, and the New Jersey State Council for the Arts. He was awarded a doctorate of humane letters from Malcolm X College in Chicago (1972). He also served as poet laureate of New Jersey from July, 2002, until the post was abolished in July, 2003.

BIOGRAPHY

Imamu Amiri Baraka, as he has been known since 1967, was born Everett LeRoi Jones into a black middle-class family in Newark, New Jersey, the son of postal worker-elevator operator Coyette Leroy Jones and social worker Anna Lois Russ Jones. An excellent student whose parents encouraged his intellectual interests, young LeRoi Jones developed lifelong interests in literature and music at an early age. After graduating with honors from a predominately white high school, he was admitted to Rutgers University in 1951. The following year, he briefly attended Columbia University before transferring to Howard University, but he dropped out in 1954 at the age of nineteen. He would later receive M.A. degrees in philosophy from Columbia and in German literature from the New School for Social Research. Jones afterward spent more than two years in the United States Air Force, primarily in Puerto Rico, during which time he began to write. He was promoted to sergeant before receiving an undesirable discharge as a suspected communist.

By 1957, Jones was living a bohemian existence in the creative environment of Greenwich Village and New York's Lower East Side, where he embarked on his literary career while working at a variety of jobs. During the early or "Beat" stage of his career, Jones associated closely with numerous white avant-garde poets, including Robert Creeley, Allen Ginsberg, Robert Duncan, Frank O'Hara, Jack Kerouac, Charles Olson, Gilbert Sorrentino, and Diane di Prima, with whom he founded the American Theatre for Poets in 1961. Such literary figures were important in the development of his voice as a writer, demonstrating by example the many forms that poetry could assume and changing his preconceptions of what poems could or should be.

In 1958, the year he founded Totem Press, Jones married Hettie Cohen, a white woman. They edited their self-published magazine *Yugen* for five years. They had two daughters, Kellie Elisabeth and Lisa Victoria. Jones meanwhile began establishing himself as an important young radical poet, critic, and editor. Among the many magazines to which he contributed was *Down Beat*, the jazz journal where he first expressed the musical interests that had a large impact on his poetry. The political interests that dominated Jones's later work were unmistakably present as early as 1960, when, upon the invitation of Fidel Castro, he toured Cuba with a group of black intellectuals. This event sparked his perception of the United States as a corrupt bourgeois society and seems particularly significant in relation to his later socialist emphasis. Jones's growing political interest conditioned his initial collection of poetry, *Preface to a Twenty Volume Suicide Note*, and to his first produced plays, including the Obie Award-winning *Dutchman*, which anticipated a major transformation in Jones's life.

Following the assassination of Malcolm X in 1965, Jones joined the Black Nationalist movement. He separated from Hettie Cohen, severed ties with his white associates, and moved from the Village to Harlem later that same year. Turning his attention to direct action within the black community, he founded the influential although short-lived

Black Arts Repertory Theatre School (BARTS) in Harlem and, following his return to his native city in 1966, the Spirit House in Newark. In 1967, Jones married a black actress and fellow poet, Sylvia Robinson, who became Bibi Amina Baraka. The couple would have five children, one of whom, Shani Isis, was murdered in 2003. In 1967, Jones adopted his new name, Imamu Amiri Baraka, which means "Prince" (Ameer) "the blessed one" (Baraka), along with the honorary title of "Imamu" ("spiritual leader"). In 1966-1967, he lectured at San Francisco State University, just one of several institutions of higher learning where he has taught—including New School University, the University of Buffalo, Columbia, Yale, Rutgers, and George Washington universities—and added to his controversial status by penning a number of poems and articles considered anti-Semitic.

Over the next half-dozen years, as his reputation as a writer and political activist grew, Baraka helped found and mentor the Black Community Development and Defense Organization, the Congress of African Peoples (convened in Atlanta in 1970), and the National Black Political Convention (convened in Gary, Indiana, in 1972). As a leading spokesperson of the Black Arts movement, Baraka provided support for young black poets and playwrights, including Larry Neal, Ed Bullins, Marvin X, and Ron Milner. During the Newark uprising/riot of 1968 after the assassination of Martin Luther King, Jr., Baraka was arrested for unlawful possession of firearms. Although he was convicted and given the maximum sentence after the judge read his poem "Black People!" as an example of incitement to riot, the three-year sentence was reversed on appeal.

Baraka supported Kenneth A. Gibson's campaign to become the first black mayor of Newark in 1970, but he later broke with Gibson over what he perceived as the bourgeois values of the administration. This disillusionment with black politics within the American system, combined with Baraka's attendance at the Sixth Pan-African Conference at Dar es Salaam in 1974, precipitated the subsequent stage of his political evolution. While not entirely abandoning his commitment to confront the special problems of African Americans, Baraka came to interpret these problems within the framework of an overarching Marxist-Leninist-Maoist philosophy and left the Nationalist cause, which he considered racist and fascist, in favor of an anti-imperialist stance. In conjunction with this second transformation, Baraka dropped the title "Imamu" and changed the name of his Newark publishing firm from "Jihad" to "People's War." His attitudes changed again, and he publicly denounced his former biases against women, Jews, and gays, calling for black and white workers of all persuasions to work together in their class struggle for social change.

From 1979 until his retirement in 1999, Baraka taught, lectured, and conducted workshops with the Africana Studies Department at the State University of New York-Stony Brook. In his retirement, he has remained active and has continued to produce work; he has also appeared in more than twenty films, usually as himself. Baraka is noted not only for his writings but also for his influence as an intellectual on young writers and social critics. He was the editor of *Black Nation*, the organ of the League of Revolutionary Struggle, a Marxist organization disbanded in 1990. His influence extends far beyond African American culture and politics to embrace other people of color. Native American writer Maurice Kenney, for example, credited Baraka for teaching ethnic writers how to open doors to important venues for their writing, to "claim and take" their place at the cultural forefront.

ANALYSIS

Amiri Baraka's importance as a poet rests on both the diversity of his work and the singular intensity of his Black Nationalist period. In fact, Baraka's diversity gave his nationalist poetry a symbolic significance with personal, political, and aesthetic dimensions. Perhaps his most substantial achievement is his ability to force reconsideration of the relationship between the artist, his work, its audience, and the encompassing social context. Reconstructing his own vision of this relationship both at the beginning and at the end of the nationalist period, Baraka has increasingly stressed the necessity for an art that will alter the context and increase the real freedom of both artist and community.

During his Black Nationalist period, Baraka concentrated on exposing the unstated racist premises of Euro-American art while developing an alternative black aesthetic. In part because he had demonstrated mastery of Euro-American poetic modes, Baraka's Black Nationalist philosophy commanded an unusual degree of white attention. Coming from a then-unknown writer, his militant poetry might well have been dismissed as a naïve kind of propaganda. It did, in fact, alienate many earlier admirers, who came to see him as an embodiment of the civil disorders rampant in the mid-1960's. On a more profound level, however, he spurred the more thoughtful of his readers to ponder the complex logic of his transformation and to reassess the political implications of their own aesthetic stances.

Even as Baraka's relationship with the "mainstream" audience underwent this metamorphosis, his call for a militant and, if necessary, violent response to American racism received an affirmative answer from a significant number of younger African American writers. Challenging them to speak directly to and for the African American community, Baraka pursued the implications of his demand and employed his poetry as a direct political force. His subsequent turn to a socialist position, reflecting his growing conviction that simple nationalism unintentionally contributed to capitalist oppression, forced many Black Nationalists to reassess their own positions. Though Baraka again alienated a portion of his audience, he continued to generate serious debate on central issues. Throughout his career, but especially in the 1960's and early 1970's, Baraka has exerted a combined political and aesthetic influence matched by few other figures in American literary history.

Baraka's poetry falls into three distinctive periods, each reflecting an attempt to find a philosophy capable of responding adequately to what he viewed as a corrupt culture. The voice of each period is shaped in accord with a different set of assumptions concerning the nature of the cultural corruption, the proper orientation toward political action, and the poet's relationship with his audience.

During his early period, Baraka built an essentially aesthetic response on premises shared primarily with white poets and intellectuals. Although Baraka always recognized the importance of his racial and economic heritage, the intricate philosophical voice of the early period sounds highly individualistic in comparison with his later work. In his middle, Black Nationalist period, Baraka shifted emphasis to the racial dimension of American culture. The associated voice—much more accessible, though not nearly so simple as it first appears—reflects Baraka's desire to relate primarily to the African American community. Throughout his third and ongoing Marxist-Leninist-Maoist period, Baraka adopted a less emotionally charged voice in accord with his stance as a scientific analyst of capitalist corruption.

Differing from the voices of the earlier periods—which assumed an equality between Baraka and his audience, whether based on aesthetic awareness or racial experience—this socialist voice frequently takes on the didactic tones of a teacher lecturing an audience unaware of its potential identity as a revolutionary proletariat. The diversity of Baraka's work makes it extremely difficult to find a vocabulary equally relevant to the complex postmodernism of *Preface to a Twenty Volume Suicide Note*, the militant nationalism of *Black Magic*, and the uncompromising economic analysis of *Hard Facts*. Nevertheless, Baraka is not three different people, but one person expressing himself at three different stages of awareness. Anticipations and echoes of all three voices occur during each period. Throughout his career, several constants emerge, most notably a philosophical refusal to conform to the demands of what he views as a corrupt culture and an emphasis on the oral/musical nature of the poetic experience.

Baraka's early work emphasizes the relationship between psychological experience, vocal rhythm, and the poetic line. This aesthetic adapts and develops those of Euro-American poets such as Duncan, Creeley, and Olson, whose essay "Projective Verse" states many of the general premises of the group with which Baraka associated. Olson insists on "the possibilities of breath" as the central element of "Open" verse and develops the idea that "FORM IS NEVER MORE THAN THE EXTENSION OF CONTENT." Given this aesthetic, the poetic voice should embody the precise rhythm and emphasis of the poet's immediate experience and perception.

"DUNCAN SPOKE OF A PROCESS"

The poem "Duncan Spoke of a Process" both explicitly recognizes Baraka's aesthetic affinities (he also inscribed poems to Gary Snyder, Ginsberg, and Michael McClure during this period) and analyzes the experience and premises shaping his voice. The poem typifies Baraka's early work in that it is philosophical, abstract, and nonracial. Although it may obliquely relate to Baraka's experience as a black man, it is equally accessible to a reader whose emotional state derives from different circumstances. In addition, it typifies the early work in its intimation of the deep dissatisfaction with Euro-American culture that led to Baraka's political development.

Assuming an audience familiar with Duncan, Baraka meditates on the emotional and intellectual implications of Duncan's work and revises its aesthetic in accord with his own perceptions. Although he reiterates the word "repeat" three times in the first stanza, he is not simply repeating Duncan's words. The poem most closely resembles Duncan in its syntax, which mirrors the hesitations of a consciousness struggling to embody a natural process in order to find words that repeat experience "as a day repeats/ its color." Frequently "sentences" consist of a string of perceptual units with ambiguous syntactic relationships. Many sentences contain no concrete images ("Before that, what came easiest"); the images that do occur are in relation to poetic consciousness rather than external "reality." Like Duncan's, Baraka's landscape is part psychological and part mythic or archetypal. The image of unidentified people traveling across the "greenest earth" represents his struggle to unite these landscapes, to bring the nurturing archetypal world to life in the persona's mind.

The remainder of the poem, however, emphasizes the persona's inability to achieve this rejuvenating unity. He insists that all abstract ideas and assumptions be validated in relation to memory (of psychological states rather than of external experiences). His memory, however, confronts him with an internal wasteland, "a heap of broken feeling." Starting with this consuming feeling of loss—whether of lover, childhood innocence, affinity with Duncan, or spiritual resiliency remains purposefully ambiguous—the persona's process leads him increasingly toward solipsism. No longer able to distinguish between "love" and "opinion," he feels no sense of the reality of past connections; even the archetypal Eden seems to be an illusion. Existing ". . . where there/ is nothing, save myself. . . . ," he says, "I cannot fill/ myself. . . ." The isolation of the word "myself" in its own line emphasizes the isolation that momentarily overwhelms the persona. Paradoxically, the line expressing the moment of existential terror intimates the pure merging of voice and consciousness associated with the processes of nature in the first stanza.

Perhaps because of this resemblance, the moment generates in the persona a resolve to reestablish contact with the external world. His determination, however, collapses in a way that, at least in retrospect, seems to anticipate Baraka's later political development. His first reaction to the existential terror is a perception of what he "love[s] most." Rather than reassuring him, however, this engenders a cynical determination—perhaps reflecting the continuing sense of loss—that he will "not/ leave what futile lies/ I have." In a context where "love" is a "futile lie," the persona's subsequent decision to "go out to/ what is most beautiful" demands ironic revaluation. The irony increases when the persona derives his conception of the "beautiful" from the platitudinous appeal to nobility of "some noncombatant Greek/ or soft Italian prince," the originators of the Machiavellian slavocracy of Euro-American culture. The persona's concluding questions anticipate the insistence on social and political processes that characterizes Baraka's later works: "And which one/ is truly/ to rule here? And/ what country is this?" Duncan spoke of a process which was essentially mythic, natural, and psychological. While mirroring this process, Baraka's internal processes are clearly carrying him toward the political arena where questions concerning control and possession are central rather than subordinate.

"CROW JANE" AND "LEROY"

Throughout his early work, Baraka tries on a variety of personas, indicating a fascination with masks that provides the center for some of his most interesting early work. The "Crow Jane" sequence, echoing both William Butler Yeats's "Crazy Jane" poems and a blues composition by Mississippi Joe Williams, focuses on the limits of social masking. "Crow Jane," a white woman unconsciously adopting the old Jim Crow racial patterns, attempts to escape her role in "straight" America only to find herself a "wet lady of no image." Even more uncompromising in its dissatisfaction with masks that derive meaning from Euro-American cultural patterns, "An Agony. As New." develops the image of a persona being burned within a mask of "white hot metal." Tormented by the constrictions of a corrupt, mechanical white role, the persona feels itself "inside someone/ who hates me." Although that someone can easily be seen as a white self, tormenting a black soul, the poem is not developed in explicitly racial terms. It could apply, for example, to a gay person living a "straight" life or a businessperson on the verge of a breakdown. Its implications are clear, however; inexorably, the agony leads to the final line consisting only of the word "screams." Again, the "projective" merging of voice and experience is pure, but the echoes of the scream sound in a voice no longer intended for the ears of the white avant-garde.

Baraka's nationalist voice, collective where the earlier voice was individualistic, aspires to a specifically "black" purity. Even while assuming the role of teacher, Baraka claims authority for his voice only to the extent that it reflects the strength and values of his African American heritage. In "Leroy," he offers up his old voice to the black community, urging it to "pick me apart and take the/ useful parts, the sweet meat of my feelings. And leave/ the bitter . . . rotten white parts/ alone." The alienation associated with Euro-American culture, expressed in the word "alone" as a line by itself, contrasts with the expansive sense of connection felt by the Amiri who rejects the masks of his predecessor "Leroy."

It would be misleading, however, to suggest that Baraka simply rejects all masks imposed by white society in order to reveal his "true" black face. Even while rebelling against the masks associated with his avant-garde personas, Baraka continues to explore the potential of masking in relation to his new orientation. This exploration takes two distinct forms—both designed to bring Baraka closer to the black community. First, he realizes that his own family background distances him from the "black angels" and "strong nigger feeling" described in "Leroy." Even while envisioning Leroy's mother "getting into/ new blues, from the old ones," he sees her "hypnotizing" him as she stares into "the future of the soul." In relation to African American culture, the future of the black bourgeoisie appears increasingly white and alienated. To become "purely black," Baraka must to some extent mask the influence of his class origins. Second, the mask itself is a central image in both African and African American culture. Invoking both the ritual knowledge of Africa and the survival strategy of the black South, the mask has been exploited in African American literature from Charles Waddell Chesnutt and Langston Hughes through Ralph Ellison and William Melvin Kelley. To speak with a black voice, Baraka must, like Br'er Rabbit, present a variety of shifting surfaces, both to defend against and to attack the predatory forces of his environment.

CALL-AND-RESPONSE

These shifting surfaces are extremely elusive, deriving their meaning as much from audience as from speaker. Using musical forms and images as primary points of reference, Baraka explores this relationship between group and individual voices. His music criticism frequently refers to the primacy in African American culture of the call-and-response mode of work songs and spirituals. Playing off this dynamic, many of Baraka's nationalist poems identify his individual voice with that of a group leader calling for an affirmative response from his community. "Three Movements and a Coda," for example, concludes: "These are songs if you have the/ music." Baraka can provide lyrics, but if they are to come alive as songs, the music must be provided by the participation of a responsive community. The conclusion of "Black Art" makes it clear that this music is more than a purely aesthetic response: "Let the world be a Black Poem/ And Let All Black People Speak This Poem/ Silently/ or LOUD." If the world is to be a poem for the black community, a political response must accompany the aesthetic one.

Determining the precise nature of the desired response demands an awareness of the differing implications of Baraka's poetry when interpreted in relation to white and black cultural traditions. Euro-American reactions to Baraka's nationalist voice tend to attribute even its most extreme statements to the poet himself, dismissing the possibility that he is wearing a mask for political purposes. This is particularly significant in relation to the poems in which Baraka appears to suggest random violence against whites. "Three Movements and a Coda" presents the image of looting a drugstore as a guerrilla attack on the "Vampire Nazis." "Black People!" includes the exhortation: "you can't steal nothin' from a white man, he's already stole it he owes/ you anything you want, even his life." The same poem, using profanity as "magic words," pictures looting as a "magic dance in the street."

"A POEM SOME PEOPLE WILL HAVE TO UNDERSTAND"

Frequently, Baraka pictures violence in graphic images of "smashing at jelly-white faces" or "cracking steel knuckles in a jewlady's mouth." Given the unqualified intensity of these images, it hardly seems surprising that many white and less militant black readers dismiss the Baraka of this period as a reverse racist forwarding the very modes of thought he ostensibly rejects. In essence, they take the call that concludes "A Poem Some People Will Have to Understand" on a literal level. When Baraka asks: "Will the machinegunners please step forward," they respond that a military race war can end only in catastrophe for both races.

As the title of the poem suggests, however, the call should not be interpreted simplistically. To be understood, it must be seen in the context of Baraka's view of the historical response of African Americans to racist oppression. Describing a society in which "the wheel, and the wheels, wont let us alone," he points out that blacks have "awaited the coming of a natural/ phenomenon" to effect a release. Only after repeating "But none has come" three times does Baraka summon the "machinegunners." The call sounds Baraka's response to what he sees as the traditional passivity of the African American community. Recognizing that practically all black experience involves direct contact with psychological racism tied to economic exploitation, Baraka treats these shared experiences hyperbolically in order to shake his community into political action. Placed in a social context where violent group rebellion has been the exception, there is much less chance than most white readers believe that his words will be acted on literally. The use of this aesthetic of calculated overstatement demonstrates Baraka's willingness to use the tradition of masking for a new set of political purposes. Where the form of most African American masks has been dictated by their relationship to white psychology, however, Baraka shapes his new masks to elicit response from blacks. Far from oversimplifying his awareness in the nationalist period, Baraka demonstrates his developing sense of the complexity of poetry designed to function in a real social and political context.

The contextual complexity, however, adds a new dimension of seriousness to attacks on Baraka's use of anti-Semitism and racism as rhetorical strategies. Baraka negotiates extremely treacherous territory when and if he expects readers to concentrate on his desire to "Clean out the world for virtue and love" in the same poem ("Black Art") that endorses "poems that kill . . . Setting fire and death to/ whitie's ass." A similar apparent paradox occurs in "Black People!" which says both "Take their lives if need be" and "let's make a world we want black children to grow and learn in." Baraka's aesthetic approach, which vests ultimate authority in the authenticating response, raises the problematic possibility that the audience's real social actions will authenticate the destructive rhetoric rather than the constructive vision.

"IT'S NATION TIME" AND "AFRICA AFRICA AFRICA"

Baraka attempts to diminish this possibility by developing his constructive vision in celebratory nationalist poems such as "It's Nation Time" and "Africa Africa Africa," which introduce a new musical/chant mode to his work. Exhortations such as "Black Art," which, like Baraka's earlier work, manipulate punctuation and syntax to express fully the urgency of an emotional experience, also anticipate the chant poems by introducing oratorical elements reflecting participation in communal ritual. "A Poem for Black Hearts," for example, varies the opening phrase "For Malcolm's eyes" to establish a focal point for audience response. "For Malcolm's words," "For Malcolm's heart," and similar phrases provide a kind of drumbeat for Baraka's meditation on the fallen leader.

In "It's Nation Time" and "Africa Africa Africa," this drumbeat, clearly the constitutive structural element, often sounds explicitly: "Boom/ Boom/ BOOOM/ Boom." Writing primarily in short lines echoing these single drumbeats, Baraka uses reiteration and rhythmical variation to stress his vision of Pan-African unity. The first thirteen lines of "Africa Africa Africa" include no words other than "Africa" and "Africans." Anticipating Baraka's developing interest in reggae music, these poems call for the transformation of the old forms of African American culture into those of a new Pan-African sensibility. "It's Nation Time" phrases this call: "get up rastus for real to be rasta fari." Baraka rejects those "rastus" figures content to wear the passive masks imposed on Africans unaware of their heritage, and celebrates the Rastafarians, a Caribbean sect associated strongly with reggae.

AM/TRAK

The most effective poems of Baraka's socialist period redirect the music of these nationalist chants in an attempt to lead the proletariat, black and white, to a new awareness of the implications of its own experience. *AM/TRAK*, Baraka's celebration of John Coltrane, attempts to chart this new social and aesthetic awareness by relating Baraka's poetic processes to those of the great jazz saxophonist. Beginning with a section that, like the saxophonist's piercing high notes, merges "History Love Scream," Baraka explores the origins of Coltrane's art, which combines individual intensity and the communal response of the bars and churches of Coltrane's Philadelphia. At once purely black and more highly aware than any single voice from the community, Coltrane's voice combines "The vectors from all sources—slavery, renaissance/ bop Charlie Parker/ nigger absolute super-sane screams against reality."

Just as Coltrane's voice incorporates and surpasses that of Charlie "Yardbird" Parker, Baraka's incorporates Coltrane's and places it in a wider socialist perspective. Meditating on the aesthetic "difficulty" of both Coltrane's experimental sounds and his own philosophical works, Baraka considers the threat of losing the communal response: "'Trane you blows too long.'/ Screaming niggers drop out yr solos." Of course, the phrase "drop out" is ambiguous: Even as the audience refuses to make the effort to comprehend the call, the call perfectly expresses the implications of the audience's experience. Such a call, Baraka insists, can never simply fade into silence. Rather, it will receive a response from artists such as Thelonius Monk, the jazz pianist who played "Street gospel intellectual mystic survival codes." Coltrane's audience, according to Baraka, consists largely of fellow artists able to perceive the depths of his involvement with black reality.

By associating his own voice with Coltrane's, Baraka points to the developing distance between himself and his wider audience, a distance reflecting his shift to a socialist stance. The poem's final section, especially, is much more politically explicit than either the previous sections or Coltrane's music. As he does in numerous poems of the period, including "Dictatorship of the Proletariat" and "Class Struggle in Music," Baraka insists that the capitalist economic system bears full responsibility for the aesthetic and political corruption of American life. Seeing that "the money lord hovers oer us," he concludes, "only socialism brought by revolution/ can win." Meditating on Coltrane's death in relation to the Newark disorders, Baraka responds to his music as an implicit call for the socialist revolution that will "Be reality alive in motion in flame to change." The intensity of the call for change is unmistakable, in both Coltrane's music and Baraka's poetry. Baraka's identification of the change with "socialism brought by revolution," however, seems abstract and unconvincing in contrast, perhaps because of the relative flatness of diction.

As in many of the poems of the socialist period, Baraka's rhetorical strategy seems unclear. *AM/TRAK* contains few indications that the last section should be seen as some type of intricate mask. In fact, American socialist writing lacks a dominant tradition of masking and also tends to reject philosophically anything other than direct confrontation. Still, Baraka certainly retains his knowledge of the African American tradition of masking and has the ability to adjust his voice in accord with shifting social contexts. His extreme didactic stance may be intended as much to spark debate as to enforce agreement. The direct attacks on Don L. Lee (Haki R. Madhubuti) and Nikki Giovanni that occur in Baraka's works, however, suggest that such an interpretation may be overly ingenuous and that Baraka does in fact seek total agreement.

SOCIALIST VOICE

No simple aesthetic analysis suffices to explain either Baraka's new poetic voice or his difficulty in calling forth an affirmative response from either the artistic or the working-class community. Lines such as "This is the dictatorship of the proletariat/ the total domination of society by the working class" can easily be dismissed as lacking either the intellectual complexity or the emotional power of Baraka's earlier work. Such a dismissal, however, risks avoiding the issue of cultural conditioning, which Baraka has come to view as central. Arguing that capitalist control of the media deforms both the proletariat's image of itself as a revolutionary force and its response to a "pure" socialist art, Baraka attempts to shatter the psychological barriers through techniques of reiteration similar to those used in his nationalist poetry. His relationship with the proletariat audience, however, generates a new set of political and aesthetic problems. While the nationalist voice assumed authority only insofar as it was validated by the experience of the African American community, the socialist voice must take on the additional burden of convincing the proletarian audience that its interpretation of its own experience has been "incorrect." If the community does not respond to Baraka's voice as its own, the problem lies with a brainwashed response rather than with a tainted call (the source of the problem in "Leroy"). As a result, Baraka frequently adopts a "lecturer's" voice to provide the "hard facts" that will overcome resistance to political action by proving that capitalism deceives the proletariat into accepting a "dictatorship of the minority."

The lack of response to his poems based on this aesthetic may simply reflect the accuracy of his analysis of the problem. What is certain is that Baraka remains determined to resist corruption in whatever form he perceives it and that he continues to search for a voice like the one described in "Class Struggle in Music (2)," a voice that "even reached you."

SOMEBODY BLEW UP AMERICA, AND OTHER POEMS

The critically acclaimed collection *Somebody Blew Up America, and Other Poems* is dominated by the title poem, Baraka's inflammatory response to the September 11, 2001, terrorist attacks on the United States. The title poem is a sharp thorn among roses of tribute and remembrance, such as "Beginnings: Malcolm," an homage to Malcolm X that raises the issue of Christianity's contribution to the disharmonious state of affairs in the world. The title poem, read publicly beginning on September 19, 2001, and published in November of that year, caused a storm of controversy.

"Somebody Blew Up America" is a polemic that uses a terrorist act of global consequence as a jumping-off point to condemn terrorism in general, and especially the terrorism practiced by whites against minorities, particularly that which occurs in the United States. The poem gathers many threads from Baraka's traditional themes. Racism, corruption, class warfare, government, and imperialism all come under fire in an angry litany of historical outrages—slavery, murder, genocide, market manipulation, Christianity, assassination, capitalism, financial control, and political shenanigans—along with the more recent outrage of passenger-plane attacks against buildings. The poem also brings together elements of Baraka's three creative phases: the intellectual avant-garde, the Black Nationalist, and the radically political.

The structure and tone of the poem owe much to the Beat movement of the 1950's, particularly to Ginsberg's "Howl" (1956). Baraka, in fact, seems to be paying homage to Ginsberg in his repetition of the refrain "Who" and in his reference to an owl in the final stanzas. Stylistically, the poem draws on several traditions: blank verse, spur-of-the-moment rhyme, and repetitious, hip-hop rhythm. Like the Beats, Baraka is not afraid to use a full range of techniques—blunt language, emotionally charged words, racial epithets, Ebonics, slang, and street lingo—to drive home a point. He accuses both the living and the dead (naming such well-known public figures as Trent Lott, David Duke, Rudy Giuliani, Jesse Helms, George W. Bush, Colin Powell, and Condoleezza Rice) of complicity in a five-hundred-year conspiracy to eliminate undesirables, opponents, and the outspoken in an all-consuming effort to dominate the world. Baraka asks tough questions, demanding to know who has historically been the worst mass murderers; who has been the chief aggressors over the ages; who currently controls the oil, the media, and the governments around the globe; and who is responsible for the sad state of the world. The material is based on fact, innuendo, rumor, and wild speculation, making it difficult to distinguish where truth leaves off and fiction begins. The poet's anger is real, and the targets of his vituperation are legion, but he sometimes contradicts himself in his righteous vehemence. After the initial shock of "Somebody Blew Up America" wears off, the thoughtful reader is left with the myriad questions the poem raises, but is provided no answers for how to correct humankind's self-destructive nature or how to change the course of history. Even if reminded of the past, Baraka seems to say, people are condemned to repeat it.

In the poem, Baraka implies that Jews both in the United States and abroad were aware in advance of the September 11 attacks and stayed away from New York City on the day the planes crashed into the Twin Towers. Suggestions like this caused New Jersey's governor to call for Baraka to resign from his post as the state's poet laureate. Baraka, however, refused to do so, and the post was abolished in 2003, ending his appointment.

UN POCO LOW COUP

In contrast to much of Baraka's earlier poetic work, *Un Poco Low Coup* presents brief bursts of inspiration about a range of subjects. The short folio (twenty-three pages) features poems combined with illustrations, photographs, scribbles, and drawings in folk-art style to aid in understanding or to visually expand on a theme. The pieces are experiments in concision, based on the Japanese haiku, the impressionistic seventeen-syllable poem used to express small but significant or profound moments. The title of Baraka's collection (*un poco* means "a little" in Spanish) is an ironic pun on the sound of the word "haiku," in the same vein as such earlier works as *Raise Race Rays Raze: Essays Since 1965* (1971) or *Wise, Why's, Y's* (1995). "Low coup" (LOW-coo) may be presumed to have the opposite intent of the haiku, as filtered through politically motivated, radicalized African American sensibilities, wherein skepticism rules and things are not accepted at face value. The reader is warned in advance that these epigram-like or graffiti-styled efforts, though echoing the brevity of the Japanese verse, do not aim at high art, but low art, since puns are traditionally considered one of the lower forms of humor. Many pieces in *Un Poco Low Coup* do not even attempt to duplicate the precise haiku form, as though the poet, after consciously launching the collection in imitation of a well-established poetic form, found the ancient structure too confining for modern thought.

Reflecting Baraka's lifelong love of music and rhythm, the poems in *Un Poco Low Coup* are like improvisational, jazz-flavored riffs—as though scored for such traditional Japanese instruments as the koto, the shamisen, the hichiriki, or the taiko—touching on favorite themes. These nuggets of arcane, esoteric wisdom are intended as thought-provoking snacks for the brain, rather than as a filling meal for the soul. Much can be read into them, but the reader has to do most of the work; Baraka's short poems are only a beginning rather than an end, a catalyst to cogitation rather than a completed thought.

It is difficult to argue about the premise of the individual poems. Like the haiku that spawned them, the *Un Poco Low Coup* poems are so brief and so open-ended that interpretation becomes the sole responsibility of readers, all of whom will bring unique personal experiences that contribute to understanding; Baraka proposes, but each person disposes meaning.

In "Ancient Music," for example, Baraka contends that death is humankind's common enemy, and everything else pales by comparison. "In the Funk World," he posits that James Brown deserves more acclaim than Elvis Presley for his contributions to music. The wry "Monday in B-flat" suggests that dialing emergency is more efficacious than prayer in getting results. "Low Coup for Bush 2" recommends imprisonment for George W. Bush. In "Heaven," Baraka implies that the concept of servitude and the idea of slavery was an original tenet of Christianity. Ultimately, the value of the poems of *Un Poco Low Coup* can be summed up in a paraphrase of an older, haiku-like aphorism: "Profundity is in the eye—and ear—of the informed, politically aware beholder."

OTHER MAJOR WORKS

LONG FICTION: *The System of Dante's Hell*, 1965.

SHORT FICTION: *Tales*, 1967; *The Fiction of LeRoi Jones/Amiri Baraka*, 2000; *Tales of the Out and the Gone*, 2007.

PLAYS: *The Baptism*, pr. 1964; *Dutchman*, pr., pb. 1964; *The Slave*, pr., pb. 1964; *The Toilet*, pr., pb. 1964; *Experimental Death Unit #1*, pr. 1965; *Jello*, pr. 1965; *A Black Mass*, pr. 1966; *Arm Yourself, or Harm Yourself*, pr., pb. 1967; *Great Goodness of Life (A Coon Show)*, pr. 1967; *Madheart*, pr. 1967; *Slave Ship: A Historical Pageant*, pr., pb. 1967; *The Death of Malcolm X*, pb. 1969; *Bloodrites*, pr. 1970; *Junkies Are Full of (SHHH . . .)*, pr. 1970; *A Recent Killing*, pr. 1973; *S-1*, pr. 1976; *The Motion of History*, pr. 1977; *The Sidney Poet Heroical*, pb. 1979 (originally as *Sidnee Poet Heroical*, pr. 1975); *What Was the Relationship of the Lone Ranger to the Means of Production?*, pr., pb. 1979; *At the Dim'cracker Party Convention*, pr. 1980; *Weimar*, pr. 1981; *Money: A*

Jazz Opera, pr. 1982; *Primitive World: An Anti-Nuclear Jazz Musical*, pr. 1984; *The Life and Life of Bumpy Johnson*, pr. 1991; *General Hag's Skeezag*, pb. 1992; *Meeting Lillie*, pr. 1993; *The Election Machine Warehouse*, pr. 1996.

NONFICTION: "*Cuba Libre*," 1961; *The New Nationalism*, 1962; *Blues People: Negro Music in White America*, 1963; *Home: Social Essays*, 1966; *Black Music*, 1968; *A Black Value System*, 1970; *Kawaida Studies: The New Nationalism*, 1971; *Raise Race Rays Raze: Essays Since 1965*, 1971; *Strategy and Tactics of a Pan-African Nationalist Party*, 1971; *Crisis in Boston!*, 1974; *The Creation of the New Ark*, 1975; *Daggers and Javelins: Essays*, 1984; *The Autobiography of LeRoi Jones/Amiri Baraka*, 1984; *The Artist and Social Responsibility*, 1986; *The Music: Reflections on Jazz and Blues*, 1987 (with Amina Baraka); *Conversations with Amiri Baraka*, 1994 (Charlie Reilly, editor); *Jesse Jackson and Black People*, 1994; *Eulogies*, 1996; *Digging: Afro American Be/At American Classical Music*, 1999; *Bushwacked! A Counterfeit President for a Fake Democracy: A Collection of Essays on the 2000 National Elections*, 2001; *National Elections*, 2001; *Jubilee: The Emergence of African-American Culture*, 2003 (with others); *The Essence of Reparations*, 2003; *Home: Social Essays*, 2009.

EDITED TEXTS: *The Moderns: New Fiction in America*, 1963; *Black Fire: An Anthology of Afro-American Writing*, 1968 (with Larry Neal); *African Congress: A Documentary of the First Modern Pan-African Congress*, 1972; *Confirmation: An Anthology of African-American Women*, 1983 (with Amina Baraka).

MISCELLANEOUS: *Selected Plays and Prose*, 1979; *The LeRoi Jones/Amiri Baraka Reader*, 1991; *Insomniacathon: Voices Without Restraint*, 1999 (audiocassette).

BIBLIOGRAPHY

Baraka, Amiri. "Amiri Baraka." http://www.amiri baraka.com. The official Web site for the author contains a brief biography, photographs, descriptions of books, selected poems and essays, recordings of poems, and links to other sites.

_____. Interviews. *Conversations with Amiri Baraka*. Edited by Charlie Reilly. Jackson: University Press of Mississippi, 1994. Offers insights into the black experience through Baraka's experiences during the turbulent later half of the twentieth century, from his ghetto life in the 1940's through the Black Nationalist movement of the 1970's to his intellectual life in the 1990's. Baraka critiques and elucidates his works and underscores his belief in the connection between art and social criticism.

Benston, Kimberly W., ed. *Imamu Amiri Baraka (LeRoi Jones): A Collection of Critical Essays*. Englewood Cliffs, N.J.: Prentice-Hall, 1978. Benston, who also wrote *Baraka: The Renegade and the Mask* (1976), brings together essays that shed light on various aspects of his poetry and drama. Includes a bibliography.

Collins, Lisa Gail, and Margo Natalie Crawford, eds. *New Thoughts on the Black Arts Movement*. Piscataway, N.J.: Rutgers University Press, 2006. This collection of essays discusses the African American renaissance in arts and letters during the 1960's and 1970's and examines the contributions of such influential figures as Baraka.

Epstein, Andrew. *Beautiful Enemies: Friendship and Postwar American Poetry.* New York: Oxford University Press, 2006. This study examines the complex and changeable relationships among and between writers John Ashbery, Frank O'Hara, Baraka and others of various New York intellectual circles, in terms of literary, personal, and philosophical issues.

Finch, Annie Ridley Crane, and Kathrine Lore Varnes, eds. *An Exaltation of Forms: Contemporary Poets Celebrate the Diversity of Their Art.* Ann Arbor: University of Michigan Press, 2002. This collection of essays focusing on contemporary poetic techniques includes a brief piece by Baraka, "The Low Coup as a Contemporary Afro-American Verse Form," explaining his rationale behind the poems in *Un Poco Low Coup.*

Gwynne, James B., ed. *Amiri Baraka: The Kaleidoscopic Torch.* New York: Steppingstones Press, 1985. This collection of poems and essays for and about Baraka includes Richard Oyama's analysis of "The Screamers," titled "A Secret Communal Expression," as well as essays by Clyde Taylor and E. San Juan, Jr.

Smethurst, James Edward. *The Black Arts Movement: Literary Nationalism in the 1960's and 1970's.* Chapel Hill: University of North Carolina Press, 2005. Part of the John Hope Franklin Series in African American History and Culture, this profusely illustrated study focuses on the cultural side of black self-awareness that grew out of the Civil Rights and Black Power movements, including Baraka's contributions to those efforts.

Watts, Jerry Gafio. *Amiri Baraka: The Politics and Art of a Black Intellectual.* New York: New York University Press, 2001. A critical appraisal. Watts argues that Baraka's artistry declined as he became more politically active, though he considers Baraka to be an important poet and lens through which African American political history can be viewed.

Woodard, K. Komozi. *A Nation Within a Nation: Amiri Baraka (LeRoi Jones) and Black Power Politics.* Chapel Hill: University of North Carolina Press, 1999. Revises the common view of Baraka as an extremist, arguing that he became a seasoned political veteran who brought together divergent black factions.

Craig Werner
Updated by Jack Ewing

PAUL BEATTY

Born: Los Angeles, California; 1962

PRINCIPAL POETRY
Big Bank Take Little Bank, 1991
Joker, Joker, Deuce, 1994
Slam! Poetry: Heftige Dichtung aus Amerika, 1994

OTHER LITERARY FORMS

After publishing three books of poetry, Paul Beatty (BAY-tee) turned to fiction, becoming widely known as a novelist. His novels, *The White Boy Shuffle* (1996), *Tuff* (2000), and *Slumberland* (2008), are comedic satires that address the complexities of African American and mainstream American culture at the turn of the millennium. Like his poetry, Beatty's novels are praised for their urban lyricism, quick wit, and wide-reaching social commentary. Beatty has also published an eclectic and controversial collection of African American humor entitled *Hokum: An Anthology of African American Humor* (2006).

ACHIEVEMENTS

Before trying his hand at fiction, Paul Beatty was known as a preeminent hip-hop poet and performance artist. He was crowned the Grand Slam Champion of the New York City-based Nuyorican Poets Café in 1991 for his work as a performance poet. That same year, the *Village Voice* named *Big Bank Take Little Bank* one of the best books of the year, and soon after *Newsweek* declared him "the premier bard of hiphop." Beatty's poetry is widely acclaimed for its sharp, postmodern edge and blend of high and low cultural references, a mix that is indebted to rap music but explodes beyond its urban borders. After carrying this hip-hop aesthetic from poetry into fiction, Beatty has secured a reputation for writing dazzling novels known for their percussive language, unflinching humor, and broad cultural references. Upon publication of his first novel, *The White Boy Shuffle*, *The New York Times* declared Beatty a new fiction writer to watch. In 2009, he received a grant from the Creative Capital Foundation. Beatty is considered a premier African American poet, novelist, satirist, and cultural commentator.

BIOGRAPHY

Paul Beatty was born in Los Angeles in 1962 and moved to West Los Angeles with his mother and two sisters when he was eight years old. In his introduction to *Hokum*, Beatty admits that by this time he had already been combing through his mother's library, reading impressive amounts of literature from E. L. Doctorow to *Mad* magazine.

Beatty, reared on cartoons and comics, was first exposed to African American literature between middle and high school, when he was given a copy of Maya Angelou's novel *I Know Why the Caged Bird Sings* (1969). He claims that after reading three pages, he discarded the work, upset by what he believed to be its maudlin content, and consequently, he did not read African American literature again until ten years later.

After high school, Beatty moved to Boston, where he earned an M.A. in psychology at Boston University. During his time as a graduate student and teaching assistant, he began to write poetry. He then moved to New York City, where he earned an M.F.A. in creative writing from Brooklyn College. Although Beatty studied with the consummate Beat poet Allen Ginsberg, his fellow graduate students and some professors often failed to understand the urban sensibilities in his work, and for a time, Beatty struggled to find his poetic voice.

Soon after he graduated, Beatty began teaching in East Harlem and performing slam poetry at the newly reopened Nuyorican Poets Café. After Beatty won the first Nuyorican Grand Slam, the Café press published Beatty's first book of poetry, *Big Bank Take Little Bank*, which was received as a rhythmic and smart collection of urban poems. Penguin published Beatty's second book of poetry, *Joker, Joker, Deuce*, as a Penguin Poets selection, establishing his reputation as a poet. Critics hailed the poems as lyrical, humorous poems that demand oral performance. Beatty was, however, uneasy with what he termed the insincerity and complacency of contemporary and performance poets and admitted in a *BOMB Magazine* interview that after a time, "poetry got boring." After his short story "'What Set You from, Fool?'" appeared in Eric Liu's *Next: Young American Writers on the New Generation* (1994), Beatty crossed over to literature with his first novel, *The White Boy Shuffle*.

The receipt of a grant in 1996 allowed Beatty to move to Berlin, where he started writing his second novel, *Tuff*. After returning to the United States, he published several short stories, including "A Spoonful of Borscht" (2000), which appeared in the literary journal *Transition*. Beatty also published essays and another novel, *Slumberland*. His novels have been translated and are studied in academic publications.

ANALYSIS

Reviewers and critics often call Paul Beatty a hip-hop poet, a categorization that Beatty himself finds easy and superficial. He admits to being influenced by hip-hop, but resists wholly defining his poetry in those terms. Like hip-hop itself, Beatty's poetry lives on the page as a model of innovation and change, yet resists being formulaically labeled as part of the African American oral tradition. For Beatty, the vernacular tradition, from the oral poems of the Greeks to the rhymes of hip-hop artists, is founded on multiplicity of meaning. He believes these forms should be looked to as a way to balance and blend seemingly incompatible things, such as playwright William Shakespeare's timeless wit with rap artist Biggie Smalls's keen grandiloquence. Recognizing this, critics also attempt to situate Beatty's work as postmodern due to its ironic blending of multiple narratives across time and culture. Indeed, his influences range from blues and jazz music to cartoons, Japanese literature and film, the Enlightenment philosopher Voltaire, and comedian Richard Pryor.

For Beatty, who wrote two books of poetry while performing spoken word, recording language is a difficult, meandering process that cannot be bound by audience needs and expectations. While performing his poetry, Beatty found that his audiences, often solely white or multiracial, missed many of the cultural references readily understood by black culture. Rather than adjusting his style, Beatty decided to allow readers to have their own struggles when accessing his work and eventually found that audiences who gained exposure to hip-hop or urban language would come to appreciate and understand his work. Limiting his poetic voice was never an option, and by forging ahead, Beatty found much fun and absurdity in observing audience responses to his far-reaching and irreverent work.

On the page, Beatty's poems take on an intentionally rollicking form and rely on the placement of words on the page and the use of white space to control the movement of language. Read aloud, the rhythms of rap and hip-hop are evident as the poems speed to their often elusive conclusions. Beatty's imagery and dramatic situations freely borrow from both "the 'hood" and "the academy" as well as from everywhere in between. In doing so, the poems attempt to reconcile the false notion that low and high culture are mutually exclusive. The resulting collections showcase how critical comparisons of seemingly incompatible cultural forms can often yield rich readings. Forging these connections against a backdrop of concern and sometimes anger, Beatty's poems remain quick and light, strikingly satirical and funny. Beatty's work is often anthologized and discussed in book reviews, journal articles, and in interviews with the author.

BIG BANK TAKE LITTLE BANK

Beatty's first book of poems, *Big Bank Take Little Bank* was well-received, despite the fact that the language and style were unfamiliar to many readers. The title phrase, "big bank take little bank," is an expression that refers to the circumstance under which the person with the most possessions will eventually acquire all others' property. With its urban, insider orientation, the title forecasts the poetry's linguistic mix of street culture and pop references. One *Library Journal* reviewer cited the text as a "pop-modern" deluge that records how the poet experienced the 1980's. Beatty's poems are not only funny, but also explosive, taking on dynamic forms that scatter words and lines across the page. The effect mimics hip-hop rhythms and shows a poet attempting to find his voice through experimentation and play.

The most anthologized poem in the collection, "Aa Bb Cc . . . Xx Yy and Zzing," is an epigram that questions an elementary teacher's assumption that the tenets of equality and opportunity found in the Declaration of Independence can be an inspiration to all young students, regardless of race and class. True to the form, the poem is short, witty, and unapologetically cross-referential, as it smugly compares the speaker's chances of becoming the president to the famous panda bear Ling Ling's cubs' chances of surviving. As it jaunts through inner-city America and explores the lines between black authenticity and appropriation, the collection is concerned about the social and political state of young African Americans, but it is not overtly political. Instead, it trades somber messages for wily observation and intense humor.

JOKER, JOKER, DEUCE

Beatty's second collection, *Joker, Joker, Deuce*, gains velocity and hurtles through what seems to be the poet's mounting anger at and frustration with racial politics and poetic chicanery. Rather than rant, however, Beatty again relies on satire, humor, and volatile rhythms to critique and caricature American culture. In "That's Not in My Job Description," Beatty turns the tables on traditional racial discourse by posing as an ethnographer embedded in a corporate environment to study the habits of "whitey." The white boys invite him out for an awkward, obligatory drink, and although they presume to know something about being black in the United States, the speaker, unlike Beatty, resentfully holds his tongue. Beatty also explores the differences between white and black humor in "Why That Abbott and Costello Vaudeville Mess Never Worked with Black People." This poem, masquerading as a haiku, simply reads: "who's on first?/ i don't know, your mama."

No one, including African Americans, is untouched by Beatty's critical ire. He deconstructs what it means to act black in a society that increasingly commodifies black culture, and he struggles to meaningfully challenge racial injustice. He parodies the use of famous black figures to sell items such as tennis shoes by imagining the civil rights leader Martin Luther King, Jr., sporting Nike shoes throughout his many civic demonstrations. In "Verbal Mugging," a title that critics have used to describe the tone of the collection, Beatty confronts performance poetry itself by drawing attention to insincerity on the part of the poet and the audience: "you don't have to think// cause i illustrate my words/ with some cheesy rip off diana ross four tops hand gestures." Throughout its shouts and slams, *Joker, Joker, Deuce*, like all Beatty's poetry, remains mirthful and slick, adroitly dodging any phraseology that would nail down his racial or social allegiances.

OTHER MAJOR WORKS

LONG FICTION: *The White Boy Shuffle*, 1996; *Tuff*, 2000; *Slumberland*, 2008.
EDITED TEXTS: *Hokum: An Anthology of African American Humor*, 2006.

BIBLIOGRAPHY

Ashe, Bertram. "Paul Beatty's *White Boy Shuffle* Blues: Jazz Poetry, John Coltrane, and the Post-Soul Aesthetic." In *Thriving on a Rift: Jazz and Blues Influences in African*

American Literature and Film, edited by Graham Lock and David Murray. New York: Oxford University Press, 2009. This chapter examining *The White Boy Shuffle* deals with jazz poetry and Beatty's style.

Grassian, Daniel. *Writing the Future of Black America: Literature of the Hip-hop Generation*. Columbia: University of South Carolina Press, 2009. Contains a chapter on Paul Beatty.

Rankin, Thomas. "*Joker, Joker, Deuce.*" In *Masterplots II: African American Literature*, edited by Tyrone Williams. Rev. ed. Pasadena, Calif.: Salem Press, 2009. Provides an in-depth analysis of this work.

Selinger, Eric Murphy. "Trash, Art, and Performance Poetry." Review of *Joker, Joker, Deuce*. *Parnassus: Poetry in Review* 23, nos. 1/2 (1998): 356-382. Reviews *Joker, Joker, Deuce* in the context of Beatty's production as a performance poet. One of the few full-length analyses of Beatty's poetry, this article provides insight into the work's motivations and impact.

Svboda, Terese. "Try Bondage." Review of *Joker, Joker, Deuce*. *Kenyon Review* 17, no. 2 (1995): 154-160. Reviews Beatty's book *Joker, Joker, Deuce* along with collections by Lois-Ann Yamanaka, Sapphire, and Marilyn Chin. Shows how Beatty deconstructs African American myths through his edgy, explosive rhymes while it praises the collection's veracity, sharp wit, and moral stance.

Thomas, Lorenzo. "'Stuck in the Promised Land': African American Poets at the Edge of the Twenty-first Century." In *Black Liberation in the Americas*, edited by Fritz Gysin and Christopher Mulvey. Munster, Germany: Lit Verlag, 2001. Discusses the work of five young African American poets writing in the 1990's and closely reads selections from Beatty's *Joker, Joker, Deuce*. Attempts to situate their poetry as simultaneously responding to and breaking away from earlier African American literary traditions in the face of an increasingly commodified and postmodern cultural landscape.

Lindsay Christopher

ARNA BONTEMPS

Born: Alexandria, Louisiana; October 13, 1902
Died: Nashville, Tennessee; June 4, 1973

PRINCIPAL POETRY
"Hope," 1924
Personals, 1963

OTHER LITERARY FORMS

Arna Bontemps (bon-TAHM) contributed to many genres of literature. He decided to concentrate on writing poetry after moving to Harlem in 1924 and because he felt that the mind-set of the early artists, writers, and musicians who lived there was particularly attuned to the rhythm and sound of poetry. In the 1930's, he turned to the novel as a vehicle for attempting to right the wrongs of an educational system that minimized black contributions to society, often devoting only two paragraphs to blacks—one dealing with Africa and the other with slavery in the Americas. His best-known novel, *Black Thunder* (1936), told the story of Gabriel Prosser, a slave who orchestrated an unsuccessful revolt in 1800. Hoping to gain a readership whose minds were less skeptical and more malleable than adults, he collaborated on several children's books with Langston Hughes and Jack Conroy and wrote several of his own, including *You Can't Pet a Possum* (1934). He later began to concentrate on history and biography for children with such books as *The Story of George Washington Carver* (1954) and *Frederick Douglass: Slave, Fighter, Freeman* (1959). He wanted young blacks to understand their racial past and gain a sense of pride in what blacks had achieved despite the obstacles they faced. Bontemps, indeed a prolific writer, was writing his autobiography when he died in 1973.

ACHIEVEMENTS

Arna Bontemps was showered with awards and recognition for his literary works. He won the Alexander Pushkin Award for Poetry from *Opportunity: A Journal of Negro Life* for "Golgotha Is a Mountain" in 1926 and for "The Return" in 1927. Also in 1927, he was awarded First Prize in Poetry for "Nocturne at Bethesda" by *The Crisis*, published by the National Association for the Advancement of Colored People (NAACP). He went on to win *Opportunity*'s short-story prize in 1932 for "A Summer Tragedy," a powerful tale that is included in many anthologies. He was granted two Julius Rosenwald Fellowships for travel, study, and writing, the first in 1938-1939 and the other in 1942-1943, and two Guggenheim Fellowships in 1949 and 1954. He received the Jane Addams Children's Book Award in 1956 for *The Story of the Negro*.

Arna Bontemps
(Library of Congress)

BIOGRAPHY

Arna Wendell Bontemps was born in Alexandria, Louisiana, in 1902, to a Roman Catholic brick mason and accomplished trombonist, Paul Bismark Bontemps, and a Methodist schoolteacher, Marie Carolina Pembrooke. His father, who left the Roman Catholic Church to become a lay minister with the Seventh-day Adventists, was a somewhat distant, practical man who hoped his son would join the family trade in building construction and masonry. From the start, however, Bontemps's mother instilled in him a love of reading and encouraged him to give his imagination free rein. Her free-spirited creativity had a great influence on him.

Bontemps had just turned three when the family moved to the Watts area of California because his father had grown tired of the indignities suffered by blacks in the South. Bontemps's father had been walking down the sidewalk when a pair of drunken white men grew close; when they hurled an epithet, his father, following convention, had stepped down into the street to avoid a confrontation. The three-year-old Bontemps was too young to understand the full implications of the incident, and when at age twelve, after his mother's death, he was sent to San Fernando Academy, a mostly white boarding school, he misunderstood his father's admonition that he not "act all colored" at the school. He saw this warning not as the safety measure it was designed to be, but as an attempt to make him forget his past, to negate everything in him that was black. His father was trying both to protect him and to get him away from the influence of his uncle Buddy, who drank heavily, loved tall tales told in dialect, and believed in ghosts. The young Bontemps, however, admired and enjoyed Uncle Buddy's energy and good humor. Physical separation did not remove his uncle from his mind; Bontemps even based the main character of his first novel, *God Sends Sunday* (1931), on him.

The idea that he was being miseducated, that he was expected to assimilate into white society and to be no different, stayed with Bontemps for many years and perhaps created in him a desire to change things, to learn about his heritage, and to alter misconceptions about black people. Because he believed that fiction was often more successful than scholarly writings in conveying history, he decided to become a writer. After receiving a bachelor of arts degree from Pacific Union College in Angwin, California, in 1923, he moved to Harlem to be among like-minded people with interests in literature, art, and music, and to teach at Harlem Academy, the largest Seventh-day Adventist school in the nation. He published his first poem, "Hope," in 1924 in *The Crisis*. He married Alberta Johnson in 1926; the couple would have six children.

In 1931, Bontemps accepted a teaching position at Oakwood Junior College, in Huntsville, Alabama. He loved the softness of the South, the greenery, the agriculture, and the slower life. Unfortunately, he was in Alabama during a turbulent time when nine young men (known as the Scottsboro boys) were wrongfully accused and ultimately convicted of raping two white girls. The trial in nearby Decatur, Georgia, attracted the attention of the nation, and many friends from his Harlem days—Hughes and Countée Cullen among them—stopped to visit Bontemps and his family on their way to hold protests at the courthouse where the trial was held. The school administration became concerned because of the influx of black activists as well as Bontemps's mail orders for black history books. He was told that if he wanted to keep his position, he would have to burn some of his more radical works, such as books by W. E. B. Du Bois and Frederick Douglass. The administrators wanted some public display of his break from radical politics. Appalled, Bontemps quietly resigned at the end of the spring semester, 1934.

About a year later, he accepted a position at the Shiloh Academy in Chicago. In 1938, he became an editorial supervisor for the Federal Writers' Project of the Illinois Works Progress Administration, where he met writers such as Conroy, Nelson Algren, Richard Wright, Margaret Walker, and Saul Bellow. His third novel, *Drums at Dusk*, was published in 1939, and he continued to write children's books, as he would into the 1970's. He received a master's degree in library science from the University of Chicago in 1943 and was appointed a librarian at Fisk University in Atlanta, where he would remain until his retirement in 1965. At Fisk, he found just the kind of life for which he had hoped. He became instrumental in building up the library's African American archives, bringing in Hughes's papers and developing a serious focus on black writers, artists, and musicians. With Hughes and later on his own, Bontemps edited several collections of poetry and other works by African Americans. His only collection of poetry, *Personals*, containing twenty-three poems from the 1920's, was published in 1963. In his later years, he served as curator of the James Weldon Johnson Collection at Yale University, visiting scholar at the University of Illinois, and poet-in-residence at Fisk University.

ANALYSIS

Several themes dominate Arna Bontemps's poetry: protest against social inequity, the decline in religious belief, and the search for identity through examination of the past. His social protest was more suggested than directly stated, however. He always wrote in a brooding, sad way, never showing joy or laughter. His dismay at what he considered the loss of right behavior, ethics, responsibility, and faith is pronounced in some of his poetry. However, his greatest interest was in exploring roots, most often African, summoning up the past by returning to it and seeing what could be learned. The return could be to a memory or be an actual relocation to a place or to a loved one. The Africa of his poetry is a bit idealized, with verdant grasses and scarlet birds in lush palms and tom-toms beating out hypnotic rhythms and never sounding warnings of impending danger.

"GOLGOTHA IS A MOUNTAIN"

Often, further study is necessary for a complete understanding of Bontemps's poetry, in which biblical references abound. For example, the poem "Golgotha Is a Mountain" refers to Golgotha, a hill near Jerusalem believed to be the site of the crucifixion of Jesus Christ. The name of the hill comes from an Aramaic word that means "place of the skull." Golgotha is a place of death, as evidenced through Bontemps's oblique reference to those who ". . . hanged two thieves there,/ And another man," causing a flood of tears then and now, enough to make a river. Romans and Jews in biblical times carried out executions on the outskirts of cities, preferably on elevated spots so that the executions would serve as warnings to passersby. In this poem, Bontemps may be linking the suffering of Jesus with that of blacks. The excavation at the mountain could serve as a reminder that the Africans who dig precious stones out of mountains get no recompense. The mountains are theirs, but the wealth eludes them.

"THE RETURN"

"The Return" describes the poet's attempt to summon up the past and understand it, one of Bontemps's major themes. The poet states, "The throb of rain is the throb of muffled drums;/ darkness brings the jungle to our room// . . . This is a night of love/ retained from those lost nights our fathers slept/ in huts; this is a night that cannot die." He hopes that calling up the sounds and smells of Africa will give life to racial memory, saying,

"Oh let us go back and search the tangled dream." He knows that such trips are only temporary, soon interrupted by reality, with street noise, weather, and birds.

"NOCTURNE AT BETHESDA"

The Bethesda of the poem "Nocturne at Bethesda" is the biblical site of miracles, where the afflicted gather and wait for angels to stir up the waters of a pond. Those who enter the pool before the water settles are released from pain. According to the biblical account, a man, hobbled for thirty-eight years, was too crippled to reach the pool in time, so Jesus healed him. In modern times, a person might wait at that ancient pool for some kind of revelation or cleansing, but it will not come. Bontemps reflects on the twentieth century's demise of faith and concludes that the forces that once sustained people no longer have the power to heal or transform. He laments that the healing waters are no longer there to help blacks, noting, ". . . This ancient pool that Healed/ A host of bearded Jews does not awake// . . . No Saviour comes/ with healing in his hands. . . ." There is no solace for blacks at this site, causing him to ask ". . . why/ Do our black faces search empty sky?" He looks for an answer and mourns the loss of spiritual values where God was once immanent: "I may pass through centuries of death/ with quiet eyes, but I'll remember still/ a jungle tree with burning scarlet birds.// I shall be seeking ornaments of ivory,/ I shall be dying for a jungle fruit."

"A BLACK MAN TALKS OF REAPING"

The last poem in *Personals*, "A Black Man Talks of Reaping," is probably the most anthologized. In this poem, a man who has prepared his land well, planting his seeds deeply enough to save them from the wind and birds, takes pride in rows that could, in his mind, run from "Canada to Mexico." However, the times are bad and the crops have not done well. The man, like many blacks after the Emancipation, is either a tenant farmer or a sharecropper, and finds that he has nothing to pass down to his children. He says his children "glean" or take from "fields" they have not sown and "feed on bitter fruit." Bontemps feels it is unnatural and disastrous for humans not to be able to reap what they sow, but he credits blacks for their endurance and for believing that a better day will come. In "Day-Breakers," he wrote lines conveying this mind-set: "Yet would we die as some have done./ Beating a way for the rising sun."

OTHER MAJOR WORKS

LONG FICTION: *God Sends Sunday*, 1931; *Black Thunder*, 1936; *Drums at Dusk*, 1939.

SHORT FICTION: *The Old South*, 1973.

PLAY: *St. Louis Woman*, pr. 1946 (with Countée Cullen).

NONFICTION: *Father of the Blues*, 1941 (with W. C. Handy; biography); *They Seek a City*, 1945 (with Jack Conroy; revised as *Anyplace but Here*, 1966); *One Hundred Years of Negro Freedom*, 1961; *Free at Last: The Life of Frederick Douglass*, 1971; *Arna Bontemps—Langston Hughes Letters: 1925-1967*, 1980.

CHILDREN'S LITERATURE: *Popo and Fifina: Children of Haiti*, 1932 (with Langston Hughes); *You Can't Pet a Possum*, 1934; *Sad-Faced Boy*, 1937; *The Fast Sooner Hound*, 1942 (with Conroy); *We Have Tomorrow*, 1945; *Slappy Hooper: The Wonderful Sign Painter*, 1946 (with Conroy); *Story of the Negro*, 1948; *Chariot in the Sky: A Story of the Jubilee Singers*, 1951; *Sam Patch*, 1951 (with Conroy); *The Story of George Washington Carver*, 1954; *Lonesome Boy*, 1955; *Frederick Douglass: Slave, Fighter, Freeman*, 1959; *Famous Negro Athletes*, 1964; *Mr. Kelso's Lion*, 1970; *Young Booker: Booker T. Washington's Early Days*, 1972; *The Pasteboard Bandit*, 1997 (with Hughes); *Bubber Goes to Heaven*, 1998.

EDITED TEXTS: *The Poetry of the Negro*, 1949, 1971 (with Hughes); *The Book of Negro Folklore*, 1958 (with Hughes); *American Negro Poetry*, 1963; *Great Slave Narratives*, 1969; *Hold Fast to Dreams*, 1969; *The Harlem Renaissance Remembered*, 1972.

BIBLIOGRAPHY

Bloom, Harold, ed. *Black American Poets and Dramatists of the Harlem Renaissance*. New York: Chelsea House, 1995. Contains an essay on Bontemps that places him within the greater context of the Harlem Renaissance.

Bontemps, Arna. *Personals*. 1963. Reprint. Alexandria, Va.: Chadwyck-Healey, 1998. Bontemps's preface to his poetry collection details his great excitement at reaching Harlem in 1924, describing the city as a "foretaste of paradise."

_____, ed. *American Negro Poetry: An Anthology*. Rev. ed. New York: Hill and Wang, 1996. In his eloquent introduction, Bontemps discusses the importance of poetic expression in African American culture.

Drew, Bernard A., ed. *One Hundred Most Popular African American Authors: Biographical Sketches and Bibliographies*. Westport, Conn.: Libraries Unlimited, 2007. Contains an entry on Bontemps that describes his life and lists his works.

Gates, Henry Louis, Jr., and Evelyn Brooks Higginbotham, eds. *Harlem Renaissance Lives: From the African American National Biography*. New York: Oxford University Press, 2009. Contains an informative introduction as well as a section with a comprehensive discussion of the life and works of Bontemps. Especially good for its biographical time line.

Jones, Kirkland C. *Renaissance Man from Louisiana: A Biography of Arna Wendell Bontemps*. Westport, Conn.: Greenwood Press, 1992. This biography of Bontemps stresses his many talents in various areas.

Pettis, Joyce Owens. *African American Poets: Lives, Works, and Sources*. Westport, Conn.: Greenwood Press, 2002. Contains an entry on Bontemps that looks at his life and poetic works.

Gay Pitman Zieger

GWENDOLYN BROOKS

Born: Topeka, Kansas; June 7, 1917
Died: Chicago, Illinois; December 3, 2000

PRINCIPAL POETRY

A Street in Bronzeville, 1945
Annie Allen, 1949
"We Real Cool," 1959
The Bean Eaters, 1960
Selected Poems, 1963
"The Wall," 1967
In the Mecca, 1968
Riot, 1969
Family Pictures, 1970
Aloneness, 1971
Black Steel: Joe Frazier and Muhammad Ali, 1971
Aurora, 1972
Beckonings, 1975
Primer for Blacks, 1980
To Disembark, 1981
Black Love, 1982
The Near-Johannesburg Boy, 1986
Blacks, 1987
Gottschalk and the Grande Tarantelle, 1988
Winnie, 1988
Children Coming Home, 1991
In Montgomery, 2003
The Essential Gwendolyn Brooks, 2005

OTHER LITERARY FORMS

In addition to the poetry on which her literary reputation rests, Gwendolyn Brooks published a novel, *Maud Martha* (1953); a book of autobiographical prose, *Report from Part One* (1972); and volumes of children's verse. An episodic novel, *Maud Martha* makes some use of autobiographical materials and shares many of the major concerns of Brooks's poetry, particularly concerning the attempts of the person to maintain integrity in the face of crushing environmental pressures. *Report from Part One* recounts the personal, political, and aesthetic influences that culminated in Brooks's movement to a black nationalist stance in the late 1960's. She also wrote introductions to, and edited anthologies of, the works of younger black writers. These introductions frequently provide insight into her own work. Several recordings of Brooks reading her own work are available.

ACHIEVEMENTS

Working comfortably in relation to diverse poetic traditions, Gwendolyn Brooks has been widely honored. Early in her career, she received numerous mainstream literary awards, including the Pulitzer Prize in poetry in 1950 for *Annie Allen*. She became poet laureate of Illinois in 1969 and has received more than fifty honorary doctorates. Equally significant, numerous writers associated with the Black Arts movement recognized her as an inspirational figure linking the older and younger generations of black poets. Brooks's ability to appeal both to poetic establishments and to a sizable popular audience, especially among young blacks, stems from her pluralistic voice, which echoes a wide range of precursors while remaining unmistakably black. Her exploration of the United States in general and Chicago in particular links her with Walt Whitman and Carl Sandburg. Her exploration of the interior landscape of humanity in general and women in particular places her in the tradition of Emily Dickinson and Edna St. Vincent Millay. At once the technical heir of Langston Hughes in her use of the rhythms of black street life and of Robert Frost in her exploration of traditional forms such as the sonnet, Brooks nevertheless maintains her integrity of vision and voice.

This integrity assumes special significance in the context of African American writing of the 1950's and 1960's. A period of "universalism" in black literature, the 1950's brought prominence to such poets as Brooks, LeRoi Jones (Amiri Baraka), and Robert Hayden. During this period of intellectual and aesthetic integration, Brooks never abandoned her social and racial heritage to strive for the transcendent (and deracinated) universalism associated by some African American critics with T. S. Eliot. Responding to William Carlos Williams's call in *Paterson* (1946-1958) to "make a start out of particulars and make them general," Brooks demonstrated that an African American writer need not be limited in relevance by concentrating on the black experience.

The 1960's, conversely, encouraged separatism and militancy in African American writing. Even while accepting the Black Arts movement's call for a poetry designed to speak directly to the political condition of the black community, Brooks continued to insist on precision of form and language. Although Jones changed his name to Amiri Baraka and radically altered his poetic voice, Brooks accommodated her new insights to her previously established style. An exemplar of integrity and flexibility, she both challenges and learns from younger black poets such as Haki R. Madhubuti (Don L. Lee), Sonia Sanchez, Carolyn Rodgers, and Etheridge Knight. Like Hughes, she addresses the black community without condescension or pretense. Like Frost, she wrote technically stunning "universal" poetry combining clear surfaces and elusive depths.

Brooks, a recipient of more than fifty honorary doctorates, was also appointed to the Presidential Commission on the National Agenda for the 1980's; she was the first black woman elected to the National Institute of Arts and Letters. She was named consultant in poetry (poet laureate) to the Library of Congress for 1985-1986. Her honors include the Shelley Memorial Award (1976) and the Frost Medal (1989), both awarded by the Poetry Society of America; the Langston Hughes Award (1979); the Aiken Taylor Award in Modern American Poetry from *Sewanee Review* (1992); and the Medal for Distinguished Contribution to American Letters from the National Book Foundation (1994). She also received the Academy of American Poets Fellowship in 1999.

BIOGRAPHY

Gwendolyn Elizabeth Brooks's poetry bears the strong impress of Chicago, particularly of the predominantly black South Side where she lived most of her life. Although she was born in Topeka, Kansas, Brooks was taken to Chicago before she was a year old. In many ways, she devoted her career to the physical, spiritual, and, later, political exploration of her native city.

Brooks's life and writings are frequently separated into two phases, with her experience at the 1967 Black Writers' Conference at Fisk University in Nashville serving as a symbolic transition. Before the conference, Brooks was known primarily as the first black Pulitzer Prize winner in poetry. Although not politically unaware, she held to a somewhat cautious attitude. The vitality she encountered at the conference crystallized her sense of the insufficiency of universalist attitudes and generated close personal and artistic friendships with younger black poets such as Madhubuti, Walter Bradford, and Knight. Severing her ties with the mainstream publishing firm of Harper and Row, which had published her first five books, Brooks transferred her work and prestige to the black-owned and operated Broadside Press of Detroit, Third World Press of Chicago, and Black Position Press, also of Chicago. Her commitment to black publishing houses remained unwavering despite distribution problems that rendered her later work largely invisible to the American reading public.

Educated in the Chicago school system and at Wilson Junior College, Brooks learned her craft under Inez Cunningham Stark (Boulton), a white woman who taught poetry at the South Side Community Art Center in the late 1930's and 1940's. Brooks's mother, who had been a teacher in Topeka, had encouraged her literary interests from an early age. Her father, a janitor, provided her with ineffaceable images of the spiritual strength and dignity of "common" people. Brooks married Henry Blakely in 1939, and her family concerns continued to play a central role in shaping her career. The eleven-year hiatus between the publication of *Annie Allen* and *The Bean Eaters* resulted at least in part from her concentration on rearing her two children, born in 1940 and 1951. Her numerous poems on family relationships reflect both the rewards and the tensions of her own experiences. Her children grown, Brooks concentrated on teaching, supervising poetry workshops, and speaking publicly. These activities brought her into contact with a wide range of younger black poets, preparing her for her experience at Fisk. As poet laureate of Illinois, she encouraged the development of younger poets through personal contact and formal competitions.

The division between the two phases of Brooks's life should not be overstated. She evinced a strong interest in the Civil Rights movement during the 1950's and early 1960's; her concern with family continued in the 1980's. Above all, Brooks lived with and wrote of and for the Chicagoans whose failures and triumphs she saw as deeply personal, universally resonant, and specifically black. She died in Chicago on December 3, 2000, at the age of eighty-three.

ANALYSIS

The image of Gwendolyn Brooks as a readily accessible poet is at once accurate and deceptive. Capable of capturing the experiences and rhythms of black street life, she frequently presents translucent surfaces that give way suddenly to reveal ambiguous depths. Equally capable of manipulating traditional poetic forms such as the sonnet, rhyme royal, and heroic couplet, she employs them to mirror the uncertainties of characters or personas who embrace conventional attitudes to defend themselves against internal and external chaos. Whatever form she chooses, Brooks consistently focuses on the struggle of people to find and express love, usually associated with the family, in the midst of a hostile environment. In constructing their defenses and seeking love, these people typically experience a disfiguring pain. Brooks devotes much of her energy to defining and responding to the elusive forces, variously psychological and social, which inflict this pain. Increasingly in her later poetry, Brooks traces the pain to political sources and expands her concept of the family to encompass all black people. Even while speaking of the social situation of blacks in a voice crafted primarily for blacks, however, Brooks maintains the complex awareness of the multiple perspectives relevant to any given experience. Her ultimate concern is to encourage every individual, black or white, to "Conduct your blooming in the noise and whip of the whirlwind" ("The Second Sermon on the Warpland").

A deep concern with the everyday circumstances of black people living within the whirlwind characterizes many of Brooks's most popular poems. From the early "Of De Witt Williams on His Way to Lincoln Cemetery" and "A Song in the Front Yard" through the later "The Life of Lincoln West" and "Sammy Chester Leaves 'Godspell' and Visits UPWARD BOUND on a Lake Forest Lawn, Bringing West Afrika," she focuses on characters whose experiences merge the idiosyncratic and the typical. She frequently draws on black musical forms to underscore the communal resonance of a character's outwardly undistinguished life. By tying the refrain of "Swing Low Sweet Chariot" to the repeated phrase "Plain black boy," Brooks transforms De Witt Williams into an Everyman figure. Brooks describes his personal search for love in the pool rooms and dance halls, but stresses the representative quality of his experience by starting and ending the poem with the musical allusion.

"WE REAL COOL"

"We Real Cool," perhaps Brooks's single best-known poem, subjects a similarly representative experience to an intricate technical and thematic scrutiny, at once loving and critical. The poem is only twenty-four words long, including eight repetitions of the word "we." It is suggestive that the subtitle of "We Real Cool" specifies the presence of only seven pool players at the "Golden Shovel." The eighth "we" suggests that poet and reader share, on some level, the desperation of the group-voice that Brooks transmits. The final sentence, "We/ die soon," restates the carpe diem motif in the vernacular of Chicago's South Side.

On one level, "We Real Cool" appears simply to catalog the experiences of a group of dropouts content to "sing sin" in all available forms. A surprising ambiguity enters into the poem, however, revolving around the question of how to accent the word "we" that ends every line except the last one, providing the beat for the poem's jazz rhythm. Brooks said that she intended that the "we" not be accented. Read in this way, the poem takes on a slightly distant and ironic tone, emphasizing the artificiality of the group identity that involves the characters in activities offering early death as the only release from pain. Conversely, the poem can be read with a strong accent on each "we," affirming the group identity. Although the experience still ends with early death, the pool players metamorphose into defiant heroes determined to resist the alienating environment. Their confrontation with experience is felt, if not articulated, as existentially pure. Pool players, poet, and reader cannot be sure which stress is valid.

Brooks crafts the poem, however, to hint at an underlying coherence in the defiance. The intricate internal rhyme scheme echoes the sound of nearly every word. Not only do the first seven lines end with "we," but also the penultimate words of each line in each stanza rhyme (cool/school, late/straight, sin/gin, June/soon). In addition, the alliterated consonant of the last line of each stanza is repeated in the first line of the next stanza (Left/lurk, Strike/sin, gin/June) and the first words of each line in the middle two stanzas are connected through consonance (Lurk/strike, Sing/thin). The one exception to this suggestive texture of sound is the word "Die," which introduces both a new vowel and a new consonant into the final line, breaking the rhythm and subjecting the performance to ironic revaluation. Ultimately, the power of the poem derives from the tension between the celebratory and the ironic perspectives on the lives of the plain black boys struggling for a sense of connection.

"THE MOTHER"

A similar struggle informs many of Brooks's poems in more traditional forms, including "The Mother," a powerful exploration of the impact of an abortion on the woman who has chosen to have it. Brooks states that the mother "decides that *she*, rather than her world, will kill her children." Within the poem itself, however, the motivations remain unclear. Although the poem's position in Brooks's first book, *A Street in*

Bronzeville, suggests that the persona is black, the poem neither supports nor denies a racial identification. Along with the standard English syntax and diction, this suggests that "The Mother," like poems such as "The Egg Boiler," "Callie Ford," and "A Light and Diplomatic Bird," was designed to speak directly of an emotional, rather than a social, experience, and to be as accessible to whites as to blacks. Re-creating the anguished perspective of a persona unsure whether she is victim or victimizer, Brooks directs her readers' attention to the complex emotions of her potential Everywoman.

"The Mother" centers on the persona's alternating desire to take and to evade responsibility for the abortion. Resorting to ambiguous grammatical structures, the persona repeatedly qualifies her acceptance with "if" clauses ("If I sinned," "If I stole your births"). She refers to the lives of the children as matters of fate ("Your luck") and backs away from admitting that a death has taken place by claiming that the children "were never made." Her use of the second person pronoun to refer to herself in the first stanza reveals her desire to distance herself from her present pain. This attempt, however, fails. The opening line undercuts the evasion with the reality of memory: "Abortions will not let you forget." At the start of the second stanza, the pressure of memory forces the persona to shift to the more honest first-person pronoun. A sequence of spondees referring to the children ("damp small pulps," "dim killed children," "dim dears") interrupts the lightly stressed anapestic-iambic meter that dominates the first stanza. The concrete images of "scurrying off ghosts" and "devouring" children with loving gazes gain power when contrasted with the dimness of the mother's life and perceptions. Similarly, the first stanza's end-stopped couplets, reflecting the persona's simplistic attempt to recapture an irrevocably lost mother-child relationship through an act of imagination, give way to the intricate enjambment and complex rhyme scheme of the second stanza, which highlight the mother's inability to find rest.

The rhyme scheme—and Brooks can rival both Robert Frost and William Butler Yeats in her ability to employ various types of rhyme for thematic impact—underscores her struggle to come to terms with her action. The rhymes in the first stanza insist on her self-doubt, contrasting images of tenderness and physical substance with those of brutality and insubstantiality (forget/get, hair/air, beat/sweet). The internal rhyme of "never," repeated four times, and "remember," "workers," and "singers," further stresses the element of loss. In the second stanza, Brooks provides no rhymes for the end words "children" in line 11 and "deliberate" in line 21. This device draws attention to the persona's failure to answer the crucial questions of whether her children did in fact exist and of whether her own actions were in fact deliberate (and perhaps criminal). The last seven lines of the stanza end with hard "d" sounds as the persona struggles to forge her conflicting thoughts into a unified perspective. If Brooks offers coherence, though, it is emotional rather than intellectual. Fittingly, the "d" rhymes and off-rhymes focus on physical and emotional pain (dead/instead/made/afraid/said/died/cried). Brooks provides no easy answer to the anguished question: "How is the truth to be told?" The persona's concluding cry of "I loved you/ All" rings with desperation. It is futile but it is not a lie. To call "The Mother" an antiabortion poem distorts its impact. Clearly portraying the devastating effects of the persona's action, it by no means condemns her or lacks sympathy. Like many of Brooks's characters, the mother is a person whose desire to love far outstrips her ability to cope with her circumstances and serves primarily to heighten her sensitivity to pain.

Perhaps the most significant change in Brooks's poetry involves her analysis of the origins of this pervasive pain. Rather than attributing the suffering to some unavoidable psychological condition, Brooks's later poetry indicts social institutions for their role in its perpetuation. The poems in her first two volumes frequently portray characters incapable of articulating the origins of their pain. Although the absence of any father in "The Mother" suggests sociological forces leading to the abortion, such analysis amounts to little more than speculation. The only certainty is that the mother, the persona of the sonnet sequence "The Children of the Poor," and the speaker in the brilliant sonnet "My Dreams, My Works Must Wait Till After Hell" share the fear that their pain will render them insensitive to love. The final poem of *Annie Allen*, "Men of Careful Turns," intimates that the defenders of a society that refuses to admit its full humanity bear responsibility for reducing the powerless to "grotesque toys." Despite this implicit accusation, however, Brooks perceives no "magic" capable of remedying the situation. She concludes the volume on a note of irresolution typical of her early period: "We are lost, must/ Wizard a track through our own screaming weed." The track, at this stage, remains spiritual rather than political.

POLITICS

Although the early volumes include occasional poems concerning articulate political participants such as "Negro Hero," Brooks's later work frequently centers on specific black political spokespeople such as Malcolm X, Paul Robeson, John Killens, and Don L. Lee. As of the early 1960's, a growing anger informs poems as diverse as the ironic "The Chicago *Defender* Sends a Man to Little Rock," the near-baroque "The Lovers of the Poor," the imagistically intricate "Riders to the Blood-Red Wrath," and the satiric "Riot." This anger originates in Brooks's perception that the social structures of white society value material possessions and abstract ideas of prestige more highly than individual human beings. The anger culminates in Brooks's brilliant narrative poem "In the Mecca," concerning the death of a young girl in a Chicago housing project, and in her three "Sermons on the Warpland."

"SERMONS ON THE WARPLAND"

The "Sermons on the Warpland" poems mark Brooks's departure from the traditions of Euro-American poetry and thought represented by T. S. Eliot's *The Waste Land* (1922). The sequence typifies her post-1967 poetry, in which she abandons traditional stanzaic forms, applying her technical expertise to a relatively colloquial free verse.

This technical shift parallels her rejection of the philosophical premises of Euro-American culture. Brooks refuses to accept the inevitability of cultural decay, arguing that the "waste" of Eliot's vision exists primarily because of people's "warped" perceptions. Seeing white society as the embodiment of these distortions, Brooks embraces her blackness as a potential counterbalancing force. The first "Sermon on the Warpland" opens with Ron Karenga's black nationalist credo: "The fact that we are black is our ultimate reality." Clearly, in Brooks's view, blackness is not simply a physical fact; it is primarily a metaphor for the possibility of love. As her poem "Two Dedications" indicates, Brooks sees the Euro-American tradition represented by the Chicago Picasso as inhumanly cold, mingling guilt and innocence, meaningfulness and meaninglessness, almost randomly. This contrasts sharply with her inspirational image of the Wall of Heroes on the South Side. To Brooks, true art assumes meaning from the people who interact with it. The wall helps to redefine black reality, rendering the "dispossessions beakless." Rather than contemplating the site of destruction, the politically aware black art that Brooks embraces should inspire the black community to face its pain with renewed determination to remove its sources. The final "Sermon on the Warpland" concludes with the image of a black phoenix rising from the ashes of the Chicago riot. No longer content to accept the unresolved suffering of "The Mother," Brooks forges a black nationalist politics and poetics of love.

"THE BLACKSTONE RANGERS"

Although her political vision influences every aspect of her work, Brooks maintains a strong sense of enduring individual pain and is aware that nationalism offers no simple panacea. "The Blackstone Rangers," a poem concerning one of the most powerful Chicago street gangs, rejects as simplistic the argument, occasionally advanced by writers associated with the Black Arts movement, that no important distinction exists between the personal and the political experience. Specifically, Brooks doubts the corollary that politically desirable activity will inevitably increase the person's ability to love. Dividing "The Blackstone Rangers" into three segments—"As Seen by Disciplines," "The Leaders," and "Gang Girls: A Rangerette"—Brooks stresses the tension between perspectives. After rejecting the sociological-penal perspective of part one, she remains suspended between the uncomprehending affirmation of the Rangers as a kind of government-in-exile in part two, and the recognition of the individual person's continuing pain in part three.

Brooks undercuts the description of the Rangers as "sores in the city/ that do not want to heal" ("As Seen by Disciplines") through the use of off-rhyme and a jazz rhythm reminiscent of "We Real Cool." The disciplines, both academic and corrective, fail to perceive any coherence in the Rangers' experience. Correct in their assumption that the Rangers do not want to "heal" themselves, the disciplines fail to perceive the gang's strong desire to "heal" the sick society. Brooks suggests an essential coherence in the Rangers' experience through the sound texture of part one. Several of the sound patterns echoing through the brief stanza point to a shared response to pain (there/thirty/ready, raw/sore/corner). Similarly, the accent cluster on "Black, raw, ready" draws attention to the pain and potential power of the Rangers. The descriptive voice of the disciplines, however, provides only relatively weak end rhymes (are/corner, ready/city), testifying to the inability of the distanced, presumably white, observers to comprehend the experiences they describe. The shifting, distinctively black, jazz rhythm further emphasizes the distance between the voices of observers and participants. Significantly, the voice of the disciplines finds no rhyme at all for its denial of the Rangers' desire to "heal."

This denial contrasts sharply with the tempered affirmation of the voice in part two, which emphasizes the leaders' desire to "cancel, cure and curry." Again, internal rhymes and sound echoes suffuse the section. In the first stanza, the voice generates thematically significant rhymes, connecting Ranger leader "*Bop*" (whose name draws attention to the jazz rhythm that is even more intricate, though less obvious, in this section than in part one) and the militant black leader "*Rap*" Brown, both nationalists whose "country is a Nation on no *map*." "Bop" and "Rap," of course, do not rhyme perfectly, attesting to Brooks's awareness of the gang leader's limitations. Her image of the leaders as "Bungled trophies" further reinforces her ambivalence. The only full rhyme in the final two stanzas of the section is the repeated "night." The leaders, canceling the racist association of darkness with evil, "translate" the image of blackness into a "monstrous pearl or grace." The section affirms the Blackstone Rangers' struggle; it does not pretend to comprehend fully the emotional texture of their lives.

Certain that the leaders possess the power to cancel the disfiguring images of the disciplines, Brooks remains unsure of their ability to create an alternate environment where love can blossom. Mary Ann, the "Gang Girl" of part three, shares much of the individual pain of the characters in Brooks's early poetry despite her involvement with the Rangers. "A rose in a whiskey glass," she continues to live with the knowledge that her "laboring lover" risks the same sudden death as the pool players of "We Real Cool." Forced to suppress a part of her awareness—she knows not to ask where her lover got the diamond he gives her—she remains emotionally removed even while making love. In place of a fully realized love, she accepts "the props and niceties of non-loneliness." The final line of the poem emphasizes the ambiguity of both Mary Ann's situation and Brooks's perspective. Recommending acceptance of "the rhymes of Leaning," the line responds to the previous stanza's question concerning whether love will have a "gleaning." The full rhyme paradoxically suggests acceptance of off-rhyme, of love consummated leaning against an alley wall, without expectation of safety or resolution. Given the political tension created by the juxtaposition of the disciplines and the leaders, the "Gang Girl" can hope to find no sanctuary beyond the reach of the whirlwind. Her desperate love, the more moving for its precariousness, provides the only near-adequate response to the pain that Brooks saw as the primary fact of life.

OTHER MAJOR WORKS

LONG FICTION: *Maud Martha*, 1953.

NONFICTION: *The World of Gwendolyn Brooks*, 1971; *Report from Part One*, 1972; *Young Poet's Primer*, 1980; *Report from Part Two*, 1996.

CHILDREN'S LITERATURE: *Bronzeville Boys and Girls*, 1956; *The Tiger Who Wore White Gloves*, 1974; *Very Young Poets*, 1983.

EDITED TEXT: *Jump Bad: A New Chicago Anthology*, 1971.

BIBLIOGRAPHY

Bloom, Harold, ed. *Gwendolyn Brooks*. Philadelphia: Chelsea House, 2000. From the series Modern Critical Views. Includes an introduction by Bloom and provides a solid introduction to Brooks.

Bolden, B. J. *Urban Rage in Bronzeville: Social Commentary in the Poetry of Gwendolyn Brooks, 1945-1960*. Chicago: Third World Press, 1999. A critical analysis focused on the impact of Brooks's early poetry. Bolden examines *A Street in Bronzeville*, *Annie Allen*, and *The Bean Eaters* in clear historical, racial, political, cultural, and aesthetic terms.

Bryant, Jacqueline Imani, ed. *Gwendolyn Brooks and Working Writers*. Chicago: Third World Press, 2007. Contains seventeen essays by writers, educators, and friends of Brooks describing encounters with the poet and how she influenced them.

"Gwendolyn's Words: A Gift to Us." *Essence* 31, no. 11 (March, 2001): A18. Begins with an account of Brooks's early life and documents the sequence of her compositions. Also covers her professional relationship with Haki R. Madhubuti, who helped publish her works.

Kent, George E. *A Life of Gwendolyn Brooks*. Lexington: University Press of Kentucky, 1990. This biography, completed in 1982 just before Kent's death, is based on interviews with Brooks and her friends and family. Integrates discussions of the poetry with a chronicle of her life. Especially valuable is an extensive recounting of the events and speeches at the 1967 Fisk conference, which changed the direction of her poetry. D. L. Melhem's afterword provides an update to 1988.

Melhem, D. L. *Gwendolyn Brooks: Poetry and the Heroic Voice*. Lexington: University Press of Kentucky, 1987. Beginning with a biographical chapter, Melhem employs a generally laudatory tone as he subsequently looks closely at the earlier poetry collections. He surveys the later works within a single chapter and also examines *Maud Martha* and *Bronzeville Boys and Girls*. Melhem's treatment gives attention to both structures and themes. The bibliography of her works is organized by publisher, to show her commitment to small black-run presses after the late 1960's.

Mickle, Mildred, ed. *Gwendolyn Brooks*. Pasadena, Calif.: Salem Press, 2009. Part of the Critical Insights series, this collection of critical essays examines aspects of Brooks's work such as her relation to the Harlem Renaissance and her legacy.

Mootry, Maria K., and Gary Smith, eds. *A Life Distilled: Gwendolyn Brooks, Her Poetry and Fiction*. Urbana: University of Illinois Press, 1987. Looks at Brooks's sense of place, her aesthetic, and the militancy that emerged in her "second period." The middle section comprises essays on individual collections, while the book's final two essays examine *Maud Martha*. The selected bibliography lists Brooks's works and surveys critical sources in great detail, including book reviews and dissertations.

Washington, Mary Helen. "An Appreciation: A Writer Who Defined Black Power for Herself." *Los Angeles Times*, December 8, 2000, p. E1. Discusses the young Brooks who attended the 1967 Fisk University Writers' Conference, encountered young black militants led by Amiri Baraka, and was converted. She branded her earlier writing "white writing" and resolved to change.

Wright, Stephen Caldwell, ed. *On Gwendolyn Brooks: Reliant Contemplation*. Ann Arbor: University of Michigan Press, 1996. This resource judiciously selects and assembles the most important writings to date about the works of Brooks in the form of reviews and essays. Three-part organization helpfully separates the reviews from the essays and the later essays from the rest.

Craig Werner

STERLING A. BROWN

Born: Washington, D.C.; May 1, 1901
Died: Takoma Park, Maryland; January 13, 1989

PRINCIPAL POETRY
Southern Road, 1932
The Last Ride of Wild Bill, and Eleven Narrative Poems, 1975
The Collected Poems of Sterling A. Brown, 1980

OTHER LITERARY FORMS

Sterling A. Brown produced several studies of African American literature: *Outline for the Study of the Poetry of American Negroes* (1931), *The Negro in American Fiction* (1937), and *Negro Poetry and Drama* (1937). With Arthur P. Davis and Ulysses Lee, he edited *The Negro Caravan* (1941). Brown also published numerous scholarly pieces in leading journals on subjects relating to African American culture and literature.

ACHIEVEMENTS

Sterling A. Brown is considered an important transitional figure between the Harlem Renaissance era and the period immediately following the Depression. Brown's fame is based not only on his poetry but also on his achievements as a critic, folklorist, scholar, and university teacher. As an acknowledged authority on African American culture, Brown served on many committees and boards and participated in numerous scholarly and research activities. Among these were the Carnegie-Myrdal Study, the American Folklore Society, the Institute of Jazz Studies, the editorial board of *The Crisis*, the Federal Writers' Project, and the Committee on Negro Studies of the American Council of Learned Societies.

Brown's poems and critical essays have been anthologized widely, and he was a memorable reader of his own poetry, especially on such recordings as *The Anthology of Negro Poets* (Folkways) and *A Hand's on the Gate*. He cowrote an article with Rayford Logan on the American Negro for *Encyclopaedia Britannica*. Brown was a Guggenheim Fellow (1937-1938) and a Julius Rosenwald Fellow (1942). He was an eminent faculty member at Howard University in Washington, D.C., from 1929 to 1969. *The Collected Poems of Sterling A. Brown* was selected for the National Poetry Series in 1979. Brown won the Lenore Marshall Poetry Prize in 1981, the Langston Hughes Award in 1982, and the Frost Medal, awarded by the Poetry Society of America, in 1987.

BIOGRAPHY

Born into an educated, middle-class African American family, Sterling Allen Brown was the last of six children and the only son of Adelaide Allen Brown and the Reverend Sterling Nelson Brown. His father had taught in the School of Religion at Howard University since 1892, and the year Brown was born, his father also became the pastor of Lincoln Temple Congregational Church. The person who encouraged Brown's literary career and admiration for the cultural heritage of African Americans, however, was his mother, who had been born and reared in Tennessee and graduated from Fisk University. Brown also grew up listening to tales of his father's childhood in Tennessee, as well as to accounts of his father's friendships with noted leaders such as Frederick Douglass, Blanche K. Bruce, and Booker T. Washington.

Brown attended public schools in Washington, D.C., and graduated from the well-known Dunbar High School, noted for its distinguished teachers and alumni; among the latter were many of the nation's outstanding black professionals. Brown's teachers at Dunbar included literary artists such as Angelina Weld Grimké and Jessie Redmon Fauset. Moreover, Brown grew up on the campus of Howard University, where there were many outstanding African American scholars, such as historian Kelly Miller and critic and philosopher Alain Locke.

Brown received his A.B. in 1922 from Williams College (Phi Beta Kappa) and his M.A. in 1923 from Harvard University. Although he pursued further graduate study in English at Harvard, he never worked toward a doctorate degree; however, he eventually received honorary doctorates from Howard University, the University of Massachusetts, Northwestern, Williams College, Boston University, Brown, Lewis and Clark College, Lincoln University (Pennsylvania), and the University of Pennsylvania. In September, 1927, he was married to Daisy Turnbull, who shared with him an enthusiasm for people, a sense of humor, and a rejection of pretentious behavior; she was also one of her husband's sharpest critics. She inspired Brown's poems "Long Track Blues" and "Against That Day." Daisy Turnbull Brown died in 1979. The Browns had one adopted child, John L. Dennis.

In 1927, "When de Saints Go Ma'ching Home" won first prize in an *Opportunity* writing contest. From 1926 to 1929, several of the poems that Brown later published in *Southern Road* were printed in *Crisis*, *Opportunity*, *Contempo*, and *Ebony and Topaz*. His early work is often identified with the outpouring of black writers during the New Negro movement, for he shared with those artists (Claude McKay, Countée Cullen, Jean Toomer, and Langston Hughes) a deep concern for a franker self-revelation and a respect for the folk traditions of his people; however, Brown's writings did not reflect the alien-and-exile theme so popular with the writers of the Renaissance.

Brown's teaching career took him to Virginia Seminary and College, Lincoln University (Missouri), and Fisk University. He began teaching at Howard in 1929 and remained there until his retirement in 1969. He was also a visiting professor at Atlanta

University, New York University, Vassar College, the University of Minnesota, the New School, and the University of Illinois (Chicago Circle). Several years after coming to Howard, Brown became an editor with the Works Progress Administration's Federal Writers Project. Along with a small editorial staff, he coordinated the Federal Writers Project studies by and about blacks. Beginning in 1932, Brown supervised an extensive collection of narratives by former slaves and initiated special projects such as *The Negro in Virginia* (1940), which became the model for other studies. His most enduring contribution to the project was an essay, "The Negro in Washington," which was published in the guidebook *Washington: City and Capital* (1937).

Brown's first fifteen years at Howard were most productive. During this period (1929-1945), he contributed poetry as well as reviews and essays on the American theater, folk expressions, oral history, social customs, music, and athletics to *The New Republic, Journal of Negro Education, Phylon, Crisis, Opportunity*, and other journals. His most outstanding essay, "Negro Characters as Seen by White Authors," which appeared in *Journal of Negro Education* in 1933, brought attention to the widespread misrepresentation of black characters and life in American literature. Only after Brown's retirement from Howard in 1969 did he begin reading his poems regularly there. This long neglect has been attributed to conservative faculty members' reluctance to appreciate a fellow professor whose interests were in blues and jazz. Brown was widely known as a raconteur. Throughout his career, he challenged fellow African American writers to choose their subject matter without regard to external pressures and to avoid the error of "timidity." He was a mentor who influenced the black poetry movement of the 1960's and 1970's, and poets such as Margaret Walker, Gwendolyn Brooks, Langston Hughes, and Arna Bontemps, along with critics such as Addison Gayle and Houston Baker, learned from him.

In the five years before his retirement, Brown began to exhibit stress caused by what he perceived to be years of critical and professional neglect as well as unfulfilled goals. Inclined toward periods of deep depression, he was occasionally hospitalized in his later years. He died in Takoma Park, Maryland, on January 13, 1989.

ANALYSIS

The poetry of Sterling A. Brown is imbued with the folk spirit of African American culture. For Brown, there was no wide abyss between his poetry and the spirit inherent in slave poetry; indeed, his works evidence a continuity of racial spirit from the slave experience to the African American present and reflect his deep understanding of the multitudinous aspects of the African American personality and soul.

The setting for Brown's poetry is primarily the South, through which he traveled to listen to the folktales, songs, wisdom, sorrows, and frustrations of his people, and where the blues and ballads were nurtured. Brown respected traditional folk forms and employed them in the construction of his own poems; thus he may be called "the poet of the soul of his people."

SOUTHERN ROAD

Brown's first published collection of poems, *Southern Road*, was critically acclaimed by his peers and colleagues James Weldon Johnson and Alain Locke, because of its rendering of the living speech of African Americans, its use of the raw material of folk poetry, and its poetic portrayal of African American folk life and thought. Later critics such as Arthur P. Davis, Jean Wagner, and Houston Baker have continued to praise his poetry for its creative and vital use of folk motifs. Some of the characters in Brown's poetry, such as Ma Rainey, Big Boy Davis, and Mrs. Bibby, are based on real people. Other characters, such as Maumee Ruth, Sporting Beasley, and Sam Smiley seem real because of Brown's dramatic and narrative talent. He is also highly skilled in the use of poetic techniques such as the refrain, alliteration, and onomatopoeia, and he employs several stanzaic forms with facility. Brown's extraordinary gift for re-creating the nuances of folk speech and idiom adds vitality and authenticity to his verse.

Brown is successful in drawing on rich folk expressions to vitalize the speech of his characters through the cadences of southern speech. Though his poems cannot simply be called dialect poetry, Brown does imitate southern African American speech, using variant spellings and apostrophes to mark dropped consonants. He uses grunts and onomatopoeic sounds to give a natural rhythm to the speech of his characters. These techniques are readily seen in a poem that dramatizes the poignant story of a "po los boy" on a chain gang. This poem follows the traditional folk form of the work song to convey the convict's personal tragedy.

Brown's work may be classed as protest poetry influenced by poets such as Carl Sandburg and Robert Frost; he is able to draw on the entire canon of English and American poetry as well as African American folk material. Thus he is fluent in the use of the sonnet form, stanzaic forms, free-verse forms, and ballad and blues forms.

In *Southern Road*, several themes express the essence of the southern African American's folk spirit and culture. Recurring themes and subjects in Brown's poetry include endurance, tragedy, and survival. The theme of endurance is best illustrated in one of his most anthologized poems, "Strong Men," which tells the story of the unjust treatment of black men and women from the slave ship, to the tenant farm, and finally to the black ghetto. The refrain of "Strong Men" uses rhythmic beats, relentlessly repeating an affirmation of the black people's ability and determination to keep pressing onward, toward freedom and justice. The central image comes from a line of a Carl Sandburg poem, "The strong men keep coming on." In "Strong Men," Brown praises the indomitable spirit of African Americans in the face of racist exploitation. With its assertive tone, the rhythm of this poem suggests a martial song.

Some of the endurance poems express a stoic, fatalistic acceptance of the tragic fate of African Americans, as can be seen in "Old Man Buzzard," "Memphis Blues," and "Riverbank Blues." Another important aspect of the endurance theme as portrayed by Brown is the poetic characters' courage when they are confronted with tragedy and injustice. In the poem "Strange Legacies," the speaker gives thanks to the legendary Jack Johnson and John Henry for their demonstration of courage.

"THE LAST RIDE OF WILD BILL"

Brown's poems reflect his understanding of the often tragic destinies of African Americans in the United States. No poet before Brown had created such a comprehensive poetic dramatization of the lives of black men and women in America. Brown depicts black men and women as alone and powerless, struggling nevertheless to confront an environment that is hostile and unjust. In this tragic environment, African American struggles against the schemes of racist whites are seen in "The Last Ride of Wild Bill," published in 1975 as the title poem of a collection. A black man falls victim to the hysteria of a lynch mob in "Frankie and Johnnie," a poem that takes up a familiar folktale and twists it to reflect a personal tragedy that occurs as a result of an interracial relationship. Brown emphasizes that in this story the only tragic victim is the black man. The retarded white girl, Frankie, reports her sexual experience with the black man, Johnnie, to her father and succeeds in getting her black lover killed; she laughs uproariously during the lynching. "Southern Cop" narrates the mindless killing of a black man who is the victim of the panic of a rookie police officer.

However, Brown's poems show black people as victims not only of whites but also of the whole environment that surrounds them, including natural forces of flood and fire as well as social evils such as poverty and ignorance. Rural blacks' vulnerability to natural disasters is revealed in "Old King Cotton," "New St. Louis Blues," and "Foreclosure." In these poems, if a tornado does not come, the Mississippi River rises and takes the peasant's arable land and his few animals, and even traitorously kills his children by night. These poems portray despairing people who are capable only of futile questions in the face of an implacable and pitiless nature. The central character of "Low Down" is sunk in poverty and loneliness. His wife has left and his son is in prison; he is convinced that bad luck is his fate and that in the workings of life someone has loaded the dice against him. In "Johnny Thomas," the title character is the victim of poverty, abuse by his parents and society, and ignorance. (He attempts to enroll in a one-room school, but the teacher throws him out.) Johnny ends up on a chain gang, where he is killed. The poem that most strongly expresses African American despair for the entire race is "Southern Road," a convict song marked by a rhythmic, staccato beat and by a blues line punctuated by the convict's groaning over his accursed fate:

> My ole man died—hunh—
> Cussin' me;
> Old lady rocks, bebby,
> huh misery.

SLIM GREER POEMS

The African American's ability to survive in a hostile world by mustering humor, religious faith, and the expectation of a utopian afterlife is portrayed in poems depicting the comical adventures of Slim Greer and in one of Brown's popular poems, "Sister Lou." The series of Slim Greer poems, "Slim Greer," "Slim Lands a Job," "Slim in Atlanta," and "Slim in Hell," reveal Brown's knowledge of the life of the ordinary black people and his ability to laugh at the weaknesses and foolishness of blacks and whites alike. With their rich exaggerations, these poems fall into the tall tale tradition of folk stories. They show Slim in Arkansas passing for white although he is quite dark; or Slim in Atlanta, laughing in a "telefoam booth" because of a law that keeps blacks from laughing in the open. In "Slim Lands a Job," the poet mocks the ridiculous demands that southern employers make on their black employees. Slim applies for a job in a restaurant. The owner is complaining about the laziness of his black employees when a black waiter enters the room carrying a tray on his head, trays in each hand, silver in his mouth, and soup plates in his vest, while simultaneously pulling a red wagon filled with other paraphernalia. When the owner points to this waiter as one who is lazy, Slim makes a quick exit. In "Slim in Hell," Slim discovers that Hell and the South are very much alike; when he reports this discovery to Saint Peter, the saint reprimands him, asking where he thought Hell was if not the South.

"SISTER LOU"

In "Sister Lou," one of his well-known poems, Brown depicts the simple religious faith that keeps some blacks going. After recounting all the sorrows in Sister Lou's life, the poem pictures Heaven as a place where Sister Lou will have a chance to allow others to carry her packages, to speak personally to God without fear, to rest, and most of all to take her time. In "Cabaret," however, Brown shows the everyday reality that belies the promises God made to his people: The black folk huddle, mute and forlorn, in Mississippi, unable to understand why the Good Lord treats them this way. Moreover, in poems such as "Maumee Ruth," religion is seen as an opium that feeds people's illusions. Maumee Ruth lies on her deathbed, ignorant of the depraved life led by her son and daughter in the city, and needing the religious lies preached to her to attain a peaceful death.

"REMEMBERING NAT TURNER"

Brown's poems embrace themes of suffering, oppression, and tragedy, yet always celebrate the vision and beauty of African American people and culture. One such deeply moving piece is "Remembering Nat Turner," a poem in which the speaker visits the scene of Turner's slave rebellion, only to hear an elderly white woman's garbled recollections of the event; moreover, the marker intended to call attention to Turner's heroic exploits, a rotting signpost, has been used by black tenants for kindling. A stoic fatalism can be seen in the poem "Memphis Blues," which nevertheless praises the ability of African Americans to survive in a hostile environment because of their courage and willingness to start over when all seems lost: "Guess we'll give it one more try." In the words of Brown, "The strong men keep a-comin' on/ Gittin' stronger."

OTHER MAJOR WORKS

NONFICTION: *Outline for the Study of the Poetry of American Negroes*, 1931; *The Negro in American Fiction*, 1937; *Negro Poetry and Drama*, 1937; *A Son's Return: Selected Essays of Sterling A. Brown*, 1996 (Mark A. Sanders, editor).

EDITED TEXT: *The Negro Caravan*, 1941 (with Arthur P. Davis and Ulysses Lee).

BIBLIOGRAPHY

Davis, Arthur P. "Sterling Brown." In *From the Dark Tower: Afro-American Writers, 1900-1960*. Washington, D.C.: Howard University Press, 1982. A comprehensive study by the dean of African American critics, who knew Brown personally and taught with him at Howard University on African American writers during the 1950's. The essays on individual writers are supplemented by ample introductory material, and there is also an extensive bibliography, listed by author.

Ekate, Genevieve. "Sterling Brown: A Living Legend." *New Directions: The Howard University Magazine* 1 (Winter, 1974): 5-11. A tribute to the life and works of Brown in a magazine published by the university where he taught for forty years. This article analyzes Brown's literary influence on younger poets and assesses his importance in the African American literary canon.

Sanders, Mark A. *Afro-Modernist Aesthetics and the Poetry of Sterling A. Brown*. Athens: University of Georgia Press, 1999. Criticism and interpretation of Brown and his poetry in the context of twentieth century African American literature and intellectual life.

Thelwell, Ekwueme Michael. "The Professor and the Activists: A Memoir of Sterling Brown." *Massachusetts Review* 40, no. 4 (Winter, 1999/2000): 617-638. A fond memoir of Brown written by one of his students at Howard University. Offers a glimpse into Brown's personality, political bent, and place as a black intellectual during the tumultuous 1960's.

Tidwell, John Edgar, and Steven C. Tracy, eds. *After Winter: The Art and Life of Sterling Brown*. New York: Oxford University Press, 2009. A collection of critical essays on Brown's works, as well as interviews with those who knew him. Also contains a bibliography and discography.

Wagner, Jean. "Sterling Brown." In *Black Poets of the United States, from Paul Laurence Dunbar to Langston Hughes*. Urbana: University of Illinois Press, 1973. A comprehensive and insightful study of the poetry of Brown, covering the subjects, themes, and nuances of his poetry. Wagner's writing on Brown is warm and appreciative.

Betty Taylor-Thompson

LUCILLE CLIFTON

Born: Depew, New York; June 27, 1936
Died: Baltimore, Maryland; February 13, 2010

OTHER LITERARY FORMS

In addition to her poetry, Lucille Clifton wrote prose, often for children but also for adults. *Generations: A Memoir* (1976), is included as a part of *Good Woman*. She began publishing books for children in 1970 with *Some of the Days of Everett Anderson*, short poems in a picture-book format that spawned a series about the life of a young black boy. *The Times They Used to Be* (1974) is written as a narrative poem. She wrote other picture books in prose: *The Boy Who Didn't Believe in Spring* (1973), *All Us Come Cross the Water* (1973), *My Brother Fine with Me* (1975), *Three Wishes* (1976), and *Amifika* (1977), as well as a short novel, *The Lucky Stone* (1979). In response to questions her own six children had, Clifton wrote *The Black BC's* (1970), an alphabet book that blends poetry with prose. A departure from her usual perspective, *Sonora Beautiful* (1981) features a white girl as the protagonist.

ACHIEVEMENTS

In 2007, Lucille Clifton became the first African American to be awarded the Ruth Lilly Poetry Prize from the Poetry Foundation in recognition of her lifetime achievement. In 1988, she became the only poet ever to have two books, *Next* and *Good Woman*, nominated for the Pulitzer Prize in the same year. Clifton won the National Book Award for *Blessing the Boats* in 2000; previously, she was a National Book Award finalist for *The*

Terrible Stories. She also won the Coretta Scott King Award for *Everett Anderson's Goodbye* in 1984. Other honors include an Emmy Award from the American Academy of Television Arts and Sciences, the Charity Randall Citation (1991), the Shelley Memorial Award (1992), a grant from the Eric Mathieu King Fund (1996), the Shestack Prize from *American Poetry Review* (1988), the Lannan Literary Award for Poetry (1996), the Lila Wallace-*Reader's Digest* Writers' Award (1998), the Anisfield-Wolf Book Award for lifetime achievement (2001), the Langston Hughes Award (2003), the Frost Medal from the Poetry Society of America (2010), and three fellowships from the National Endowment for the Arts (1969, 1970, 1972). She held honorary degrees from the University of Maryland and Towson State University. Clifton was elected to the American Academy of Arts and Sciences and served as chancellor of the Academy of American Poets (1999-2005). In 1991, Clifton became a distinguished professor of humanities at St. Mary's College in Columbia, Maryland. She retired in 2007.

BIOGRAPHY

Lucille Clifton was born Thelma Lucille Sayles, daughter of Samuel L. Sayles and Thelma Moore Sayles, in Depew, New York, and grew up with two half sisters and a brother. Her father worked for the New York steel mills. Her mother was a launderer, homemaker, and aspiring poet but once had to burn all her poems because her husband told her, "Ain't no wife of mine going to be no poetry writer."

Ironically, both parents encouraged Clifton to be anything she wanted to be. She was named for her great-grandmother, who, according to her father, was the first black woman to be legally hanged in the state of Virginia. The first in her family to finish high school or consider attending college, Clifton entered college at Howard University at the age of sixteen, having earned a full scholarship. After majoring in drama and attending for two years, Clifton lost her scholarship. She told her father,

> I don't need that stuff. I'm going to write poems. I can do what I want to do! I'm from Dahomey women!

After transferring to Fredonia State Teachers College in 1955, Clifton worked as an actor and began her writing career. While at Fredonia, she met novelist Ishmael Reed at a writers' group, and he showed some of her poems to Langston Hughes, who was the first to publish Clifton's writing.

In 1958, she married Fred James Clifton. They had four daughters, Sidney, Fredrica, Gillian, and Alexia, and two sons, Channing and Graham. In 1969, poet Robert Hayden entered her poems into competition for the Young Men's-Young Women's Hebrew Association Poetry Center Discovery Award. Clifton won the award and with it the publication of her first volume of poems, *Good Times*, which was chosen as one of the ten best books of the year by *The New York Times*. Prior to 1971, when she became poet-in-residence at the historically black Coppin State College in Baltimore, Maryland, Clifton had worked in state and federal government positions. She remained at Coppin until 1974. From 1979 through 1982, she was poet laureate of the state of Maryland. From 1982 to 1983, she was a visiting writer at Columbia University School of the Arts and at George Washington University. Subsequently, she taught literature and creative writing at the University of California, Santa Cruz, and later at St. Mary's College. In addition to appearing in more than one hundred anthologies of poetry, her poems have come to popular attention through her numerous television appearances.

ANALYSIS

Distinguished by her minimalist style, Lucille Clifton is sometimes compared with poets Gwendolyn Brooks and Emily Dickinson. Clifton is usually considered one of the prominent black aesthetic poets, along with Sonia Sanchez and Amiri Baraka, who were consciously breaking with Eurocentric conventions in their work. The characteristics of Clifton's craft—her concise, often untitled free verse, use of vernacular speech, repetition, puns and allusions, lowercase letters, sparse punctuation, and focused use of common words—became her trademark style, which is clearly unfettered by others' expectations. Without worrying about convention, about boundaries—created either physically or emotionally—Clifton shares her perceptions of life by writing about the feelings humans share. Her rationale for writing poetry was to assert the importance of being human. In an interview with Michael Glaser, Clifton stated that

> writing is a way of continuing to hope. When things sometimes feel as if they're not going to get any better, writing offers a way of trying to connect with something beyond that obvious feeling . . . a way of remembering I am not alone

She further stated that she sees writing as a way to bear witness, to hold back the darkness by acknowledging the pain of the past and then choosing a more joyful future.

GOOD TIMES

Clifton's early work was frequently inspired by her family, especially her children, and was often a celebration of African American ancestry, heritage, and culture. In the title poem of *Good Times*, Clifton reminds all children, "oh children think about the/ good times." She juxtaposes society's perceptions and her own in the opening poem of the collection—"in the inner city/ or/ like we call it/ home"—to honor the place where she lives. Believing in the humanity of all people, she calls on each person, regardless of ancestry, to take control of his or her life. Of Robert, in the poem by the same name, she states he "married a master/ who whipped his mind/ until he died," suggesting through the image that the union was one of mutual consent. Her impatience with humans of all kinds who do not strive to improve their lot is a theme begun with this collection and continued throughout her life. Another theme that arises here is optimism, as in "Flowers": "Oh/ here we are/ flourishing for the field/ and the name of the place/ is Love."

GOOD WOMAN

One theme of the poems in *Good Woman* involves Clifton's ethnic pride, as is reflected in "After Kent State": "white ways are/ the way of death/ come into the/ black/ and live." This volume also contains a section called "Heroes," which directly extends this first theme, and ends the book with a section called "Some Jesus."

> I have learned
> some few things
> like when a man
> walk manly
> he don't stumble
> even in the lion's den.

Although the gender in this poem is male, Clifton would not limit the message to men. Overall, her early work heralds African Americans for their resistance to oppression and their survival of racism.

AN ORDINARY WOMAN

An Ordinary Woman includes poems divided into two sections, beginning with "Sisters," a celebration of family and relationships. "The Lesson of the Falling Leaves" includes the following lines:

> the leaves believe
> such letting go is love
> such love is faith
> such faith is grace
> such grace is god
> i agree with the leaves.

It is a testimony to hope, a theme that runs throughout her work. Consistently juxtaposing past with present, Clifton provides wisdom to guide the future, as in the example of "Jackie Robinson":

> ran against walls
> without breaking.
> in night games
> was not foul
> but, brave as a hit
> over whitestone fences,
> entered the conquering dark.

TWO-HEADED WOMAN

Two-Headed Woman, which invokes the African American folk belief in a "Two-Headed Woman," with its overtones of a voodoo conjurer, begins with a section entitled

"Homage to Mine," moves onto "Two-Headed Woman," and concludes with "The Light That Came to Lucille Clifton." While Clifton's works often have allusions to Christianity, as in the "Some Jesus" series in *Good News About the Earth*, she refers to other faiths as well, including the Hindu goddess Kali, from "An Ordinary Woman," providing evidence of her openness to multiple ways of knowing. As a "Two-Headed Woman," in the opening poem of that section, Clifton says she has "one face turned outward/ one face/ swiveling slowly in." Spirituality and mysticism pervade this collection, as the final poem attests, with its reference to the "shimmering voices" of her ancestors, whom the poet has heard singing in the "populated air."

QUILTING

In five parts, each of the first four named for traditional quilt patterns, "Log Cabin," "Catalpa Flower," "Eight-Pointed Star," and "Tree of Life," *Quilting* seems pieced together, like a quilt. It ends with a single poem, "Blessing the Boats," in "prayer," as if the spiritual life serves as the connecting threads. Clifton honors those whose roles in history have brought about change, as in "February 11, 1990," dedicated to "Nelson Mandela and Winnie," and "Memo," which is dedicated "to Fannie Lou Hamer." The poem's "questions and answers" ends with "the surest failure/ is the unattempted walk."

THE TERRIBLE STORIES

In *The Terrible Stories*, Clifton chronicles the terrible stories of her own life, which include her struggle with breast cancer, and the terrible stories of her people, which include slavery and the prejudice that has survived time. The last section in the book, "From the Book of David," concludes with a question from the poem "What Manner of Man." Referring to the biblical David, the poet asks how this David will be remembered "if he stands in the tents of history/ bloody skull in one hand, harp in the other?" Clifton's ability to look at history—ancient, contemporary, or personal—and find redemption in it gives humanity a way to face and survive its failures; this perspective shows her consistent faith in grace.

BLESSING THE BOATS

Blessing the Boats includes new poems as well as selected poems from *Next*, sometimes called a collection of sorrow songs, as loss is the overriding theme. Once more, "New Poems," the opening section of the anthology, records and comments on contemporary events of the twentieth century, such as school shootings, referred to in "The Times," and the bombing of black churches, referred to in "Alabama 9/15/63." It also addresses private occurrences, such as the traumas that gave rise to such poems as "Dialysis" and "Donor."

VOICES

In *Voices*, which is divided into the three sections "hearing," "being heard," and "ten oxherding pictures," Clifton continues with the themes and motifs of her earlier volumes. The first section is "a collection of persona" and personification, according to reviewer Cameron Conaway, for characters, animals, historical figures, and abstract ideas (as in the poem "sorrows") are given life and voice. Most poignant are the interior monologues of three characters seen only on cardboard boxes: Aunt Jemima, Uncle Ben, and the Cream of Wheat man. Each longs to know about home and family, common themes in Clifton's work, but it is the Cream of Wheat man who relates their collective wanderings and whose longing is the most poignant: "we return to our shelves/ our boxes ben and jemima and me/ we pose and smile I simmer what/ is my name." Clifton's thematic concern for recapturing lost names is also emphasized in the monologues "mataoka" and "witko," as the poems respectively have subtitles that reveal more about the names of the Native Americans: "(actual name of Pocahontas)" and "aka crazy horse." In the monologues, Clifton subtly forces readers to look beyond what they think they know to acknowledge the depths of the lives of those who have been denied voice.

The issue of loss extends not only to names but also to the land. Such loss is examined in the second section with the poem "in 1844 explorers John Fremont and Kit Carson discovered Lake Tahoe," in which Clifton characteristically uses repetition of words and structure to emphasize time and another group of Native Americans—the Washoe—whose history has also been overshadowed: "in 1841 Washoe children// in 1842 Washoe warriors began to dream// in 1843 Washoe elders began to speak// in 1844 Fremont and Carson." The final line of the poem speaks volumes of the loss through its terseness.

Clifton's interest in the realm of the spiritual is also evident in *Voices*. In the first section, animals—a horse and a raccoon—express prayers, and in a "dog's god," the deity of the canine not only blesses the dog with "four magnificent legs" but also "two-legs to feed him." In the second section, Clifton moves to the personal—she is most often the speaker—and acknowledges that "the gods/ are men"; in the poem "dad," her father thinks that such ". . . gods might/ understand/ a man like me."

The third section, "ten oxherding pictures," contains a group of poems previously issued in 1988 as a limited-edition chapbook. Clifton acknowledges that these poems are based on "an allegorical series composed as a training guide for Chinese Buddhist monks," yet she wrote her poems having only a knowledge of the titles of the pictures. Nonetheless, her poems coincide with the pictures: Both are guides to enlightenment as one journeys in search of self. In the eighth poem of the series, Clifton concludes "man is not ox/ i am not ox/ no thing is ox/ all things are ox": Alone, nothing is the self; together, all is the self. This revelation is the converse of an idea expressed earlier in the collection in "mirror," where people are ". . . not understanding/ what we are or what we/ had hoped to be." However, through the meditation on the ten pictures, *Voices* ends with

Clifton's characteristic theme of hope—that its readers come to understand what and who they are and what they hope to be through "hearing" and "being heard."

NONFICTION: *Generations: A Memoir*, 1976.

CHILDREN'S LITERATURE: *The Black BC's*, 1970; *Some of the Days of Everett Anderson*, 1970; Everett Anderson's Christmas Coming, 1971; *All Us Come Cross the Water*, 1973; *The Boy Who Didn't Believe in Spring*, 1973; *Everett Anderson's Year*, 1974; *The Times They Used to Be*, 1974; *My Brother Fine with Me*, 1975; *Everett Anderson's Friend*, 1976; *Three Wishes*, 1976; *Amifika*, 1977; *Everett Anderson's 1-2-3*, 1977; *Everett Anderson's Nine Month Long*, 1978; *The Lucky Stone*, 1979; *Sonora Beautiful*, 1981; *Everett Anderson's Goodbye*, 1983; *One of the Problems of Everett Anderson*, 2001.

BIBLIOGRAPHY

Anaporte-Easton, Jean. "Healing Our Wounds: The Direction of Difference in the Poetry of Lucille Clifton and Judith Johnson." *Mid-American Review* 14, no. 2 (1994). This essay suggests that Clifton's voice is distinctive because of her use of physical imagery, particularly of the body, in order to write a work that seeks to unite it with both mind and spirit.

Bennett, Bruce. "Preservation Poets." Review of *Quilting. The New York Times Book Review*, March 1, 1992, pp. 22-23. Poet and critic Bennett discusses Clifton's *Quilting*, noting that the first four sections are named after traditional quilting designs, yet the final section, "prayer," consists of a single poem. He believes readers familiar with Clifton's work will witness recurrent themes section by section: importance of history on the present and future, celebration of women, and life as a personal journey of spiritual growth and discovery.

Clifton, Lucille. "A Conversation with Lucille Clifton." Interview by Alexs Pate. *Black Renaissance* 8, no. 2/3 (Summer, 2008): 12-19. Author and professor Pate interviews Clifton as part of a series of conversations with authors who represent excellence in African American literature sponsored by the Givens Foundation for African American Literature and the University of Minnesota. Clifton discusses many African Americans she has known and says poetry is "mind and soul and heart, a balancing act."

_____. "Lucille Clifton." Interview by Shirley Marie Jordan. In *Broken Silences: Interviews with Black and White Women Writers*, edited by Jordan. New Brunswick, N.J.: Rutgers University Press. 1993. Jordan and Clifton explore the differences in perception between black and white women and how that affects their approaches to writing. Focuses on *Sonora Beautiful*, one of the few works by a female African American writer told from the perspective of a white protagonist.

Evans, Mari, ed. *Black Women Writers (1950-1980): A Critical Evaluation.* Garden City, N.Y.: Anchor Press/Doubleday, 1984. Devotes three substantial essays to Clifton and her work, including "Lucille Clifton," written by Clifton herself. The other two selections are Audrey T. McCluskey's "Tell the Good News: A View of the Works of Lucille Clifton" and Haki Madhubti's "Lucille Clifton: Warm Water, Greased Legs, and Dangerous Poetry."

Holladay, Hilary. *Wild Blessings: The Poetry of Lucille Clifton.* Baton Rouge: Louisiana State University Press, 2004. A study of Clifton's work, including an interview with the poet.

Koontz, Tom, and Dolores Anindon D'Angelo. "The Poetry of Lucille Clifton." In *Masterplots II: African American Literature,* edited by Tyrone Williams. Rev. ed. Pasadena, Calif.: Salem Press, 2009. Provides an in-depth analysis of Clifton's poetry that looks at her life and how it influenced the themes of her poetry and children's literature.

Lupton, Mary Jane. *Lucille Clifton: Her Life and Letters.* Westport, Conn.: Praeger, 2006. This full-length biography of the poet explores Clifton's life and work and offers insight and analysis.

White, Mark Bernard. "Sharing the Living Light: Rhetorical, Poetic, and Social Identity in Lucille Clifton." *CLA Journal* 40, no. 3 (1997): 288-305. An evaluation of Clifton's presentation of her self-identity, especially focusing on the poems "An Ordinary Woman" and "Two-Headed Woman."

Woo, Elaine. "Lucille Clifton, 1936-2010: Poet Weathered Tragedies, Celebrated Survival in Work." *Los Angeles Times,* February 21, 2010, p. A36. This obituary provides a short biography and notes her accomplishments and expression of optimism in her poems, despite her many hardships.

Alexa L. Sandmann
Updated by Paula C. Barnes

COUNTÉE CULLEN

Born: New York, New York; or Louisville, Kentucky; or Baltimore, Maryland;
   May 30, 1903
Died: New York, New York; January 9, 1946

OTHER LITERARY FORMS

Countée Cullen (KUH-lehn) wrote nearly as much prose as he did poetry. While serving from 1926 through most of 1928 as literary editor of *Opportunity*, a magazine vehicle for the National Urban League, Cullen wrote several articles, including book reviews, and a series of topical essays for a column called "The Dark Tower" about figures and events involved in the Harlem Renaissance. He also wrote many stories for children, most of which are collected in *My Lives and How I Lost Them* (1942), the "autobiography" of Cullen's own pet, Christopher Cat, who had allegedly reached his ninth life. Earlier, in 1932, the poet had tried his hand at a novel, publishing it as *One Way to Heaven* (1932). In addition to articles, reviews, stories, and a novel, the poet translated or collaborated in the writing of four plays, one of them being a musical. In 1935, Cullen translated Euripides' *Medea* for the volume by the same name; in 1942, Virgil Thomson set to music the seven verse choruses from Cullen's translation. With Owen Dodson, Cullen wrote the one-act play *The Third Fourth of July*, which appeared posthumously in 1946. The musical was produced at the Martin Beck Theater on Broadway, where it ran for 113 performances; this production also introduced Pearl Bailey as the character Butterfly.

ACHIEVEMENTS

Countée Cullen's literary accomplishments were many. While he was a student at DeWitt Clinton High School, New York City, he published his first poems and made numerous and regular contributions to the high school literary magazine. From DeWitt, whose other distinguished graduates include Lionel Trilling and James Baldwin, Cullen went to New York University. There he distinguished himself by becoming a member of Phi Beta Kappa and in the same year, 1925, by publishing *Color*, his first collection of

Countée Cullen
(Library of Congress)

poems. In June, 1926, the poet took his second degree, an M.A. in English literature from Harvard University. In December, 1926, *Color* was awarded the first Harmon Gold Award for literature, which carried with it a cash award of five hundred dollars. Just before publication in 1927 of his second book, *Copper Sun*, Cullen received a Guggenheim Fellowship for a year's study and writing in France. While in France, he worked on improving his French conversation by engaging a private tutor and his knowledge of French literature by enrolling in courses at the Sorbonne. Out of this experience came *The Black Christ, and Other Poems*. In 1944, the poet was offered the chair of creative literature at Nashville's Fisk University, but he refused in order to continue his teaching at the Frederick Douglass Junior High in New York City.

BIOGRAPHY

Countée Cullen was born Countée LeRoy Porter, although scholars remain uncertain as to the place of his birth. He was raised by Elizabeth Porter, who is thought to be his grandmother and who brought him to Harlem. When Porter died in 1918, Cullen was adopted by the Reverend and Mrs. Frederick A. Cullen; the Reverend Cullen was minister of the Salem Methodist Episcopal Church of Harlem. The years spent with the Cullens in the Methodist parsonage made a lasting impression on the young poet; although he experienced periods of intense self-questioning, Cullen appears never to have discarded his belief in Christianity.

During his undergraduate years at New York University, the young poet became heavily involved with figures of the Harlem Renaissance; among these Harlem literati were Zora Neale Hurston, Langston Hughes, Carl Van Vechten (a white writer who treated black themes), and Wallace Thurman. After the appearance of *Color* in 1925 and the receipt of his Harvard M.A. in June, 1926, Cullen assumed the position of literary editor of *Opportunity*. At the end of October, 1926, he wrote one of the most important of his "Dark Tower" essays about the appearance of that great treasure of the Harlem Renaissance, the short-lived but first black literary and art quarterly *Fire* (issued only once). He contributed one of his best poems, "From the Dark Tower," to *Fire*. About the solitary issue, Cullen wrote that it held great significance for black American culture, because it represented "a brave and beautiful attempt to meet our need for an all-literary and artistic medium of expression."

On April 10, 1928, Cullen married Nina Yolande Du Bois, daughter of one of the most powerful figures of twentieth century black American culture, W. E. B. Du Bois; the two were married at Salem Methodist Episcopal Church. This union proved to be of short duration, however; while Cullen was in Paris on his Guggenheim Fellowship, his wife was granted a decree of divorce. The marriage had not lasted two years. Much of Cullen's poetry deals with disappointment in love, and one senses that the poet was himself often disappointed in such matters.

In 1940, however, after Cullen had taught for several years at the Frederick Douglass Junior High School of New York, he married a second time; on this occasion he chose Ida Mae Roberson, whom he had known for ten years. Ida Mae represented to the poet the ideal woman; she was intelligent, loyal, and empathetic, if not as beautiful and well-connected as his former wife.

When Cullen died of uremic poisoning on January 9, 1946, only forty-two years old, the New York newspapers devoted several columns to detailing his career and praising him for his distinguished literary accomplishments. However, nearly thirty years after Cullen's death, Houston A. Baker deplored (in *A Many-Colored Coat of Dreams: The Poetry of Countée Cullen*, 1974) the fact that no collection of his poetry had been published since the posthumous *On These I Stand*, nor had any of his previously published volumes been reprinted. Indeed, many volumes of this important Harlem Renaissance poet can be read only in rare-book rooms of university libraries.

ANALYSIS

In his scholarly book of 1937, *Negro Poetry and Drama*, Sterling A. Brown, whose poems and essays continue to exert formidable influence on black American culture, remarked that Countée Cullen's poetry is "the most polished lyricism of modern Negro poetry." About his own poetry and poetry in general, Cullen himself observed, "Good poetry is a lofty thought beautifully expressed. Poetry should not be too intellectual. It should deal more, I think, with the emotions." In this definition of "good poetry," Cullen reflects his declared, constant aspiration to transcend his color and to strike a universal chord. However, the perceptive poet, novelist, essayist and critic James Weldon Johnson asserted that the best of Cullen's poetry "is motivated by race. He is always seeking to free himself and his art from these bonds."

The tension prevalent in Cullen's poems, then, is between the objective of transcendence—to reach the universal, to enter the "mainstream"—and his ineluctable return to the predicament his race faces in a white world. This tension causes him, on one hand, to demonstrate a paramount example of T. S. Eliot's "tradition and the individual talent" and, on the other, to embody the black aesthetic (as articulated during the Harlem Renaissance). In his best poems, he achieves both. Transcending the bonds of race and country, he produces poetry that looks to the literature and ideas of the past while it identifies its creator as an original artist; yet, at the same time, he celebrates his African heritage, dramatizes black heroism, and reveals the reality of being black in a hostile world.

"Yet Do I Marvel"

"Yet Do I Marvel," perhaps Cullen's most famous single poem, displays the poet during one of his most intensely lyrical, personal moments; however, this poem also illustrates his reverence for tradition. The sonnet, essentially Shakespearean in rhyme scheme, is actually Petrarchan in its internal form. The Petrarchan form is even suggested in the rhyme scheme; the first two quatrains rhyme *abab*, *cdcd* in perfect accord with the Shakespearean scheme. The next six lines, however, break the expected pattern of yet another quatrain in the same scheme; instead of *efef* followed by a couplet *gg*, the poem adopts the scheme *eeffgg*. While retaining the concluding couplet (*gg*), the other two (*eeff*) combine with the final couplet, suggesting the Petrarchan structure of the sestet. The poem is essentially divided, then, into the octave, wherein the problem is stated, and the sestet, in which some sort of resolution is attempted.

Analysis of the poem's content shows that Cullen chose the internal form of the Petrarchan sonnet but retained a measure of the Shakespearean form for dramatic effect. By means of antiphrastic statements or ironic declaratives in the first eight lines of the poem, the poem's speaker expresses doubt about God's goodness and benevolent intent, especially in his creation of certain limited beings. The poem begins with the assertion that "I doubt not God is good, well-meaning, kind" and then proceeds to reveal that the speaker actually believes just the opposite to be true; that is, he actually says, "I do doubt God is good." For God has created the "little buried mole" to continue blind and "flesh that mirrors Him" to "some day die." Then the persona cites two illustrations of cruel, irremediable predicaments from classical mythology, those of Tantalus and Sisyphus. These mythological figures are traditional examples: Tantalus, the man who suffers eternal denial of that which he seeks, and Sisyphus, the man who suffers the eternal drudgery of being forced to toil endlessly again and again only to lose his objective each time he thinks he has won it.

The illustration of the mole and the man who must die rehearses the existential pathos of modern human beings estranged from God and thrust into a hostile universe. What appeared to be naïve affirmations of God's goodness become penetrating questions that reveal Cullen himself in a moment of intense doubt. This attitude of contention with God closely resembles that expressed by Gerard Manley Hopkins in his sonnet "Thou Art Indeed Just, Lord." The probing questions, combined with the apparent resolve to believe, are indeed close; one might suggest that Cullen has adapted Hopkins's struggle for certainty to the black predicament, the real subject of Cullen's poem. The predicaments of Tantalus and Sisyphus (anticipating Albert Camus's later essay) comment on a personal problem, one close to home for Cullen himself. The notion of men struggling eternally toward a goal, thinking they have achieved it but having it torn from them, articulates the plight of black artists in the United States. In keeping with the form of the Petrarchan sonnet, the ninth line constitutes the *volta* or turn toward some sort of resolution. From ironic questioning, the persona moves to direct statement, even to a degree of affirmation. "Inscrutable His ways are," the speaker declares, to a mere human being who is too preoccupied with the vicissitudes of his mundane existence to grasp "What awful brain compels His awful hand," this last line echoing William Blake's "The Tyger." The apparent resolution becomes clouded by the poem's striking final couplet: "Yet do I marvel at this curious thing:/ To make a poet black, and bid him sing!"

The doubt remains; nothing is finally resolved. The plight of the black poet becomes identical with that of Tantalus and Sisyphus. Like these figures from classical mythology, the black poet is, in the contemporary, nonmythological world, forced to struggle endlessly toward a goal he will never, as the poem suggests, be allowed to reach. Cullen has effectively combined the Petrarchan and the Shakespearean sonnet forms; the sestet's first four lines function as an apparent resolution of the problem advanced by the octave. The concluding couplet, however, recalling the Shakespearean device of concentrating the entire poem's comment within the final two lines, restates the problem of the octave by maintaining that, in the case of a black poet, God has created the supreme irony. In "Yet Do I Marvel," Cullen has succeeded in making an intensely personal statement; as Johnson suggested, this poem "is motivated by race." Nevertheless, not only race is at work here. Rather than selecting a more modern form, perhaps free verse, the poet employs the sonnet tradition in a surprising and effective way, and he also shows his regard for tradition by citing mythological figures and by summoning up Blake.

REGARD FOR TRADITION

Cullen displays his regard for tradition in many other poems. "The Medusa," for example, by its very title celebrates once again the classical tradition; in this piece, another sonnet, the poet suggests that the face of a woman who rejected him has the malign power of the Medusa. In an epitaph, a favorite form of Cullen, he celebrates the poetry of John Keats, whose "singing lips that cold death kissed/ Have seared his own with flame." Keats was Cullen's avowed favorite poet, and Cullen celebrates him in yet a second poem, "To John Keats, Poet at Spring Time." As suggested by Cullen's definition of poetry, it was Keats's concern for beauty which attracted him: "in spite of all men say/ Of Beauty, you have felt her most."

"HERITAGE"

Beauty and classical mythology were not the only elements of tradition that Cullen revered. Indeed, he forcefully celebrated his own African heritage, exemplifying the first of the tenets of the black aesthetic. "Heritage" represents his most concentrated effort to reclaim his African roots. This 128-line lyric opens as the persona longs for the song of "wild barbaric birds/ Goading massive jungle herds" from which, through no fault of his own, he has been removed for three centuries. He then articulates Johnson's observation that this poet is ever "seeking to free himself and his art" from the bonds of this heritage. The poem's speaker remarks that, although he crams his thumbs against his ears and keeps them there, "great drums" always throb "through the air." This duplicity of mind and action force upon him a sense of "distress, and joy allied." Despite this distress, he continues to conjure up in his mind's eye "cats/ Crouching in the river reeds," "silver snakes," and "the savage measures of/ Jungle boys and girls in love." The rain has a particularly dramatic effect on him; "While its primal measures drip," a distant, resonant voice beckons him to "'strip!/ Off this new exuberance./ Come and dance the Lover's Dance!'" Out of this experience of recollection and reclaiming his past comes the urge to "fashion dark gods" and, finally, even to dare "to give You [the one God]/ Dark despairing features."

THE BLACK CHRIST

The intense need expressed here, to see God as literally black, predicts the long narrative poem of 1929, *The Black Christ*. This poem, perhaps more than any other of Cullen's poems, represents his attempt to portray black heroism, the second tenet of the black aesthetic. Briefly the poem tells the tale of Jim, a young black man who comes to believe it is inevitable that he will suffer death at the hands of an angry lynch mob. Miraculously, after the inevitable lynching has indeed occurred, the young man appears to his younger brother and mother, much as Jesus of Nazareth, according to the Gospels, appeared before his disciples. Christ has essentially transformed himself into black Jim. Although the poem contains such faults as a main character who speaks in dialect at one point and waxes eloquent at another, and one speech by Jim who, pursued by the mob, speaks so long that he cannot possibly escape (one may argue that he was doomed from the start), it has moments of artistic brilliance.

Jim "was handsome in a way/ Night is after a long, hot day." He could never bend his spirit to the white man's demands: "my blood's too hot to knuckle." Like Richard Wright's Bigger Thomas, Jim was a man of action whose deeds "let loose/ The pent-up torrent of abuse," which clamored in his younger brother "for release." Toward the middle of the poem, Jim's brother, the narrator, describes Jim, after the older brother has become tipsy with drink, as "Spring's gayest cavalier"; this occurs "in the dim/ Half-light" of the evening. At the end, "Spring's gayest cavalier" has become the black Christ, Spring's radiant sacrifice, suggesting that "Half-light" reveals only selective truths, those one may be inclined to believe are true because of one's human limitations, whereas God's total light reveals absolute truth unfettered. Following this suggestion, the image "Spring's gayest cavalier" becomes even more fecund. The word "cavalier" calls up another poem by Hopkins, "The Windhover," which is dedicated to Christ. In this poem, the speaker addresses Christ with the exclamation, "O my chevalier!" Both "cavalier" and "chevalier" have their origins in the same Latin word, *caballarius*. Since Cullen knew both French and Latin and since Hopkins's poems had been published in 1918, it is reasonable to suggest a more than coincidental connection. At any rate, "Spring's gayest cavalier" embodies an example of effective foreshadowing.

Just before the mob seizes Jim, the narrator maintains that "The air about him shaped a crown/ Of light, or so it seemed to me," similar to the nimbus so often appearing in medieval paintings of Christ, the holy family, the disciples, and the saints. The narrator describes the seizure itself in an epic simile of nine lines. When Jim has been lynched, the younger brother exclaims, "My Lycidas was dead. There swung/ In all his glory, lusty, young,/ My Jonathan, my Patrocles." Here Cullen brings together the works of John Milton, the Bible, and Homer into one image that appears to syncretize them all. Clearly, the poet is attempting to construct in Jim a hero of cosmic proportions while at the same time managing to unify, if only for a moment, four grand traditions: the English, the biblical, the classical, and, of course, the African American.

"HARLEM WINE"

While *The Black Christ* dramatizes black heroism, it also suggests what it means to be black in a hostile, white world. Not all the black experience, however, is tainted with such unspeakable horror. In "Harlem Wine," Cullen reveals how blacks overcome their pain and rebellious inclinations through the medium of music. The blues, a totally black cultural phenomenon, "hurtle flesh and bone past fear/ Down alleyways of dreams." Indeed, the wine of Harlem can its "joy compute/ with blithe, ecstatic hips." The ballad stanza of this poem's three quatrains rocks with rhythm, repeating Cullen's immensely successful performance in another long narrative poem, *The Ballad of the Brown Girl*.

"FROM THE DARK TOWER"

Although not as notable a rhythmic performance as "Harlem Wine" or *The Ballad of the Brown Girl*, "From the Dark Tower" is, nevertheless, a remarkable poem. It contains a profound expression of the black experience. Important to a reading of the poem is the fact that the Dark Tower was an actual place located on New York's 136th Street in the heart of Harlem; poets and artists of the Harlem Renaissance often gathered there to discuss their writings and their art. Perhaps this poem grew out of one of those gatherings. The poem is more identifiably a Petrarchan or Italian sonnet than "Yet Do I Marvel"; as prescribed by the form, the octave is arranged into two quatrains, each rhyming *abbaabba*, while the sestet rhymes *ccddee*. The rhyme scheme of the sestet closely resembles that in "Yet Do I Marvel."

The octave of "From the Dark Tower" states the poem's problem in an unconventional, perhaps surprising manner by means of a series of threats. The first threat introduces the conceit of planting, to which the poem returns in its last pair of couplets. The poet begins, "We shall not always plant while others reap/ The golden increment of bursting fruit." The planting conceit suggests almost immediately the image of slaves working the fields of a Southern plantation. Conjuring up this memory of the antebellum South but then asserting by use of the future tense ("We *shall* not") that nothing has changed—that is, that the white world has relegated modern African Americans to their former status as slaves, not even as good as second-class citizens—Cullen strikes a minor chord of deep, poignant bitterness felt by many blacks during his lifetime. However, what these blacks produce with their planting is richly fertile, a "bursting fruit"; the problem is that "others reap" this "golden increment." The poet's threat promises that this tide of gross, unjust rapine will soon turn against its perpetrators.

The next few lines compound this initial threat with others. These same oppressed people will not forever bow "abject and mute" to such treatment by a people who have shown by their oppression that they are the inferiors of their victims. "Not everlastingly" will these victims "beguile" this evil race "with mellow flute"; the reader can readily picture scenes of supposedly contented, dancing "darkies" and ostensibly happy minstrel men. "We were not made eternally to weep" declares the poet in the last line of the octave. This line constitutes the *volta* or turning point in the poem. All the bitterness and resentment implied in the preceding lines is exposed here. An oppressed people simply will not shed tears forever; sorrow and self-pity inevitably turn to anger and rebellion.

The first four lines of the sestet state cases in defense of the octave's propositions that these oppressed people, now identified by the comparisons made in these lines as the black race, are "no less lovely being dark." The poet returns subtly to his planting conceit by citing the case of flowers that "cannot bloom at all/ In light, but crumple, piteous, and fall." From the infinite heavens to finite flowers of Earth Cullen takes his reader, grasping universal and particular significance for his people and thereby restoring and bolstering their pride and sense of worth.

Then follow the piercing, deep-felt last lines: "So, in the dark we hide the heart that bleeds,/ And wait, and tend our agonizing seeds." As with "Yet Do I Marvel," Cullen has effectively combined the structures of the Petrarchan and Shakespearean sonnets by concluding his poem with this trenchant, succinct couplet. The planting conceit, however, has altered dramatically. What has been "golden increment" for white oppressors will yet surely prove the "bursting fruit" of "agonizing seeds." The poem represents, then, a sort of revolutionary predeclaration of independence. This "document" first states the offenses sustained by the downtrodden, next asserts their worth and significance as human beings, and finally argues that the black people will "wait" until an appropriate time to reveal their agony through rebellion. Cullen has here predicted the anger of James Baldwin's *The Fire Next Time* (1963) and the rhetoric of the Black Armageddon, a later literary movement led by such poets as Amiri Baraka, Sonia Sanchez, and Nikki Giovanni.

Whereas these figures of the Black Armageddon movement almost invariably selected unconventional forms in which to express their rebellion, Cullen demonstrated his respect for tradition in voicing his parallel feelings. Although Cullen's work ably displays his knowledge of the traditions of the Western world, from Homer to Keats (and even Edna St. Vincent Millay), it equally enunciates his empathy with black Americans in its celebration of the black aesthetic. At the same time that his poetry incorporates classicism and English Romanticism, it affirms his black heritage and the black American experience.

OTHER MAJOR WORKS

LONG FICTION: *One Way to Heaven*, 1932.

PLAYS: *Medea*, pr., pb. 1935 (translation of Euripides); *One Way to Heaven*, pb. 1936 (adaptation of his novel); *St. Louis Woman*, pr. 1946 (adaptation of Arna Bontemps's novel *God Sends Sunday*); *The Third Fourth of July*, pr., pb. 1946 (one act; with Owen Dodson).

CHILDREN'S LITERATURE: *The Lost Zoo (A Rhyme for the Young, but Not Too Young)*, 1940; *My Lives and How I Lost Them*, 1942.

EDITED TEXT: *Caroling Dusk*, 1927.

MISCELLANEOUS: *My Soul's High Song: The Collected Writings of Countee Cullen, Voice of the Harlem Renaissance*, 1991 (Gerald Early, editor).

BIBLIOGRAPHY

Baker, Houston A., Jr. *A Many-Colored Coat of Dreams: The Poetry of Countée Cullen.* Detroit: Broadside Press, 1974. This brief and somewhat difficult volume examines Cullen's poetry in the context of a black American literature that is published and criticized largely by a white literary establishment. Presents a new view of Cullen's poetry by holding it up to the light of black literary standards.

Ferguson, Blanche E. *Countée Cullen and the Negro Renaissance.* New York: Dodd, Mead, 1966. The only book-length study of Cullen for many years, this volume is a highly fictionalized biography. In a pleasant and simple style, Ferguson walks readers through major events in Cullen's life. Includes eight photographs, a brief bibliography, and an index.

Hutchinson, George, ed. *The Cambridge Companion to the Harlem Renaissance.* New York: Cambridge University Press, 2007. This work on the Harlem Renaissance contains a chapter comparing Cullen and Langston Hughes.

Onyeberechi, Sydney. *Critical Essays: Achebe, Baldwin, Cullen, Ngugi, and Tutuola.* Hyattsville, Md.: Rising Star, 1999. A collection of Onyeberechi's criticism and interpretation of the work of several African American authors. Includes bibliographic references.

Perry, Margaret. *A Bio-Bibliography of Countée Cullen.* Westport, Conn.: Greenwood Press, 1971. After a brief biographical sketch, Perry offers a valuable bibliography of Cullen's works and a sensitive reading of the poetry.

Pettis, Joyce. *African American Poets: Lives, Works, and Sources.* Westport, Conn.: Greenwood Press, 2002. This work on African American poets contains an entry describing the life and works of Cullen.

Schwarz, A. B. Christa. *Gay Voices of the Harlem Renaissance.* Bloomington: Indiana University Press, 2003. Schwarz examines the work of four leading writers from the Harlem Renaissance—Cullen, Langston Hughes, Claude McKay, and Richard Bruce Nugent— and their sexually nonconformist or gay literary voices.

Shucard, Alan R. *Countée Cullen.* Boston: Twayne, 1984. A basic biography detailing the life and works of Cullen.

Tuttleton, James W. "Countée Cullen at 'The Heights.'" In *The Harlem Renaissance: Revaluations,* edited by Amritjit Singh, William S. Shiver, and Stanley Brodwin. New York: Garland, 1989. Examines Cullen's years at New York University and analyzes his senior honors thesis on Edna St. Vincent Millay. Tuttleton argues that this period was very important to Cullen's emergence as a poet.

Washington, Shirley Porter. *Countée Cullen's Secret Revealed by Miracle Book: A Biography of His Childhood in New Orleans.* Bloomington, Ind.: AuthorHouse, 2008. This work by Cullen's niece asserts that Cullen was born James S. Carter, Jr., in New Orleans to James S. Carter, Sr., the first licensed African American dentist in Louisiana, and to Gussie Yeager Carter.

John C. Shields

OWEN DODSON

Born: Brooklyn, New York; November 28, 1914
Died: New York, New York; June 21, 1983

PRINCIPAL POETRY
Powerful Long Ladder, 1946
Cages, 1953
The Confession Stone, 1968 (revised and enlarged as *The Confession Stone: Song Cycles*, 1970)
The Harlem Book of the Dead, 1978 (with James Van Der Zee and Camille Billops)

OTHER LITERARY FORMS

Owen Dodson's contribution to the theater is significant, from his first involvement at Bates College in 1933 to his work on a production of his own play, *Till Victory Is Won* (first produced in 1965), by the Carnegie Hall Opera Ebony four months before his death in 1983. He published or produced eight plays between 1935 and 1965. Dodson wrote two autobiographical novels, *Boy at the Window* (1951), reprinted as *When Trees Were Green* (1967), and *Come Home Early, Child* (1977). In addition, he wrote short fiction, published in various anthologies, as well as a screenplay and radioplays.

ACHIEVEMENTS

Although poetry was Owen Dodson's first love, his need for drama led him to writing plays, but they were poetic drama. Throughout his time at Yale, he attempted to devote himself totally to drama, but continued to write poetry. The impact of his first collection of poetry, *Powerful Long Ladder*, was such that his peers and seniors assimilated him into the canon of standard African American poetry; his poems appeared in principal black poetry anthologies of the 1950's, although he had stopped writing poetry.

While at Yale, Dodson was awarded a stipend of $3,200 from the Rockefeller General Board for his expressed interest in "forming a Negro Theater where Negroes may have plays presented." With this end in mind, Dodson wrote numerous plays. In 1943, following his service in the U.S. Navy, he received a Rosenwald Fellowship to write plays for an African American theater, but failed to fulfill his obligation. In 1952, after finishing *Boy at the Window*, Dodson, with the help of poet W. H. Auden, secured a Guggenheim Fellowship "for creative activity in the field of fiction," in the amount of $3,500.

BIOGRAPHY

Owen Vincent Dodson was the ninth and last child born to Sarah Goode Dodson and Nathaniel Dodson on November 28, 1914, in Brooklyn, New York. Dodson's father, a journalist, member of the American Press Association, and editor of the Negro News Service, exerted enormous influence on his son through his literary associations. Dodson's mother died when he was eleven, and his father died the following year, so Dodson was raised by Lillian Dodson, his oldest sibling. She moved the family near Thomas Jefferson High School, which Dodson attended from 1928 to 1932.

In high school, Dodson achieved excellence in poetry reading and won various prizes in elocution. He wrote poems mostly dealing with the deaths of members of his family. Befriended by the well-known Folger family, owners of Standard Oil, Dodson and his brother Kenneth helped matriarch Mary Wells with family dinners and babysitting, and, in return, were allowed to accompany her to musical programs, motion pictures, lectures, and plays—all encouraging Dodson's love of theater. He graduated from high school with a B average, with As in elocution, and received a scholarship for Bates College in Lewiston, Maine.

As a freshman at Bates, while studying John Keats's poetry, Dodson boasted to his professor that he could write a sonnet as good as one of Keats. His professor commanded him to each week submit a sonnet he had written until either he could surpass Keats or he graduated. At Bates, Dodson refined his poetry, primarily sonnets, publishing some of them in small publications. However, despite his passion for poetry, he continued playwriting, receiving an invitation to enroll in Yale School of Drama. During his three years at Yale, he achieved a reputation for notable productions of his own plays. In 1939, with his M.F.A. in hand, Dodson accepted a teaching position at Spelman College in Atlanta, Georgia, where he mingled with the black intelligentsia and experienced racism in the South. In 1940, his beloved brother Kenneth died.

In 1941, Dodson became a visiting professor of drama at the newly established department of communication of the Hampton Institute in Virginia. Within six months, however, Dodson, fearful of German domination of the United States, enlisted in the U.S. Navy. While in the Navy, he produced a weekly program honoring black servicemen and featuring morale-boosting plays. He continued to write poetry largely because of his realization that a great many individuals had suffered. His poetry was published in *The Negro Caravan* (1941; Sterling A. Brown, Arthur P. Davis, and Ulysses Lee, editors), an anthology of black literature, in which he was described as an "aware" black poet.

In 1946, Dodson published his first volume of poetry, *Powerful Long Ladder*. The following year, he accepted the position of professor of drama at Howard University, in Washington D.C., where he remained for twenty-five years, writing and producing his plays. He retired from Howard in 1967, suffering from ill health. His second volume of verse, *The Confession Stone*, was published in 1968. He died of heart failure in 1983.

ANALYSIS

As Owen Dodson was unable or unwilling to confine himself to any specific genre, his poems are also far-ranging in subject, style, and form. Reflecting his classical, humanistic education, his poetry frequently alludes to mythological or classical figures. Just as his drama is poetic, his poetry is dramatic and intense. Although highly skilled in the writing of sonnets, he also wrote free verse. Unlike most of the African American poets of his day, who attempted to lay bare the black experience in the United States, Dodson, instead, speaks emotionally, expressing pain and sorrow for those who have no voice.

POWERFUL LONG LADDER

Powerful Long Ladder is permeated with sorrow throughout—sorrow for those individuals suffering from the domination and brutality of racism, from conditions of war, and from grief over the deaths of loved ones. Some of Dodson's verse written while he was in the U.S. Navy focuses on his awareness of the suffering of others. "Black Mother Praying" (1943), written in free verse, is one of his most famous poems. Dodson relates an African American woman's anguished pleading for God's help in response to the brutal treatment of African Americans during the summer, 1943, race riots, sparked by competition between blacks and whites for higher-wage jobs in war industries. Another poem dating from his service period, "Jonathan's Song, A Negro Saw a Jewish Pageant, 'We Will Never Die,'" was engendered by Dodson's visit to a Jewish celebration of life. Dodson and a Jewish friend attended a candlelight ceremony commemorating Jews who had died as a result of racial hatred; Dodson's recognition of the suffering of the Jews produced a passionate emotional poem mingling the suffering of the two races. In 1940, during the Battle of Britain, Dodson composed "Iphigenia," whose reference to mythological Agamemnon's daughter, who was sacrificed in order for the Argive fleet to fulfill its mission, comments on the sacrifice of the innocent English people being slaughtered to satisfy the world's corrupt people. Dodson uses a tone of great sorrow as he internalizes the world's pain.

In "Poems For My Brother, Kenneth," in the first poetry selection, Dodson presents various perspectives of his brother. Kenneth appears regularly in Dodson's dreams, giving him directions, and then disappears back into his grave; in every thought, Dodson is overcome with memories of Kenneth. Dodson questions the relevance of World War II to him in view of Kenneth's death. Much as his mother's death years earlier had eroded Dodson's faith in God, Kenneth's death has now destroyed any hope of life after death for Dodson. He perceives Kenneth's body in the ground as "awaiting nothing." Dodson proclaims, "There will be no resurrection."

Dodson's concern for the dignity of black people in a white world of almost universal disrespect for them compelled him to compose poems in memory of African Americans whose accomplishments and personal virtues were exceptional. Poems in *Power-*

ful Long Ladder include a tribute to Samuel Chapman Armstrong, founder of Hampton Institute, and to "Miss Packard and Miss Giles," founders of Spelman College, and a eulogy for fellow poet, Countée Cullen. The book also contains three choruses from his verse drama *Divine Comedy* (pr. 1938); *Some Day We're Gonna Tear Them Pillars Down*, a drama that cries out for freedom; and "Sorrow Is the Only Faithful One," a personal poem that sets forth sorrow as his enduring lone companion.

THE CONFESSION STONE

The Confession Stone, begun in 1960 and finished after he had retired from Howard University, spans the three days from Good Friday to Easter morning. The poems are grouped into cycles involving Jesus' entire family: poems or letters from Joseph to Mary; entries from "Journals of Magdalene"; Joseph's letters to Martha, sister of Lazarus; Joseph's letters to Pontius Pilate, Judas, and God; and a single response from God. The title of the work refers to a rock whereon individuals kneel and wrestle with pain and misery, and the characters in the collection appear to be on the hard stone of confession. Dodson's purpose in writing the poems, as is the purpose of most of his poetry, is to reach some reconciliation or terms with God. In the poem, Dodson appeals to God for some sign of recognition and promises not to speak of Calvary. God's cryptic response insists that Dodson has not been deserted.

The cycle of poems originated with Dodson's appearance on stage in 1941 as Judas in Lenore J. Coffee and William Joyce Cowen's *Family Portrait* (first produced in 1939) in which the Holy Family is portrayed as human beings. Dodson began the cycles with a sorrowful Mary mourning for her son—poems that composer Robert Fleming set to music and arranged for contralto Maureen Forrester to perform at Carnegie Hall. The cycle of songs continues to be sung at Easter Services.

THE HARLEM BOOK OF THE DEAD

Other Dodson poems were published in *The Harlem Book of the Dead*, a book of photographs taken by noted photographer of rituals, James Van Der Zee, who recorded funerals in the 1920's, 1930's, and 1940's for the benefit of relatives and posterity. The book was a collaborative effort between Van Der Zee, who also was the subject of an interview; Camille Billops, who furnished a text; Owen Dodson, whose poems accompanied, largely in juxtaposition, the photographs; and Toni Morrison, who provided an introduction. For one photograph of a woman arrayed in funeral attire, Dodson juxtaposed his "Allegory of Seafaring Black Mothers," in which he mythically speaks of mothers telling fortunes, milking goats, and scrubbing the ship's deck while sailing on the sea. Beneath the photograph of another deceased woman, Dodson deals with images of death's decay, but announces a resurrection so glorious and vivid that it startles the angels.

OTHER MAJOR WORKS

LONG FICTION: *Boy at the Window*, 1951 (also known as *When Trees Were Green*, 1967); *Come Home Early, Child*, 1977.

SHORT FICTION: "The Summer Fire," 1956.

PLAYS: *Deep in Your Heart*, pr. 1935; *The Poet's Caprice*, pb. 1935 (appeared in the December, 1935, issue of *Garnet*); *Including Laughter*, pr. 1936; *Divine Comedy*, pr. 1938 (music by Morris Mamorsky); *The Garden of Time*, pr. 1939 (music by Shirley Graham); *The Ballad of Dorrie Miller*, pr., pb. 1943 (also known as *The Ballad of Dorie Miller*, 2002); *Everybody Join Hands*, pr., pb. 1943; *Freedom the Banner*, pr. 1943; *New World A-Coming*, pr. 1943; *The Third Fourth of July*, pb. 1946 (with Countée Cullen); *Bayou Legend*, pr. 1948; *Till Victory Is Won*, pr. 1965 (with Mark Fax; opera); *The Shining Town*, pb. 1991 (wr. 1937).

SCREENPLAY: *They Seek a City*, 1945.

RADIO PLAYS: *Old Ironsides*, 1942; *Robert Smalls*, 1942; *The Midwest Mobilizes*, 1943; *Dorrie Miller*, 1944; *New World A-Coming*, 1945; *St. Louis Woman*, c. 1945 (adaptation of Cullen and Arna Bontemps's play); *The Dream Awake*, 1969.

NONFICTION: "Twice a Year," 1946-1947; "College Troopers Abroad," 1950; "Playwrights in Dark Glasses," 1968; "Who Has Seen the Wind? Playwrights and the Black Experience," 1977; "Who Has Seen the Wind? Part II," 1980.

BIBLIOGRAPHY

Grant, Nathan L. "The Unpublished Poetry of Owen Dodson." *Callaloo* 20, no. 3 (Summer, 1997): 619-626. Contains selections of Dodson's unpublished poetry, scavenged from handwritten or typewritten papers and found in various folders. Some are early versions of later published poems or represent mere ideas, abandoned as failures.

Hatch, James V. *Sorrow Is the Only Faithful One: The Life of Owen Dodson*. Urbana, Ill.: University of Chicago Press, 1993. Sympathetic, well-detailed biography of Dodson written by his friend.

"Owen Vincent Dodson." In *Contemporary Black Biography*, edited by Ashyia Henderson. Vol. 38. Farmington Hill, Mich.: Gale Group, 2003. Informative article on Dodson, his background, deaths of family members, education, literary accomplishments, homosexuality, struggles with segregation, alcoholism, and illness.

Shuman, R. Baird. "Poetry of Owen Dodson." In *Masterplots II: African American Literature*, edited by Tyrone Williams. Rev. ed. Pasadena, Calif.: Salem Press, 2009. Provides in-depth analysis of Dodson's poetry, including themes and meanings and the critical context.

Weixlmann, Joe. "A Review of Owen Dodson's *Jazz in Praise of the Lord*." *Black American Literature Forum* 14, no. 2 (Summer, 1980): 53-54. Discussion of Dodson's taped performance of his own selected poems.

Mary Hurd

RITA DOVE

Born: Akron, Ohio; August 28, 1952

OTHER LITERARY FORMS

Rita Dove has published *Fifth Sunday* (1985), a collection of short stories; *Through the Ivory Gate* (1992), a novel; and *The Poet's World* (1995), a collection of essays. *The Darker Face of the Earth*, a verse drama, appeared in 1994.

ACHIEVEMENTS

Rita Dove's literary honors include grants and fellowships from the National Endowment for the Arts, the Academy of American Poets, the Guggenheim Foundation, and the General Electric Foundation. She spent 1988-1989 as a Senior Mellon Fellow at the National Humanities Center in North Carolina. She served as poet laureate consultant in poetry to the Library of Congress from 1993 to 1995 and poet laureate of the Commonwealth of Virginia from 2004 to 2006. She also was a special bicentennial consultant (poet laureate) to the Library of Congress along with poets W. S. Merwin and Louise Glück in 1999-2000. She became a chancellor of the Academy of American Poets in 2006.

In 1987, her collection *Thomas and Beulah* made her the first black woman since Gwendolyn Brooks to win the Pulitzer Prize. She has also been awarded the Peter I. B. Lavan Younger Poets Award (1986), several Ohioana Book Awards for Poetry (1990, 1994, 2000), the Charles Frankel Prize/National Humanities Medal (1996), the Heinz Award in the Arts and Humanities (1996), the Sara Lee Frontrunner Award (1997), Levinson Prize from *Poetry* magazine (1998), the John Frederick Nims Translation Award (1999; together with Fred Viebahn), the Duke Ellington Lifetime Achievement Award (2001), the Emily Couric Leadership Award (2003), the Common Wealth Award of Distinguished Service (2006; with others), the Lifetime Achievement Award from the Library of Virginia (2008), and the Fulbright Lifetime Achievement Medal and the Premio Capri (both in 2009).

BIOGRAPHY

Born in 1952 in Akron, Ohio, Rita Francis Dove is the daughter of Ray Dove and Elvira (Hord) Dove. She received a B.A. in 1973 from Miami University (Ohio) and then studied modern European literature at the University of Tübingen, Germany, on a Fulbright Fellowship. She returned to the United States to earn an M.F.A. at the highly regarded Iowa Writers' Workshop at the University of Iowa in 1977. She held a number of teaching posts and traveled widely in Europe and the Middle East, later becoming a professor of English at the University of Virginia. During the summer of 1998, the Boston Symphony Orchestra performed her song cycle of a woman's life, *Seven for Luck*, with music by John Williams. From January, 2000, to January, 2002, she wrote a weekly column, "Poet's Choice," for *The Washington Post*. Dove married Fred Viebahn, a writer, in 1979; they had a daughter, Aviva Chantal Tamu Dove-Viebahn in 1983.

ANALYSIS

In a period when much American poetry is condemned as being merely an exercise in solipsistic navel gazing, and when African American poetry more specifically seems to have lapsed into hibernation after the vigorous activity of the Black Arts movement, Rita Dove steps forth with a body of work that resoundingly answers such criticism. Hers is a poetry characterized by discipline and technical proficiency, surprising breadth of reference, a willingness to approach emotionally charged subjects with aesthetic objectivity, and a refusal to define herself only in terms of blackness. She combines a novelist's eye for action and gesture with the lyric poet's exalted sense of language. Dove's distinguishing feature is her ability to turn a cold gaze on the larger world with which she has to interact as a social being—and as an African American woman. That gaze is filtered through an aesthetic sensibility that regards poetry as a redemptive force, a transformational power.

The startling scope of Dove's learning opens for her poetry a correspondingly vast range of topics and concerns, but the most persistent, and the one that most distinguishes her work from that of poets in the 1970's and 1980's, is history. She is constantly laboring to bring into focus the individual struggle in the ebb and flow of the historical tide. A second major concern is cultural collision, the responses of an outsider to a foreign culture, and she pursues this theme in a number of travel poems. Dove also plumbs the circumstances of her life as a way of confronting the puzzle of her own identity—as an African American, as a woman, as a daughter, as a parent—but she manages self-dramatization without self-aggrandizement.

Dove has been lauded for her technical acumen. Although much modern poetry is best characterized by a certain casualness and laxity, she has created poetry in which no verse is "free." Each poem gives the impression of having been chiseled, honed, and polished. Her poems evolve into highly individual structures, rather than traditional forms, although it is possible to find an occasional sonnet neatly revised and partially hidden. More often she stresses rhythm and sound and uses interior rhyme, slant rhyme, and feminine rhyme to furnish her stanzas with a subtle organizing principle, what she calls the "sound cage" of a poem. Her idiom is predominantly colloquial, but she can adopt the stiffened, formal diction of the eighteenth and nineteenth centuries when evoking personas from those periods. In her mastery of the craft, Dove reveals an attitude toward poetry itself—a deeply felt love and respect—that also influences the approach a reader must take to it. Her work makes demands on the reader because of that love.

Dove's first two volumes, _The Yellow House on the Corner_ and _Museum_, provide a balance between the personal or individual and the social or cultural. Each is divided into sections that allow the author to address concerns that she wishes for now to remain separate. It has also been noted that the titles of these two books signal a shift in Dove's emphasis from the homely and familiar, "the yellow house," to the more sophisticated and arcane "museum." This generalization should not, however, obscure the fact that the poet's interests in these books overlap considerably. _Museum_ is the more consciously organized, with its sections pointedly titled and each dealing with a central topic—history and myth, art and artifact, autobiography and the personal past, life in the modern world.

Dove's next volume, _Thomas and Beulah_, represents her coming of age critically, a step into the position of a leading African American poet. It allows her to extend her continual dissertation on the single person striving in the midst of historical flux; at the same time, she can pursue her abiding interest in her own family romance, the question of heritage. Following _Thomas and Beulah_, and still availing itself of a variety of themes, _Grace Notes_ is by far the most intensely autobiographical of her works, becoming a study in limitation and poignant regret. How, she seems to ask here, does one grant to daily life that ornament or variation that magically transforms it? _On the Bus with Rosa Parks_ examines the panoply of human endeavor, exploring the intersection of individual fates with the grand arc of history.

THE YELLOW HOUSE ON THE CORNER

Poems in _The Yellow House on the Corner_ often depict the collision of wish with reality, of heart's desire with the dictates of the world. This collision is made tolerable by the working of the imagination, and the result is, for Dove, "magic," or the existence of an unexplainable occurrence. It is imagination and the art it produces that allow the speaker in "This Life" to see that "the possibilities/ are golden dresses in a nutshell." "Possibilities" have the power to transform this life into something distinct and charmed. Even the woman driven mad with grief over the loss of her son (or husband?)

in "The Bird Frau" becomes a testament to possibility in her desire to "let everything go wild!" She becomes a bird-woman as a way of reuniting with her lost airman, who died in the war over France. Although her condition may be perceived as pathetic, Dove refuses to indulge sentimentality, instead seeing her madness as a form of undying hope.

The refusal to indulge sentimentality is a mark of Dove's critical intelligence. It allows her to interpose an objectifying distance between herself and the subject. She knows the absolute value of perspective, so that while she can exult in the freedom that imagination makes possible, she recognizes that such liberty has its costs and dangers too. Two poems in particular reveal this desire and her wariness: "Geometry" and "Sightseeing." In the former, Dove parallels the study of points, lines, and planes in space with the work of the poet: "I prove a theorem and the house expands:/ the windows jerk free to hover near the ceiling,/ the ceiling floats away with a sigh." Barriers and boundaries disappear in the imagination's manipulation of them, but that manipulation has its methodology or aesthetic: "I *prove* a theorem. . . ."

In "Sightseeing," the speaker, a traveler in Europe after World War II, comes upon what would seem to be a poem waiting to happen. The inner courtyard of a village church has been left just as it was found by the villagers after an Allied bombing raid. It is filled with the shattered cherubim and seraphim that had previously decorated the inner terrace of the building: "What a consort of broken dolls!" Nevertheless, the speaker repudiates any temptation to view the sight as the villagers must—"A terrible sign. . . ." Instead she coolly ponders the rubble with the detached air of a detective: "Let's look/ at the facts." She "reads" the scene and the observers' attention to it as a cautionary lesson. The "children of angels" become "childish monsters." Since she distinguishes herself from the devout villagers, she can also see herself and her companion in the least flattering light: "two drunks" coming all the way across the town "to look at a bunch of smashed statues."

This ability to debunk and subvert expectations is a matter of artistic survival for Dove and a function of her calm intelligence. As an African American poet, she is aware of the tradition of letters into which she steps. Two other poems imply that this tradition can be problematic. In "Upon Meeting Don L. Lee, in a Dream" Dove encounters Lee (now known as Haki R. Madhubuti), a leading figure in the Black Arts movement, which attempted to generate a populist, specifically black aesthetic. The figure that emerges from Dove's poem, however, is unable to change except to self-destruct: "I can see caviar/ Imbedded like buckshot between his teeth." Her dream-portrait of Lee deflates not only his masculinity but his status as cultural icon as well. In "Nigger Song: An Odyssey," Dove seems to hark back further for a literary forebear and finds one in Brooks, the first black woman to win the Pulitzer Prize. Although by 1967 Brooks would have come to embrace the black nationalism that Lee embodied, Dove's poem echoes the Brooks of an earlier time, the composer of "We Real Cool." In her evocation of "the nigger night," Dove captures the same vibrant energy that Brooks both celebrates and laments with the realization that the energy of urban African American youth is allowed no purposeful outlet and will turn on itself. She writes: "Nothing can catch us./ Laughter spills like gin from glasses."

Some of the most compelling poems in Dove's first book are in a group of vignettes and portraits from the era of American slavery. These poems not only reveal her historical awareness but also allow her to engage the issue of race from a distance. Dove wants her poetry to produce anger, perhaps, but not to be produced only by anger. One example of this aesthetic distance from emotion might be "The Abduction," a brief foray in the voice of Solomon Northrup. Northrup is a free black lured to Washington, D.C., by "new friends" with the promise of good work, and then kidnapped and sold into bondage. Dove dwells on the duplicity of these men and Northrup's susceptibility to them, yet no pronouncements are made. The poem ends with the end of freedom, but that ending has been foreshadowed by the tightly controlled structure of the poem itself, with each stanza shortening as the scope of the victim's world constricts to this one-line conclusion: "I woke and found myself alone, in darkness and in chains." The indignation and disgust that such an episode could call forth are left entirely to the reader.

MUSEUM

Dove's next volume, *Museum*, is itself, as the title suggests, a collection of historical and aesthetic artifacts. The shaping impulse of the book seems to be retrospective, a looking back to people and things that have been somehow suspended in time by legend, by historical circumstance, by all-too-human emotional wish. Dove intends to delve beneath the publicly known side of these stories—to excavate, in a sense, and uncover something forgotten but vital. The book is filled with both historical and mythical figures, all sharing the single trait of muted voice. Thus, "Nestor's Bathtub" begins: "As usual, legend got it all/ wrong." The private torment of a would-be martyr is made public in "Catherine of Alexandria." In "The Hill Has Something to Say," the poet speculates on the buried history of Europe, the cryptic messages that a culture sends across time. In one sense, the hill is a metaphor for this book, a repository of signs and images that speak only to that special archaeologist, the reader.

In the section titled "In the Bulrush," Dove finds worthy subjects in unlikely places and draws them from hiding. "Banneker" is another example of her flair for evoking the antebellum world of slavery, where even the free man is wrongly regarded because of his race. In the scientist Benjamin Banneker, she finds sensitivity, eloquence, and intelligence, all transformed by prejudice into mere eccentricity. Banneker was the first black man to devise an almanac and served on Thomas Jefferson's commission to lay out the city of Washington, D.C., but the same qualities that lifted him to prominence made him suspect in the eyes of white society. Dove redeems this crabbed conception of the man in an alliterative final passage that focuses attention on his vision:

> Lowering his eyes to fields
> sweet with the rot of spring, he could see
> a government's domed city
> rising from the morass and spreading
> in a spiral of lights . . .

A third section of the book is devoted entirely to poems about the poet's father, and they represent her efforts to understand him. It is a very personal grouping, made to seem all the more so by the preceding sections in which there is little or nothing directly personal at all.

In the final section, "Primer for the Nuclear Age," Dove includes what is one of her most impressive performances. Although she has not shown herself to be a poet of rage, she is certainly not inured to the social and political injustice she observes. Her work is a way of channeling and controlling such anger; as she says in "Primer for the Nuclear Age," "if you've/ got a heart at all, someday/ it will kill you." "Parsley," the final poem of *Museum*, summons up the rank insanity of Rafael Trujillo, dictator of the Dominican Republic, who, on October 2, 1957, ordered twenty thousand black Haitians killed because they could not pronounce the letter *r* in *perejil*, Spanish for parsley. The poem is divided into two sections; the first is a villanelle spoken by the Haitians; the second describes General Trujillo on the day of his decision. The second section echoes many of the lines from the Haitians' speech, drawing murderer and victim together, suggesting a disturbing complicity among all parties in this episode of unfettered power. Even though Dove certainly wants to draw attention to this event, the real subject here is the lyric poet's realm—that point at which language intersects with history and actually determines its course.

THOMAS AND BEULAH

Thomas and Beulah garnered the Pulitzer Prize, but it is more important for the stage it represents in Dove's poetic development. Her first two books reveal a lyric poet generally working within the bounds of her medium. The lyric poem denies time, process, change. It becomes a frozen moment, an emotion reenacted in the reading. In *Thomas and Beulah*, she pushes at the limitations of the form by stringing together, "as beads on a necklace," a whole series of these lyric moments. As the poems begin to reflect on one another, the effect is a dramatic unfolding in which the passing of time is represented, even though the sequence never establishes a conventional plot. To accomplish this end, Dove creates a two-sided book: Thomas's side ("Mandolin," twenty-one poems) followed by Beulah's ("Canary in Bloom," twenty-one poems).

The narrative moves from Thomas's riverboat life and the crucial death of his friend Lem to his arrival in Akron and marriage, through the birth of children, jobs, illness, and death. Beulah's part of the book then begins, moving through her parents' stormy relationship, her courtship with Thomas, marriage, pregnancy, work, and death. These two lives transpire against the historical backdrop of the great migration, the Depression, World War II, and the March on Washington; however, these events are practically the only common elements in the two sides of the story. Thomas and Beulah seem to live separate lives. Their communication with each other is implicit in the survival of the marriage itself. Throughout, Dove handles the story through exacting use of imagery and character.

Thomas emerges as a haunted man, dogged by the death of his friend Lem, which occurs in the opening poem, "The Event." Thomas drunkenly challenges Lem to swim from the deck of the riverboat to an island in the Mississippi. Lem drowns in the attempt to reach what is probably a mirage, and Thomas is left with "a stinking circle of rags/ the half-shell mandolin." In "Courtship," he begins to woo Beulah, but the poem implies that the basis of their relationship will be the misinterpreted gesture and that Thomas's guilt has left him with a void. He casually takes a yellow silk scarf from around his neck and wraps it around her shoulders; "a gnat flies/ in his eye and she thinks/ he's crying." Thomas's gift, rather than a spontaneous transfer of warmth, is a sign of his security in his relative affluence. The show of vulnerability and emotional warmth is accidental. The lyric poet in Dove allows her to compress this range of possibility in the isolated gesture or image. Beulah's life is conveyed as a more interior affair, a process of attaining the wisdom to understand her world rather than to resist it openly. In "The Great Palace of Versailles," Beulah's reading becomes her secret escape from the nastiness of the whites for whom she works in Charlotte's Dress Shoppe. As she lies dying in the final poem, "The Oriental Ballerina," the contemplation of the tiny figurine seems a similar invitation to fantasy, but her sensibilities have always been attuned to seeing the world as it is, as it has to be, and the poem ends in a brief flurry of realistic details and an air of acceptance; there is "no cross, just the paper kiss/ of a kleenex above the stink of camphor,/ the walls exploding with shabby tutus. . . ."

GRACE NOTES

Grace Notes marks Dove's return to the purely lyric mode, but an autobiographical impulse dominates the work to an unprecedented degree. More than in any of her previous collections, the poet can be seen as actor in her own closet drama, whether as a young child learning a rather brutal lesson in the southern black school of survival ("Crab-Boil") or as a mother groping for a way to reveal feminine mysteries to her own little girl ("After Reading *Mickey in the Night Kitchen* for the Third Time Before Bed"). The willingness to become more self-referential carries with it the danger of obscurity, the inside joke that stays inside. Dove, however, seems to open herself to a kind of scrutiny and challenge that offer no hiding place, and that assay extends to her own poetic practice. In "Dedication," a poem in the manner of Czeslaw Milosz, Dove seems to question the veracity of her own technical expertise: "What are music or books if not ways/ to trap us in rumors? The freedom of fine cages!"

In the wickedly ironic "Ars Poetica," she places herself on the literary chain of being with what might pass for self-deprecation. Her ambition is to make a small poem, like a ghost town, a minute speck on the "larger map of wills." "Then you can pencil me in as a hawk:/ a traveling x-marks-the-spot." However, this hawk is not a songbird to be taken lightly. The very next poem in the book unleashes the bird of prey in Dove (a pun she surely intends); in the aptly titled "Arrow," she exposes the sexism and racism of an "eminent scholar" in all of its condescending glory. This focus on the autobiographical element is not to imply that the range of subjects in *Grace Notes* is not still wide-ranging and surprising. Echoes of her earlier books sound clearly; so does the wit that makes them always engaging: "Here's a riddle for Our Age: when the sky's the limit,/ how can you tell you've gone too far?"

MOTHER LOVE

In *Mother Love*, Dove survives her overused source material, the myth of Demeter and Persephone, by transforming it into something deeply personal. She allows herself to be inhabited by the myth, and Dove's Demeter consciousness reveals that every time a daughter walks out the door, the abduction by Hades begins again. Dove's persona adopts Persephone's stance in "Persephone in Hell"; here, Dove recalls, at twenty, enjoying the risks of visiting Paris. She felt her mother's worry but asserts, "I was doing what she didn't need to know," testing her ripeness against the world's (man's) treachery. Dove employs loose sonnet shapes in these poems, giving herself license in order to provide authentic contemporary voices. At once dramatic, narrative, and highly lyrical, these poems more than fulfill the expectations of those who anointed her at the outset of her career.

ON THE BUS WITH ROSA PARKS

On the Bus with Rosa Parks is a more miscellaneous collection, but with several cohesive groupings. The "Cameos" sequence provides sharply etched vignettes of working-class life, a recurrent subject in Dove's writings. The closing sequence, from which the entire collection takes its name, explores the interface of public and private lives in contemporary African American history. As ever, Dove is a superb storyteller whose filmlike poems are energized by precise imagery and tonal perfection.

AMERICAN SMOOTH

The title, *American Smooth*, refers to the name Dove herself gave to a ballroom dance in which the partners separate and become free to improvise and express themselves individually. In the title poem, two partners achieve such perfect harmony in their dancing that for a few seconds they forget technical points like keeping their frame and instead feel as if they are flying. Dance imagery shows up in several other poems in this collection, which displays Dove's cosmopolitanism. In "Rhumba," each short line takes place during one measure of this three-step dance, and there is an unspoken dialogue between the two partners. In "Fox Trot Fridays," a couple escapes from the grinds of their daily existence by going dancing for one night each week and, for a short time, perhaps just the length of one song, find happiness. Another couple finds passion when they dance together in "Bolero." The only African American woman at a country club dance wears a red dress, makes a grand entrance, and waltzes in "Brown." "The Castle Walk" refers to a ballroom dance created by Vernon and Irene Castle, who taught ballroom dancing to the social elite of New York during the early twentieth century. In this poem, based on an actual event before World War I, they engage an African American band to play at a society dance. The band puts forth their best effort, although they know that their audience is incapable of truly appreciating their ragtime-style music. Men dance the cake-walk at a picnic in "Samba Summer" for the benefit of the women and children in attendance. Using different points of view, including the title character's, Dove describes one of the most famous dancing performances in history in "The Seven Veils of Salome."

Dove delves into African American history with seven poems that salute the 369th Infantry Regiment of the U.S. Army. During World War I, this African American unit spent 191 days in the trenches. "The Passage" describes their voyage across the Atlantic from Newport News, Virginia, to France. The well-educated narrator suffers from sea sickness, worries about German submarines and stormy weather, and thinks he sees a whale from the ship one day. In "Alfonzo Prepares to Go over the Top," a soldier prepares to leave the relative safety of his trench and take part in a bayonet charge during the Battle of Belleau Wood. The regiment marches in a 1919 victory parade on Fifth Avenue in New York in "The Return of Lieutenant James Reese Europe." Decades later in "Ripont," an African American family attends a memorial service at a battlefield where the regiment once fought.

Another event in African American history forms the subject of "Hattie McDaniel Arrives in Coconut Grove." The accomplishments of McDaniel create a sense of ambivalence in many blacks: She was the first African American actor to win an Academy Award, but she did so playing Mammy, a stereotypical role as a black servant, in *Gone with the Wind* (1939).

OTHER MAJOR WORKS

LONG FICTION: *Through the Ivory Gate*, 1992.

SHORT FICTION: *Fifth Sunday*, 1985.

PLAY: *The Darker Face of the Earth*, pb. 1994, 2000 (verse drama).

NONFICTION: *The Poet's World*, 1995.

EDITED TEXTS: *The Best American Poetry, 2000*, 2000; *Conversations with Rita Dove*, 2003 (Earl G. Ingersoll, editor).

BIBLIOGRAPHY

Bloom, Harold, ed. *African American Poets: Robert Hayden Through Rita Dove.* Philadelphia: Chelsea House, 2003. Contains a short biography on Dove and the essay "Rita Dove's Shakespeares," by Peter Erickson.

Dove, Rita. Interviews. *Conversations with Rita Dove.* Edited by Earl G. Ingersoll. Jackson: University Press of Mississippi, 2003. Part of the Literary Conversations series, this work gathers numerous interviews with Dove, many of them looking at the process of writing.

McDowell, Robert. "The Assembling Vision of Rita Dove." *Callaloo* 9 (Winter, 1986): 61-70. This article provides an excellent overview of Dove's accomplishments in her first three books and places her in the larger context of American poetry. McDowell argues that Dove's distinction is her role as "an assembler," someone who pulls together the facts of this life and presents them in challenging ways.

Newson, Adele S. Review of *On the Bus with Rosa Parks. World Literature Today* 74, no. 1 (Winter, 2000): 165-166. Newson examines the collection section by section, suggesting that the book forms an overall story bonded by related imagery and linked through digressions. In it, readers hear "the voice of a community's history and human response."

Pereira, Malin. *Rita Dove's Cosmopolitanism.* Urbana: University of Illinois Press, 2003. A critical analysis of Dove's poetry, literary criticism, drama, and fiction. Pereira states that Dove is most responsible for initiating a new era in African American poetry.

Righelato, Pat. *Understanding Rita Dove.* Columbia: University of South Carolina Press, 2006. Provides literary analysis of Dove's work through *American Smooth.*

Shoptaw, John. Review of *Thomas and Beulah. Black American Literature Forum* 21 (Fall, 1987): 335-341. This review isolates specific verbal tactics that Dove employs. It also addresses the problem of narrative and the difficult task Dove set for herself in telling the story as she did.

Steffen, Theresa. *Crossing Color: Transcultural Space and Place in Rita Dove's Poetry, Fiction, and Drama.* New York: Oxford University Press, 2001. Examines both Dove's linguistic devices and the cultural contexts of her work.

Vendler, Helen. *The Given and the Made: Strategies of Poetic Redefinition.* Cambridge, Mass.: Harvard University Press, 1995. One of the foremost literary critics of poetry discusses Dove's poetry in this collection of lectures.

Walters, Jennifer. "Nikki Giovanni and Rita Dove: Poets Redefining." *Journal of Negro History* 85 (Summer, 2000): 210-217. Discusses Giovanni and Dove as African American women who found their voices through writing.

Nelson Hathcock; Philip K. Jason
Updated by Thomas R. Feller

PAUL LAURENCE DUNBAR

Born: Dayton, Ohio; June 27, 1872
Died: Dayton, Ohio; February 9, 1906

PRINCIPAL POETRY
Oak and Ivy, 1893
Majors and Minors, 1895
Lyrics of Lowly Life, 1896
Lyrics of the Hearthside, 1899
Lyrics of Love and Laughter, 1903
Lyrics of Sunshine and Shadow, 1905
Complete Poems, 1913

OTHER LITERARY FORMS

Though Paul Laurence Dunbar is best known for his poetry, he was a fiction writer as well. His achievements in fiction include four volumes of short stories and four novels. Criticism of Dunbar's short fiction suggests that the stories contained in *Folks from Dixie* (1898) represent his best accomplishment in this literary form. His novels *The Uncalled* (1898) and *The Sport of the Gods* (1902) acquired more critical acclaim than his other two novels, *The Love of Landry* (1900) and *The Fanatics* (1901).

In addition to his work in these more traditional literary forms, Dunbar wrote an assortment of lyrics and libretti for a variety of theatrical productions. He also wrote essays for newspapers and attempted to establish a periodical of his own.

ACHIEVEMENTS

Paul Laurence Dunbar's literary career was brilliant, extending roughly across two decades. He can be credited with several first-time accomplishments: He was the first to use dialect poetry as a medium for the true interpretation of African American character and psychology, and he was the first African American writer to earn national prominence. In range of style and form, Dunbar is one of the most versatile of African American writers.

BIOGRAPHY

Paul Laurence Dunbar was born to former slaves Joshua Dunbar and Matilda J. Murphy Dunbar on June 27, 1872. He spent his early childhood in Dayton, Ohio, where he attended Central High School. Dunbar began to write at age sixteen and gained early patronage for his work, and he was introduced to the Western Association of Writers in 1892.

The next few years of his life found him in the presence of great black leaders. He met

Paul Laurence Dunbar
(Library of Congress)

Frederick Douglass, Mary Church Terrell, and Ida B. Wells at the World's Columbian Exposition in Chicago in 1893. He met W. E. B. Du Bois in 1896 and Booker T. Washington in 1897. These encounters influenced Dunbar's literary tone and perspective significantly. He blended the creative perspective of Washington with the social philosophy of Du Bois in order to present a valid scenario of African Americans after the Civil War.

Major James B. Pond, a Dunbar enthusiast, sponsored a trip to England for the writer that extended from February to August of 1897. Upon his return to the United States, Dunbar married Alice Moore and decided to earn his living as a writer. Between 1898 and 1903, Dunbar wrote essays for newspapers and periodicals, primarily addressing the issues of racial equality and social justice. He attempted to establish his own journalistic voice through a periodical that he named the *Dayton Tattler* in 1890. This effort failed. During the latter years of his life, Dunbar wrote lyrics, including those for the school song for Tuskegee Institute. He died in Dayton, Ohio, on February 9, 1906.

ANALYSIS

The body of poetry produced by Paul Laurence Dunbar illustrates some of the best qualities found in lyrical verse. It is obvious that the poet concentrated on a creation of mood and that he was an innovator who experimented with form, meter, and rhyme. Equally apparent is the fact that Dunbar's creative style was influenced by the great British poetic innovators of the seventeenth and nineteenth centuries. Dunbar's commitment to speak to his people through his verse is reflected in his dialect poetry. Writing in all the major lyrical forms—idyll, hymn, sonnet, song, ballad, ode, and elegy—Dunbar established himself as one of the most versatile poets in American literature.

The more than four hundred poems written by Dunbar are varied in style and effect. It is clear, however, that his dominant aim was to create an empathetic poetic mood resulting from combinations of elements such as meter, rhyme, diction, sentence structure, characterization, repetition, imagery, and symbolism. His most memorable poems display the influence of such masters as William Wordsworth; Robert Herrick; Alfred, Lord Tennyson; John Donne; Robert Browning; and John Keats.

Such an array of influences would ordinarily render one's genius suspect. There are common threads, however, that organically characterize the poetic expressions of Dunbar. The undergirding strain in his poetry is his allegiance to lyrical qualities. He carries mood through sound patterns, creates images that carry philosophical import, shapes dramatic events in the pattern of movement in his syntactic forms, and develops a rhythmic pattern that is quite effective in recitation. These lyrical qualities predominate in the best of Dunbar's poetry. Indeed, one might easily classify Dunbar's poetry in typical Romantic lyrical categories: The bulk of his poems can be classified as love lyrics, reflective lyrics, melancholic lyrics, or nature lyrics. Sometimes these moods overlap in a single poem. Consequently, an analysis of the features in Dunbar's poetry is necessarily complex, placing his lyrical qualities in the poetic traditions that shape them.

LYRICS OF THE HEARTHSIDE

Dunbar's lyricism is substantially displayed in his love poetry in *Lyrics of the Hearthside*. In "A Bridal Measure," the poet's persona beckons maidens to the bridal throne. His invitation is spirited and triumphant yet controlled, reminiscent of the tradition in love poetry established by Ben Jonson. The tone, however, more closely approximates the carpe diem attitude of Herrick.

> Come, essay a sprightly measure,
> Tuned to some light song of pleasure.
> Maidens, let your brows be crowned
> As we foot this merry round.

The rhyming couplets carry the mood and punctuate the invitation. The urgency of the moment is extended further in the direct address: "Phyllis, Phyllis, why be waiting?/ In the woods the birds are mating." The poem continues in this tone, while adopting a pastoral simplicity.

> When the year, itself renewing,
> All the world with flowers is strewing,
>   Then through Youth's Arcadian land,
>   Love and song go hand in hand.

The accentuation in the syntactic flow of these lines underlines the poet's intentions. Though the meter is irregular, with some iambs and some anapests, the force of the poet's exhortation remains apparent.

Dunbar frequently personifies abstractions. In "Love and Grief," Dunbar espouses a morbid yet redemptive view of love. While the reflective scenario presented in this poem recalls Tennyson's meditations on death and loss, the poetic event echoes Wordsworth's faith in the indestructibility of joy. Utilizing the heroic couplet, Dunbar makes an opening pronouncement:

> Out of my heart, one treach'rous winter's day,
> I locked young Love and threw the key away.
> Grief, wandering widely, found the key,
> And hastened with it, straightway, back to me.

The drama of grief-stricken love is thus established. The poet carefully clarifies his position through an emphatic personification of Grief's behavior: "He unlocked the door/ and bade Love enter with him there and stay." Being a lyric poet of redemptive sensibility, Dunbar cannot conclude the poem on this note. The "table must turn," as it does for Wordsworth in such situations. Love then becomes bold and asks of Grief: "What right hast thou/ To part or parcel of this heart?" To justify the redemptive quality he presents, Dunbar attributes the human frailty of pride to Love, a failing that invites Grief. In so doing, the poet's philosophical intuitiveness emerges with a measure of moral decorum. Through the movement in the syntactic patterns, the intensity of the drama is heightened as the poem moves to resolution. Dunbar utilizes a variety of metrical patterns, the most significant of which is the spondee. This poetic foot of two accented syllables allows the poet to proclaim emphatically: "And Love, pride purged, was chastened all his life." Thus, the principal emotion in the poem is redeemed.

The brief, compact lyrical verse, as found in Browning, is among Dunbar's typical forms. "Love's Humility" is an example:

> As some rapt gazer on the lowly earth,
>   Looks up to radiant planets, ranging far,
> So I, whose soul doth know thy wondrous worth
>   Look longing up to thee as to a star.

This skillfully concentrated simile elevates love to celestial heights. The descriptive detail enhances the power of the feeling the poet captures and empowers the lyrical qualities of the poem with greater pathos.

LYRICS OF LOVE AND LAUGHTER

Dunbar's *Lyrics of Love and Laughter* is not the best of his collections, but it contains some remarkable dialect verse. "A Plea" provides an example of this aspect of his reputation. Speaking of the unsettling feelings experienced by one overcome with love, Dunbar exhorts a lover's love object to "treat him nice."

> I ain't don a t'ing to shame,
> Lovahs all ac's jes de same:
> Don't you know we ain't to blame?
>   Treat me nice!

Rendering a common experience in the African American idiom, Dunbar typifies the emotionally enraptured lover as one who has no control over his behavior:

> Whut a pusson gwine to do,
> W'en he come a-cou'tin' you
> All a-trimblin' thoo and thoo?
>   Please be nice.

The diction in this poem is not pure dialect. Only those portions that describe the emotions and behavior of the lover are stated in dialect, highlighting the primary emotions and enhancing the pathetic mood, which is apparently Dunbar's principal intent. Typical of Dunbar's love lyrics, "A Plea" is rooted in the experience of a particular culture yet remains universal in its themes. Through his use of diction, meter, and stanzaic form, Dunbar captures fundamental human emotions and renders them with intensity and lyrical compassion.

LYRICS OF LOWLY LIFE

Reflective lyrics form a large segment of Dunbar's poetry. Some of his best poems of this type are found in *Lyrics of Lowly Life*, including the long stanzaic poem "Ere Sleep Comes Down to Soothe the Weary Eyes." This poem uses one sensory impression as a focal point for the lyrical evolution in the style of Keats. The sleep motif provides an avenue through which the persona's imagination enters the realm of reflection.

Through sleep's dream the persona is able to "make the waking world a world of lies—/ of lies palpable, uncouth, forlorn." In this state of subconscious reflection, past pains are revisited as they "come thronging through the chambers of the brain." As the poem progresses, it becomes apparent that the repetitive echo of "ere sleep comes down to soothe the weary eyes" has some significance. This refrain begins and ends each stanza of the poem except the last. In addition to serving as a mood-setting device, this expression provides the channel of thought for the literary journey, which is compared with the "spirit's journeying." Dunbar's audience is thus constantly reminded of the source of his revelations.

Dunbar reveals his poetic thesis in the last stanza. He uses images from the subconscious state of life, sleep, to make a point about death. Prior to making this point, Dunbar takes the reader to the realm of reflective introspection: "So, trembling with the shock of sad surprise,/ The soul doth view its awful self alone." There is an introspective confrontation of the soul with itself, and it resolves:

> When sleep comes down to seal the weary eyes,
>
> . . . .
>
> Ah, then, no more we heed
> the sad world's cries,
> Or seek to probe th' eternal mystery,
> Or fret our souls at long-withheld replies.

The escape from pain and misery is death; there is no intermediary state that will eradicate that fact of life. Dunbar presents this notion with sympathy and sincerity. His metaphorical extensions, particularly those relative to the soul, are filled with compassion. The soul is torn with the world's deceit; it cries with "pangs of vague inexplicable pain." The spirit, an embodiment of the soul, forges ahead to seek truth as far as fancy will lead. Questioning begins then, and the inner sense confronts the inner being until truth emerges. Dunbar's presentation of the resolution is tender and gentle.

Dunbar wrote reflective lyrics in the vernacular as well. "Accountability" espouses the philosophy of divine intention. In this poem, the beliefs and attitudes of the persona are revealed in familiar language.

> Folks ain't got no right to
>   censuah othah
>   folks about dey habits;
>
> . . . .
>
> We is all constructed diff'ent,
>   d'ain't no two of
>   us de same;
>
> . . . . . .
>
> But we all fits into places dat
>   no othah ones
>   could fill.

Each stanza in this poem presents a thesis and develops that point. The illustrations from the natural world support a creationist viewpoint. The persona obviously accepts the notion that everything has a purpose. The Creator gave the animals their members shaped as they are for a reason and so, "Him dat giv' de squr'ls de bushtails made de bobtails fu' de rabbits." The variations in nature are by design: "Him dat built de gread big mountains hollered out de little valleys"; "Him dat made de streets an' driveways wasn't shamed to make de alley." The poet establishes these notions in three quatrains, concluding in the fourth quatrain: "When you come to think about it, how it's all planned out it's splendid./ Nuthin's done er evah happens, dout hit's somefin' dat's intended." The persona's position that divine intention rules the world is thereby sealed.

Introspection is a feature of Dunbar's reflective lyrics. In "The Lesson," the persona engages in character revelation, interacts with the audience toward establishment of appropriate resolution, and participates in the action of the poem. These qualities are reminiscent of Browning's dramatic monologues. As the principal speaker sits by a window in his cottage, reflecting, he reports:

> And I thought of myself so sad and lone,
> And my life's cold winter that knew no spring;
> Of my mind so weary and sick and wild,
>   Of my heart too sad to sing.

The inner conflict facing the persona is revealed in these lines and the perspective of self-examination is established. The persona must confront his sadness and move toward resolution. The movement toward resolution presents the dramatic occasion in the poem: "A thought stole into my saddened heart,/ And I said, 'I can cheer some other soul/ By a carol's simple art.'" Reflective introspection typically leads to improved character, a fundamental tenet in the Victorian viewpoint. Sustained by his new conviction and outlook, the persona "sang a lay for a brother's ear/ In a strain to soothe his bleeding heart."

The lyrical quality of "The Lesson" is strengthened by the movement in the poet's syntactic patterns. Feelings of initial despair and resulting joy and hope are conveyed through the poet's syntax. The sequential conjoining of ideas as if in a rushing stream of thought is particularly effective. The latter sections of the poem are noteworthy in this regard. This pattern gives the action more force, thereby intensifying the feeling. Dunbar presents an emphatic idea—"and he smiled . . ."—and juxtaposes it to an exception—"Though mine was a feeble art." He presents a responsive result—"But at his smile I smiled in turn"—connected to a culminating effect—"And into my soul there came a ray." With this pronouncement, the drama comes full circle from inner conflict through conversion to changed philosophical outlook. Dunbar captures each moment with appropriate vigor.

"YESTERDAY AND TO-MORROW"

The subjects of love and death are treated in Dunbar's lyrics of melancholy, the third major mood found in the poet's lyrical verse. "Yesterday and To-morrow," in *Lyrics of*

Sunshine and Shadow, is an example of Dunbar's lyric of melancholy. The mood of this poem is in the tradition of the British Romantic poets, particularly that of Wordsworth. Dunbar treats the melancholy feelings in this poem with tenderness and simplicity. The persona expresses disappointment with the untimeliness of life's events and the uncertainties of love. This scenario intimates a bleak future.

"Yesterday and To-morrow" is developed in three compact quatrains. Each quatrain envelops a primary emotion. The first stanza unfolds yesterday's contentment in love. The lover remembers the tender and blessed emotion of closeness with his lover: "And its gentle yieldingness/ From my soul I blessed it." The second stanza is reminiscent of the metaphysical questionings and imagery of Donne: "Must our gold forever know/ Flames for the refining?" The lovers' emotions are compared with precious metal undergoing the fire of refinement: Their feelings of sadness are released in this cynical question.

In the third quatrain, Dunbar feeds the sad heart with more cynicism. Returning to the feelings of disappointment and uncertainty, the persona concludes: "Life was all a lyric song/ Set to tricksy meter." The persona escapes in cynicism, but the poem still ends on a hopeless note.

"COMMUNION"

"Communion," from *Lyrics of the Hearthside*, is another of Dunbar's melancholy lyrics and focuses on the theme of love and death. The situation in the poem again evokes a cynical attitude, again reminiscent of Donne. The poem presents a struggle between life's memories and death. Life's memories are primarily of the existence of the love relationship, and death symbolizes its demise. This circumstance unfolds in a dramatic narrative in the style of Browning.

The first two stanzas of the poem introduce the situation, and the mood begins to evolve in stanza 3. The poet uses images from nature to create the somber mood. The "breeze of Death," for example, sweeps his lover's soul "Out into the unsounded deeps." On one hand, the Romantic theme of dominance of nature and humanity's helplessness in the face of it creeps through; on the other hand, faith in love as the superior experience resounds. The conflict between conquering Death, symbolized in nature, and Love creates tension in the poem. Consequently, though the breeze of Death has swept his bride away, the persona announces that "Wind nor sea may keep me from/ Soft communing with my bride." As these quatrains of iambic pentameter unfold, the poem becomes somewhat elegiac in tone.

The persona solemnly enters into reflective reminiscence in the fifth stanza and proclaims: "I shall rest my head on thee/ As I did long days of yore." Continuing in stanza 6, he announces: "I shall take thy hand in mine,/ And live o'er the olden days." Leading up to the grief-stricken pledge of eternal love, the melancholic feeling is intensified. The mourner details his impression as follows:

> Tho' the grave-door shut between,
> Still their love lights o'er me steal.
>
> I can see thee thro' my tears,
> As thro' rain we see the sun.

The comfort that comes from such memories brings a ray of light; the lover concludes:

> I shall see thee still and be
>   Thy true lover evermore,
> And thy face shall be to me
>   Dear and helpful as before.

The drama cannot end unless the persona interacts with his audience. The audience is therefore included in the philosophical conclusion: "Death may vaunt and Death may boast,/ But we laugh his pow'r to scorn." Dunbar illustrates an ability to overcome the causes of melancholy in his lyrics of this mood. He works with contrasting feelings, cynicism, and determinism to achieve this goal. His melancholic mood is therefore less gloomy than one might expect.

"IN SUMMER"

Because Dunbar was greatly influenced by the British Romantic writers, it is not surprising that he also wrote nature lyrics. "In Summer," from *Lyrics of the Hearthside*, and "The Old Apple-Tree," from *Lyrics of Lowly Life*, are representative of his nature lyrics. "In Summer" captures a mood of merriment that is stimulated by nature. The common man is used as a model of one who possesses the capacity to experience this natural joy. Summer is a bright, sunny time; it is also a time for ease, as presented in the second stanza. Introducing the character of the farm boy in stanza 3, Dunbar presents a model embodiment of the ease and merriment of summer. Amid the blades of green grass and as the breezes cool his brow, the farm boy sings as he plows. He sings "to the dewy morn" and "to the joys of life." This behavior leads to some moralizing, to which the last three stanzas of the poem are devoted. The poet's point is made through a contrast:

> O ye who toil in the town.
>   And ye who moil in the mart,
> Hear the artless song, and your faith made strong
>   Shall renew your joy of heart.

Dunbar admonishes the reader to examine the behavior of the farm boy. Elevation of the simple, rustic life is prevalent in the writings of early British Romantic poets and postbellum African American writers alike. The admonition to reflect on the rustic life, for example, is the same advice Wordsworth gives in "The Old Cumberland Beggar." Both groups of writers agree that there are lessons to be learned through an examination of the virtues of the rustic life. In this vein, Dunbar advises: "Oh, poor were the worth of the world/ If never a song were heard." He goes further by advising all to "taunt old Care with a merry air."

"THE OLD APPLE-TREE"

The emphasis on the rustic life is also pervasive in "The Old Apple-Tree." The primary lyrical quality of the poem is that the poetic message evolves from the poet's memory and imagination. Image creation is the medium through which Dunbar works here: His predominant image, dancing in flames of ruddy light, is an orchard "wrapped in autumn's purple haze."

Dunbar proceeds to create a nature scene that provides a setting for the immortalization of the apple tree. Memory takes the persona to the scene, but imagination re-creates events and feelings. The speaker in the poem admits that it probably appears ugly "When you look the tree all over/ Unadorned by memory's glow." The tree has become old and crooked, and it bears inferior fruit. Thus, without the nostalgic recall, the tree does not appear special at all.

Utilizing the imaginative frame, the speaker designs features of the simple rustic life, features that are typically British Romantic and peculiarly Wordsworthian. The "quiet, sweet seclusion" realized as one hides under the shelter of the tree and the idle dreaming in which one engages dangling in a swing from the tree are primary among these thoughts. Most memorable to the speaker is the solitary contentment he and his sweetheart found as they courted beneath the old apple tree.

> Now my gray old wife is Hallie,
> An I'm grayer still than she,
> But I'll not forget our courtin'
> 'Neath the old apple-tree.

The poet's ultimate purpose, to immortalize the apple tree, is fulfilled in the last stanza. The old apple tree will never lose its place in nature or its significance, for the speaker asks:

> But when death does come a-callin',
> This my last request shall be,—
> That they'll bury me an' Hallie
> 'Neath the old apple-tree.

The union of humanity and nature at the culmination of physical life approaches a notion expressed in Wordsworth's poetry. This tree has symbolized the ultimate in goodness and universal harmony; it symbolizes the peace, contentment, and joy in the speaker's life. Here Dunbar's indebtedness to the Romantic traditions that inform his entire oeuvre is most profoundly felt.

OTHER MAJOR WORKS

LONG FICTION: *The Uncalled*, 1898; *The Love of Landry*, 1900; *The Fanatics*, 1901; *The Sport of the Gods*, 1901 (serial), 1902 (book).

SHORT FICTION: *Folks from Dixie*, 1898; *The Strength of Gideon, and Other Stories*, 1900; *In Old Plantation Days*, 1903; *The Heart of Happy Hollow*, 1904; *The Best Stories of Paul Laurence Dunbar*, 1938; *The Complete Stories of Paul Laurence Dunbar*, 2006 (Gene Andrew Jarrett and Thomas Lewis Morgan, editors).

MISCELLANEOUS: *In His Own Voice: The Dramatic and Other Uncollected Works of Paul Laurence Dunbar*, 2002 (Herbert Woodward Martin and Ronald Primeau, editors).

BIBLIOGRAPHY

Alexander, Eleanor. *"Lyrics of Sunshine and Shadow": The Tragic Courtship and Marriage of Paul Laurence Dunbar and Alice Ruth Moore*. Albany: State University of New York Press, 2001. Traces the tempestuous romance of the noted African American literary couple. Draws on love letters, diaries, journals, and autobiographies to tell the story of Dunbar and Moore's affair, their elopement, Dunbar's abuse of Moore, their marriage, and the violence that ended their marriage. An examination of a celebrated couple in the context of their times, fame, and cultural ideology.

Bennett, Paula Bernat. "Rewriting Dunbar: Realism, Black Women Poets, and the Genteel." In *African-American Poets: 1700's-1940's*, edited by Harold Bloom. New York: Chelsea House, 2009. Bennett examines Dunbar from a modern feminist perspective.

Best, Felton O. *Crossing the Color Line: A Biography of Paul Laurence Dunbar*. Dubuque, Iowa: Kendall/Hunt, 1996. Discusses Dunbar's life and works, including racial issues.

Harrell, Willie J., Jr. *We Wear the Mask: Paul Laurence Dunbar and the Politics of Representative Reality*. Kent, Ohio: Kent State University Press, 2010. This collection of essays contains several on Dunbar's poetry, covering topics such as the tradition of masking as expressed in his poetry, his use of dialect, and his portrayal of soldiers.

Hudson, Gossie Harold. *A Biography of Paul Laurence Dunbar*. Baltimore: Gateway Press, 1999. A detailed biography of Dunbar with bibliographical references.

Leonard, Keith D. *Fettered Genius: The African American Bardic Poet from Slavery to Civil Rights*. Charlottesville: University of Virginia Press, 2006. Contains a chapter on Dunbar, "Writ on Glory's Scroll: Paul Laurence Dunbar's Moral Heroism," and chapters on the African American bardic tradition that provided context for understanding Dunbar.

Martin, Jay, ed. *A Singer in the Dawn: Reinterpretations of Paul Laurence Dunbar*. New York: Dodd, Mead, 1975. Contains biographical "reminiscences" and essays about Dunbar's poetry and fiction.

Primeau, Ronald, et al. *Being a Collection of Essays on Paul Laurence Dunbar by Members of the Society for the Study of Midwestern Literature*. East Lansing, Mich.: Midwestern Press, 2006. This collection of essays, presented at a conference about Dunbar and his work, contains several surveys of his poetry.

Reef, Catherine. *Paul Laurence Dunbar: Portrait of a Poet*. Berkeley Heights, N.J.: Enslow, 2000. A basic biography of Dunbar that focuses on his poetry.

Patricia A. R. Williams

JAMES A. EMANUEL

Born: Alliance, Nebraska; June 15, 1921

OTHER LITERARY FORMS

James A. Emanuel's first book was written in prose, not poetry. His book *Langston Hughes* (1967) was one of the first detailed studies of Hughes's work. Unsatisfied with the scant critical attention given to black authors, Emanuel worked with Theodore L. Gross and edited *Dark Symphony: Negro Literature in America* (1968), the first book of its kind in nearly thirty years. A few years later, in 1972, he collaborated on another book, *How I Write Two*, this time with MacKinlay Kantor and Lawrence Osgood. *How I Write Two* explores the writing processes of several black poets, including Emanuel, Sonia Sanchez, and Gwendolyn Brooks. He served as general editor of the Broadside Critics series from 1970 to 1975. He has written a memoir, *The Force and the Reckoning* (2001), complete with poems and photos. Many of Emanuel's literary essays and book reviews appeared in books, periodicals, and journals.

ACHIEVEMENTS

Although James A. Emanuel has been called one of the most overlooked poets of modern times, he has garnered some recognition as a critic. Arguably, his most notable achievement is the promotion of critical attention for black writers' work. He received the John Hay Whitney Fellowship (1952, 1953) and the Saxton Memorial Fellowship (1964). In 1966, Emanuel developed the first course in African American poetry to be offered at City College of New York. He also ran for a position on the Mount Vernon, New York, school board, but was defeated. "For 'Mr. Dudley,' a Black Spy" (from *Black Man Abroad*) describes the difficult experience. He was awarded two Fulbright scholarships, a professorship at the University of Grenoble in France from 1968 to 1969 and a professorship at the University of Warsaw in Poland from 1975 to 1976. Emanuel also received a Black American Literature Forum Special Distinction Award for poetry in 1978. In 1979, the American Biographical Institute named him among its Notable Americans. Emanuel invented the jazz-and-blues haiku during the 1990's. The form combines elements of jazz, blues, and the Japanese haiku. For his invention, he received the Sidney Bechet Creative Award in 1996. In 2007, he was honored with the Dean's Award for Distinguished Achievement from Columbia University.

BIOGRAPHY

James Andrew Emanuel, the fifth of seven children, was born in Alliance, Nebraska, to Cora Ann Mance and Alfred A. Emanuel, a farmer and railroad worker. Early on, Emanuel's parents instilled a love of language and narrative in him. He read widely, and by junior high school, he was writing detective stories and poetry. In 1939, he graduated high school and was named the class valedictorian. He took a job in Washington, D.C., as the confidential secretary to General Benjamin O. Davis, assistant inspector general of the War Department in the United States Army, and he later joined the United States Army, where he served as a staff sergeant with the Ninety-third Infantry Division in the Pacific. After World War II, he enrolled in Howard University in Washington, D.C., where he earned a B.A. degree. In 1950, he married Mattie Etha Johnson, whom he met after moving to Chicago, where he had begun attending Northwestern University and working as a civilian chief in the preinduction section of the Army and Air Force Induction Station. The couple had one child, James, Jr., who committed suicide in 1983. The couple was divorced in 1974. After earning an M.A. in 1953, Emanuel moved to New York and enrolled in a Ph.D. program at Columbia University. He earned the degree in 1962. Emanuel became an assistant professor at the City College of New York in 1962, where he would teach until 1984.

Emanuel's early work was published in college journals, but in 1958, his work began to appear in periodicals such as *The New York Times*, *Midwest Quarterly*, and *Freedomways*. In 1967, Emanuel published a critical study of Hughes, and in 1968, he coedited an anthology of African American literature, *Dark Symphony*. His first book of poetry, a collection of previously published poems, *The Treehouse, and Other Poems*, was also published in 1968.

In October of 1968, Emanuel moved to Seyssins and taught at the University of Grenoble, where he served as a Fulbright professor of American literature for a year. While living in France, he began working on poems later printed in *Panther Man*. From 1970 to 1975, he worked as general editor of the Broadside Critics Series, which published books about black poets, including Countée Cullen, Claude McKay, and Phillis Wheatley.

Emanuel served as a visiting professor of American literature at the University of Toulouse (1971-1973, 1979-1981) and Fulbright professor of American literature at the University of Warsaw (1975-1976). After his retirement from the City University of New York, Emanuel began to travel and live in Europe. Emanuel is often excluded from major anthologies, but some of his works, correspondence, and other documents are at the Library of Congress, Manuscript Division, Washington, D.C. Additional manuscripts and documents are housed in the collection at the Jay B. Hubbell Center for American Literary Historiography at Duke University in Durham, North Carolina.

ANALYSIS

James A. Emanuel's earlier poetry was largely influenced by English poets such as John Keats and William Shakespeare, but his relationship with Hughes and his close study of Hughes's work also influenced him. Some of Emanuel's poems contain vernacular, and many of them experiment with genres of music, including blues and jazz. Critics say his poems are precise and that he is adept at creating subtle phrases. Unlike the poems of many of the African American poets writing during the 1960's, Emanuel's poems rarely contain alternate spellings or innovative forms. Instead, his poems usually have rhymed quatrains and regular lines and stanzas. They are about youth, black experiences, war, manhood, and love.

THE TREEHOUSE, AND OTHER POEMS

Most of the poems in *The Treehouse, and Other Poems* were previously published in anthologies and periodicals, such as *Phylon*, *The New York Times*, and *Negro Digest*. The poems are traditional, but some reflect blues and jazz influence. Emanuel's serious poems are often about African Americans who were killed because of racism. Emmett Till, the fourteen-year-old boy who was tortured, murdered, and thrown into the Tallahatchie River in Mississippi in 1955 for whistling at a white woman, is coupled with the fairy river boy who swims forever. "Where Will Their Names Go Down?" remembers the unnamed who were subjected to similar hate crimes. "Fisherman" was inspired by time Emanual spent with his son. Other poems are about war, heroes, and the poetic process. Scholars suggest that *The Treehouse, and Other Poems* received little critical attention because the poems do not adhere to the militant, direct style of some of the African American poetry published during that time.

PANTHER MAN

Dedicated to Emanuel's City College of New York students, *Panther Man*, angry in tone, argues against racism in the United States. In the preface, Emanuel calls the volume "a reflection of personal, racially meaningful predicaments" compelled by "my feelings about the most abysmal evil in the modern world: American racism." The tone is harsher and more militant than that of *The Treehouse, and Other Poems*. Most of the poems mark Emanuel's distancing himself from the traditional poetic forms found in his earlier collection. The title poem is based on the 1969 slaying by Chicago police officers of Black Panthers Mark Clark and Fred Hampton, while "Whitey, Baby" criticizes systemic racism. *Panther Man* also contains tributes to African Americans, particularly poet Hughes and Muslim leader Malcolm X. "For the Fourth Grade, Prospect School: How I Became a Poet" and "Black Poet on the Firing Range" are about poets and how they compose, while "Fourteen" and "Sixteen, Yeah" are about youth.

BLACK MAN ABROAD

Black Man Abroad has four sections of poems arranged thematically: "The Toulouse Poems, Parts I and II," "The Warsaw Experiment," and "Occasionals." Most of the poems are set in Toulouse or another city in Western Europe, and many of them are longer and more complex than poems in earlier collections. The poems reveal speakers tackling themes that appear across Emanuel's oeuvre: childhood innocence, manhood, and racism. This volume includes the author's first romantic love poems, poems inspired by Marie-France Passard, a travel guide and librarian he met while in Europe, including "For 'Mee'" and "Lovelook Back," as well as poems about parental love. The speakers of the poems are often concerned with how the past affects the present. In some of the poems, such as "Didn't Fall in Love," the speaker refuses to allow himself to get involved in a new relationship because of past experiences. In "Goodbye No. 1," the speaker is sad because he loses something he thought he had. "Ass on the Beach, in Spain" explores the power and lure of feminine beauty over that of men. "After the Poetry Reading, Black" describes audience members' disappointment when Emanuel reads poems that do not seem to situate him as a black poet.

WHOLE GRAIN

A number of haiku, in addition to the haiku that serve as prefaces to each part of the collection, make up the 215 poems in *Whole Grain*, a collection of Emanuel's work from 1958 to 1989. Other forms are represented as well, including sonnets ("For a Farmer" and "Sonnet for a Writer"), free verse ("Topless, Bottomless Bar, Manhattan"), and rhymed quatrains ("Experience" and "I Wish I Had a Red Balloon"). Organized by themes, the collection contains poems about love, sex, race, and youth. Many of the poems, such as "Treehouse," "Whitey, Baby," "Emmett Till," and "Fisherman," are favorites among Emanuel's readers.

JAZZ FROM THE HAIKU KING

Jazz from the Haiku King, an innovative collection of various types of jazz-and-blues haiku, indicates how jazz, an African American form of music, and haiku, a Japanese form of poetry, can be complementary means of expression. "Dizzy Gillespie (News of

His Death)" and "Duke Ellington" pay tribute to musicians, while "Farmer" explores the connection between a farmer and jazz. "Sleek Lizard Rhythms" describes the rhythm of jazz music. "Jackhammer," "Ammunition," and "Impressionist" speak directly to African Americans, asking them to liberate themselves and fight against injustice.

OTHER MAJOR WORKS

NONFICTION: *Langston Hughes*, 1967; *How I Write Two*, 1972 (with MacKinlay Kantor and Lawrence Osgood); *The Force and the Reckoning*, 2001 (autobiography).

EDITED TEXT: *Dark Symphony: Negro Literature in America*, 1968 (with Theodore L. Gross).

BIBLIOGRAPHY
Bloom, Harold. *Modern Black American Poets and Dramatists*. New York: Chelsea House, 1995. Provides a biography of Emanuel and excerpts from book reviews and critical essays about his work. It also includes an excerpt from "The Task of the Negro Writer as Artist: A Symposium," an essay Emanuel wrote explaining that all writers, regardless of race or ethnicity, must create work that is beautiful, powerful, and true.

Emanuel, James A. "James A. Emanuel." http://www .james-a-emanuel.com. The official Web site for Emanual contains a brief biography, a bibliography, and interviews with the author.

Fabre, Michel. *From Harlem to Paris: Black American Writers in France, 1840-1980*. Champaign: University of Illinois Press, 1993. The chapter titled "James Emanuel: A Poet in Exile" discusses Emanuel's life in France, particularly how people, sights, and experiences in and around Paris inspired his creativity, leading him to write poems such as "Lovelook Back," "Clothesline, Rue Marie," and "For Alix, Who Is Three."

Hakutani, Yoshinobu. *Cross-Cultural Visions in African American Modernism: From Spatial Narrative to Jazz Haiku*. Columbus: Ohio State University Press, 2006. The chapter titled "James Emanuel's Jazz Haiku and African American Individualism" focuses on Emanuel's *Jazz from the Haiku King*.

Holdt, Marvin. Review of *Black Man Abroad*. *Black American Literature Forum* 13, no. 3 (Autumn, 1979): 79-85. Offers an extensive examination of the work and its message.

Watson, Douglas. "James Andrew Emanuel." In *Dictionary of Literary Biography: Afro-American Poets Since 1955*, edited by Thadious M. Davis and Trudier Harris. Vol. 41. Farmington Hills, Mich.: Gale, 1985. Provides a well-developed biography and criticism of Emanuel's work.

KaaVonia Hinton

NIKKI GIOVANNI

Born: Knoxville, Tennessee; June 7, 1943

PRINCIPAL POETRY

Black Feeling, Black Talk, 1968
Black Judgement, 1968
Black Feeling, Black Talk, Black Judgement, 1970
Poem of Angela Yvonne Davis, 1970
Re: Creation, 1970
Spin a Soft Black Song: Poems for Children, 1971, 1987 (juvenile)
My House, 1972
Ego-Tripping, and Other Poems for Young People, 1973 (juvenile)
The Women and the Men, 1975
Cotton Candy on a Rainy Day, 1978
Vacation Time: Poems for Children, 1980 (juvenile)
Those Who Ride the Night Winds, 1983 (juvenile)
Knoxville, Tennessee, 1994 (juvenile)
Life: Through Black Eyes, 1995
The Genie in the Jar, 1996 (juvenile)
The Selected Poems of Nikki Giovanni, 1996
The Sun Is So Quiet, 1996 (juvenile)
Love Poems, 1997
Blues: For All the Changes, 1999
Quilting the Black-Eyed Pea: Poems and Not Quite Poems, 2002
The Collected Poetry of Nikki Giovanni, 1968-1998, 2003
Acolytes, 2007
Bicycles: Love Poems, 2009

OTHER LITERARY FORMS

Besides her volumes of verse, Nikki Giovanni (jee-oh-VAH-nee) has made several poetry recordings. Some, such as *Truth Is on Its Way* (1971), have gospel music accompaniment. Her recordings, as well as her many public performances, have helped to popularize the black oral poetry movement. Her two books of conversations with older, established African American writers, *A Dialogue: James Baldwin and Nikki Giovanni* (1973) and *A Poetic Equation: Conversations Between Nikki Giovanni and Margaret Walker* (1974), offer the contrasting attitudes of two generations of African American writers on the aims of African American literature in white America. The first book is especially interesting for its spirited discussion about the changing relationships between black men and black women, a topic of many of Giovanni's poems. The second clarifies her literary development and contains an impassioned plea for African Americans to seize control of their destinies.

Gemini: An Extended Autobiographical Statement on My First Twenty-five Years of Being a Black Poet (1971), which was nominated for a National Book Award in 1973, offers scenes from her life as a child and mother. While little is seen of the experiences and influences that shaped her art and thought, the book does contain essays about the black cultural revolution of the 1960's that serve as companion pieces to her poems. She has edited several texts, written syndicated columns—"One Woman's Voice" (*The New York Times*) and "The Root of the Matter" (*Encore American and Worldwide News Magazine*)—and contributed essays to many black magazines and journals. *Sacred Cows . . . and Other Edibles* (1988) collects a number of her essays. A collection of her work has been established at the Muger Memorial Library, Boston University.

ACHIEVEMENTS

Nikki Giovanni has earned an impressive array of honors throughout her literary career. In the late 1960's, she won grants from the Ford Foundation, National Endowment for the Arts, and the Harlem Cultural Council. She was named one of ten Most Admired Black Women by the *Amsterdam News* in 1969. In 1971, she won an outstanding achievement award from *Mademoiselle*, an Omega Psi Phi Fraternity Award for outstanding contribution to arts and letters, and a Prince Matchabelli Sun Shower Award; in 1972, a National Association of Radio and Television Announcers Award for her recording of *Truth Is on Its Way* and a Woman of the Year Youth Leadership Award from *Ladies' Home Journal*; in 1973, a National Book Award nomination for *Gemini* and a Best Books for Young Adults citation from the American Library Association for *My House.*

Giovanni was named Woman of the Year by the Cincinnati Chapter of the Young Women's Christian Association (1983), an Outstanding Woman of Tennessee (1985), and Woman of the Year by the Lynchburg chapter of the National Association for the Advancement of Colored People (NAACP; 1989). She was inducted into the Ohio Women's Hall of Fame in 1985 and won the Post-Corbett Award (1986), the Ohioana Library Award for *Sacred Cows . . . and Other Edibles* (1988), and the Children's Reading Roundtable of Chicago Award for *Vacation Time* (1988). She won the Tennessee Writer's Award (1994) and the Jeanine Rae Award for the Advancement of Women's Culture (1995). In 1996, she won the Langston Hughes Award, the Tennessee Governor's Award in the Humanities, the Outstanding Humanitarian Award from the Kentucky House of Representatives, the Parents' Choice Award for *The Sun Is So Quiet*, and the Contributor's Arts Award from the Gwendolyn Brooks Center, which named her to the National Literary Hall of Fame for Writers of African Descent in 1998. She received the NAACP Image Award for *Love Poems* in 1998, *Blues* in 2000, *Quilting the*

Black-Eyed Pea in 2003, *Acolytes* in 2008, and *Hip Hop Speaks to Children: A Celebration of Poetry with a Beat* in 2009. Other awards in 1998 include the Tennessee Governor's Award in the Arts, the Appalachian Medallion Award from the University of Charleston, and the Belle Ringer Image Role Model Award from Bennett College.

Giovanni received the Virginia Governor's Award for the Arts (2000), the SHero Award for Lifetime Achievement (2002), the Rosa Parks Women of Courage Award (2002), the American Library Association's Black Caucus Award for *Quilting the Black-Eyed Pea* (2003), the East Tennessee Writers Hall of Fame Award for Poetry (2004), the John Henry "Pop" Lloyd Humanitarian Award (2005), the ALC Lifetime Achievement Award (2005), the Oppenheim Toy Portfolio Best Book Award for *Rosa* (2005), the African American Literary Legends and Legacies Award for Poetry for *Acolytes* (2007), the Gwendolyn Brooks/John O. Killens Award (2007), Carl Sandburg Literary Award (2007), Women of Power Legacy Award (2008), and the American Book Award from the Before Columbus Foundation for *The Collected Poetry of Nikki Giovanni* (2008).

She has received numerous honorary degrees from academic institutions, including Wilberforce University, Fisk University, the University of Maryland (Princess Anne Campus), Ripon University, Smith College, Indiana University, Albright College, Cabrini College, Allegheny College, Wilmington University, Pace University, West Virginia University, Florida A&M University (Tallahassee), and Dillard University. Several cities have honored her with keys to the city, including Dallas, New York City, Cincinnati, Miami, New Orleans, and Los Angeles.

BIOGRAPHY

Nikki Giovanni was born Yolande Cornelia Giovanni in Knoxville, Tennessee, but grew up in Wyoming and Lincoln Heights, Ohio, suburbs of Cincinnati, where she made her home. She described her childhood as "quite happy" in the poem "Nikki-Rosa," and her reminiscences in *Gemini* testify to her devotion to relatives, especially her sister Gary (who nicknamed her "Nikki") and her grandparents, John Brown Watson, one of the first graduates of Fisk University, and his wife, Louvenia, whose strength of character she admired and emulated. Giovanni herself entered Fisk at the age of sixteen and was graduated magna cum laude in 1967 with a bachelor of arts degree in history. At Fisk, her independent spirit led to her being expelled after one semester, but when she reentered in 1964, she immediately became involved in politics, reestablishing the university's chapter of the Student Nonviolent Coordinating Committee (SNCC). She also became greatly interested in literature and participated in John Oliver Killens's writers' workshop. She also briefly attended the School of Social Work at the University of Pennsylvania. It was black politics and black art, however, that held her interest. In 1967, a Ford Foundation grant enabled her to complete and publish her first book of poetry, *Black Feeling, Black Talk*, and its success led to a National Foundation of the Arts grant on which she attended Columbia University's School of Fine Arts in 1968. Instead of completing her proposed novel or work toward a graduate degree, she continued to work on a volume of poetry, *Black Judgement*, published through a grant by the Harlem Cultural Council on the Arts.

Her impact on African American literature was immediate and electric. Her celebration of blackness and her militancy placed her in the avant-garde of black letters. Hailed as the Princess of Black Poetry, she began touring the United States, lecturing to college audiences, spreading her message of black cultural nationalism, "ego-tripping," and love. To raise black cultural awareness and to foster black art, she became an assistant professor of black studies at Queens College, Flushing, New York, in 1968 and taught creative writing at Livingston College, Rutgers University, from 1968 to 1970. She organized the Black Arts Festival in Cincinnati in 1967, editing *Love Black*, a magazine of the people; participated in the 1970 National Educational Television program "Soul!"; and took part in the two-week African American festival "Soul at the Center" at Lincoln Center in New York in 1972.

The core of Giovanni's life and work is love and service; the focus is the family: her own, the black community, and humanity. In 1969, her son Thomas Watson Giovanni was born: Her concern for him—indeed for all children—was the springboard for her volumes of children's poetry, which include *Spin a Soft Black Song*, *Ego-Tripping, and Other Poems for Young Readers*, *Vacation Time*, and *The Genie in the Jar*. She also worked with the Reading Is Fundamental (RIF) Program in Harlem, the Jackie Robinson Foundation, and the President's Committee on the International Year of the Child (1979). Her poetry reflects a life of meditation and domesticity. She is also an active member of African American service organizations and an editorial consultant and columnist for *Encore American and Worldwide News Magazine*, a black news monthly with a Third World focus.

In the 1980's and 1990's, she taught at a number of colleges and universities throughout the country, both as a faculty member and visiting professor, including College of Mount St. Joseph on the Ohio, as professor of creative writing; Ohio State University, Columbus, as visiting professor of English; and Texas Christian University, as visiting professor in humanities. She started her long tenure as professor at Virginia Tech, Blacksburg, Virginia, in 1987. She also contributes a great deal of her time to public service and directing a variety of art festivals and writing workshops. She directs the Warm Hearth Writers' Workshop, was appointed to the Ohio Humanities Council in 1987, served from 1990 to 1993 as a member of the board of directors for Virginia Foundation for Humanities and Public Policy, and participated in the Appalachian Community Fund from 1991 to 1993 and the Volunteer Action Center from 1991 to 1994. She was a featured poet at the International Poetry Festival in Utrecht, Holland, in 1991. She gives numerous poetry readings and lectures worldwide and appears on numerous television talk shows.

ANALYSIS

From the beginning of her career, Nikki Giovanni has combined private with public concerns, and her development has been toward the exploration of the inner life of one black female—herself—as a paradigm for black women's aspirations in contemporary America. An individualist who early admired Ayn Rand's concept of rational self-interest, Giovanni has a unique black identity. Her example of self-actualization embodied in her poetry has been not only influential but also inspirational, especially to black youth.

In *The Souls of Black Folk* (1903), W. E. B. Du Bois expressed the dilemma of the black American writer—a double consciousness of being both an American and a black. Giovanni, however, has never felt this division. In *Gemini*, she asserts, "I've always known I was colored. When I was Negro I knew I was colored; now that I'm Black I know which color it is. Any identity crisis I may have had never centered on race." The transition from Negro to black represents for her, as for Amiri Baraka and other adherents of the Black Consciousness movement, a transvaluation: black becomes a "sacrament." It is an outward and visible sign of an inward and spiritual grace, making a poetry reading a "service" and a play a "ritual." Rather than a mask that prevents the inner man from being seen, as in Ralph Ellison's *Invisible Man* (1952), color becomes a sign of worth itself. In her early poems and pronouncements, Giovanni proves herself a true Gemini, dividing the world into mutually exclusive categories. Everything is literally black or white: "Perhaps the biggest question in the modern world is the definition of a genus—huemanity. And the white man is no hueman." Her concerns, in her first two books of poems, like the audience she both addresses and represents, are exclusively black. Her early ideas about poetry are closely connected with her ideas about race. In her essay "The Weather as a Cultural Determiner," she elaborates on the thesis that African Americans are naturally poets: Indeed "we are our own poems": "Poetry is the culture of a people. We are poets even when we don't write poems; just look at our life, our rhythms, our tenderness, our signifying, our sermons and our songs." Her poems were originally composed for polemical, not lyrical, ends—for the black community: Poetry is "just a manifestation of our collective historical needs. And we strike a responsive chord because the people will always respond to the natural things."

POLITICAL POEMS

Throughout Giovanni's poetry run two main themes, revolution and love—one destructive, the other creative. Even in her earliest verse, both strands are evident: only the emphasis shifts from the former to the latter. For example, in an early poem, "Detroit Conference of Unity and Art (For HRB)," the "most valid" of the resolutions passed "as we climbed Malcolm's ladder" was "Rap chose me." The revolution that she calls for in *Black Judgement* is, on one level, literal: In "Reflections on April 4, 1968," the date of the assassination of Martin Luther King, Jr., even her poetic structure collapses in the face of the need for violence:

> What can I, a poor Black woman, do to destroy America?
> This is a question, with appropriate variations, being
> asked in every Black heart. There is one answer—
>   I can kill.
> There is one compromise—I can protect those who kill.
> There is one cop-out—I can encourage others to kill.
> There are no other ways.

The revolution is also symbolic, striking out at the poisonous racial myths that have devalued blacks in America. In "Word Poem (Perhaps Worth Considering)," she writes: "as things be/come/ let's destroy/ then we can destroy/ what we be/come/ let's build/ what we become/ when we dream." The destruction here is of values and attitudes, seemingly in accord with the statement in *Gemini:* "Nobody's trying to make the system Black; we're trying to make a system that's human so that Black folks can live in it. This means we're trying to destroy the existing system." Giovanni's poems attack the American political establishment in a sweeping, generalized way; her analysis is simple— exterminate the white beast. Her real contempt is directed toward "Negroes" still in the service of white America: "The True Import of Present Dialogue, Black vs. Negro" is "Can you kill/ Can you kill a white man/ Can you kill the nigger/ in you." Her "Black Judgement" is upon ". . . niggerish ways." Aware that with children lies the future, she urges in "Poem for Black Boys" new revolutionary games:

> Ask your mother for a Rap Brown gun
> Santa just may comply if you wish hard enough
> Ask for CULLURD instead of Monopoly
> DO NOT SIT IN DO NOT FOLLOW KING
> GO DIRECTLY TO STREETS
> This is a game you can win.

Poetry of denial, vilification, and decreation (what she calls her "nigger-nigger" phrase) is essentially dead-ended; the main rhetorical problem of the new black poets was how to restore value to the black experience. Giovanni accomplished such a restoration through the affirmation of her own life and the transforming power of poetry. In *Cotton Candy on a Rainy Day*, "The Beep Beep Poem" has a "song of herself" almost like Walt Whitman's:

> i love the aloneness of the road
> when I ascend descending curves
> the power within my toes delights me
> and i fling my spirit down the highway
> i love the way i feel
> when i pass the moon and i holler to the stars
> i'm coming through

Such elation, however, is unusual. The tone of "Nikki-Rosa," "Mothers," and "Legacies" is more bittersweet. Giovanni gradually realized that writing itself creates value: She says in "Boxes," "i write/ because/ i have to." In the 1960's, writing appeared to be a luxury: In "For Saundra," she notes:

> maybe i shouldn't write
> at all
> but clean my gun
> and check my kerosene supply
> perhaps these are not poetic
> times
> at all.

MY HOUSE

In the 1960's, poetry was to be a witness of the times—"it's so important to record" ("Records"), but her poetry proved to be her house: *My House* shows her assimilation and transformation of the world into her castle. In "Poem (For Nina)," she begins by asserting that "We are all imprisoned *in the castle of our skins*," though her imagination will color her world "Black Gold": "my castle shall become/ my rendezvous/ my courtyard will bloom with hyacinths and jack-in-the-pulpits/ my moat will not restrict me but will be filled/ with dolphins. . . ." In "A Very Simple Wish," she wants through her poetry to make a patchwork quilt of the world, including all that seems to be left behind by world history: "i've a mind to build/ a new world/ want to play."

In *My House*, Giovanni began to exhibit increased sophistication and maturity. Her viewpoint had broadened beyond a rigid black revolutionary consciousness to balance a wide range of social concerns. Her rhymes had also become more pronounced, more lyrical, more gentle. The themes of family love, loneliness, and frustration, which Giovanni had defiantly explored in her earlier works, find much deeper expression in *My House*. Her change from an incendiary radical to a nurturing poet is traced in the poem "Revolutionary Dreams": from dreaming "militant dreams/ of taking over america," she

> . . . awoke and dug
> that if i dreamed natural
> dreams of being a natural
> woman doing what a woman
> does when she's natural
> i would have a revolution

This changed perspective accords with the conclusion of "When I Die": "And if ever i touched a life i hope that life knows/ that i know that touching was and still is and will/ always be the true/ revolution." Love and sex form the subject matter of many of her poems. She will "scream and stamp and shout/ for more beautiful beautiful beautiful/ black men with outasight afros" in "Beautiful Black Men" and propose "counterrevolutionary" sex in "Seduction" and "That Day": "if you've got the dough/ then i've got the heat/ we can use my oven/ til it's warm and sweet."

This bold and playful manner, however, is usually modulated by the complications of any long-term relationship between men and women. While she explains in *Gemini:* "to me sex is an essence. . . . It's a basic of human relationships. And sex is conflict; it could be considered a miniwar between two people," marriage is "give and take—you give and he takes." In "Woman," her acknowledgment of the difficulty of a black man maintaining his self-respect in America has led to her acceptance of his failings: "she decided to become/ a woman/ and though he still refused/ to be a man/ she decided it was all/ right."

COTTON CANDY ON A RAINY DAY

The title poem of *Cotton Candy on a Rainy Day*, like many others in the collection, bespeaks the tempering of her vision. When Giovanni published this volume, critics viewed it as one of her most somber works. They noted the focus on emotional ups and downs, fear and insecurity, and the weight of everyday responsibilities. The title poem tells of "the gray of my mornings/ Or the blues of every night" in a decade known for "loneliness." Life is likened to nebulous cotton candy: "The sweet soft essence/ of possibility/ Never quite maturing." Her attitude tired, her potential stillborn, she is unable to categorize life as easily as before, "To put a three-dimensional picture/ On a one-dimensional surface."

One reason for her growth in vision seems to be her realization of the complexity of a woman's life. The black woman's negative self-image depicted in "Adulthood" was not solved by adopting the role of Revolutionary Black Poet. In "Woman Poem," "Untitled," "Once a Lady Told Me," "Each Sunday," and "The Winter Storm," the women with compromised lives are other women. In "A Poem Off Center," however, she includes herself in this condition: "maybe i shouldn't feel sorry/ for myself/ but the more i understand women/ the more i do." A comparison of "All I Gotta Do" ("is sit and wait") to "Choice," two poems alike in their subject matter and their syncopated beat, shows that a woman's only choice is to cry.

AFRICA AND BLACK MUSIC

Two other themes in her poetry also ally Giovanni with the new black poets—Africa and black music. The romantic and exotic Africa of the Harlem Renaissance writers appears only in "Ego-Tripping," where Africa is personified as a beautiful woman. Her own African experience has produced poems that give a balanced recognition of the African's separate identity. In "They Clapped," African Americans are treated like any other tourists and African life is seen realistically.

> they stopped running when they learned the packages
> on the women's heads were heavy and that babies didn't
> cry and disease is uncomfortable and that villages are fun
> only because you knew the feel of good leather on good
> pavement.

Her conclusion—"despite the dead/ dream they saw a free future"—opens the way for a new hope in Africa: "i dream of black men and women walking/ together side by side into a new world/ described by love and bounded by difference."

Black music forms the basis of many of her poems: Aretha Franklin emerges as her personal idol, lines from popular songs are woven into "Revolutionary Music" and "Dreams," and several of her poems are based on traditional black American music. She has written a blues tune, "Master Charge Blues," in which a modern woman lets her credit card cure her troubles, and a song that could be set to music, "The Only Song I'm Singing."

The use of the ballad stanza in "On Hearing 'The Girl with the Flaxen Hair'" is effective in building a narrative about white and black art: The girl with flaxen hair gets a song; the black woman does not because her man is tired after working. Her most successful adaptation of musical form comes in "The Great Pax White," which recalls gospel music. Here Pax Whitie (a bitter parody of the Pax Romana) is described first in an inversion of the words beginning Saint John's gospel: The word "was death to all life." Western history, its wars and brutality, is recounted with two alternating calls and responses: "ain't they got no shame?" and "ain't we got no pride?" Her historical account is heavily ironic:

> So the great white prince
> Was shot like a nigger in texas
> And our Black shining prince was murdered
> like that thug in his cathedral
> While our nigger in memphis
> was shot like their prince in dallas.

The irony here and in other political poems, such as "Oppression," would be directed in *Cotton Candy on a Rainy Day* toward herself in "Being and Nothingness" and "The New Yorkers."

HUMAN RELATIONSHIPS

As Giovanni's poems turned toward human relationships, there was a marked increase in her lyricism and especially in her use of imagery, both decorative and structural. Her lover's hands are compared to butterflies in "The Butterfly"; she feels like a falling leaf after a night of passion in "Autumn Poems"; getting rid of a lover is just so much "Housecleaning." "Make Up" sustains the image of cosmetics to talk about the life of pretense that a woman must live. On the whole, her verse descends from William Carlos Williams and Hughes, but her voice is her own. While she is not a stylistic innovator, nor a stunning image-maker, she has an ingratiating style, one that proceeds from the energy of her personality, and an increasingly sure command of phrasing.

In "The Wonder Woman (A New Dream—for Stevie Wonder)," Giovanni reviewed her life up to 1971: "i wanted to be/ a sweet inspiration in my dreams/ of my people but the times/ require that i give/ myself willingly and become/ a wonder woman." If her subsequent history has fallen short of this ideal, it is still her strong clear voice that one remembers after reading her poetry; her poems are ultimately the self-expression of a black woman who has discovered that "Black love is Black wealth" and who has brought many people, both black and white, to poetry.

CHILDREN'S POETRY

Giovanni devoted a great deal of her writing to children's poetry in the 1980's and early 1990's. She describes her writing for children as an opportunity to "share a bit of the past with children. Black kids deserve to hear their history. My kids books are serious but not dour." Her movement toward this type of poetry reflected her time spent as a mother and enjoying her extended family. More than anything, the poems in her children's collection *Vacation Time* showcased her growing lightness of spirit and inner stability. Similarly, *Those Who Ride the Night Winds* revealed a new and innovative form and brought forth Giovanni's heightened self-knowledge and imagination. In *Those Who Ride the Night Winds*, she echoed the political activism of her early verse as she dedicated various pieces to Phillis Wheatley, Martin Luther King Jr., and Rosa Parks. A decade passed between the publication of *Those Who Ride the Night Winds* and her 1994 title *Knoxville, Tennessee*, a time during which she devoted energy to public causes and arts development, wrote essays, and contributed to edited texts.

THE SELECTED POEMS OF NIKKI GIOVANNI AND LOVE POEMS

During the 1980's and the 1990's—Giovanni's "middle years"—her work continued to reflect her changing concerns and perspectives. *The Selected Poems of Nikki Giovanni*, which spanned the first three decades of her career, was lauded by critics as a "rich synthesis [that] reveals the evolution of Giovanni's voice and charts the course of the social issues that are her muses, issues of gender and race."

Her collection titled *Love Poems* has an interesting pop-culture twist to it. Ever an unwavering supporter of Black youth, Giovanni was devastated by the murder of rap singer Tupac Shakur in 1997 and had the words "Thug Life" tattooed on her left forearm in his honor. She then dedicated *Love Poems* to Shakur. "A lover whose love was often misunderstood," begins the dedication. Giovanni noted in an interview that she was frustrated with those who would confuse the message and the messenger:

Rap is expressing the violence that's there, and we weren't even looking at that until rap came up and talked about it. It gave voice to the conditions that people are living under.

While there are somber, sociopolitical pieces here—the burning of black churches and the role of "gansta rap"—most of the poems find Giovanni upbeat and domestic. Most of the poems are about friendship and sexuality, children and motherhood, loneliness and sharing, "beautiful black men" and "our faith and our energy and loving our mamas and ourselves and the world and all the chances we took in trying to make everything better." Her celebration of creative energy and the family spirit of African American communities dominates this collection.

BLUES

As the twentieth century came to a close, readers found a bit of the younger, more political Giovanni in several of the poems of her collection *Blues*. While sociopolitical commentary in poetry often fails because it loses touch with humanity, Giovanni continues to keep focus on people: Here she spars with ills that confront Americans but places a human face on every struggle. A real estate developer is destroying the woodland adjacent to Giovanni's home in preparation for a new housing development ("Road Rage"); a young basketball star ("Iverson"), harassed for his youth and style, finds a compassionate but stern sister in Giovanni; and President Bill Clinton is subject to Giovanni's forthright opinions ("The President's Penis"). Giovanni writes in this collection with an authority informed by experience and shared with heart-stealing candor.

Pop culture and pleasure find a place in the collection as well. She writes about tennis player Pete Sampras and her own tennis playing; pays tribute to Jackie Robinson, soul singer Regina Belle, the late blues singer Alberta Hunter, and Betty Shabazz, the late widow of Malcolm X. She also writes fondly of her memories of going to the ballpark with her father to see the Cincinnati Reds.

Her battle with illness is captured in "Me and Mrs. Robin," which deals with Giovanni's convalescence from cancer surgery and the family of robins she observed with delight and sympathy from her window. However, this gentle poem also revisits the real estate developer, who, the poem notes, has destroyed trees and "confused the birds and murdered the possum and groundhog." As she identifies with an injured robin, Giovanni's language invokes a gnostic cosmogony: God takes care of individuals; Mother Nature wreaks havoc left and right. "No on2e ever says 'Mother Nature have mercy.' Mother nature don't give a damn," Giovanni says; "that's why God is so important."

THE COLLECTED POETRY OF NIKKI GIOVANNI, 1968-1998

The Collected Poetry of Nikki Giovanni, 1968-1998 provides the reader with a comprehensive portrait of a significant poet. The poems, spanning three decades, are arranged chronologically and serve as a testament to Giovanni's growth as a poet and activist. In the interview by singer and poet Jill Scott included in this volume, Giovanni states, "The collection really shows my growth, my understanding. . . . [and] I want to keep growing." The interview captures the unique, powerful voice of Giovanni, reinforcing her focus on African Americans as her inspiration. The poems in the collection are arranged chronologically. Other features include a biographical time line, annotations to the poems, and indexes of titles and first lines. The introduction by Virginia C. Fowler was published previously in *The Selected Poems of Nikki Giovanni*. This collection reveals the essence of the poet as insightful observer, viewing the endurance of African Americans through both a universal and personal lens.

ACOLYTES

Giovanni began writing *Acolytes* "with my feet propped on my mother's hospital bed." She clearly identifies with the acolytes. Defining herself as a follower, she articulates the toll of loss and the importance of courage and faith. Moreover, she celebrates inspirational people, including civil rights leader Parks in "The Rosa Parks" and "The Seamstress of Montgomery" and poet Gwendolyn Brooks in "Remembering Gwen."

With these eighty new poems and short prose pieces, she clearly provides connections within the literary canon of African American works through allusions to Brooks, Hughes, Baraka, and Richard Wright, among others. Always the Princess of Black Poetry, she reaffirms the connectedness among artists and revels in the ability to unite and inspire others. In "Paint Me Like I Am," she encourages others to grow, to create: "We owe it to ourselves to re-create ourselves/ and find a different if not better way to live."

With its twenty-seven prose pieces, the collection's focus is on narration, with storytelling the primary strategy and gathering and inspiring people toward a common purpose the main goal. In the prose piece "We Gather," she says, "We are gathered to fulfill a covenant . . . a vow. . . ." Each piece seems to amplify her views on writing, imprisonment, slavery, loss, and other poets. In one, she rejoices in domesticity because it brings about order as does poetry to language. In "Saturday Days," she says that she likes housekeeping because order "brings peace and comfort."

Giovanni uses personal insight and experiences to guide her writing, and her poems embody what she advises other writers, as stated in a 2000 interview: "The authority of the writer always overcomes the skepticism of the reader. If you know what you're talking about, or if you feel that you do, the reader will believe you." Whether it is preparing leaders, as described in "Sanity (To Be Continued)," or defining them, as in "A Library," her authoritative voice shines through—and her readers believe her and in her.

BICYCLES

In *Bicycles*, Giovanni uses a bicycle as a metaphor for love, which also "requires trust and balance." She captures the diverse types of love, including romantic love, love between friends, and self-love. She also describes the loss of love, as in "A Substitute for You": "I'm just saying/ What we had is gone// I need a substitute/ for you." Through sixty-five poems, she identifies the dynamics of personal relationships and honestly and with humor chronicles their ups and downs.

A companion to *Love Poems*, this collection pairs bicycles—vehicles for movement and change—with love. "Bicycles," the title poem, illustrates the metaphoric relationship in the lines: "Midnight poems are bicycles/ Taking us on safer journeys." The concept of love as a journey is also depicted in "Letting the Air Out" (subtitled "Of My Tires") and many other poems.

The sensual nature of romantic love is dramatized in "I Like the Dance." The poem succinctly captures the sensual sway of love through dance, as in the "gentle sway" and ". . . the way I feel/ in your arms." Similarly, in "Your Shower," the persona, or poetic voice, moves over the body of the loved one with sexual intensity and playfulness: "Tickle my way/ Down to your lips."

Equally important is self-love. As exemplified in several poems, including "Dinner at Nine" and "My Muse," the importance of loving oneself is essential to happiness. In "Dinner at Nine," by the way the solitary diner interacts with her surroundings, the focus is shown to be not on others, but on the woman diner herself, yet when her order is ready, the waiter appears confused: "When my order arrives/ The waiter doesn't understand/ Why there is only/ me." Giovanni is clearly comfortable in her position as poet, and "My Muse" confirms her delight in her role: "I am my own/ Muse." She is her own inspiration without reservation and without conceit.

Love, however, is not without consequence or self-discovery. In "My Beer," she identifies that love is not without conflict and strife: "If I could learn to like beer// I could change my life/ I'd have somewhere/ To put my tears/ When we fight." In "Love (and the Meaning of Love)," she incorporates the way in which reasoning often precludes love: "I understood/ Why we shouldn't// So you declined/ And we didn't." In "Deal or No Deal," she infuses humor into the gambling nature of love by using pop culture, specifically an allusion to a popular game show. In fact, as the poem concludes, to play the game of love, one must be willing "To make a fool/ Of yourself."

In her final poem of the volume, "We Are Virginia Tech," she pays reverence to those killed in the April 16, 2007, shooting at the college where she has taught since 1987, and urges strength and courage for those who remain. The persistent repetition of the title phrase reinforces the importance of community. Ultimately, she challenges the college community to prevail, to be open to possibilities, "To invent the future// Through our blood and tears/ Through all this sadness."

OTHER MAJOR WORKS

NONFICTION: *Gemini: An Extended Autobiographical Statement on My First Twenty-five Years of Being a Black Poet*, 1971; *A Dialogue: James Baldwin and Nikki Giovanni*, 1973; *A Poetic Equation: Conversations Between Nikki Giovanni and Margaret Walker*,

1974; *Sacred Cows . . . and Other Edibles*, 1988; *Conversations with Nikki Giovanni*, 1992 (Virginia C. Fowler, editor); *Racism 101*, 1994; *The Prosaic Soul of Nikki Giovanni*, 2003 (includes *Gemini, Sacred Cows*, and *Racism 101*); *On My Journey Now: Looking at African-American History Through the Spirituals*, 2007.

CHILDREN'S LITERATURE: *The Girls in the Circle*, 2004; *Rosa*, 2005; *The Grasshopper's Song: An Aesop's Fable Revisited*, 2008; *Hip Hop Speaks to Children: A Celebration of Poetry with a Beat*, 2008; *Lincoln and Douglass: An American Friendship*, 2008.

EDITED TEXTS: *Night Comes Softly: Anthology of Black Female Voices*, 1970; *Appalachian Elders: A Warm Hearth Sampler*, 1991 (with Cathee Dennison); *Grand Mothers: Poems, Reminiscences, and Short Stories About the Keepers of Our Traditions*, 1994; *Shimmy Shimmy Shimmy Like My Sister Kate: Looking at the Harlem Renaissance Through Poems*, 1996; *Grand Fathers: Reminiscences, Poems, Recipes, and Photos of the Keepers of Our Traditions*, 1999.

BIBLIOGRAPHY

Baldwin, James, and Nikki Giovanni. *A Dialogue: James Baldwin and Nikki Giovanni*. Philadelphia: Lippincott, 1973. Based on a conversation aired by the Public Broadcasting Service as *Soul!* in 1971, this friendly, informal conversation sheds light on Giovanni's opinions regarding race and gender identity in the United States—foundational themes in much of her poetry. Includes a foreword by Ida Lewis and an afterword by Orde Coombs.

Fowler, Virginia C. *Nikki Giovanni*. New York: Twayne, 1992. An introductory biography and critical study of selected works by Giovanni. Includes bibliographical references and index.

Giovanni, Nikki. "Nikki Giovanni." http://www.nikki- giovanni.com. Giovanni's official Web site offers a biography, biographical time line, lists of her published works and recordings, and several videos.

McDowell, Margaret B. "Groundwork for a More Comprehensive Criticism of Nikki Giovanni." In *Belief vs. Theory in Black American Literary Criticism*, edited by Joseph Weixlmann and Chester J. Fontenot. Greenwood, Fla.: Penkevill, 1986. An excellent source; McDowell points out biases and inconsistencies in criticism addressing Giovanni's writings and sketches areas in need of further research.

Milne, Ira Mark, ed. *Poetry for Students*. Vol. 28. Detroit: Thomson/Gale Group, 2008. Contains an analysis of Giovanni's "Ego-Tripping."

Mullen, Harryette. "'Artistic Expression Was Flowing Everywhere': Alison Mills and Ntozake Shange, Black Bohemian Feminists in the 1970's." *Meridians: Feminism, Race, Transnationalism* 4, no. 2 (2004). Although briefly noted, Giovanni's focus on both the beauty and danger of black men in her work of the 1970's is included. The reference to her work is placed in context with other Black female artists of the Black Arts movement.

Page, Yolanda Williams, ed. *Encyclopedia of African American Women Writers.* Westport, Conn.: Greenwood Press, 2007. Contains a short biographical essay on Giovanni.

Reid, Margaret Ann. *Black Protest Poetry: Polemics from the Harlem Renaissance and the Sixties.* Vol. 8 in *Studies in African and African-American Culture.* New York: Peter Lang, 2008. This work on the Harlem Renaissance and the 1960's discusses Giovanni and places her in context.

Walters, Jennifer. "Nikki Giovanni and Rita Dove: Poets Redefining." *The Journal of Negro History* 85, no. 3 (Summer, 2000): 210-217. The poetry of Giovanni and Rita Dove is discussed. Both women are examples of self-defined African American women who found a voice through writing.

White, Evelyn C. "The Poet and the Rapper." *Essence* 30, no. 1 (May, 1999): 122-124. Discusses the views of Giovanni and rapper and actor Queen Latifah on racism, rap music, and politics, topics that have abundantly influenced Giovanni's poetry.

Honora Rankine-Galloway; Sarah Hilbert
Updated by Cynthia S. Becerra

GEORGE MOSES HORTON

Born: Northampton County, North Carolina; c. 1797
Died: Possibly Philadelphia, Pennsylvania; c. 1883

PRINCIPAL POETRY

The Hope of Liberty, 1829 (revised as *Poems by a Slave*, 1837)
The Poetical Works of George M. Horton, the Colored Bard of North Carolina: To Which Is Prefixed the Life of the Author Written by Himself, 1845
Naked Genius, 1865
The Black Bard of North Carolina: George Moses Horton and His Poetry, 1997 (Joan Sherman, editor)

OTHER LITERARY FORMS

During his final years in Philadelphia, George Moses Horton wrote stories for Sunday school texts. A 229-page manuscript from that period, *The Museum*, was lost.

ACHIEVEMENTS

In the Chapel Hill, North Carolina, area, George Moses Horton achieved a local reputation for his ability to compose and dictate poetry before he could write. His poem "On Liberty and Slavery" (published in the *Lancaster Gazette*, 1828) was the first poem in which a slave reflected on slavery as it affected him. His first volume of poetry, *The Hope of Liberty*, was the first book published by an African American in the South. In 1996, Horton was inducted into North Carolina's Literary Hall of Fame. The following year, Chatham County named him the county's historic poet laureate and the George Moses Horton Society for the Study of African American Poetry was formed.

BIOGRAPHY

Although records of the life of George Moses Horton are minimal, the consensus is that he probably was born in 1797 and died in 1883. According to his own account, he was born on a Northampton County, North Carolina, plantation belonging to William Horton, who later moved to more fertile land in Chatham County, near Pittsboro. For several years, George was in charge of the cows. Although William seems to have favored him somewhat, George remained illiterate. Early on, he showed musical talent and facility in rhyme, and he gradually taught himself to read by listening to children's spelling lessons and by using fragments of spelling books, his mother's Wesley hymnal, and the Bible.

When George was about seventeen, William's estate was distributed to his children, and George was separated from his nine siblings, becoming the property of William's son James. Initially, his job was plowing, but soon George was being sent to Chapel Hill's weekly farmers market to sell plantation produce. University of North Carolina (UNC) students quickly learned that George could compose acrostic love poems based on their sweethearts' names, and they paid him twenty-five cents per poem. Some also gave him books of poetry by writers such as Homer, Vergil, William Shakespeare, John Milton, and Lord Byron.

Using money he received from his poems, George "bought" some time from James and spent more time in Chapel Hill, where he met novelist Caroline Lee Hentz, the wife of a UNC professor. Impressed by George's talent, Hentz tutored him in poetic composition and arranged for some of his poems to be published, primarily in northern newspapers.

Throughout his life, George Moses Horton continually tried to gain his freedom. In 1828, three North Carolinians attempted to buy his freedom, but James Horton refused a premium offer. The next year, his friends' efforts resulted in the publication of *The Hope of Liberty*, a collection of twenty-one poems, the expressed purpose of which was to raise money to send Horton to Liberia. The effort was unsuccessful; however, Horton did arrange to "buy" more of his time (for twenty-five cents a week), staying in Chapel Hill and working for UNC president Joseph Calwell. However, his hopes of being purchased by Calwell were never realized.

In 1833, Horton married a slave from the Snipes farm. To this unhappy union were born a son named Free and a daughter named Rody. Horton had only limited contact with his wife and children.

In 1843, Horton published a poem in the *Southern Literary Messenger*. He hoped this rare accomplishment for a southern slave poet might lead to his purchase by William Lloyd Garrison, but Garrison failed to respond to his letters. Horton then published *The Poetical Works of George M. Horton, the Colored Bard of North Carolina* (1845), forty-three poems with an autobiographical preface. Horton, still attempting to purchase his freedom, sold this volume for fifty cents a copy.

In his mid-fifties, Horton appealed to UNC president Donald Swain to buy his freedom, citing his increasing difficulty in walking the eight miles to Chapel Hill. Swain suggested he appeal to Horace Greeley, but both appeals were unsuccessful.

In 1859, Horton delivered the speech "An Address: The Stream of Liberty and Science" to UNC students, discussing his life, his views about slavery, and his general philosophy. The American Civil War soon ended his connection with UNC students, however, and he lost the market for his poems until the Union Army arrived in 1865. Befriended by Captain William H. S. Banks (Ninth Michigan Cavalry Volunteers), Horton began to travel with the U.S. Army. Banks helped Horton publish *Naked Genius*, which was advertised as a way to benefit disabled Union veterans.

In 1866, Horton moved to Philadelphia, where he apparently attempted unsuccessfully to become part of the literary scene. According to most reports, he wrote stories for

Sunday school texts and worked for various old friends from North Carolina until his death. There is no extant account of his last years, though there are references to *The Museum*, a 229-page manuscript, now lost.

ANALYSIS

Although George Moses Horton originally gained fame for composing and reciting love poems and acrostics, his poems actually encompass a variety of conventional forms, including quatrains, couplets, ballads, and blank verse. Generally the rhymes are highly conventional, strongly influenced by the poems and hymns Horton read. The diction is the essentially archaic language of hymnals: "wilt," "thee," "'twas," "oft," "lea," and "clement." The syntax frequently is stilted and artificial, reflecting a neoclassical influence. Other neoclassical echoes include personified abstractions (Winter and Spring) and numerous classical allusions (Helen, Troy, Phoebus, and Philomela).

THE HOPE OF LIBERTY

The Hope of Liberty begins with an introduction that explains Horton's status as a slave and how he came to write the twenty-one poems. It states that the intent of this publication is to earn money so that Horton can buy his freedom and go to Liberia. Horton's hopes for freedom are clear in "On Hearing of the Intention of a Gentleman to Purchase the Poet's Freedom." He rejoices at the prospect of help in purchasing his freedom, comparing the news to sunshine breaking through storms, spring coming after winter, and ultimately as inspiring as the Aeolian harp of Greek mythology. He believes Providence has intervened in his life, preparing him for freedom and guiding him, even through the depths of despair.

The collection also contains poems on themes that would be continued in Horton's later volumes, including religion ("Praise of Creation"), slavery ("On Liberty and Slavery"), love, death ("On Death"), and nature ("On Winter"). In a series of quatrains, "On Summer" details the activities of various creatures in nature—birds, insects, oxen, horses, cattle—as well as the farmer and the orchards and fields.

THE POETICAL WORKS OF GEORGE M. HORTON

The Poetical Works of George M. Horton, the Colored Bard of North Carolina contained forty-three poems and an autobiography. Several of the poems deal with religious subjects. For example, "Reflections from the Flash of a Meteor" uses a series of quatrains to develop the meteor as a symbol for human life, specifically the life of the poet-persona. Similarly, "Rise up, my soul" (a fragment included in his autobiography) traces the poet's role as a guest at the "gospel feast." "Excited upon Reading the Obedience of Nature to Her Lord in the Vessel on the Sea" retells the story of Jesus' calming the sea and saving the disciples' boat. Another poem fragment (included in Horton's autobiographical essay) recounts the fleeing Israelites' rejoicing as they see the destruction of the pursuing Egyptians. Even a poem such as "The Retreat from Moscow" is used for religious instruction. The inhabitants run like quail fleeing from an eagle. The destruction of Moscow parallels that of Gomorrah, and nature's creatures (dogs, horses, oxen, cattle, pigeons, and chickens) scatter much like humans on Judgment Day.

Other poems deal with philosophical concepts. Some, such as "True Friendship," (written in ballad stanzas) are essentially abstract and conventional, but others employ nature imagery and even humor. A frequently anthologized poem, "The Woodsman and Money Hunter," develops the traditional conflict between Nature and money; the woodsman eventually finds that Nature supplies all his needs except money, and he decides money is not important enough for him to chase. Humor is an important element in poems such as "The Creditor to His Proud Debtor." The poet-persona, who seems to live a simple life, sees a man who owes him money. The well-dressed debtor is described as a "crowing" fashion plate, wearing a cravat and bell-crowned hat, sitting in the shade, and smoking expensive cigars. His pockets are full of the poet-persona's money, and the poet-persona speculates how different the situation would be if he demanded his money and insisted that the sheriff force the debtor to pay his debts. Humor also figures prominently in "Troubled with the Itch and Rubbing with Sulphur." The poet-persona considers his itch a plague only temporarily relieved by scratching. He associates this itch with the devil because treating it with sulphur blackens his clothes and makes him stink; he not only resembles the devil, but also finds sleeping impossible.

Although Horton wrote many religious and philosophical poems, modern critics more highly praise his poems about nature, his ambitions as a poet, and his situation as a slave. These poems are among Horton's most personal. "The Happy Bird's Nest" deals with the day's end: The bee leaves the flower, the bird returns to its nest, the gazelle bounds over the mountains, darkness grows as the sun sets and the moon rises, the night bird sings, and the laborer has earned his rest. "The Fate of an Innocent Dog" recounts the story of Tiger, a dog that tries to stop other dogs from killing sheep but is himself killed instead. For Horton, this story provides a parallel to people who venture out into the world and suffer for the offenses of others. Horton insists that in order to survive in the world, a man needs a friend from home.

Several poems are tributes to people Horton admired. "Eulogy" is a tribute to Horton's benefactor Hentz. This Elizabethan sonnet praises Hentz's work, asserting that her fame will be eternal, outlasting her life and that of the world itself. The more ceremonial "Death of Gen. Jackson—An Eulogy" emphasizes the importance of freedom as Horton describes a world filled with gloom at the death of a brave and heroic man who refused to live as a slave. The general's fame bloomed like a flower, but now it has set like a star. Also heroic is Henry Clay in "Mr. Clay's Reception at Raleigh: April, 1844," whose brilliance is said to equal that of ten thousand stars. This hope for unity ends with "Clay's Defeat," as Horton demonstrates the changes resulting from Clay's electoral defeat: Summer turns into winter, the bird is too chilled to sing, and generally the music ends.

The dark side of slavery is seen in "Division of an Estate." Using the metaphor of a man beheaded, Horton describes the reaction of the "body" (the slaveholder's various possessions). He begins by describing the sorrow and confusion of the animals (the sheep, cattle, horses, dogs, and swine). Even the sun and stars are affected by the actions of the ungrateful heirs, but the greatest distress is suffered by the slaves, whose fate is most uncertain. As they are divided right and left, they may be headed to Heaven or Hell.

NAKED GENIUS

Naked Genius contained ninety new poems and about forty from Horton's 1845 publication. In "George Moses Horton, Myself," the aging poet recalls his youthful talent, limited by his lack of freedom: "My genius from a boy/ Has fluttered like a bird within my heart;/ But could not thus confined her powers employ." Although he recognizes the impossibility of recovering the past, he still expresses hope for future achievement, using the symbol of the soaring bird to represent his enduring soul:

> She like a restless bird,
> Would spread her wings, her power to be unfurl'd,
> And let her songs be loudly heard,
> And dart from world to world.

BIBLIOGRAPHY

Andrews, William L., ed. *The North Carolina Roots of African American Literature: An Anthology*. Chapel Hill: University of North Carolina Press, 2006. Contains a selection of Horton's works and an introduction providing biographical information and critical analysis.

Bryant, Earle V. "The Poetry of George Moses Horton." In *Masterplots II: African American Literature*, edited by Tyrone Williams. Rev. ed. Pasadena, Calif.: Salem Press, 2009. Examines Horton's poetry in detail, looking at themes and the critical context.

Gates, Henry Louis, Jr,. and Nellie Y. McKay, ed. *The Norton Anthology of African American Literature*. New York: W. W. Norton, 2004. This anthology presents several poems with a biographical and critical introduction.

"The George Moses Horton Project." Chatham County Arts Council. http://www .chathamarts.org/horton. This Web site for the George Moses Horton Project, an educational program of the Chatham County Arts Council, contains a biographical sketch and discussion of the project, as well as links to a fact sheet and some of Horton's writings.

Pettis, Joyce Owens. *African American Poets: Lives, Works, and Sources*. Westport, Conn.: Greenwood Press, 2002. Contains an entry on Horton that looks at his life and works.

Richmond, M. A. *Bid the Vassal Soar: Interpretive Essays on the Life and Poetry of Phillis Wheatley and George Moses Horton*. Washington, D.C.: Howard University Press, 1974. Comparative analysis of these early African American poets.

Sherman, Joan R., ed. *The Black Bard of North Carolina: George Moses Horton and His Poetry*. Chapel Hill: University of North Carolina Press, 1997. Collects sixty-two poems, some previously unpublished, and contains a biography, bibliography, critical evaluation, and editorial notes.

Walser, Richard. "George Moses Horton." In *Southern Writers: A Biographical Dictionary*, edited by Robert Bain, Joseph M. Flora, and Louis D. Rubin, Jr. Baton Rouge: Louisiana State University Press, 1979. Brief biographical sketch and evaluation with limited bibliography.

Charmaine Allmon Mosby

LANGSTON HUGHES

Born: Joplin, Missouri; February 1, 1902
Died: New York, New York; May 22, 1967

OTHER LITERARY FORMS

In addition to his prolific production of poetry, Langston Hughes wrote, translated, edited, and collaborated on works in a number of other genres. He wrote two novels, *Not Without Laughter* (1930) and *Tambourines to Glory* (1958), and produced several volumes of short stories, including *The Ways of White Folks* (1934), *Laughing to Keep from Crying* (1952), and *Something in Common, and Other Stories* (1963). Hughes's short fiction also includes several collections of stories about his urban folk philosopher, Jesse B. Semple (Simple): *Simple Speaks His Mind* (1950), *Simple Takes a Wife* (1953), *Simple Stakes a Claim* (1957), *The Best of Simple* (1961), and *Simple's Uncle Sam* (1965).

Langston Hughes
(Library of Congress)

Hughes published several works for young people, including the story *Popo and Fifina: Children of Haiti* (1932), with Arna Bontemps; biographies of black Americans in *Famous American Negroes* (1954), *Famous Negro Music Makers* (1955), and *Famous Negro Heroes of America* (1958); and a series of "first book" histories for young people, such as *The First Book of Negroes* (1952), *The First Book of Jazz* (1955), and *The First Book of Africa* (1960).

Hughes's histories for adult readers include *Fight for Freedom: The Story of the NAACP* (1962) and two pictorial histories in collaboration with Milton Meltzer, *A Pictorial History of the Negro in America* (1956) and *Black Magic: A Pictorial History of the Negro in American Entertainment* (1967). Other experimental volumes of photo essays are *The Sweet Flypaper of Life* (1955), with photographs by Roy DeCarava, and *Black Misery* (1969), with illustrations by Arouni.

Major translations by Hughes include *Cuba Libre* by Nicolás Guillén (1948), with Ben Carruthers; *Gypsy Ballads* by Federico García Lorca (1951); and *Selected Poems of Gabriela Mistral* (1957).

Hughes was also productive as a playwright, although his plays did not enjoy much critical or financial success. They include *Mulatto* (pb. 1935), *Little Ham* (pr. 1935), *Simply Heavenly* (pr. 1957), based on the characters in his Simple stories; and *Tambou-*

rines to Glory (pr., pb. 1963), adapted from his novel. The last play was billed as a "gospel song-play," and Hughes created several other plays in that category: *Black Nativity* (pr. 1961), *Jerico-Jim Crow* (pr. 1964), and *The Prodigal Son* (pr. 1965). These productions are of interest mainly because they underscore Hughes's heartfelt sympathy with the black folk life of America, a love affair he carried on throughout his works.

Hughes wrote the libretti for several operas, a screenplay—*Way Down South* (1939), with Clarence Muse—radio scripts, and song lyrics. His most famous contribution to musical theater, however, was the lyrics he wrote for Kurt Weill and Elmer Rice's musical adaptation of Rice's *Street Scene* (pr., pb. 1947).

Over the years, Hughes also wrote several nonfiction articles, mainly focused on his role as a poet and his love of black American music—jazz, gospel, and the blues. Perhaps his most important article was his first: "The Negro Artist and the Racial Mountain," published in *The Nation* on June 23, 1926, in defense of the idea of a black American literary style, voice, and subject matter.

Anthologies of Hughes's work include *The Langston Hughes Reader* (1958), and *Five Plays* (1963), edited by Walter Smalley. Hughes himself edited many volumes of work by black American writers, including *The Poetry of the Negro, 1746-1949* (1949), with Arna Bontemps; *The Book of Negro Folklore* (1959), also with Bontemps; *New Negro Poets: U.S.A.* (1964); *The Book of Negro Humor* (1966); and *The Best Short Stories by Negro Writers: An Anthology from 1899 to the Present* (1967).

He also wrote two volumes of autobiography, *The Big Sea: An Autobiography* (1940) and *I Wonder as I Wander: An Autobiographical Journey* (1956). A planned third volume was not completed.

ACHIEVEMENTS

All the works of Langston Hughes illustrate the depth of his commitment to a celebration of black American life in all its forms and make immediately evident the reason why he has been proclaimed the poet laureate of black America. As a young poet, he won prizes in contests sponsored by *The Crisis* and *Opportunity*, and his first two volumes of poetry, *The Weary Blues* and *Fine Clothes to the Jew*, won critical acclaim. He won the Witter Brynner Prize for best poetry by an undergraduate (1926), a Harmon Gold Award (1930) for his novel *Not Without Laughter*, a Guggenheim Fellowship (1935), a National Institute of Arts and Letters Award (1946), an Anisfeld-Wolfe Book Award (1954) for *Simple Takes a Wife*, and the Spingarn Medal from the National Association for the Advancement of Colored People (NAACP) in 1960. Hughes's receipt of a Rosenwald Fund Fellowship in 1941 enabled him to make his first cross-country reading tour. He became a member of the American Academy of Arts and Letters in 1961.

His stature as a humorist grew from his creation of Jesse B. Semple, also known as Simple, a Harlem barstool philosopher in the tradition of American folk humor ranging from Davy Crockett to Mr. Dooley. Hughes wrote about Simple in columns published in the *Chicago Defender*, begun in the 1940's and continuing into the 1960's. His Simple columns also appeared in the *New York Post* between 1962 and 1965. Publication of his five books of Simple sketches increased the readership of that sage of Harlem with his views on life in white America.

Although Hughes never had any one big seller, his efforts in so many fields of literary endeavor earned for him the admiration and respect of readers in all walks of life. Certainly, too, Hughes is a major poetic figure of his time and perhaps the best black American poet.

BIOGRAPHY

James Mercer Langston Hughes (the first two names were soon dropped) was born in Joplin, Missouri, on February 1, 1902. His parents, James Nathaniel Hughes and Carrie Mercer Langston Hughes, separated when Hughes was young; by the time he was twelve, he had lived in several cities: Buffalo, N.Y.; Cleveland; Lawrence and Topeka, Kansas; Colorado Springs, and Mexico City (where his father lived). Until 1914, however, Hughes lived mainly with his maternal grandmother in Lawrence.

Hughes began writing poetry during his grammar school days in Lincoln, Illinois. While attending Cleveland's Central High School (1916-1920), Hughes wrote his first short story, "Mary Winosky," and published poems in the school's literary publications. The first national publication of his work came in 1921, when *The Crisis* published "The Negro Speaks of Rivers." The poem had been written while Hughes was taking a train on his way to see his father in Mexico City, a visit that the young man dreaded making. His hatred for his father, fueled by his father's contempt for poor people who could not make anything of themselves, actually led to Hughes's being hospitalized briefly in 1919.

Hughes's father did, however, send his son to Columbia University in 1921. Although Hughes did not stay at Columbia, his experiences in Harlem laid the groundwork for his later love affair with the city within a city. Equally important to Hughes's later work was the time he spent at sea and abroad during this period of his life. His exposure to American blues and jazz players in Paris nightclubs and his experiences in Europe, and especially in Africa, although brief, provided a rich source of material that he used over the next decades in his writing.

The years between 1919 and 1929 have been variously referred to as the Harlem Renaissance, the New Negro movement, and the Harlem Awakening. They were years of rich productivity within the black artistic community, and Hughes was an important element in that renaissance. While working as a busboy in the Wardman Park Hotel in Washington, D.C., in 1925, Hughes showed some of his poems—"Jazzonia," "Negro Dancers," and "The Weary Blues"—to Vachel Lindsay, who read them during one of his performances that same evening. The next day, Hughes was presented to the local press as "the busboy poet." With that introduction, and with the aid of people such as writer Carl Van Vechten and Walter White (of the NAACP), Hughes's popularity began to grow. He published *The Weary Blues* in 1926 and entered Lincoln University in Pennsylvania, where he completed his college education. The 1920's also saw the publication of his second volume of poems, *Fine Clothes to the Jew*, and the completion of his first novel, *Not Without Laughter*.

During much of the early 1930's, Hughes traveled abroad. He went to Cuba and Haiti during 1931-1932 and joined a group of young writers and students from Harlem on a film-making trip to Russia in 1932-1933. Publishing articles in Russian journals enabled him to extend his own travels in the Far East; he also began to write short stories during that time. By 1934, he had written the fourteen stories that he included in *The Ways of White Folks*.

During the mid-1930's, several of Hughes's plays were produced: *Mulatto* and *Little Ham* were among them. In the course of having these plays performed, Hughes started the Harlem Suitcase Theatre (1938), the New Negro Theatre in Los Angeles (1939), and the Skyloft Players of Chicago (1941).

After the publication of his first autobiographical volume, *The Big Sea*, Hughes spent time in Chicago with the group he had founded there. When America entered World War II, Hughes produced material for the war effort, ranging from "Defense Bond Blues" to articles on black American participation in the war. In addition, during the 1940's, he began work on his translations of the poetry of Guillén, wrote essays for such diverse magazines as the *Saturday Review of Literature* and *Negro Digest*, wrote the lyrics for *Street Scene*, and published volumes of poetry, including *Shakespeare in Harlem*, *Fields of Wonder*, and *One Way Ticket*.

Also in the 1940's, Hughes "discovered" Jesse B. Semple. Drawing inspiration from a conversation he had in a bar with a worker from a New Jersey war plant—during which the man complained to his nagging girlfriend, "You know white folks don't tell colored folks what cranks crank"—Hughes developed the framework for his Simple stories. He combined his own authorial voice, the voice of Simple's learned interrogator (eventually named Boyd), and the voice of Simple himself to weave a mixture of folk humor that has direct ties back to the "old southwest" humor of Mark Twain and his contemporaries.

The next decades saw continued production of poetry and other writing by Hughes. He wrote his pictorial histories and his "first books" for children. He continued his public readings, often accompanied by piano or jazz orchestra—a prototype of the Beat poets. His second volume of autobiography, *I Wonder as I Wander*, was published in 1956, and *The Langston Hughes Reader*, an extensive collection of his work in several genres, appeared two years later. The last two volumes of new poetry, *Ask Your Mama* and *The Panther and the Lash*, continued his experimentation with incorporating jazz and folk elements in his poetry.

Hughes spent the last years of his life living and working in Harlem. He encouraged younger black writers, publishing several stories by newcomers in his *The Best Short Stories by Negro Writers*, as well as including works by established older writers such as Ralph Ellison and Richard Wright. Hughes died on May 22, 1967, in Harlem, the city that so inspired and informed his best work. No one caught the magic that Harlem represented during his lifetime in quite the way that Hughes did.

ANALYSIS

Langston Hughes often referred to three poets as his major influences: Paul Laurence Dunbar, Carl Sandburg, and Walt Whitman. If one were to assay what qualities of Hughes's poetry show the influence of which poet, one might say that Hughes got his love of the folk and his lyric simplicity from Dunbar, his attraction to the power of the people—especially urban dwellers— and his straightforward descriptive power from Sandburg, and his fascination with sensual people—people of the body rather than the mind—and his clear sense of rhythm from Whitman. No one would draw such a clear delineation, but the elements described are essential elements of Hughes's poetry. His work explores the humor and the pathos, the exhilaration and the despair, of black American life in ways that are sometimes conventional and sometimes unique. He explored the blues as a poetic form, and he peopled his poems with Harlem dancers, as well as with a black mother trying to explain her life to her son. He worked with images of dreams and of "dreams deferred"; he looked at life in the middle of America's busiest black city and at the life of the sea and of exploration and discovery. Always, too, Hughes examined the paradox of being black in mostly white America, of being not quite free in the land of freedom.

The poetry of Hughes is charged with life and love, even when it cries out against the injustice of the world. He was a poet who loved life and loved his heritage. More than any other black American writer, he captured the essence of the complexity of a life that mixes laughter and tears, joy and frustration, and still manages to sing and dance with the spirit of humanity.

THE WEARY BLUES

Hughes's first collection of poetry, *The Weary Blues*, contains samples of many of the poetic styles and themes of his poetry in general. The collection begins with a celebration of blackness ("Proem") and ends with an affirmation of the black American's growing sense of purpose and equality "Epilogue" ("I, Too, Sing America"). In between, there are poems that sing of Harlem cabaret life and poems that sing the blues. Some of the nonblues poems also sing of a troubled life, as well as an occasional burst of joy. Here, too, are the sea poems drawn from Hughes's traveling experiences. All in all, the sparkle of a love of life in these poems was that which caught the attention of many early reviewers.

The titles of some of the poems about cabaret life suggest their subject: "Jazzonia,"

"Negro Dancers," "The Cat and the Saxophone (2 A.M.)," and "Harlem Night Club." "The Cat and the Saxophone (2 A.M.)" is especially intriguing because it intersperses a conversation between two "jive" lovers with the first chorus of "Everybody Loves My Baby," producing the effect of a jazz chorus within the song's rhythmic framework.

Part of the controversy that flared in the black community during the Harlem Renaissance involved whether an artist should present the "low-life" elements or the more conventional middle-class elements in black American life. Hughes definitely leaned toward the former as the richer, more exciting to portray in his poetry. Because the blues tradition is more tied to the common folk than to the middle class, Hughes's interest in the possibilities of using the blues style in his poetry is not surprising. He took the standard three-line blues stanza and made it a six-line stanza to develop a more familiar poetic form; the repetition common in the first and second lines in the blues becomes a repetition of the first/second and third/fourth lines in Hughes's poems. As in the traditional blues, Hughes varies the wording in the repeated lines—adding, deleting, or changing words. For example, here is a stanza from "Blues Fantasy":

> My man's done left me,
> Chile, he's gone away.
> My good man's left me,
> Babe, he's gone away.
> Now the cryin' blues
> Haunts me night and day.

Often exclamation points are added to suggest more nearly the effect of the sung blues.

There are not as many blues poems in this first collection as there are in later ones such as *Fine Clothes to the Jew* and *Shakespeare in Harlem*. (The latter contains a marvelous seven-poem effort titled "Seven Moments of Love," which Hughes subtitled "An Un-Sonnet Sequence in Blues.") The title poem of his first collection, "The Weary Blues," is an interesting variation because it has a frame for the blues that sets up the song sung by a blues artist. The poet recalls the performance of a blues singer/pianist "on Lenox Avenue the other night" and describes the man's playing and singing. Later, the singer goes home to bed, "while the Weary Blues echoed through his head." Over the years, Hughes wrote a substantial number of blues poems and poems dealing with jazz, reflecting clearly his love for the music that is at the heart of the black American experience.

Some of the poems in *The Weary Blues* are simple lyrics. They are tinged with sadness ("A Black Pierrot") and with traditional poetic declarations of the beauty of a loved one ("Ardella"). The sea poems are also, by and large, more traditional than experimental. Again, their titles reflect their subject matter: "Water-Front Streets," "Port Town," "Sea Calm," "Caribbean Sunset," and "Seascape."

A few of these early poems reflect the gentle but insistent protest that runs through

Hughes's poems; they question the treatment of black Americans and search for a connection with the motherland, Africa. The last section of the book is titled "Our Land," and the first poem in the section, "Our Land: Poem for a Decorative Panel," explores the idea that the black American should live in a land of warmth and joy instead of in a land where "life is cold" and "birds are grey." Other poems in the section include "Lament for Dark Peoples," "Disillusion," and "Danse Africaine." Perhaps the most poignant poem in the book is also in this last section: "Mother to Son." The poem is a monologue in dialect in which a mother encourages her son to continue the struggle she has carried on, which she likens to climbing a rough, twisting staircase: "Life for me ain't been no crystal stair./ It's had tacks in it . . . And places with no carpet on the floor—/ Bare." The collection's final poem, "Epilogue" ("I, Too, Sing America"), raises the hope that some day equality will truly be reached in America for the "darker brother" who is forced "to eat in the kitchen/ When company comes." Taken together, the poems of *The Weary Blues* make an extraordinary first volume of poetry and reveal the range of Hughes's style and subject matter.

The next two principal volumes of poetry, *Fine Clothes to the Jew* and *The Dream Keeper, and Other Poems*, present more of Hughes's blues poems (the latter volume is primarily in that genre) and more poems centering on Harlem's night life. The final two volumes, *Ask Your Mama* and *The Panther and the Lash*, continue the experiment of combining musical elements with poetry and offer some of Hughes's strongest protest poetry.

ASK YOUR MAMA

Ask Your Mama is dedicated to "Louis Armstrong—the greatest horn blower of them all." In an introductory note, Hughes explains that "the traditional folk melody of the 'Hesitation Blues' is the leitmotif for this poem." The collection was designed to be read or sung with jazz accompaniment, "with room for spontaneous jazz improvisation, particularly between verses, when the voice pauses." Hughes includes suggestions for music to accompany the poetry. Sometimes the instructions are open ("delicate lieder on piano"), and sometimes they are more direct ("suddenly the drums roll like thunder as the music ends sonorously"). There are also suggestions for specific songs to be used, including "Dixie" ("impishly"), "When the Saints Go Marchin' In," and "The Battle Hymn of the Republic." As a final aid, Hughes includes at the end of his collection "Liner Notes" for, as he says, "the Poetically Unhep."

Throughout, the poems in *Ask Your Mama* run the current of protest against "the shadow" of racism that falls over the lives of Earth's darker peoples. Shadows frequently occur as images and symbols, suggesting the fear and the sense of vague existence created by living in oppression. "Show Fare, Please" summarizes the essence of the poet's feeling of being left out because he does not have "show fare," but it also suggests that "the show" may be all illusion anyway. Not all the poems are so stark; the humor of Hughes's earlier work is still very much in evidence. In "Is It True," for example, Hughes notes that "everybody thinks that Negroes have the *most* fun, but, of course, secretly hopes they do not—although curious to find out if they do."

THE PANTHER AND THE LASH

The Panther and the Lash, the final collection of Hughes's new poetry, published the year he died, also contains some of his most direct protest poetry, although he never gives vent to the anger that permeated the work of his younger contemporaries. The collection is dedicated "To Rosa Parks of Montgomery who started it all . . ." in 1955 by refusing to move to the back of a bus. The panther of the title refers to a "Black Panther" who "in his boldness/ Wears no disguise,/ Motivated by the truest/ Of the oldest/ Lies"; the lash refers to the white backlash of the times (in "The Backlash Blues").

The book has seven sections, each dealing with a particular part of the subject. "Words on Fire" has poems on the coming of the Third World revolution, while "American Heartbreak" deals with the consequences of "the great mistake/ That Jamestown made/ Long ago"; that is, slavery. The final section, "Daybreak in Alabama," does, however, offer hope. In spite of past and existing conditions, the poet hopes for a time when he can compose a song about "daybreak in Alabama" that will touch everybody "with kind fingers."

OTHER MAJOR WORKS

LONG FICTION: *Not Without Laughter*, 1930; *Tambourines to Glory*, 1958.

SHORT FICTION: *The Ways of White Folks*, 1934; *Simple Speaks His Mind*, 1950; *Laughing to Keep from Crying*, 1952; *Simple Takes a Wife*, 1953; *Simple Stakes a Claim*, 1957; *The Best of Simple*, 1961; *Something in Common, and Other Stories*, 1963; *Simple's Uncle Sam*, 1965; *The Return of Simple*, 1994; *Short Stories*, 1996.

PLAYS: *Little Ham*, pr. 1935; *Mulatto*, pb. 1935; *Troubled Island*, pr. 1935 (opera libretto); *Don't You Want to Be Free?*, pb. 1938; *Freedom's Plow*, pb. 1943; *Street Scene*, pr., pb. 1947 (lyrics; music by Kurt Weill and Elmer Rice); *Simply Heavenly*, pr. 1957 (opera libretto); *Black Nativity*, pr. 1961; *Five Plays*, 1963 (Walter Smalley, editor); *Tambourines to Glory*, pr., pb. 1963; *Jerico-Jim Crow*, pr. 1964; *The Prodigal Son*, pr. 1965.

SCREENPLAY: *Way Down South*, 1939 (with Clarence Muse).

NONFICTION: *The Big Sea: An Autobiography*, 1940; *The Sweet Flypaper of Life*, 1955 (photographs by Roy De Carava); *A Pictorial History of the Negro in America*, 1956 (with Milton Meltzer); *I Wonder as I Wander: An Autobiographical Journey*, 1956; *Fight for Freedom: The Story of the NAACP*, 1962; *Black Magic: A Pictorial History of the Negro in American Entertainment*, 1967 (with Meltzer); *Black Misery*, 1969 (illustrated by Arouni); *Arna Bontemps—Langston Hughes Letters: 1925-1967*, 1980; *Remember Me to Harlem: The Letters of Langston Hughes and Carl Van Vechten, 1925-1964*, 2001 (Emily Bernard, editor).

TRANSLATIONS: *Masters of the Dew*, 1947 (of Jacques Roumain; with Mercer Cook); *Cuba Libre*, 1948 (of Nicolás Guillén; with Ben Carruthers); *Gypsy Ballads*, 1951 (of Federico García Lorca); *Selected Poems of Gabriela Mistral*, 1957.

CHILDREN'S LITERATURE: *Popo and Fijina: Children of Haiti*, 1932 (story; with Arna Bontemps); *The First Book of Negroes*, 1952; *Famous American Negroes*, 1954; *The First Book of Rhythms*, 1954; *Famous Negro Music Makers*, 1955; *The First Book of Jazz*, 1955; *The First Book of the West Indies*, 1955; *Famous Negro Heroes of America*, 1958; *The First Book of Africa*, 1960.

EDITED TEXTS: *The Poetry of the Negro, 1746-1949*, 1949 (with Bontemps); *The Book of Negro Folklore*, 1959 (with Bontemps); *New Negro Poets: U.S.A.*, 1964; *The Book of Negro Humor*, 1966; *The Best Short Stories by Negro Writers: An Anthology from 1899 to the Present*, 1967.

MISCELLANEOUS: *The Langston Hughes Reader*, 1958; *The Collected Works of Langston Hughes*, 2001-2004 (16 volumes).

BIBLIOGRAPHY
Berry, Faith. *Langston Hughes: Before and Beyond Harlem*. New York: Wings Books, 1995. The first biography based on primary sources and interviews, which sets out to re-create the historical context in which Hughes lived and worked. Berry quotes an unusual number of poems in their entirety and includes extensive discussions of his poetry throughout the biography.
Dace, Letitia, and M. Thomas Inge, eds. *Langston Hughes: The Contemporary Reviews*. New York: Cambridge University Press, 2009. Collects critical reviews of Hughes's work during the time the works were written and published.
Haskins, James. *Always Movin' On: The Life of Langston Hughes*. Trenton, N.J.: Africa World Press, 1993. A good biography of Hughes.
Leach, Laurie F. *Langston Hughes: A Biography*. Westport, Conn.: Greenwood Press, 2004. An overview of Hughes's life and development as a playwright, poet, and journalist.
Ostrom, Hans A. *A Langston Hughes Encyclopedia*. Westport, Conn.: Greenwood Press, 2002. A comprehensive reference work that looks at his life and his works, including his poetry.
Rager, Cheryl R., and John Edgar Tidwell, eds. *Montage of a Dream: The Art and Life of Langston Hughes*. Columbia: University of Missouri Press, 2007. Most of the essays here are previously unpublished and all offer interesting new ways of looking at Hughes's writing. Included in the discussion are many of his lesser known works, including his autobiographies and translations.
Rampersad, Arnold. *The Life of Langston Hughes*. 2 vols. 2d ed. New York: Oxford University Press, 2002. This major critical biography illustrates not only the triumphs but also the struggles of the man and the writer. The importance of Hughes in

the Harlem Renaissance and his symbolic significance in the developing artistic and imaginative consciousness of African American writers come alive in concrete examples in volume 1, *I, Too, Sing America*, and volume 2, *I Dream a World*. These titles, drawn from Hughes's poetry, reveal the themes illustrating the writer's life and the points in his own characterization of his struggle.

Schwarz, A. B. Christa. *Gay Voices of the Harlem Renaissance*. Bloomington: Indiana University Press, 2003. Schwarz examines the work of four leading writers from the Harlem Renaissance—Countée Cullen, Langston Hughes, Claude McKay, and Richard Bruce Nugent—and their sexually nonconformist or gay literary voices.

Wallace, Maurice O. *Langston Hughes: The Harlem Renaissance*. New York: Marshall Cavendish Benchmark, 2008. This biography of Hughes covers his life, the Harlem of his time, his legacy, and his major works. Contains a chapter on his poetry.

Edward E. Waldron

JAMES WELDON JOHNSON

Born: Jacksonville, Florida; June 17, 1871
Died: Wiscasset, Maine; June 26, 1938

OTHER LITERARY FORMS

James Weldon Johnson was known mainly for his poetry, but he also wrote a novel, *The Autobiography of an Ex-Coloured Man* (1912), and an autobiography, *Along This Way: The Autobiography of James Weldon Johnson* (1933), as well as numerous essays.

ACHIEVEMENTS

James Weldon Johnson was the first African American in his county—and probably all of Florida—to pass the bar through an open state court examination since Reconstruction. Johnson was Fisk University's first Adam K. Spence Professor of Creative Writing (1932-1938) and a visiting professor at New York University (1934-1937). He earned honorary degrees from Atlanta University, Talladega College, and Howard University. He received the Spingarn Medal for achievement from the National Association for the Advancement of Colored People (NAACP). He also earned the W. E. B. Du Bois Literature Prize, the Harmon Gold Award for *God's Trombones* (1927), and a Julius Rosenwald Fellowship (1929). While he was principal at the Edwin M. Stanton School in Jacksonville, he began offering high school courses; this curriculum enabled African Americans to graduate from high school in Jacksonville for the first time.

Johnson's writings brought increased respect to him and to African Americans everywhere. His *Lift Every Voice and Sing*—set to music by John Rosamond Johnson— became the theme song of the NAACP. In 1990, the *Congressional Record* entered "Lift Every Voice and Sing" as the official African American national hymn. After

James Weldon Johnson
(Library of Congress)

Johnson's death, both his "Lift Every Voice and Sing" and his "The Creation" became picture books for children in 1993 and 1994, respectively. Yale University Library opened its James Weldon Johnson Memorial Collection in 1950, and the U.S. Postal Service honored Johnson with a twenty-two-cent stamp in 1988.

BIOGRAPHY

James William Johnson (who became James Weldon Johnson in 1913) and John Rosamond Johnson were the two surviving children of headwaiter and minister James Johnson and Helen Louise Dillet Johnson. Johnson's mother was a musician and was the first African American female to teach in a Florida public grammar school, the Edwin M. Stanton School, where she taught her son. Because there was no local high school for African Americans, the young Johnson enrolled in Atlanta University's preparatory school in 1887. By 1894, he had a B.A. from Atlanta University, had toured with a male quartet, was the principal at Stanton School, and was studying law. After passing the bar, he practiced law part-time (1898-1901).

At Stanton, Johnson developed a set of courses that allowed the school's African American students to earn a high school education. In 1895, he started *The Daily American*, Jacksonville's—and possibly the United States'—first daily African American newspaper. His "Lift Every Voice and Sing," written in 1900, became nationally known.

Johnson moved to New York after a fire destroyed the Stanton School in 1901. With his brother, John Rosamond Johnson, and Robert Cole, a performer, producer, and composer, Johnson wrote more than two hundred songs. He studied at Columbia (1903-1906), earned an M.A. from Atlanta University, and completed a European theatrical tour. The two brothers campaigned for Theodore Roosevelt and wrote his campaign song: "You're All Right, Teddy." James Weldon Johnson resigned from his job as internal revenue collector to accept U.S. president Roosevelt's appointment as Venezuelan consul (1907). While he was the Nicaraguan consul (1909-1912), Johnson married Grace Nail (1910) and wrote his only novel, *The Autobiography of an Ex-Coloured Man*.

Johnson adopted a new middle name in 1913. He worked as an editorial writer for the African American periodical *New York Age* (1914-1927) and as a member of the staff of the NAACP (1916-1920). After acting as NAACP secretary (1918-1920), he became the organization's first nonwhite general secretary (1920-1930).

Johnson urged using the press to address inequalities and celebrate achievements. He published his first verse collection, *Fifty Years, and Other Poems*, in 1917. During the Harlem Renaissance of the 1920's, Johnson edited *The Book of American Negro Poetry* (1922), *The Book of American Negro Spirituals* (1925), and *The Second Book of American Negro Spirituals* (1926). The latter two works were reprinted together in *The Books of American Negro Spirituals* (1926), which included his brother's piano arrangements. Johnson's critical introductions offer insights into these often-ignored genres. These works publicized the literary contributions of African Americans in ways other than dialect writings and minstrel shows, enhanced the Harlem Renaissance, and performed a service for all.

In 1927, he published *God's Trombones*, a poetry collection based on a trip to Georgia while he was in college. That same year, Johnson lectured at the University of North Carolina—an opportunity not often granted to an African American. Later, he lectured at New York University, Northwestern University, Yale University, Oberlin College, and Swarthmore College.

In *Black Manhattan* (1930), Johnson detailed three centuries of African American life and literature, culminating in the Harlem Renaissance. In 1930, he obtained a part-time position in the creative writing department at Fisk University. In the following years, he published an autobiography, *Along This Way*, and his last verse collection, *Saint Peter Relates an Incident*. His book-length essay *Negro Americans, What Now?* (1934) is an argument favoring racial integration.

In 1938, Johnson and his wife, Grace, were in a car-train accident. His wife survived, but Johnson died. His funeral was at Salem Methodist Church, Harlem, and he was buried in Brooklyn's Greenwood Cemetery with *God's Trombones* in his hands.

ANALYSIS

James Weldon Johnson had many roles—lawyer, activist, politician, diplomat, journalist, songwriter, and anthologist—but he is perhaps best remembered for his writings, including his inspirational poetry. The lasting popularity and public interest in Johnson's writings is demonstrated by the numerous reprints of his works.

LIFT EVERY VOICE AND SING

Johnson wrote *Lift Every Voice and Sing* to celebrate Abraham Lincoln's birthday in 1900; his brother John Rosamond Johnson set the poem to music. The rhyme scheme is *aabccdeee*. The popular composition is the voice of free African Americans expressing their hopes for the future of the United States. It served as the NAACP's theme song and as the African American national hymn. Johnson's elation each time he heard it is noted in *Complete Poems*.

FIFTY YEARS, AND OTHER POEMS

Johnson's first verse collection, *Fifty Years, and Other Poems*, compiled twenty years of writing. Johnson wrote the poem "Fifty Years" in Nicaragua in commemoration of the fiftieth anniversary of the Emancipation Proclamation. The twenty-four-stanza poem, with a rhyme scheme of *abab*, originally was forty-one stanzas. *The New York Times* published the poem on the fiftieth anniversary (1912) of the Emancipation Proclamation.

Many of the poems are about racial discrimination. "Color Sergeant" descrbies a man with "color black" who gives his life in warfare. Although "despised of men" for his color, the sergeant remains true "to his duty." The poem reminds readers of the military contributions of African Americans. The five-stanza poem uses the rhyme scheme of *abcb*. The unrhymed "Brothers" is a graphic description of a mob's burning an African American at the stake. The final words of the victim are "'Brothers in spirit, brothers in deed are we.'" The poem ends with the mob pondering what the victim meant by these words.

The last poems in the volume employ dialect, suggestive of the writings of Johnson's friend Paul Laurence Dunbar. This writing is offensive to some readers and critics but pleasing to others. Two of the poems employing dialect—"Nobody's Lookin' but de Owl and de Moon: A Negro Serenade" and "You's Sweet to Yo' Mammy Jes de Same: Lullaby"—were lyrics taken from the songs written in New York by the Johnson brothers and Cole.

GOD'S TROMBONES

Johnson wrote the poetic sermons in *God's Trombones* after having visited many churches. "The Creation," written in 1920, was the first of the sermons; the remaining six were completed by 1926. Johnson conveys rhythm without strict rhyme schemes. He avoids the misspellings and mispronunciations that others often use to convey African American speech. Instead, he captures the beauty and the dignity of the sermons he had heard in order to convey the religious spirit of African Americans. He uses standard English and some dialect for effect; for example, Johnson compares God making a person from dust to a mammy bending over her baby.

Johnson duplicates some of the oratorical techniques that an accomplished speaker might use to involve his congregation. In "The Creation," Johnson uses repetition, using the phrase "That's good!" again and again. He employs hyperbole; for example, Johnson says valleys were produced by God's footsteps. The poet uses alliteration: God "spat out the seven seas." Johnson's descriptions enable the reader to visualize scenes: lightning flashing when God bats his eyes, lakes cuddling in the hollows, and a rainbow curling around God's shoulders.

SAINT PETER RELATES AN INCIDENT

The title of the collection *Saint Peter Relates an Incident* is taken from the poem "Saint Peter Relates an Incident of the Resurrection Day," which describes the opening of the Tomb of the Unknown Soldier on Judgment Day. A crowd waits to see the unknown military hero who emerges; the watchers are astonished when they see that the occupant is an African American. Johnson wrote the poem in response to the unfair treatment that mothers of deceased black soldiers received on a nationally sponsored trip to Europe. As in his other works, he advocates empowerment, pride, self-assertion, communication, and cooperation among all people. The rhyme scheme of the lines in part 1 of the title poem is *aabb*. Part 4 has fourteen stanzas, and each verse has four lines with a rhyme scheme of *aabb*. No dialect is apparent. The stanzas in part 2, however, are irregular: One stanza has three lines, one has five lines, and the others have four lines. Parts 5 and 6 have verses with lines of no regular rhyme pattern and no set number of lines. This lack of structure is cited as a weakness by some critics. Interestingly, the soldier sings some lines from the spiritual "Deep River" as he climbs toward heaven. The poem concludes with a description of the emotion from heaven in response to the revelation of the identity of the unknown soldier; the emotion is a mixture of laughter and tears.

Johnson advanced pride in African Americans in his poems, including "O Black and Unknown Bards." Johnson uses misspellings in some of the other poems in the collection, and some of these poems draw on songs and folklore, such as "Brer Rabbit, You's de Cutes' of 'Em All" and "Sence You Went Away."

COMPLETE POEMS

Complete Poems includes an introduction, a chronology, and the collections *God's Trombones, Fifty Years, and Other Poems*, and *Saint Peter Relates an Incident*. In the third part, "College Years, and Other Poems," editor Sondra Kathryn Wilson includes some poems that had never before appeared in print. Most of the poems in this last section were written by Johnson while he was at Atlanta University, but some date from after the turn of the twentieth century. Some of Johnson's poems from his college years imitate those of other poets. "Moods," for example, is suggestive of "I Love You" by Ella Wheeler Wilcox. His "Christmas Carol" reminds the reader of other familiar poems about the holiday season. Johnson's "Ode to Florida" is similar to "Ode on a Grecian Urn" by John Keats.

OTHER MAJOR WORKS

LONG FICTION: *The Autobiography of an Ex-Coloured Man*, 1912.

NONFICTION: *The Changing Status of Negro Labor*, 1918; *The Washington Riots: An N.A.A.C.P. Investigation*, 1919; *Black Manhattan*, 1930; *Along This Way: The Autobiography of James Weldon Johnson*, 1933; *Negro Americans, What Now?*, 1934; *The Selected Writings of James Weldon Johnson*, 1995 (2 volumes; Sondra Kathryn Wilson, editor); *James Weldon Johnson: Writings*, 2004.

TRANSLATION: *The English Libretto of "Goyescas,"* 1915.

CHILDREN'S LITERATURE: *Lift Every Voice and Sing*, 1970 (illustrated by Mozelle Thompson); *Lift Every Voice and Sing*, 1993 (illustrated by Elizabeth Catlett); *The Creation*, 1994 (illustrated by James Ransome).

EDITED TEXTS: *The Book of American Negro Poetry*, 1922; *The Book of American Negro Spirituals*, 1925; *The Second Book of American Negro Spirituals*, 1926.

BIBLIOGRAPHY

Fleming, Robert E. "The Composition of James Weldon Johnson's 'Fifty Years.'" In *Critical Essays on James Weldon Johnson*, edited by Kenneth M. Price and Lawrence J. Oliver. New York: Prentice Hall International, 1997. Examines "Fifty Years" and how it was written by Johnson.

_____. *James Weldon Johnson*. Boston: Twayne, 1987. A basic biography of Johnson with critical analysis of his poetry and other works.

Gates, Henry Lewis, and Gene Andrew Jarrett, eds. *The New Negro: Readings on Race, Representation, and African American Culture, 1892-1938*. Princeton, N.J.: Princeton University Press, 2007. Contains several essays by Johnson about the role of African Americans as well as numerous essays about African American poetry and poets that shed light on the era in which Johnson wrote.

Gebbhard, Caroline. "Inventing a 'Negro Literature': Race, Dialect, and Gender in the Early Work of Paul Laurence Dunbar, James Weldon Johnson, and Alice Dunbar-

Nelson." In *African American Poets: 1700's-1940's*, edited by Harold Bloom. New York: Bloom's Literary Criticism/Chelsea House, 2009. Examines what these early African American writers felt that literature should be, including questions about dialect.

Johnson, James Weldon. *The Essential Writings of James Weldon Johnson*. Edited by Rudolph P. Byrd. New York: Modern Library, 2008. Contains an informative introduction by Byrd and a profile by the poet Michael S. Harper. Contains selections from his poetry, fiction, and nonfiction.

Napierkowski, Marie Rose, and Mary K. Ruby, eds. *Poetry for Students*. Detroit: Gale, 1998. Contains an analysis of "The Creation."

Wintz, Cary R., ed. *Harlem Speaks: A Living History of the Harlem Renaissance*. Naperville, Ill.: Sourcebooks, 2007. This history of the Harlem Renaissance contains a chapter on Johnson.

Anita Price Davis

BOB KAUFMAN

Born: New Orleans, Louisiana; April 18, 1925
Died: San Francisco, California; January 12,
1986

PRINCIPAL POETRY
Solitudes Crowded with Loneliness, 1965
Golden Sardine, 1967
The Ancient Rain: Poems, 1956-1978, 1981
Cranial Guitar: Selected Poems, 1996

OTHER LITERARY FORMS

Bob Kaufman is known primarily for his poetry, but he was a contributing editor for *Beatitude*, a mimeographed literary magazine first published in San Francisco in 1959. Kaufman's poetry, which began as a form of oral literature, crosses over into theater because he was a San Francisco poet known for his spontaneous performances on the streets of the city and at the Co-existence Bagel Shop.

ACHIEVEMENTS

Bob Kaufman's "Bagel Shop Jazz" was nominated for the Guinness Prize for Poetry in 1961 and appeared in Volume 4 of *The Guinness Book of Poetry, 1959-1960* (1961). In 1979, Kaufman received a fellowship from the National Endowment for the Arts. His *Cranial Guitar* won a PEN Center USA West Poetry Award in 1997.

Because Kaufman applied the improvisational jazz style of saxophonist and composer Charlie Parker to poetry, Kaufman became known as the Original Bebop Man. In addition, because Kaufman followed the examples of Surrealism and Dadaism, creating extraordinarily imagistic combinations of words that eluded explication, some critics refer to Kaufman as the Black American Rimbaud. Although Kaufman made little effort to collect his writings, his poems still appear in major anthologies of African American and Beat generation writing. Both National Public Radio and the Public Broadcasting Service have produced programs on Kaufman.

BIOGRAPHY

Separating the legend of Robert Garnell Kaufman from the verifiable details of his life is a difficult task. Kaufman himself contributed to the development of his legend, and various biographical sources have recorded unverifiable information that has been reproduced in other sources.

The legend indicates that Kaufman's father was an orthodox Jew of German ancestry and his mother was a Catholic from Martinique who had some acquaintance with voodoo. Perhaps Kaufman's grandfather was partly Jewish, but Kaufman's siblings report that the New Orleans family was middle class and Catholic. His father, Joseph Kaufman, was a Pullman porter who worked on trains running between New Orleans and Chicago; his mother, Lillian, was a schoolteacher who made her book collection and piano important parts of the family home. The couple had thirteen children.

The legend suggests that Kaufman joined the United States Merchant Marine at age thirteen, traveled around the world numerous times, and developed his interest in literature when a shipmate influenced him and loaned him books. However, Kaufman probably did not enter the merchant marine until he was eighteen, and thereafter, he became an active member of the National Maritime Union. This union of merchant sailors faced federal review because it reputedly had ties to communist organizations, and Kaufman was one of two thousand sailors driven from the merchant marine because of his political views.

Kaufman moved to New York, where he studied for a time at the New School of Social Research and lived on the lower East Side. It was in New York that he met Allen Ginsberg and William Burroughs. Kaufman returned to San Francisco in 1958. Later that year, he married Eileen Singe.

Kaufman emerged as a literary artist in San Francisco in the late 1950's. *Abomunist Manifesto* was published as a broadside in 1959 by City Lights, and Kaufman's witty and innovative poem made him famous in the North Beach section of San Francisco. *Life* magazine (November 30, 1959) published Paul O'Neil's scathing report on the Beat generation, and a posed photo mocking Beatniks in their "pad" included Kaufman's broadside as an example of standard Beatnik reading. City Lights published two additional broadsides by Kaufman, *Does the Secret Mind Whisper?* and *Second April.* In 1960, Kenneth Tynan's *We Dissent*, a ninety-minute British television program included Kaufman among the featured Beatnik writers. Kaufman also was shown in Ron Rice's underground film *The Flower Thief* (1960), which dealt with the Beat generation in North Beach. As Kaufman became more flamboyant as a street poet in San Francisco, he came into conflict with the police and was often arrested and sometimes beaten. To be free of such treatment, he briefly went to New York, where he read poetry in Greenwich Village. He returned to San Francisco in 1963.

In 1965, New Directions published *Solitudes Crowded with Loneliness*, which included the broadsides and a selection of other poems. In 1967, City Lights published *Golden Sardine*, and in 1981, New Directions published *The Ancient Rain.*

The legend says that Kaufman took a vow of silence when John F. Kennedy was assassinated and maintained it until after the war in Vietnam ended. At a local gathering place, Kaufman is reported to have ended his silence in 1975 by reciting from T. S. Eliot's *Murder in the Cathedral* (pr., pb. 1935) and performing his own composition, "All Those Ships That Never Sailed."

Weakened by drug dependency and emphysema, Kaufman died in San Francisco in 1986. In tribute, a procession of artists, family members, and friends followed a New Orleans jazz band through the North Beach section of San Francisco to view the sites that Kaufman frequented during his career in poetry.

Through the collaboration of Eileen Kaufman (Kaufman's wife), Gerald Nicosia, and David Henderson, *Cranial Guitar*, a selection of poems by Kaufman, was published in 1996. Critical attention to Kaufman grew after its publication, and slowly critics began recognizing that categories such as Beat poet, jazz poet, and Surrealist poet only partially describe Kaufman.

ANALYSIS

As presented in Bob Kaufman's *Solitudes Crowded with Loneliness*, "Abomunist Manifesto" is a sequence of eleven parts. The title plays on *Manifest der Kommunistischen Partei* (1848; *The Communist Manifesto*, 1850) by Karl Marx and Friedrich Engels, but in the conversion of "com" to "abom," Kaufman calls attention to the world's focus on the A-bomb, or atomic bomb. The Abomunists contrast with communists and capitalists and have a modified language and special world perspective that Kaufman's manifesto humorously and provocatively discloses. For example, the Abomunists "vote against everyone by not voting for anyone." Never accepting candidacy, the Abomunists insist, "The only office Abomunists run for is the unemployment office." The worldview of the Abomunists is suggested in apparent contradictions: "Abomunists do not feel pain, no matter how much it hurts." Kaufman adds, "Laughter sounds orange at night, because/ reality is unrealizable while it exists."

Kaufman lends the sequence dramatic proportions when he indicates that the author is "Bomkauf," apparently a fusion of "Bomb" and "Kaufman" that humorously suggests the atomic bomb and the author's name, but also supplies a variation on *dummkopf*, a German word meaning idiot. Bomkauf extends the dramatic proportions of the poem when he indicates that "Further Notes," the third part in the sequence, is "taken from 'Abomunismus und Religion' by Tom Man," apparently a reference to Thomas Mann, and, for some readers, Tom Paine.

"Excerpts from the Lexicon Abomunon," the fifth part of the sequence, is a brief comical dictionary of Abomunist terms "compiled by BIMGO," or Bill Margolis, who, among others, collaborated with Kaufman on the editing of *Beatitude*, the mimeographed magazine in which "Abomunist Manifesto" first appeared. Kaufman's lexical game is shown in entries such as "Abomunize," which means "to carefully disorganize." An "Abomunasium" is a "place in which abomunastics occur, such as bars, coffee shops, USO's, juvenile homes, pads, etc."

The speakers in "Still Further Notes Dis- and Re-Garding Abomunism" include Bomkauf (with his associates, since he says "We"), who provides an introductory passage for five diary entries by Jesus from "the Live Sea Scrolls." The entries comically chronicle the last days of Jesus, who speaks in hipster language, complaining, "Barabbas gets suspended sentence and I make the hill. What a drag. Well, that's poetry, and I've got to split now."

For "Abominist Rational Anthem," a sound poem that defies logical interpretation, Schroeder, the child pianist from the comic strip Peanuts, is cited as the composer of the music. "Abomunist Documents," which includes two pieces of eighteenth century correspondence, one written by Hancock (founding father John Hancock) and the other by Benedict (traitor Benedict Arnold), is material that, according to Bomkauf, was "*discovered during ceremonies at the Tomb of the Unknown Draftdodger*."

The final entry in "Abomunist Manifesto" is "Abomnewscast . . . on the Hour . . . ," in which an unnamed newscaster presents comical headlines that refer to people, current events, and history. The newscast is "sponsored by your friendly neighborhood Abomunist." Kaufman satirizes society's quest for material gratification even as society stands on the brink of a nuclear apocalypse. The newscaster refers to a bomb shelter available in "decorator colors" with a "barbecue unit that runs on radioactivity." In a cemetery, one can acquire "split-level tombs." Norman Rockwell's charming interpretation of American life in "The Spelling Bee" becomes "The Lynching Bee" in the newscast, and the image is so American that the Daughters of the American Revolution give the work an award. The world spins forward with its population explosion, Cold War, arms race, and television programs, and the newscaster warns that the pending "emergency signal" will not be a drill. He advises, ". . . turn the TV off and get under it."

BAGEL SHOP JAZZ

Kaufman frequented the Co-existence Bagel Shop in San Francisco, and the shop became a forum for his presentations. In "Bagel Shop Jazz," Kaufman analyzes and describes the "shadow people" and the "nightfall creatures" who populate the bagel shop and give it a special atmosphere. Among the people at the shop are "mulberry-eyed girls in black stockings." The girls are "love tinted" and "doomed," yet ". . . they fling their arrow legs/ To the heavens,/ Losing their doubts in the beat." There are also "angel guys" who have "synagogue eyes." These men are "world travelers on the forty-one bus" and they blend "jazz with paint talk." They are "lost in a dream world,/ Where time is told with a beat." In contrast to the guys and girls are "coffee-faced Ivy Leaguers, in Cambridge jackets." These men discuss "Bird and Diz and Miles" (jazz musicians Charlie "Bird" Parker, Dizzie Gillespie, and Miles Davis) and flash "cool hipster smiles" even as they hope that "the beat is really the truth."

Though the community of bagel-shop patrons poses no apparent threat, these people become "brief, beautiful shadows, burned on walls of night" because "the Guilty police arrive" and end the interaction the bagel shop encourages. The patrons are probably Abomunistic in their attitude, and society, as represented by the police, cannot tolerate their individuality and edginess.

THE ANCIENT RAIN

The title poem of *The Ancient Rain* is topical and prophetic, satirical and tender, as well as symbolic and surreal. A prose poem set in stanzas that often begin with the refrain "The Ancient Rain . . . ," Kaufman's "The Ancient Rain" honors the history of the United States and decries social injustice. The falling of the Ancient Rain is an apocalyptic event that strikes down evil and honors the righteous. The Ancient Rain has godlike powers: "The Ancient Rain is supreme and is aware of all things that have ever happened." Kaufman adds, "The Ancient Rain is the source of all things, the Ancient Rain knows all secrets, the Ancient Rain illuminates America." Kaufman foresees a destructive world war, but he also sees that the Ancient Rain will prevail over the war, giving righteous triumph to those who are just.

Among the heroes Kaufman names in the poem are Abraham Lincoln, George Washington, John F. Kennedy, Franklin Delano Roosevelt, Nathan Hale, Crispus Attucks, Hart Crane, Federico García Lorca, Ulysses S. Grant, John Brown, and Martin Luther King, Jr. Among the villains are George Custer, D. W. Griffith, the members of the Ku Klux Klan, Julius Caesar, Robert E. Lee, warmongers, and bigoted and hypocritical immigrants. Kaufman draws his greatest inspiration from Attucks, the black man who was the first to die in the American Revolution, and García Lorca, whose poetry lifted Kaufman into "crackling blueness" and led him to "seek out the great Sun of the Center."

BIBLIOGRAPHY

Anderson, T. J. *Notes to Make the Sound Come Right: Four Innovators of Jazz Poetry.* Fayetteville: University of Arkansas Press, 2004. Examines the jazz poetry of Bob Kaufman, as well as of Nathaniel Mackey, Stephen Jonas, and Jayne Cortez. Anderson provides overviews on jazz poetry as well as chapters on each of the poets. He studies Kaufman's appropriation of the rhythms and tones of jazz.

Christian, Barbara. "Whatever Happened to Bob Kaufman?" In *The Beats: Essays in Criticism*, edited by Lee Bartlett. Jefferson, N.C.: McFarland, 1981. Christian calls attention to social protest and jazz in Kaufman's work.

Damon, Maria. "'Unmeaning Jargon'/Uncanonized Beatitude: Bob Kaufman, Poet." In *The Dark End of the Street: Margins in American Vanguard Poetry*. Minneapolis: University of Minnesota Press, 1993. Examines the poetic works of Kaufman and the language he used.

_____, ed. "Bob Kaufman: Poet A Special Section." *Callaloo: A Journal of African American and African Arts and Letters* 25, no. 1 (Winter, 2002): 105-231. This special section in *Callaloo* presents articles on Kaufman by Aldon Lynn Nielsen, James Smethurst, Amor Kohli, Jeffrey Falla, Rod Hernandez, and Horace Coleman.

Henderson, David. Introduction to *Cranial Guitar*, by Bob Kaufman. Minneapolis: Coffee House Press, 1996. Henderson explains Kaufman's career and quotes extensively from a radio documentary on Kaufman.

Kohli, Amor. "Black Skins, Beat Masks: Bob Kaufman and the Blackness of Jazz." In *Reconstructing the Beats*. New York: Palgrave Macmillan, 2004. Kohli sees jazz performance as a means of protest.

Lawlor, William T. *"Cranial Guitar."* In *Masterplots II: African American Literature*, edited by Tyrone Williams. Rev. ed. Pasadena, Calif.: Salem Press, 2009. Provides in-depth analysis of *Cranial Guitar*, paying attention to themes and meanings. Also contains brief biography of Kaufman.

Thomas, Lorenzo. "'Communicating by Horns': Jazz and Redemption in the Poetry of the Beats and the Black Arts Movement." *African American Review* 26, no. 2 (1992): 291-299. Thomas draws a connection between jazz artists and rebellion against conformity.

Winans, A. D. "Bob Kaufman." *American Poetry Review* 29, no. 3 (May-June, 2000): 19-20. Winans offers a compact review of Kaufman's life.

William T. Lawlor

YUSEF KOMUNYAKAA

James Willie Brown

Born: Bogalusa, Louisiana; April 29, 1947

PRINCIPAL POETRY

Dedications and Other Darkhorses, 1977
Lost in the Bonewheel Factory, 1979
Copacetic, 1984
I Apologize for the Eyes in My Head, 1986
Toys in the Field, 1986
Dien Cai Dau, 1988
February in Sydney, 1989
Magic City, 1992
Neon Vernacular: New and Selected Poems, 1993
Thieves of Paradise, 1998
Talking Dirty to the Gods, 2000
Pleasure Dome: New and Collected Poems, 2001
Taboo, 2004
Gilgamesh: A Verse Play, 2006 (with Chad Gracia)
Warhorses, 2008

OTHER LITERARY FORMS

Despite his impressive poetic output—averaging more than a book of poems every other year since 1977 and publication in all the major poetry journals—Yusef Komunyakaa (koh-muhn-YAH-kuh) has not been content to stay within these traditional confines. He has made a number of sound and video recordings of his readings of his work. One of the more interesting of these is *Love Notes from the Madhouse* (1997), a live reading performed with a jazz ensemble led by John Tchicai. He has written two libretti, "Slip Knot," with T. J. Anderson, about an eighteenth century slave, and "Testimony" (1999), about jazz great Charlie Parker. On *Thirteen Kinds of Desire* (2000), vocalist Pamela Knowles sings lyrics by Komunyakaa. Of his fight against traditional poetic boundaries, he notes: "I am always pushing against the walls [categories] create. I will always do this. . . . Theater and song won't be the last of me."

Blue Notes: Essays, Interviews, and Commentaries (1999), edited by Radiclani Clytus, is an eclectic mix of seven interviews with the poet from 1990 to 1999, as well as twelve short impressionistic essays by him and five new poems with commentary by the author. With Sascha Feinstein, he edited *The Jazz Poetry Anthology* (volume 1, 1991; volume 2, 1996). Together with Martha Collins, Komunyakaa translated the work of

Vietnamese poet Nguyen Quang Thieu. His own poetry has been translated into Vietnamese as well as Russian, Korean, Czech, French, and Italian.

ACHIEVEMENTS

Many readers, critics, and fellow poets have long recognized Yusef Komunyakaa as a major poet of his generation. His poems about the Vietnam War place him among the finest writers who have explored this difficult terrain. His use of jazz and blues rhythms places him in the tradition of poet Langston Hughes and the best southern writers. Of his many awards and honors, perhaps the most impressive is the 1994 Pulitzer Prize in poetry for *Neon Vernacular*, which also won the Kingsley Tufts Award and the William Faulkner Prize. *Thieves of Paradise* was a finalist for the National Book Critics Circle Award. Komunyakaa has also won the Thomas Forcade Award, the Hanes Poetry Prize, the San Francisco State Poetry Center Book Award (1986), the Levinson Prize from *Poetry* magazine (1997), the Morton Dauwen Zabel Award (1998), and the Union League Civic and Arts Poetry Prize (1998). He served as a chancellor of the Academy of American Poets from 1999 to 2005 and became a member of the American Academy of Arts and Letters in 2009. He received the Ruth Lilly Poetry Prize (2001), the Shelley Memorial Award (2004), the Louisiana Writer Award (2007), the John William Corrington Award for Literary Excellence from Centenary College of Louisiana (2006-2007), and the Jean Kennedy Smith New York University Creative Writing Award of Distinction (2009).

Komunyakaa has been awarded creative writing fellowships from the National Endowment for the Arts, the Fine Arts Center in Provincetown, Massachusetts, and the Louisiana Arts Council. He has served as a judge for numerous poetry competitions and has been on the advisory board for the *Encyclopedia of American Poetry* (1998, 2001). His work has appeared in all the major poetry journals, as well as national magazines such as *The Atlantic* and *The New Republic*. One indication of Komunyakaa's appeal is the number of diverse anthologies that include his work. He appears repeatedly in the annual *The Best American Poetry*, collections of verse about Vietnam, and numerous periodicals.

BIOGRAPHY

Yusef Komunyakaa was born James Willie Brown. The oldest of five children, he had a strained relationship with his father, which he chronicled vividly years later in a fourteen-sonnet sequence titled "Songs for My Father," which appears in *Neon Vernacular*. The Bogalusa of Komunyakaa's childhood was a rural community in southern Louisiana that held few opportunities economically or culturally, especially for a young black man. The main industry was the single paper mill, one that turned "workers into pulp," according to one poem. There was a racially charged atmosphere. The public library admitted only whites; the Ku Klux Klan was still active. In "Fog Galleon," Komunyakaa writes of these difficulties:

> I press against the taxicab
> Window. I'm black here, interfaced
> With a dead phosphorescence;
> The whole town smells
> Like the world's oldest anger.

Daydreaming and reading were ways of escaping and coping with a slow life. Daydreaming, which Komunyakaa now sees as an important creative act of his youth, is evident in his early identification with his grandfather's West Indian heritage. He took the name Komunyakaa from his grandfather, who, according to family legend, came to the United States as a stowaway from Trinidad. In the poem "Mismatched Shoes," Komunyakaa writes of this identification:

> The island swelled in his throat
> & calypso leapt into the air,
>
> . . . .
> I picked up those mismatched shoes
> & slipped into his skin. Komunyakaa.
> His blues, African fruit on my tongue.

The Bible and a set of supermarket encyclopedias were his first books. He has noted the influence of the Bible's "hypnotic cadence," sensitizing him to the importance of music and metaphor. James Baldwin's *Nobody Knows My Name* (1961), discovered in a church library when Komunyakaa was sixteen, inspired him to become a writer. Jazz and blues radio programs from New Orleans, heard on the family radio, formed a third important influence. Komunyakaa speaks fondly of those early days of listening to jazz and acknowledges its importance in his work.

After graduation from high school in 1965, Komunyakaa traveled briefly and in 1969 enlisted in the U.S. Army. He was sent to Vietnam. He served as a reporter on the front lines and later as editor of *The Southern Cross*, a military newspaper. The experience of being flown in by helicopter to observe and then report on the war effort laid the groundwork for the powerful fusion of passion and detached observation that is a hallmark of his war poems, written years later. He was awarded the Bronze Star for his service in Vietnam.

Upon being discharged, Komunyakaa enrolled at the University of Colorado, where he majored in English and sociology, earning a bachelor's degree in 1975. A creative writing course there inspired him to pursue a master's degree in creative writing at Colorado State University, which he earned in 1978. He received his master of fine arts degree from the University of California, Irvine, in 1980. During this period, he published limited editions of his first two short books of poems, *Dedications and Other Darkhorses* and *Lost in the Bonewheel Factory*.

Komunyakaa taught poetry briefly in public school before joining the creative writing faculty at the University of New Orleans, where he met Mandy Sayer, whom he married in 1985; they were divorced in 1995. Also in 1985, he became an associate professor at Indiana University at Bloomington, where he was named Lilly Professor of Poetry in 1989. In the 1990's, he began a relationship with Reetika Vazirani, with whom he had a son, Jehan. In 2003, Vazirani and Jehan were found dead in an apparent murder-suicide. Komunyakaa became a professor in the Council of Humanities and Creative Writing Program at Princeton University in 1997. In 2005, he joined the faculty of New York University as distinguished senior poet.

ANALYSIS

Because Yusef Komunyakaa's poetry is so rich in imagery, allusion, metaphor, musical rhythms, and ironic twists, it possesses a freshness and a bittersweet bite whether the subject is the raw beauty of nature or the passions and follies of human nature. He has said that poetry does not work for him without "surprises." His poetry surprises both in its technique—the juxtaposition of disparate images and sudden shifts in perspective—and in its subjects. Generally his poems have a sensual quality even though the subject matter varies greatly: childhood memories, family feuds, race, war, sex, nature, and jazz. Scholar Radiclani Clytus commented early in Komunyakaa's career that the poet's interpretation of popular mythology and legend gave readers "alternative access to cultural lore. Epic human imperfections, ancient psychological profiles, and the haunting resonance of the South are now explained by those who slow drag to Little Willie John and rendezvous at MOMA." Komunyakaa's comment that "a poem is both confrontation and celebration" aptly captures the essence of his own work.

COPACETIC

Two early books, the first of Komunyakaa's published by a major university press, introduce many of his subjects and techniques and were the first to win for him critical acclaim. *Copacetic* focuses primarily on memories of childhood and the persuasive influence of music. The narrator speaks of "a heavy love for jazz," and in fact musical motifs run throughout Komunyakaa's poetry. He has compared poetry to jazz and blues in its emphasis on feeling and tone, its sense of surprise and discovery, and its diversity within a general structure. Poems such as "Copacetic Mingus," "Elegy for Thelonious," and "Untitled Blues" convey the power of this kind of music, in which "Art & life bleed into each other." Depending on the poem, music can serve as escape, therapy, or analogy. Often it is combined with richly sensual images, as in "Woman, I Got the Blues."

I APOLOGIZE FOR THE EYES IN MY HEAD AND DIEN CAI DAU

I Apologize for the Eyes in My Head continues this motif while adding new subjects and themes. The ugly side of race relations in the United States is suggested in several poems. Komunyakaa also begins to explore the pain of the Vietnam War. "For the

Walking Dead" is a moving account of "boyish soldiers on their way to the front" who seek respite with Veronica in a local bar.

The past wounds and present scars of the Vietnam War are the subjects of *Dien Cai Dau*, whose title means "crazy" in Vietnamese. The powerful yet exquisitely sensitive—and sensual—way in which Komunyakaa conveys the pain, loss, and psychic confusion of his experience in Vietnam found a receptive audience. Most present a moment or a reflection in a richly nuanced but undogmatic way. In "We Never Know," he juxtaposes a delicate image of dancing with a woman with the reality of an enemy in the field, whom he kills and whose body he then approaches. The moral ambiguity of the moment is highlighted by the tenderness with which the soldier regards the body:

> When I got to him,
> a blue halo
> of flies had already claimed him.
> I pulled the crumbled photograph
> from his fingers.
> There's no other way
> to say this: I fell in love.
> The morning cleared again,
> except for a distant mortar
> & somewhere choppers taking off.
> I slid the wallet into his pocket
> & turned him over, so he wouldn't be
> kissing the ground.

Poems such as "Tu Du Street" and "Thanks" are even more complex in their multiple, often conflicting, images. The former presents the bizarre reality of racial prejudice even in Vietnam, "where only machine gun fire bring us together." The women with whom the soldiers seek solace provide one common denominator:

> There's more than a nation
> inside us, as black & white
> soldiers touch the same lovers
> minutes apart, tasting
> each other's breath,
> without knowing these rooms
> run into each other like tunnels
> leading to the underworld.

In "Thanks," the narrator gives thanks to an unspecified being for the myriad coincidences that saved him one day in the jungle as he "played some deadly/ game for blind gods." The poet provides no resolution or closure, just a series of powerful, haunting images:

> Again, thanks for the dud
> hand grenade tossed at my feet
> outside Chu Lai. I'm still
> falling through its silence.

THIEVES OF PARADISE

Komunyakaa won an American Academy of Arts and Letters award given to writers with "progressive and experimental tendencies." This book is an example of this artist's ability to experiment with form and ease the reader into accepting poetry that is unfamiliar. Much of the subject matter is familiar—the grim reality of war and its psychological aftermath, the body's hungers and betrayals, the allure of memory and imagination—but the presentation is fresh and intriguing. "Palimpsest" is a seemingly random, kaleidoscopic series of four-quatrain poems that move from "slavecatchers" to tanks in Beijing's Tiananmen Square to the backwoods to jazz musician Count Basie. By confronting uncomfortable truths, the poet writes, "I am going to teach Mr. Pain/ to sway, to bop."

Several, such as "Nude Interrogation," "Phantasmagoria," and "Frontispiece," are prose poems that force one to rethink the nature of the form, while Komunyakaa's images work on the emotions. "The Glass Ark" is a five-page dialogue between two paleontologists.

This collection includes the libretto "Testimony," about Charlie Parker, written in twenty-eight fourteen-line stanzas. It captures the reckless allure of the man and the time:

> Yardbird
> could blow a woman's strut
> across the room. . . . pushed moans
>   through brass. . . . High
> heels clicking like a high hat.
> Black-beaded flapper. Blue satin
> Yardbird, he'd blow pain & glitter.

TALKING DIRTY TO THE GODS

Talking Dirty to the Gods stands apart from earlier works in its adherence to a strict, traditional form. Each of its 132 poems consists of sixteen lines, in four unrhymed quatrains. Much of the appeal of this collection stems from the freedom and friction Komunyakaa creates by presenting his unusual images and bizarre juxtapositions in a tightly controlled format. The gods he discusses are taken from the ancient and the modern worlds, the exotic and the commonplace. Whether discussing the maggot ("Little/ Master of earth"), Bellerophon, or Joseph Stalin, he is able to humanize his subject enough to win at least some sympathy from the reader.

NEON VERNACULAR

Neon Vernacular won considerable critical acclaim as well as the Pulitzer Prize. In addition to culling the best from earlier books, it adds gems of its own, including the un-rhymed sonnet sequence "Songs for My Father," a powerful fourteen-poem sequence that chronicles the poet's complicated relationship with his dad. In "At the Screen Door," in which a former soldier murders because he cannot separate the past from the present, Komunyakaa returns to the psychological aftermath of Vietnam.

PLEASURE DOME

The publication of *Pleasure Dome* led to laudatory reviews not only for the book's poetic achievement but also for its high purpose: "Nearly every page of these collected poems will pull you from your expectations, tell you something you did not know, and leave you better off than you were," said a reviewer for *Library Journal*, while *Booklist* praised Komunyakaa's "fluent creative energy, and his passion for living the examined life." *Pleasure Dome* is an extraordinarily rich collection of more than 350 poems. All earlier books except *Talking Dirty to the Gods* are represented. There is also a section ti-tled "New Poems" and another, "Early Uncollected." Among the new poems is "Tenebrae," a moving meditation on Richard Johnson, the black Indiana University music professor who committed suicide. The lines "You try to beat loneliness/ out of a drum" are woven throughout the poem with a cumulative, haunting effect.

OTHER MAJOR WORKS

NONFICTION: *Blue Notes: Essays, Interviews, and Commentaries*, 1999 (Radiclani Clytus, editor).

TRANSLATION: *The Insomnia of Fire*, 1995 (with Martha Collins; of poetry by Nguyen Quang Thieu).

EDITED TEXTS: *The Jazz Poetry Anthology*, 1991 (with Sascha Feinstein); *The Second Set: The Jazz Poetry Anthology, Volume 2*, 1996 (with Feinstein).

BIBLIOGRAPHY

Chow, Balance. "The Poetry of Yusef Komunyakaa." In *Masterplots II: African American Literature*, edited by Tyrone Williams. Rev. ed. Pasadena, Calif.: Salem Press, 2009. Provides biographical information about the poet as well as thorough analysis of his development as a poet and the poetry itself.

Conley, Susan. "About Yusef Komunyakaa: A Profile." *Ploughshares* 23, no. 1 (Spring, 1997): 202-207. Conley gives a concise overview of the poet's career, his central themes and motifs, his views on race relations in America, and his usual method of writing poetry.

Gotera, Vincente F. "Depending on the Light: Yusef Komunyakaa's *Dien Cai Dau*." In *America Rediscovered: Critical Essays on Literature and Film of the Vietnam War*, edited by Owen W. Gilman, Jr., and Lorrie Smith. New York: Garland, 1990. Komunyakaa differs from other war poets in his "devotion to highly textured language"; he refuses "to present Vietnam to the reader as exotica," but rather "underline[s] the existential reality" of his experience.

Jones, Kirkland C. "Folk Idiom in the Literary Expression of Two African American Authors: Rita Dove and Yusef Komunyakaa." In *Language and Literature in the African American Imagination*, edited by Carol Aisha Blackshire-Belay. Westport, Conn.: Greenwood Press, 1992. Makes a sophisticated comparison between these two poets of impeccable form and restrained passion.

Kelly, Robert. "Jazz and Poetry: A Conversation." *Georgia Review* 46 (Winter, 1992). Offers an insightful look at Komunyakaa's views on jazz and poetry in his own words.

Komunyakaa, Yusef. "Yusef Komunyakaa: Blue Note in a Lyrical Landscape." Interview by Fran Gordon. *Poets and Writers* 28, no. 6 (November/December, 2000): 26-33. Gordon terms Komunyakaa "one of America's most receptive minds" and "one of its most original voices." This interview provides a glimpse into the poet's thoughts on his background and early reading, his interest in nature and mythology, and his use of imagery and music in his poetry.

Pettis, Joyce. *African American Poets: Lives, Works, and Sources*. Westport, Conn.: Greenwood Press, 2002. Contains an entry on the life and works of Komunyakaa.

Ringnalda, Don. *Fighting and Writing the Vietnam War*. Jackson: University Press of Mississippi, 1994. Ringnalda suggests that much of the poetry about Vietnam is too safe in both form and content. Because Komunyakaa realizes that the old paradigms are shattered, he "gains the freedom to explore subterranean, prerational landscapes. This results in a poetry of rich, disturbing associations."

Salas, Angela M. *Flashback Through the Heart: The Poetry of Yusef Komunyakaa*. Selinsgrove, Pa.: Susquehanna University Press, 2004. A book-length examination of the poetic works of Komunyakaa, including discussion of how aspects of his life are represented in his poetry.

Weber, Bruce. "A Poet's Values: It's the Words over the Man." *The New York Times Biographical Service* 25 (May, 1994): 666-667. Written three weeks after Komunyakaa won the Pulitzer Prize, this brief account adds several new and interesting anecdotes about the poet's early years and his views on his craft.

Danny Robinson

AUDRE LORDE

Born: Harlem, New York; February 18, 1934
Died: Christiansted, St. Croix, Virgin Islands; November 17, 1992

OTHER LITERARY FORMS

The Cancer Journals (1980) is a personal account of the struggles of Audre Lorde (lohrd) with breast cancer. *Zami: A New Spelling of My Name, a Biomythography* (1982), is a retrospective narrative of her emerging sexuality. *Sister Outsider: Essays and Speeches* (1984) and *A Burst of Light: Essays* (1988) are collections of essays and speeches on poetry, feminism, lesbianism, and racism.

ACHIEVEMENTS

Audre Lorde received a National Endowment for the Arts grant and was a poet in residence at Tougaloo College in Jackson, Mississippi, in 1968. She also won the Creative Artists Public Service grant (1972 and 1976) and the Broadside Poets Award (1975). In 1975, she was named Woman of the Year by Staten Island Community College. She received the Borough of Manhattan President's Award for literary excellence (1987), the American Book Award from the Before Columbus Foundation for *A Burst of Light* (1989), a Walt Whitman Citation of Merit, the Bill Whitehead Award from the Publishing Triangle (1992), and two Lambda Literary Awards for Lesbian Poetry: in 1993 for *Undersong* and in 1994 for *The Marvelous Arithmetics of Distance*. She was named poet laureate of New York in 1991.

BIOGRAPHY

Audre Geraldine Lorde's parents emigrated from Grenada to New York City in 1924. Lorde, the youngest of three girls, was born in 1934. She recounted many of her childhood memories in *Zami*, identifying particular incidents that had an influence or effect on her developing sexuality and her later work as a poet. She attended the University of Mexico (1954-1955) and received a B.A. from Hunter College (1959) and an M.L.S. from Columbia University (1961). In 1962, she was married to Edwin Rollins, with whom she had two children before they were divorced in 1970.

Prior to 1968, when she gained public recognition for her poetry, Lorde supported herself through a variety of jobs, including low-paying factory work. She also served as a librarian in several institutions. After her first publication, *The First Cities*, Lorde worked primarily within American colleges and free presses. She was an instructor at City College of New York (CUNY; 1968-1970), an instructor and then lecturer at Lehman College (1969-1971), and a professor of English at John Jay College of Criminal Justice (1972-1981). From 1981 to 1987, she was a professor of English at Hunter College at CUNY and became a Thomas Hunter Professor for one year (1987-1988). She also served as poetry editor of the magazine *Chrysalis* and was a contributing editor of the journal *Black Scholar*.

In the early 1980's, she helped start Kitchen Table: Women of Color Press, a multicultural effort publishing Asian American and Latina as well as African American women writers. In the late 1980's, Lorde became increasingly concerned over the plight of black women in South Africa under apartheid, creating Sisterhood in Support of Sisters in South Africa and remaining an active voice on behalf of these women throughout the remainder of her life. She also served on the board of the National Coalition of Black Lesbians and Gays. With the companion of her last years, the writer and black feminist scholar Gloria I. Joseph, she made a home on St. Croix, U.S. Virgin Islands. Shortly before her death in 1992 she completed her tenth book of poems, *The Marvelous Arithmetics of Distance*.

ANALYSIS

Audre Lorde called herself a "black lesbian feminist warrior poet." At the heart of her work as poet, essayist, teacher, and lecturer lies an intense and relentless exploration of personal identity. Beyond the stunning portrayals of her deepest insights and emotions, her work is filled with powerful evocations of universal survival. The substance of her poetry and essays always reaches beyond the individual self into deep concerns for all humanity. Progressively, her work reveals an increasing awareness of her West Indian heritage in relation to her place in American society and its values.

All of Audre Lorde's poems, essays, and speeches are deeply personal renditions of a compassionate writer, thinker, and human being. Indeed, she drew much of her material from individual and multifaceted experience; she rendered it in writing that sought to reveal the complexity of being a black feminist lesbian poet. She expressed the feelings of being marginalized in an American society that is predominantly white, male, heterosexual, and middle class. Her writings reflected the changing constitution and perspective of American life, but she never relented to an easy optimism, nor did she make uninformed dismissals of society's ills. Her personal experiences made her compassionate toward those who suffer under oppressive regimes all over the world. By drawing from the history and mythology of the West Indies, she was able to refer to the racism and sexism that exist in other cultures.

The title of one of her essays is especially appropriate to inform her work as a poet, "The Transformation of Silence into Language and Action." In a self-characterization when she was a poet in residence at Tougaloo College, Lorde said, "I became convinced, anti-academic though I am, that all poets must teach what they know, in order to continue being." Her insistent drive to exist according to the terms of her individual desires and powers was the focal point of many of her speeches and essays. Lorde was also active on the lecture circuit, and she was invited to speak to women writers in the Soviet Union and in Berlin. She documented many of her insights into various cultures and places in essays and poems.

The various forms of her writing provided many pieces to the whole picture that made up Lorde's life and work. She was unsentimental in naming the people who have been a part of her life and in evaluating the events that make up her experiences. Her parents and her sisters are addressed with some frequency in her poems. A girlhood friend, Genevieve, appears in *Zami*, and Lorde eulogizes her death in a poem titled "Memorial II." Many women are treated in several different poems, sometimes in cycles—for example, Martha and Eudora. In these ways, Lorde documented the people and the course of her life as she charted the changes and the progress that occur; at each turn, she sought to understand more deeply the situation and to learn which detours to take next.

When she was in her forties, Lorde was diagnosed with breast cancer. *The Cancer Journals* and the essay "A Burst of Light: Living with Cancer" are important pieces of personal writing that recorded her uncertainties, fears, and doubts about her mortality. Writing mostly in the form of a diary, Lorde allowed the reader to enter into her most private thoughts and emotions, with the hope that others may be encouraged to fight cancer. From her determination to survive, Lorde converted her struggles with cancer into energy for battling on behalf of other humanitarian concerns.

She set out rigorously to combat racism, sexism, heterosexism, and homophobia in her work. At times she dealt with the issues separately, but more frequently she spoke of the whole gamut, since she perceived that each stems from human blindness about the differences among people. What was remarkable about Lorde's insight is the balance that she sought in presenting her views. Overtly political in intent and social in content, the essays and speeches ask all individuals to understand more deeply the ways in which human lives are organized. She then beckoned people to take charge of their lives, to confront the tasks at hand, and to take responsibility for making changes.

Much of Lorde's mature work evolved from her identity as a black feminist lesbian poet. These terms are essential conjunctions that expressed her existence and her vision. In the essay "The Master's Tools Will Never Dismantle the Master's House," Lorde made no apologies or defenses for her choices. She wrote, "For women, the need and desire to nurture each other is not pathological but redemptive, and it is within that knowledge that our real power is rediscovered." For Lorde, the power to exist and be alive came from her love—in all senses of the word—for women.

In her most often cited essay, "The Uses of the Erotic: The Erotic as Power," Lorde dislodged some of the negative assumptions that have sprung up around the terms "erotic" and "power," and offered new perspectives on how an individual must use her power and ability to love. For Lorde, the erotic was "a resource within each of us that lies in a deeply female and spiritual plane, firmly rooted in the power of our unexpressed or unrecognized feeling." Through a redefinition of the terms, Lorde showed how societal oppression numbs a woman's ability to feel and act deeply. Often the two—emotion and action—are in conflict with the values of a "racist, patriarchal, and anti-erotic society." Before individual human beings can come together as one society, each person must be in touch with his or her own feelings and be willing to express and share with others. These are the necessary first steps to effecting real political change.

Lorde contended that the need to share is a fundamental one that all people feel. Unfortunately, the prevailing attitudes of American society preclude true expression of individualism: If people do not fit into the norms or expectations of the dominant system of values, they are deemed "not normal" or deviant. Lorde argued against the hypocrisy of American values: Where is freedom if any forms of expression considered "unfit" are excluded? How might one such as herself, who is on the margins of all that is "normal," empower herself to take effective action?

These are the kinds of difficult questions Lorde raised from the beginning of her work as a writer and poet. She made efforts to answer them anew in much of what she produced. She emphasized the necessity of listening to others and teaching what she herself has learned in the course of her work. Always receptive to the notion of difference that exists among all people, Lorde set out to consider the meaning of her own experiences first, before she attempted to convey to others what those experiences might mean in the larger context of existence. On one hand, her work was intensely personal; it may even be considered self-absorbed at times. Yet on the other, she managed to transform her deeply private pains and joys into universal and timeless concerns.

THE FIRST CITIES AND CABLES TO RAGE

In her early collections of poetry, *The First Cities* and *Cables to Rage*, Lorde expressed a keen political disillusionment, noting the failure of American ideals of equality and justice for all. When Lorde used the pronoun "we" in her poetry, she spoke for all who have been dispossessed. In "Anniversary," for example, she wrote, "Our tears/ water an alien grass," expressing the separation between those who belong and those who do not. In poems such as "Sowing," the poet revealed the land's betrayal of its inhabitants by showing images of destruction juxtaposed to personal rage: "I have been to this place before/ where blood seething commanded/ my fingers fresh from the earth."

Lorde also demonstrated a concern for the children of this earth in "Blood-birth": Casting about to understand what it is in her that is raging to be born, she wondered how an opening will come "to show the true face of me/ lying exposed and together/ my children your children their children/ bent on our conjugating business." The image of the warrior, the one who must be prepared to go about the business of existing in an unjust world, signifies the need to take care of those not yet aware of unfulfilled promises.

Lorde was setting out to explode sexual typecasting. Certainly, there was nothing dainty about her sharp images and powerful assessments of social conditions. As she confronted harsh realities, the portrayals were necessarily clamorous. Yet the poet's rage did not lead to a blind rampage. In "Conversation in Crisis," the poet hoped to speak to her friend "for a clear meeting/ of self upon self/ in sight of our hearth/ but without fire." The poet must speak honestly and not out of false assumptions and pretenses so that real communication can occur. The reader and listener must heed the words as well as the tone in order to receive the meaning of the words. Communication, then, is a kind of contractual relationship between people.

FROM A LAND WHERE OTHER PEOPLE LIVE AND BETWEEN OUR SELVES

In the collections *From a Land Where Other People Live* and *Between Our Selves*, Lorde used a compassionate tone to tell people about the devastation of white racism on African Americans. She mixes historical fact with political reality, emphasizing the disjunction that sometimes occurs between the two. In "Equinox," Lorde observed her daughter's birth by remembering a series of events that also occurred that year: She had "marched into Washington/ to a death knell of dreaming/ which 250,000 others mistook for a hope," for few at that time understood the victimization of children that was occurring not only in the American South but also in the Vietnam War. After she heard that Malcolm X had been shot, she reread all his writings: "the dark mangled children/ came streaming out of the atlas/ Hanoi Angola Guinea-Bissau . . ./ merged into Bedford-Stuyvesant and Hazelhurst Mississippi."

From the multiplicity of world horrors, the poet returned to her hometown in New York, exhausted but profoundly moved by the confrontation of history and the facts of her own existence. In "The Day They Eulogized Mahalia," another event is present in the background as the great singer Mahalia Jackson is memorialized: Six black children died in a fire at a day care center on the South Side; "firemen found their bodies/ like huddled lumps of charcoal/ with silent mouths and eyes wide open." Even as she mourned the dead in her poems, the poet seems aware of both the power and the powerlessness of words to effect real changes. In the poem, "Power," Lorde writes,

> The difference between poetry and rhetoric
> is being ready to kill
> yourself
> instead of your children.

Once the event has occurred, one can write about it or one can try to prevent a similar event from occurring; in either case, it is not possible to undo the first event. Therefore, as a society, people must learn from their errors and their failures to care for other people. Lorde even warned herself that she must discern and employ this crucial difference between poetry and rhetoric; if she did not, "my power too will run corrupt as poisonous mold/ or lie limp and useless as an unconnected wire."

COAL, THE BLACK UNICORN, AND OUR DEAD BEHIND US

For Lorde, the process of learning all over again how to transform thought into action began with the awareness of her personal reality. In the collections *Coal*, *The Black Unicorn*, and *Our Dead Behind Us*, the poet addressed more specifically the individual human beings in her life, creating vignettes of her relationships with other people. In particular, she returned again and again to images of her mother, Linda Belmar Lorde, whose relatively light-colored skin is mentioned in many of the poems. In "Outside," she links her mother's lightness to the brutal faces of racism: "Nobody lynched my momma/ but what she'd never been/ had bleached her face of everything." When Lorde questioned, "Who shall I curse that I grew up/ believing in my mother's face," she echoed the anger that also appears in the poem "Sequelae." There she stated explicitly the rage that evolved from the mother's lies, white lies: "I battle the shapes of you/ wearing old ghosts of me/ hating you for being/ black and not woman/ hating you for being white." (*Zami* elaborates many of the specific events to which Lorde referred in her poems about her mother.)

The return to childhood allowed the poet to come to new terms with her mother. In several of Lorde's poems, she also returned to even deeper roots constituting her identity. In "Dahomey," she referred to the African goddess Seboulisa, "the Mother of us all" or the creator of the world. In embracing the mother goddess, the poet was able "to sharpen the knives of my tongue." Because the subjects of her poetry are painful ones, Lorde empowered her own speech by always calling attention to the dangers of remaining silent. In "A Song for Many Movements," she stated simply and precisely the project of her poetry: "Our labor has become/ more important/ than our silence."

UNDERSONG

Three decades of production and the work from Lorde's first five published collections form her 1993 collection titled *Undersong*, a reworking of her 1982 work, *Chosen Poems, Old and New*. It is not a "selected poems" in the usual meaning of the term, because it contains no work from her centrally important *The Black Unicorn*, which she considered too complex and too much of a unit to be dismembered by excerpting, and holds little of *Our Dead Behind Us*. Thus a large chunk of her strongest work is missing—including most of the poems in which she conjured and confronted "the worlds of Africa."

As Lorde stated in an introduction, her revision of *Chosen Poems, Old and New* was undertaken to clarify but not to recast the work—necessitating that she "propel [herself] back into the original poem-creating process and the poet who wrote it." Lorde returned to her work of *Chosen Poems, Old and New* after Hurricane Hugo wrecked her home in the Virgin Islands and she found "a waterlogged but readable copy of [the book], one of the few salvageable books from [her] library." The drama of the incident seemed to take an allegorical cast and inspired her to treat the anchoring of her poems in truth with the same fierce honesty she had devoted to confronting her childhood, her blackness, and her sexual identity. She thus seemed determined to keep her poetry under spiritual review with the same intensity that she devoted to the infinite difficulties of being an African American woman and lesbian in late twentieth century America. The changes she made in this collection seem limited to the excising of a handful of early poems, substituting others previously unpublished, and reworking line breaks and punctuation to give more space and deliberate stress to each stanza and image.

The themes of the book largely circulate on two central axes: The notion of changeable selves—the broken journey toward self—is a recurrent motif, as is her consuming involvement with issues of survival. In examining changeable selves, she juxtaposes the longing for completion with the awareness of change as a paradoxical condition of identity. In "October," Lorde appeals to the goddess Seboulisa, elsewhere described as the "Mother of us all":

> Carry my heart to some shore
> my feet will not shatter
> do not let me pass away
> before I have a name
> for this tree
> under which I am lying
> Do not let me die still
> needing to be stranger.

As the final couplet hints, the counterpoint to the search for self is the search for connection, and to that end, dialogue is used as a structuring device, creating a sense of companionship won in the face of a proudly borne singularity.

Poems with images of destruction also abound: the dead friend Genevieve; the father who "died in silence"; the "lovers processed/ through the corridors of Bellevue Mattewan/ Brooklyn State the Women's House of D./ St. Vincent's and the Tombs"; "a black boy (Emmett Till) hacked into a murderous lesson"; the lost sisters and daughters of Africa and its diaspora, whose "bones whiten/ in secret." Lorde's dual themes of the unending search for identity and a struggle for survival heightens the impact of the word "nightmare," which cycles endlessly throughout Lorde's work. The word represents her expression for history as glimpsed in surreal previsions and "Afterimages" (the title of a poem linking her memories of Till's lynching to television pictures of a Mississippi flood). One looks in vain for a "positive" counterweight, before realizing that the nightmare, for Lorde, is not a token of negativity but rather symbolizes the denied and feared aspects of experience that must be recalled and accepted for change to occur.

THE MARVELOUS ARITHMETICS OF DISTANCE

In her final collection of poems, published posthumously, Lorde displays a personal, moving, bare, and striking set of work that strives for poignant reckonings with her family. "Legacy—Hers" is about her mother, "bred for endurance/ for battle." "Inheritance—His" is about her father. She also has farewells to her sister, whom she forgives ("both you and I/ are free to go"), and to her son, whom she challenges ("In what do you believe?"). She has many bouquets for Gloria, her partner.

Lorde also visits her characteristic theme of politics in this collection. For example, she writes cinematically about the destruction wrought by U.S. foreign policy in a ferocious "Peace on Earth: Christmas, 1989":

> the rockets red glare where
> all these brown children
> running scrambling around the globe
> flames through the rubble
> bombs bursting in air
> Panama Nablus Gaza
> tear gas clouding the Natal sun.
> THIS IS A GIFT FROM THE PEOPLE OF THE UNITED
> STATES OF AMERICA
> quick cut
> the crackling Yule log
> in an iron grate.

In "Jesse Helms," which begins "I am a Black woman/ writing my way to the future," she takes on the bigotry of the U.S. senator from North Carolina with intentional crudeness:

> Your turn now jessehelms
> come on its time
> to lick the handwriting
> off the walls.

In this sparse and commanding book, perhaps the most arresting lines are those in which Lorde wrestles with the nearness of her own death. In "Today is not the day," she writes:

I am dying
but I do not want to do it
looking the other way.
Audre Lorde never looked the other way.

OTHER MAJOR WORKS

NONFICTION: *Uses of the Erotic: The Erotic as Power*, 1978; *The Cancer Journals*, 1980; *Zami: A New Spelling of My Name, a Biomythography*, 1982; *Sister Outsider: Essays and Speeches*, 1984; *I Am Your Sister: Black Women Organizing Across Sexualities*, 1985; *Apartheid U.S.A.*, 1986; *A Burst of Light: Essays*, 1988; *The Audre Lorde Compendium: Essays, Speeches, and Journals*, 1996; *Conversations with Audre Lorde*, 2004 (Joan Wylie Hall, editor); *I Am Your Sister: Collected and Unpublished Writings of Audre Lorde*, 2009.

BIBLIOGRAPHY

Bloom, Harold, ed. *Black American Women Poets and Dramatists*. New York: Chelsea House, 1996. Contains an entry on Lorde, whose gender and blackness were essential parts of who she was as a poet.

Brooks, Jerome. "In the Name of the Father: The Poetry of Audre Lorde." In *Black Women Writers (1950-1980): A Critical Evaluation*, edited by Mari Evans. Garden City, N.Y.: Doubleday, 1984. This brief chapter deals with a topic to which Lorde gives little direct attention in her own essays—the death of her father. It is a useful analysis of a focused topic that clarifies the meaning of some of the poems in which the figure of the father appears.

De Veaux, Alexis. *Warrior Poet: A Biography of Audre Lorde*. New York: W. W. Norton, 2004. Lorde's childhood in Harlem, her literary career, and her years with breast cancer are detailed in this first biography of the renowned poet.

Dilworth, Thomas. "Lorde's 'Power.'" *Explicator* 57, no. 1 (Fall, 1998): 54-57. Examines the complex imagery in Lorde's poem "Power," found in her collection *The Black Unicorn*. Argues that the poem is more than an expressive, rhetorical piece—it is a work of art.

Hull, Gloria T. "Living on the Line: Audre Lorde and *Our Dead Behind Us*." In *Changing Our Own Words: Essays on Criticism, Theory, and Writing by Black Women*, edited by Cheryl A. Wall. New Brunswick, N.J.: Rutgers University Press, 1989. A thoughtful essay on one of Lorde's collections of poetry. While it refers to some contemporary critical theory, it is an engaging and accessible study that traces the trajectory of Lorde's work. Hull also assesses various critical reviews of the collection.

Lorde, Audre. *The Cancer Journals*. San Francisco: Aunt Lute Books, 1997. A new edition with posthumous tributes from other writers and poets added to Lorde's autobiographical exploration of her breast cancer and mastectomy.

_____. "Sadomasochism: Not About Condemnation." Interview by Susan Leigh Star. In *A Burst of Light: Essays*, by Audre Lorde. Ithaca, N.Y.: Firebrand Books, 1988. Lorde talks energetically about her sexuality, setting the discussion in the context of her life's work. This interview is the first in a series of private meditations centered on her living with cancer.

Olson, Lester C. "Liabilities of Language: Audre Lorde Reclaiming Difference." *Quarterly Journal of Speech* 84, no. 4 (November, 1998): 448-470. Distortions around the naming and the misnaming of human differences are the central foci of Lorde's speech "Age, Race, Class, Sex: Women Redefining Difference," which she delivered at Amherst College in 1980.

Opitz, May, Katharine Oguntoye, and Dagmar Schultz, eds. *Showing Our Colors: Afro-German Women Speak Out*. Translated by Anne V. Adams. Amherst: University of Massachusetts Press, 1992. Addresses Lorde's exploration of her "white" side and what it meant to her. The best book to explore Lorde's complexity—and confusion—as a person.

Perreault, Jeanne. *Writing Selves: Contemporary Feminist Autobiography*. Minneapolis: University of Minnesota Press, 1995. Devotes considerable space to Lorde and her life and work. Lorde championed so many causes that one might forget that she was, first and foremost, a feminist, and Perreault speaks eloquently to that side of her.

Struthers, Ann. "The Poetry of Audre Lorde." In *Masterplots II: African American Literature*, edited by Tyrone Williams. Rev. ed. Pasadena, Calif.: Salem Press, 2009. Provides biographical information but concentrates on analyzing the themes and techniques of Lorde's poetry.

Cynthia Wong
Updated by Sarah Hilbert

CLAUDE MCKAY

Born: Sunny Ville, Jamaica; September 15, 1889
Died: Chicago, Illinois; May 22, 1948
Also known as: Eli Edwards

PRINCIPAL POETRY
Constab Ballads, 1912
Songs of Jamaica, 1912
Spring in New Hampshire, and Other Poems, 1920
Harlem Shadows, 1922
Selected Poems of Claude McKay, 1953
Complete Poems, 2004

OTHER LITERARY FORMS

Even though he is probably best known as a poet, Claude McKay's verse makes up a relatively small portion of his literary output. Although his novels, *Home to Harlem* (1928), *Banjo: A Story Without a Plot* (1929), and *Banana Bottom* (1933), do not place him at the forefront of American novelists, they were remarkable at the time for their frankness and slice-of-life realism. *Home to Harlem* was the first best-selling novel of the Harlem Renaissance, yet it was condemned by the majority of black critics, who felt that the black American art and literature emerging in the 1920's and 1930's should present an uplifting image of the African American. McKay, however, went on in his next two novels to express his admiration for the earthy ways of uneducated lower-class blacks, somewhat at the expense of black intellectuals. The remainder of McKay's published fiction appears in *Gingertown* (1932), a volume of short stories.

McKay also produced a substantial body of literary and social criticism, a revealing selection of which appears, along with a number of his letters and selections from his fiction and poetry, in *The Passion of Claude McKay: Selected Poetry and Prose, 1912-1948* (1973), edited by Wayne F. Cooper. An autobiography, *A Long Way from Home* (1937), and an important social history, *Harlem: Negro Metropolis* (1940), round out the list of his principal works.

ACHIEVEMENTS

Claude McKay received a medal from the Jamaican Institute of Arts and Sciences (1912), the National Association for the Advancement of Colored People's Harmon Foundation Award (1929) for *Harlem Shadows* and *Home to Harlem*, an award from the James Weldon Johnson Literary Guild (1937), and the Order of Jamaica. He was named that country's national poet in 1977.

Claude McKay
(Library of Congress)

McKay's contribution to American poetry cannot, however, be measured in awards and citations alone. His peculiar pilgrimage took him from Jamaica to Moscow, from communism to Catholicism, from Harlem to Marseilles. He lived and worked among common laborers most of his life, and developed a respect for them worthy of that of Walt Whitman. He rejected the critical pronouncements of his black contemporaries, and as poet and critic Melvin Tolson points out, he "was unaffected by the New Poetry and Criticism." His singular blend of modern political and social radicalism with the timeworn cadences of the sonnet won for him, at best, mixed reviews from many critics, black and white.

In any attempt to calculate his poetic achievement, however, one must realize that, with the exception of his early Jamaican dialect verse (certainly an important contribution in its own right to the little-studied literature of the British West Indies) and some rather disappointing poetry composed late in his life, his poetic career spanned little more than a decade. At the publication in 1922 of *Harlem Shadows*, the furthest extent of his poetic development, he was only thirty-three. McKay should be read as a poet on the way up, who turned his attention almost exclusively to prose after his initial success in verse.

Surely there is no more ludicrous task than to criticize a writer on the basis of his potential, and so one should take McKay as one finds him, and indeed, in those terms, he does not fare badly. His was the first notable voice of anger in modern black American poetry. Writing when he did, he had to struggle against the enormous pressure, not of white censure, but of a racial responsibility that was his, whether he wanted it or not. He could not be merely a poet—he had to be a "black poet," had to speak, to some extent, for countless others; such a position is difficult for any poet. Through it all, however, he strove for individuality, and fought to keep from being bought by any interest, black or white, right- or left-wing.

Largely through the work of McKay and of such Harlem Renaissance contemporaries as Countée Cullen and Langston Hughes, the task of being a black poet in America was made easier. *Harlem Shadows* marked a decisive beginning toward improving the predicament so concisely recorded by Cullen, who wondered aloud in the sonnet "Yet Do I Marvel" how a well-intentioned God could in his wisdom do "this curious thing:/ To make a poet black and bid him sing."

Festus Claudius McKay was born in 1889 on a small farm in Clarendon Parish, Jamaica. His parents were well-respected members of the community and of the local Baptist church. He received his early education from his older brother, a schoolteacher near Montego Bay. In 1907, he was apprenticed to a wheelwright and cabinetmaker in Brown's Town; this apprenticeship was short-lived, but it was in Brown's Town that McKay entered into a far more fruitful apprenticeship of another sort. Walter Jekyll, an English aristocrat and student of Jamaican culture, came to know young Claude and undertook the boy's literary education. As McKay recalled years later in his autobiography, *A Long Way from Home*, Jekyll opened a whole new world to him:

> I read poetry: *Childe Harold, The Dunciad, Essay on Man, Paradise Lost*, the Elizabethan lyrics, *Leaves of Grass*, the lyrics of Shelley and Keats and of the late Victorian poets, and . . . we read together pieces out of Dante, Leopardi, and Goethe, Villon and Baudelaire.

It was Jekyll who first recognized and nurtured McKay's gift for writing poetry, and who encouraged him to put that gift to work in the service of his own Jamaican dialect. The result was the publication of *Songs of Jamaica* and *Constab Ballads*. The first is a celebration of peasant life, somewhat after the manner of Robert Burns; *Constab Ballads* is more like Rudyard Kipling, drawing as it does on McKay's brief stint as a constable in Kingston, Jamaica.

Kingston gave McKay his first taste of city life and his first real taste of racism. The contempt of the city's white and mulatto upper classes for rural and lower-class blacks was an unpleasant revelation. The most blatant racism that McKay witnessed in Kingston, however, was not Jamaican in origin—it was imported in the form of American tourists. He would come to know this brand of racism much more intimately in the next few years, for, after only eight months in the Kingston constabulary, he resigned his post and left for the United States. In 1912, he enrolled, first at Tuskegee Institute, then at Kansas State College, to study agronomy. His plan was to return to Jamaica to help modernize the island's agriculture. The plan might have succeeded but for a gift of several thousand dollars from an unidentified patron—most likely Walter Jekyll—that paid McKay's way to New York, where he invested his money in a restaurant and married Eulalie Imelda Edwards, an old Jamaican sweetheart. Neither marriage nor restaurant survived long, but McKay found a certain consolation in the bustle and energy of the city. One part of town in particular seemed to reach out to him: Harlem.

In the next five years or so he worked at a variety of jobs—bar boy, longshoreman, fireman, and finally porter, then waiter, on the Pennsylvania Railroad. This was yet another apprenticeship, one in which he further developed the sympathy for the working class that remained with him all his life. Since his youth he had leaned politically toward socialism, and his years among the proletariat solidified his beliefs. His race consciousness developed hand-in-hand with his class consciousness. During this period of apprenticeship and developing awareness, he wrote. In 1918, he began a long association with Max Eastman, editor of the Communist magazine, *The Liberator*. McKay began publishing poems and essays in this revolutionary journal, and eventually became an associate editor. In 1919, in response to that year's bloody postwar race riots, McKay published in *The Liberator* what would become his most famous poem, "If We Must Die." The defiant tone and the open outrage of the poem caught the attention of the black community, and practically overnight, McKay was at the forefront of black American poets.

Then came another of the abrupt turns that were so much a part of McKay's life and work. Before his newly won reputation had a chance to flourish, he left for England where he stayed for more than a year, writing and editing for a Communist newspaper, *Workers' Dreadnought*, and, in 1920, publishing his first book of poetry since the Jamaican volumes, *Spring in New Hampshire, and Other Poems*. He returned to New York early in 1921 and spent the next two years with *The Liberator*, publishing a good bit of prose and verse and working on his principal book of poems, *Harlem Shadows*. Upon its publication in 1922, observes Wayne Cooper, McKay "was immediately acclaimed the best Negro poet since Paul Laurence Dunbar." Once again, however, he did not linger long over success. He was tired and in need of a change, especially after a chance meeting with his former wife reopened old wounds. Late in 1922, he traveled to Moscow for the Fourth Congress of the Third International. He quickly became a great favorite with Muscovites, and was allowed to address the Congress on the plight of American blacks and on the problem of racism within the Communist Party. As McKay described it, he was greeted "like a black ikon in the flesh." He was, it seemed, on the verge of a promising career as a political activist; but despite his successes in Russia, he still saw himself primarily as a writer. When he left Russia, he was "eager to resume what he considered the modern writer's proper function—namely, to record as best he could the truths of his own experience."

The 1920's were the decade of the expatriate artist, but though he spent most of his time in France until settling in Tangiers in 1931, McKay had very little to do with such writers as Ernest Hemingway and F. Scott Fitzgerald; his exile was too different from theirs. During his stay in Europe and North Africa, McKay published all his major fiction, along with a number of magazine articles. His first two novels, *Home to Harlem* and *Banjo*, were financially successful, in spite of the outraged reaction they drew from most black American critics. *Gingertown*, a collection of short stories, was not nearly so successful, and McKay's third novel, *Banana Bottom*, was a critical and financial disaster. Financially ruined, McKay was forced to end his expatriate existence.

With the help of some American friends, McKay returned to New York in 1934. He hoped to be of service to the black community, but on his return, observes Wayne Cooper, "he found a wrecked economy, almost universal black poverty, and little sense of unity among those black writers and intellectuals he had hoped to work with in years ahead." As for his literary ambitions, the Harlem Renaissance was finished; black writers were no longer in vogue. Not only could he not find a publisher, he also was unable to find any sort of a job, and wound up in Camp Greycourt, a government welfare camp outside New York City. Fortunately, Max Eastman was able to rescue him from the camp and help him get a job with the Federal Writers' Project. In 1937, he was able to publish his autobiography, *A Long Way from Home*. Once again, he was publishing articles in magazines, but his views isolated him from the mainstream black leaders; he felt, again in Cooper's words, that "their single-minded opposition to racial segregation was detrimental to any effective black community organization and to the development of a positive group spirit among blacks." McKay's thought at this time also shows a drift away from Communism, and a growing disillusionment with the fate of the "Grand Experiment" at the hands of the Soviets.

A Long Way from Home was neither a critical nor a financial success. Neither was his next and last book, *Harlem: Negro Metropolis*, a historical study published in 1940. By then, in spite of the steady work provided him by the Federal Writers' Project, his literary reputation was declining steadily. Despite his final acceptance of American citizenship in 1940, he could still not bring himself to regard the United States as home. His exile from both the black leadership and the left-wing establishment was becoming more and more total; worse still, his health began to deteriorate rapidly. Once again, like Walter Jekyll and Max Eastman in earlier years, a friend offered a hand. Ellen Terry, a Catholic writer, rescued McKay from a Harlem rooming house, and McKay's life took one last unexpected turn. As a young man he had rejected the fundamentalist Christianity of his father, and during his varied career had had little use for religion. Through his friendship with Terry, and later with the progressive Chicago bishop, Bernard Scheil, McKay experienced a change of mind and heart. In the spring of 1944, he moved to Chicago, and by fall of that year, he was baptized into the Roman Catholic Church.

At last he seemed to have found a refuge, though his letters reveal a lingering bitterness over his lot. With his newfound faith, however, came a satisfying involvement in Chicago's Catholic Youth Organization and the opportunity to go on writing. His health continued to decline, and on May 22, 1948, McKay died of heart failure. He had recently finished preparing his *Selected Poems of Claude McKay* for publication. It is probably just as well that the volume appeared posthumously, as it took five years to find a publisher; at the time of his death, all his works were out of print. After a requiem mass in Chicago, McKay was brought back to Harlem for a memorial service. He was buried in Queens, "a long way from home."

ANALYSIS

At the conclusion of his essay "The Renaissance Re-examined," which appears as the final chapter of Arna Bontemps's 1972 book, *The Harlem Renaissance Remembered*, Warrington Hudlin insists that any true appreciation of the Harlem Renaissance hinges on the realization that this celebrated literary phenomenon "opened the door" for later black writing. The Harlem Renaissance will always be remembered for this reason. It will be valued for its merits. It will come again to importance because of its idea." The poetry of Claude McKay must be read in much the same light. Though it is easy enough to find fault with much of his verse, he did help to "open the door" for those who would follow; as such, he deserves to be valued for his merits, judged by his strengths.

"INVOCATION"

Though progressive enough in thought, McKay never felt compelled to experiment much with the form of his poetry. In content, he is a black man of the twentieth century; in form, he is more an English lyricist of the nineteenth century, with Miltonic echoes here and there. The effect is, at times, a little peculiar, as in "Invocation," a sonnet in which the poet beseeches his muse to

> Let fall the light upon my sable face
> That once gleamed upon the Ethiopian's art;
> Lift me to thee out of this alien place
> So I may be, thine exiled counterpart,
> The worthy singer of my world and race.

Archaic trappings aside, there is a kind of majesty here, not bad work for a young man in his twenties. The Miltonic ring is probably no accident; McKay, it must be remembered, received something of an English gentleman's education. As the work of a black man pursuing what had been to that time primarily a white man's vocation, McKay's "Invocation" bears comparison with John Milton's "Hail native Language." One of the young Milton's ambitions was to vindicate English as poetic language, deserving of the same respect as Homer's Greek, Vergil's Latin, or Dante's Italian. McKay found himself in the position of vindicating a black man's experience of a white culture as a worthy subject for poetry.

"THE TROPICS IN NEW YORK"

Not all of McKay's verse concerns itself specifically with the theme of interracial tension. Among his poems are love lyrics, idyllic songs of country life, and harsher poems of the city, where "the old milk carts go rumbling by,/ Under the same old stars," where "Out of the tenements, cold as stone,/ Dark figures start for work." A recurring theme in McKay's work is the yearning for the lost world of childhood, which for him meant memories of Jamaica. This sense of loss is the occasion for one of his finest poems, "The Tropics in New York":

> Bananas ripe and green, and ginger-root,
> Cocoa in pods and alligator pears,
> And tangerines and mangoes and grape fruit,
> Fit for the highest prize at parish fairs.

The diction here is simple; one can almost hear Ernest Hemingway in the loving list of fruits. The speaker's memory stirs at the sight of a shop window. In the midst of the city his thoughts turn to images of "fruit-trees laden by low-singing rills,/ And dewy dawns, and mystical blue skies/ In benediction over nun-like hills." Here, in three straightforward quatrains, is the mechanism of nostalgia. From a physical reality placed by chance before him, the observer turns his eyes inward, visualizing a happy scene of which he is no longer a part. In the final stanza, his eyes are still involved in the experience, only now they have grown dim, "and I could no more gaze;/ A wave of longing through my body swept." All the narrator's senses tune themselves to grief as the quickening of smell and taste turns to a poignant hunger for "the old, familiar ways." Finally, the poem closes on a line as classically simple and tersely musical as anything in the poems of A. E. Housman: "I turned aside and bowed my head and wept."

Indeed, the poem is reminiscent of "Poem XL" in A. E. Housman's *A Shropshire Lad* (1896):

> Into my heart an air that kills
> From yon far country blows:
> What are those blue remembered hills,
> What spires, what farms are those?

It is a long way, to be sure, from Shropshire to Clarendon Parish, Jamaica, but the issue here is the long road back to lost experience, to that "land of lost content" that shines so plain, "The happy highways where I went/ And cannot come again." Any fair assessment of McKay's verse must affirm that he knew that land, those highways, all too well.

"WE WEAR THE MASK"

That same fair assessment, however, must give a prominent place to those poems on which McKay's reputation was made—his poems of protest. McKay, in the estimation of Arna Bontemps, was black poetry's "strongest voice since [Paul Laurence] Dunbar." Dunbar's "racial" verse is a good indication of the point to which black American poetry had progressed by World War I. His plantation-style dialect verse tries, with a certain ironic cheerfulness, to make the best of a bad situation. At their best, these poems exhibit a stinging wit. At their worst, they are about as dignified as a minstrel show. In his poems in literary English, Dunbar is more assertive of his racial pride but with an emphasis on suffering and forbearance, as in "We Wear the Mask." This poem speaks of the great cost at which pain and anger are contained:

> We smile, but O great Christ, our cries
> To Thee from tortured souls arise.
> We sing, but oh, the clay is vile
> Beneath our feet, and long the mile;
> But let the world dream otherwise,
> We wear the mask.

The anguish is plain enough, yet the poem, couched in a prayer, seems to view this "wearing of the mask" as an ennobling act, as a virtuous sacrifice. McKay was not inclined to view things in quite that way.

"IF WE MUST DIE"

From the spring through the fall of 1919, numerous American cities were wracked by bloody race conflicts, the worst of which was a July riot in Chicago that left dozens dead and hundreds injured or homeless. Although McKay was never the object of such violence, he and his fellow railroad waiters and porters walked to and from their trains with loaded revolvers in their pockets. Not unexpectedly, his reaction to the riots was far from mild; his concern was not with turning the other cheek, but with returning the offending slap. When the sonnet "If We Must Die" appeared in *The Liberator*, it marked the emergence of a new rage in black American poetry:

> If we must die, let it not be like hogs,
> Hunted and penned in an inglorious spot,
> While round us bark the mad and hungry dogs,
> Making their mock at our accursed lot.

Again, the form is of another century, the language dated, even by late nineteenth century standards—"O kinsmen! We must meet the common foe! . . . What though before us lies the open grave?" The message, however, is ageless, avoiding as the poem does any direct reference to race.

On the heels of much-publicized violence against black neighborhoods, the implications were clear enough, but the universality of the poem became more obvious with time. A Jewish friend of McKay's wrote him in 1939, "proclaiming that . . . ["If We Must Die"] must have been written about the European Jews persecuted by Hitler." In a more celebrated instance, Winston Churchill read the poem before the House of Commons, as if, in the words of black poet and critic, Melvin Tolson, "it were the talismanic uniform of His Majesty's field marshal." The message reaches back to Thermopylae and Masada, and forward to Warsaw, Bastogne, and beyond. In its coverage of the bloodbath at the New York State Prison at Attica, *Time* (September 27, 1971) quoted the first four lines of McKay's sonnet as the "would-be heroic" effort of an anonymous, rebellious inmate. McKay might not have minded; he stated in his autobiography that "If We Must Die" was "the only poem I ever read to the members of my [railroad] crew." A poem that touches prisoners, railroad workers, and prime ministers alike must be termed a considerable success, despite any technical flaws it may exhibit.

Even so, one must not altogether avoid the question of just how successful McKay's poems are as poems. James Giles, in his 1976 study, *Claude McKay*, remarks on the disparity "between McKay's passionate resentment of racist oppression and his Victorianism in form and diction," finding in this conflict "a unique kind of tension in many of his poems, which weakens their ultimate success." Giles is probably correct to a point. In many cases, McKay's art might have found fuller expression had he experimented more, let content more often shape form; he had shown abilities in this direction in his early Jamaican poems, and he was certainly open to experimentation in his later prose. The simple fact, however, is that he consistently chose to use traditional forms, and it would be unfair to say that it was a wholly unsuccessful strategy.

"THE LYNCHING"

Indeed, the very civility of his favorite form, the sonnet, sometimes adds an ironic tension that heightens, rather than diminishes, the effect of the poem. For example, one could imagine any number of grisly, graphic effects to be achieved in a *vers libre*, expressionistic poem about a lynching. In McKay's "The Lynching," though, one cannot help feeling the pull of an understated horror at seeing the act translated to quatrains and couplets: "and little lads, lynchers that were to be,/ Danced round the dreadful thing in fiendish glee." No further description of the "dreadful thing" is necessary. When McKay uses his poems to focus on real or imagined experience—a lynching, a cornered fight to the death, an unexpected remembrance of things past—his formal restraint probably works most often in his favor.

ANGRY SONNETS

In poems that set out to convey a self-conscious message, however, he tends to be less successful, not so much because the form does not fit the content as because poetry and causes are dangerous bedfellows. Some of McKay's other angry sonnets—"The White House," "To the White Fiends," "Baptism"—may leave readers disappointed because they preach too much. McKay's specifically sociological, political, and, later, religious views receive better expression elsewhere, in his prose. Perhaps that is why he did not devote so much of his time to poetry after the publication of *Harlem Shadows*. In any case, his position in black American poetry is secure. Perhaps he should be judged more by that which was new in his poems, and that which inspired other black writers to carry on the task, as later generations have judged the Harlem Renaissance—as a bold and determined beginning, a rolling up of the sleeves for the hard work ahead.

OTHER MAJOR WORKS

LONG FICTION: *Home to Harlem*, 1928; *Banjo: A Story Without a Plot*, 1929; *Banana Bottom*, 1933.

SHORT FICTION: *Sudom Lincha: Rasskazy o zhizni negrov v Severnoi Amerike*, 1925 (*Trial by Lynching: Stories About Negro Life in America*, 1977); *Gingertown*, 1932.

NONFICTION: *Negry v Amerike*, 1923 (*The Negroes in America*, 1979); *A Long Way from Home*, 1937 (autobiography); *Harlem: Negro Metropolis*, 1940.

MISCELLANEOUS: *My Green Hills of Jamaica, and Five Jamaican Short Stories*, 1779; *The Passion of Claude McKay: Selected Poetry and Prose, 1912-1948*, 1973 (contains social and literary criticism, letters, prose, fiction, and poetry; Wayne F. Cooper, editor).

BIBLIOGRAPHY

Brown-Rose, J. A. *Critical Nostalgia and Caribbean Migration*. New York: Peter Lang, 2009. Examines Caribbean writers including McKay, Jamaica Kincaid, Maryse Condé, and Edwidge Danticat, focusing on migration issues.

Cooper, Wayne F. *Claude McKay: Rebel Sojourner in the Harlem Renaissance*. Baton Rouge: Louisiana State University Press, 1987. This first full-length biography of McKay is a fascinating and very readable book. Special attention is paid to McKay's early life in Jamaica and the complex influences of his family. Includes nine photographs and a useful index.

Egar, Emmanuel E. *The Poetics of Rage: Wole Soyinka, Jean Toomer, and Claude McKay*. Lanham, Md.: University Press of America, 2005. Examines the poetry of McKay, Wole Soyinka, and Jean Toomer that expresses these poets' outrage over various injustices.

Gosciak, Josh. *The Shadowed Country: Claude McKay and the Romance of the Victorians*. New Brunswick, N.J.: Rutgers University Press, 2006. This biography of McKay regards him as one of the most important voices to come out of the Harlem Renaissance.

Hathaway, Heather. *Caribbean Waves: Relocating Claude McKay and Paule Mar-*

shall. Bloomington: Indiana University Press, 1999. A biographical and critical study of the lives and works of two writers and the way that their works have been shaped by their backgrounds as Caribbean immigrants.

Holcomb, Gary Edward. *Claude McKay, Code Name Sasha: Queer Black Marxism and the Harlem Renaissance*. Gainesville: University Press of Florida, 2007. This work takes a look at the life and writing career of McKay and examines his importance during the Harlem Renaissance.

James, Winston. *A Fierce Hatred of Injustice: Claude McKay's Jamaica and His Poetry of Rebellion*. New York: Verso, 2000. A critical study of McKay's early writing with a focus on the poet's use of Jamaican creole in two early collections, *Songs of Jamaica* and *Constab Ballads*, and in his previously uncollected poems for the Jamaican press. An anthology of the latter is provided together with McKay's comic sketch about Jamaican peasant life and his autobiographical essay.

Ramesh, Kotti Sree, and Kandula Nirupa Rani. *Claude McKay: The Literary Identity from Jamaica to Harlem and Beyond*. Jefferson, N.C.: McFarland, 2006. A biography that traces McKay's development from his youth through his old age.

Schwarz, A. B. Christa. *Gay Voices of the Harlem Renaissance*. Bloomington: Indiana University Press, 2003. Schwarz examines the work of four leading writers from the Harlem Renaissance—Countée Cullen, Langston Hughes, McKay, and Richard Bruce Nugent—and their sexually nonconformist or gay literary voices.

Tillery, Tyrone. *Claude McKay: A Black Poet's Struggle for Identity*. Amherst: University of Massachusetts Press, 1992. A well-documented biography tracing McKay's search for a movement with which to identify: black radical, socialist, communist, Catholic.

Richard A. Eichwald

HAKI R. MADHUBUTI
Don L. Lee

Born: Little Rock, Arkansas; February 23, 1942

OTHER LITERARY FORMS

Although Haki R. Madhubuti (MAH-dew-buh-tee) began his writing career as a poet and continues to write poems, he soon asserted that poetry was not only an aesthetic process, but also a sociopolitical act. Therefore, two themes permeating his work are also political goals: black unity and black power (through that unity). Because his efforts as a poet and writer demand total dedication to his political concerns—whether in his personal lifestyle or in his publishing ventures—Madhubuti has essentially chosen the role of poet-as-prophet. As he puts it, "*black* for the black poet is a way of life." It should come as no surprise, then, that less than half of his published writing has been poetry (despite its having been his initially favored genre), for Madhubuti does not intend to elevate his status in the black community by his writing so much as he seeks to transform the community through the writing act itself. To that end, he has become one of the foremost social essayists in the Black Nationalist movement, along with Amiri Baraka (LeRoi Jones), Maulana Ron Karenga, and Julius K. Nyerere.

Madhubuti has consistently used the social essay to espouse and develop the ideals, difficulties, and goals of what has come to be called cultural nationalism. His book *From Plan to Planet, Life Studies: The Need for Afrikan Minds and Institutions* (1973) perhaps best expresses the emphasis on "social content" in Madhubuti's use of the essay and "Blackpoetry," which, as he says in the preface to *Don't Cry, Scream*, is to "tell what's *to be* & how to *be* it," as vehicles for black liberation. The book, a collection of thirty brief essays organized into four distinct sections, is unified by the underlying premise that black survival, meaning the survival of all peoples of African descent anywhere in the world, including Africa, is threatened both by the political power of European and American governments and by the racism—latent and manifest—in those two Aryan-derived cultures.

In the attempt to unify the diaspora of African culture, Madhubuti begins by examining the individual's situation in an oppressive culture and asserts the necessity to "*create* or *re-create* an Afrikan (or black) mind in a *predominantly* European-American setting." (*Afrikan* here and throughout Madhubuti's writing is so spelled to indicate a harder *c* sound indigenous to African languages before the "contamination" of sound and spelling—implying sociopolitical domination—by European colonialism: the change in "standard" spelling is seen as a "revolutionary" act.) This first section, appropriately untitled in recognition of the difficulty involved in establishing a cultural perspective with which to begin a plan of unity, might be called "To See with Afrikan Eyes." The second section, "Life Studies," moves from the concern for the black individual to the problems inherent in the local black community. Here Madhubuti shifts from the necessity of self-esteem, or "positive identity," to the necessity for a black value system, *Nguzo Saba*, that subordinates individual success to the best interests of the black community as a whole. The code of *Nguzo Saba* nurtures self-reliance through cooperative education, business, and industry (urban or rural). To this end, he asserts that widely diverse and geographically scattered communities can form a "psychological unity" that will result in a Black Nation. Madhubuti's synthesis here achieves less theoretical complexity but more pragmatic clarity than similar ideas from his sources: Nyerere's *ujamaa*, African-based socialism; and Karenga's *kawaida*, African tradition and reason.

From this plan for cultural unity despite geographical disparity, Madhubuti focuses on the responsibility of the artist in "The Black Arts." Black artists, in these recommendations, bear the role of "culture stabilizers" who affirm racial identity, maintain political purpose, and define cultural direction in accordance with the principles of the previous section. They are, by implication, prophets who create and fulfill the prophecy of a Black Nation. Through cooperative publishing, teaching, and distribution, the artists help create new wealth, thus new power, for blacks in America—but only insofar as the black community gains unity, not merely in any sense of individual achievement. In the fourth section, "Worldview," Madhubuti extends the prior concerns for individual, community, and artist to blacks throughout the world. Loosely based on Nyerere's concepts and drawing on ideas in Frantz Fanon's *The Wretched of the Earth* (1965), as well as many other sources, he analyzes the rise of European colonialism from a cultural nationalist viewpoint and reasserts the necessity for the values defined in section two on a global as well as a national scale. While Nyerere bases his doctrine on a philosophy of issues that reaches toward love to nurture the culture, Madhubuti, revising those ideas, asserts that the "nationbuilding" of love within the community must focus on people—black people—not on issues. (*Love* is defined by him as "familyhood," "mutual involvement in one another," and "the brotherhood of man.")

The implicit contradiction throughout the essays, however, is that whites are perceived not only as the enemy of blacks in the United States, but also as "the world's enemy." No such contradiction in "a brotherhood of man" exists as long as Madhubuti speaks of blacks. In fact, it is worth noting that, aside from his condemnation of European and American colonialism (in its various forms), he argues from a problack rather than an antiwhite position. His antagonism to negative positions is explicitly stated: "Our struggle should not be based upon the *hate* of anything." In addition to this central contradiction, there are a number of flaws, particularly in unidentified sources and poor documentation, that weaken the polemic of this volume. It remains, however, an important tool in understanding the poetry of Madhubuti; in fact, considered with *Enemies: The Clash of Races* (1978), the work may be said to overshadow the poetry itself, for Madhubuti has moved increasingly to this literary form as his primary means of expressing his sociopolitical (which is to say artistic) vision.

One further major literary concern for Madhubuti has been literary criticism, especially the definition of "new Blackpoetry" in the light of the concepts of *ujamaa* and *kawaida*. His collection of critical essays, *Dynamite Voices: Black Poets of the 1960's* (1971), is significant in two respects: It established a responsibility for the black critic to evaluate seriously the merits of the emerging "cultural nationalist school" of black poets, and it provided a model for doing so (if sometimes uneven and superficial in its judgments). Here, too, Madhubuti shows a tendency for his social criticism to overrun his literary evaluation, but the book will remain an important contribution to the development of aesthetic standards for black literature. (Some of Madhubuti's insights have already been explored and expanded much more carefully and thoroughly than in his own book by Stephen Henderson and Addison Gayle, Jr.) Madhubuti regularly contributed a column, "Worldview," and book reviews to his journal *Black Books Bulletin*. Other reviews, short essays, polemical statements, and introductions are widespread in anthologies and journals such as *The Negro Digest* (later *Black World*), *Third World*, and *The Black Scholar*. In addition to his writings, recordings of Madhubuti are also available that add a great deal to the printed poem on the page. Like the work of Dylan Thomas, much of the delight in hearing Madhubuti's poetry—based as it is on the improvisations and unpredictable qualities of jazz and urban black speech patterns—is lost when his voice is absent. More so than for a great many poets, his work becomes more powerful when heard.

ACHIEVEMENTS

Perhaps Haki R. Madhubuti's single most impressive accomplishment has been not his success with new forms of poetry, his articulation of new social criticism, his formulation of new aesthetic principles, or his success as a publisher and editor, but his ability to accomplish all these goals, for which, he asserts, a black poet must struggle. Madhubuti *is* the black poet of his proposed "total dedication" to black liberation and "nationbuilding." In his embodiment of his principles and commitment, Madhubuti has reached into corners of the black community that have been heretofore untouched by black literature or liberation politics. Within four years of the publication of his first book, he had "sold more books of poetry (some 250,000 copies) than probably all the black poets who came before him combined" (*The Black Collegian*, February/March, 1971). One would be hard-pressed to name *any* American poet who could boast such a large figure in such short time—twenty-five thousand copies, 10 percent of Madhubuti's sales, might be considered a phenomenal success. Clearly, Madhubuti's popularity does not rest on library or classroom purchases; it is based on the very "market" he seeks to speak to: the black community. Having defined his audience as exclusively the blacks of the United States in his social criticism, he has found a quite remarkable response from that desired audience even though he is frequently blunt in his sarcastic ridicule of blacks who aspire to imitate whites. In taking the black community seriously as an audience, Madhubuti has discovered that the audience accepts him seriously. This interaction, then, seems to be the epitome of the "mutual involvement" between artists and community of which he writes in his social criticism.

Madhubuti's popular reception, however, has not diminished his success in a more narrowly defined black literary community. His influence on young black poets and writers of the 1970's is pervasive; one sees imitations of him and dedications to him in many black literary journals. His extensions of Baraka's theoretical positions in cultural nationalism have forced older black critics to reexamine and reevaluate their criteria for black aesthetic standards. His publishing and editing efforts have enabled many young black writers to reach print, as attested by his numerous introductions and reviews of their work. Most important, however, Madhubuti has succeeded continuously in educating (he would say *reeducating*) ever-increasing numbers of individuals within the black community to participate in that dialogue and to perpetuate it within the community. He has been, and remains, an essential leader in working toward black pride, unity, and power, or as he puts it, in giving "identity, purpose and direction" to black "nationbuilding."

BIOGRAPHY

Haki R. Madhubuti (who changed his name from Don Luther Lee to his Swahili name in 1973), was born in Little Rock, Arkansas, and moved to Chicago with his parents Jimmy and Maxine Lee midway through his childhood. After graduating from high school, Madhubuti continued his education at Wilson Junior College, Roosevelt University, and the University of Illinois at Chicago Circle. His formal education has been tempered, however, by a wide range of jobs that have increased his rapport with varied classes and individuals within the black community. After serving in the U.S. Army from 1960 to 1963, Madhubuti returned to Chicago to begin an apprenticeship as curator of the DuSable Museum of African History, which he continued until 1967. Meanwhile, he worked as a stock department clerk for Montgomery Ward (1963 to 1964), a post office clerk (1964 to 1965), and a junior executive for Spiegel's (1965 to 1966). By the end of 1967, Madhubuti's reputation as a poet and as a spokesperson for the new black poetry of the 1960's had grown sufficiently to enable him to support himself through publishing and teaching alone.

In 1968-1969, Madhubuti was writer-in-residence at Cornell University. Similar positions followed at Northeastern Illinois State College (1969-1970) and the University of Illinois at Chicago Circle (1969-1971), where he combined poet-in-residencies with teaching black literature. From 1970 to 1975, Madhubuti taught at Howard University, except for a year at Morgan State College where he was writer-in-residence for 1972-1973. The extensive popular reception of his poetry and the increasing frequency of his social essays made him a favorite if controversial reader and lecturer with black college students across the country. His influence and popularity also enabled him to found, in Chicago, the Institute of Positive Education/New Concept School in 1971. The institute published *Black Books Bulletin*, for which Madhubuti served as editor and director from 1971 to 1991. He is also the founder, publisher, and chairman of the board of Third World Press, one of the United States's largest and most successful independent African American book publishers, in operation since 1971. In conjunction with his publishing roles, Madhubuti is also a professor of English and director emeritus of the Gwendolyn Brooks Center at Chicago State University. Madhubuti has also held important executive positions with a number of Pan-African organizations such as the Congress of African People. Madhubuti's publishing, editing, teaching, and writing continue to maintain his stature within the Black Nationalist movement.

ANALYSIS

Much of Haki R. Madhubuti's poetry was initially greeted by outright condemnation on the part of white critics whose standards of aesthetic judgment were antagonistic, to say the least, toward the nationalist assumptions inherent in much of the new black poetry of the 1960's. Jascha Kessler, for example, in a review in *Poetry* (February, 1973), said that in "Lee all is converted to rant/ . . ./ [he] is outside poetry somewhere, exhorting, hectoring, cursing, making a lot of noise/ . . . you don't have to be black for that/ . . ./ it's hardly an excuse." Madhubuti's sociopolitical concerns, in short, were viewed as unfit for poetic rendering, and his urban, rap-style jazz rhythms and phrases in his poems were dismissed as simply disgruntled, militant ravings. Ironically, that sort of reception—and inability to move beyond the parameters of the New Criticism—supported exactly what the new black poets were claiming: White critical standards forced blacks to write as if they were white themselves and thereby denied them their own cultural heritage and suppressed their experience of oppression. Indeed, this is the dilemma in which the young Lee found himself; if he were to "succeed," he would need (even as a poet) to obliterate his own identity as a black man.

The writings of Amiri Baraka, probably more than any other poet's, as well as his independent studies in African culture (probably begun at the DuSable Museum), violently ruptured the assumption that accommodation to the dominant culture was the sole means by which blacks could survive in the United States. With the break from accommodationist thought, as Marlene Mosher suggests in *New Directions from Don L. Lee* (1975), Madhubuti began his struggle to create identity, unity, and power in a neo-African context that would preserve his heritage and experience while creating a possibility for the black community as a whole to free itself from the oppressive constraints of mainstream American culture. Madhubuti progressed from the accommodationist period through a reactive phase, then through a revolutionary program, to a prophetic vision. These four aspects of his poetry are distinct not only in the ideological content of his work, but also in the structure of the poems themselves. Once the prophetic vision had been embraced, it was necessary to begin a pragmatic clarification of that vision; the necessity to describe specifically the new Black Nation led, ironically, to an increasing devotion to prose, and thus Madhubuti's poetry seemed nearly to disappear—at least in publication—after his book of poems, *Book of Life*. That the vision of his poetry should result in the suspension of his poetry writing in favor of concrete description was, for those who laud his poetry, a great loss. It is not, however, incomprehensible, for Madhubuti, in urging the embodiment of his poetic vision and in describing *how* to build that vision in realistic terms, is actually carrying out what he first proposed as the goal of his work: to construct an African mind and to create a Black Nation. One assumes, then, that his activities left little time for him to pursue his poetry. Fortunately, he began again to publish books of poems in 1984.

The period of accommodation in Madhubuti's work is available only through autobiographical references found in the early poems of the reactive phase. This early "prepoetic" time is, appropriately, marked by a lack of articulation. Without his own voice, there are no poems, no prose, no statements of any kind. To speak as oneself for one's community was to react to that accommodation. Madhubuti's "confession" of that period, therefore, is marked by bitterness, hatred, and condemnation of almost everything he associated with white America, including himself. Several poems in his first book, *Think Black*, are testimonial as well as vengeful; it is clear in these poems that Madhubuti had been "liberating" himself for several years, and only then was testifying to that personal struggle through accommodation. He was to say later, in "Black Sketches" (*Don't Cry, Scream*), that he "became black" in 1963 and "everyone thought it unusual;/ even me."

THINK BLACK

Both the accommodationist period and the reactive phase are seen in *Think Black*, but the point of view is nearly always that of a reaction against accommodation. In "Un-

derstanding But Not Forgetting," Madhubuti speaks of his family life and his "early es-
cape/ period, trying to be white." Among his images are those of an intellectual
accommodationist who "still ain't hip," an uneducated grandmother "with wisdom that
most philosophers would/ envy," misery-filled weekends with "no family/ but money,"
a twenty-two-year-old sister with "five children," a mother involved in prostitution but
"providing for her family," and a cheating white newspaper distributor who kept "tell-
ing/ me what a good boy I was." Reexamining his childhood and adolescence in this
poem, Madhubuti concludes: "About positive images as a child—NONE," and further
that "About negative images as a child—all black." In his attempt to understand his
social conditioning and view it in the larger context of American culture, he is forced
to conclude that education, democracy, religion, and even the "BLACK MIDDLE
CLASS" (to which he has aspired) have failed him because of "the American System."
It is, in fact, those very outcasts of the black community itself—the grandmother and the
prostitute-mother, who "read Richard Wright and Chester Himes/ . . ./ [the] bad books,"
that offer examples of survival against overwhelming oppression.

BLACK PRIDE

Madhubuti had not, however, accomplished much more at that time than rejection of
the value system that had created his anger and despair: The awareness of *how* to "think
black" is vague. The last poem in the book, "Awareness," is a chant of only three words:
"BLACK PEOPLE THINK." In the variations of syntactical arrangement of these
words, however, one is left with the unmistakable impression that he will struggle to
learn from those outcasts of mainstream society just what it does mean to "THINK
BLACK." These lessons are the heart of his second book, *Black Pride*, which is still reactive but nevertheless substantial in its discovery of identity. Although many of these
poems remain confessional, there is an increase in the clarity of Madhubuti's sociopolitical development. In the brief lead poem, "The New Integrationist," he announces
his intention to join "negroes/ with/ black/ people." The one-word lines of the poem
force the reader to contemplate not only the irony in his use of "integration," but also the
implications inherent in the labels "negro" and "black." It is an appropriate keynote for
the fulfillment of that vague awareness with which his first book ended.

Perhaps the growth in self-identity that characterizes *Black Pride* begins, paradoxically, most clearly in "The Self-Hatred of Don L. Lee." The confessional stance of the
poet first acknowledges a love of "my color" because it allowed him to move upward in
the accommodationist period; it "opened sMall [sic]/ doors of/ tokenism." After "struggling" through a reading list of the forerunners of cultural nationalism, Madhubuti then
describes a breakthrough from "my blindness" to "pitchblack/ . . ./ awareness." His "all/
black/ . . ./ inner/ self" is now his strength, the basis for his self-identity, and he rejects
with "vehement/ hatred" his "light/ brown/ outer" self, that appearance that he had previously exploited by accepting the benefits of tokenism. While Madhubuti had escaped

accommodation by this time, he had not yet ceased to react to it; instead of having skin too dark, he had skin too light. He was, as black oral tradition puts it, "color-struck." He had, however, moved much deeper into the problem of establishing an identity based on dignity rather than denigration.

The growth of identity and black pride still remains, then, a function of what is not blackness instead of what is, or will become, Madhubuti's new Black Nation. In several poems such as "The Primitive," Madhubuti describes the loss of black values under American slavery and the subsequent efforts of blacks to imitate their oppressors who "raped our minds" with mainstream images from "Tv/ . . ./ Reader's Digest/ . . ./ tarzan & jungle jim," who offered "used cars & used homes/ reefers & napalm/ european history & promises" and who fostered "alien concepts/ of Whi-teness." His message here is blunt: "this weapon called/ civilization/ . . ./ [acts] to drive us mad/ (like them)." For all his vindictive bitterness, however, Madhubuti addresses himself to the black community more than he does to white America—self-reliance for self-preservation emerges as the crucial issue. As he suggests in the final poem "No More Marching Now," nonviolent protest and civil rights legislation have been undermined by white values; thus, "public/ housing" has become a euphemism for "concentration camps." His charge is typically blunt: "you better wake up/ . . ./ before it's too late."

Although the first two volumes of Madhubuti's poems exist in the tension between accommodation and reaction, they do show growth in the use of language as well as in identity and pride. His work, at times, suffers from clichéd rhetoric and easy catchphrases common to exhortation, but it also possesses a genuine delight in the playfulness of language even while it struggles forward in the midst of serious sociopolitical polemic. In his division of "white," for example, where the one-syllable word is frequently cut into the two-syllable "whi-te" or the second syllable is dropped completely to the next line, Madhubuti demonstrates more than typographical scoring for the sound of his poem, for he displays the fragmentation between ideals and the implementation of those ideals in American culture. In contrast, "Black man" appears frequently as one word, "blackman," sometimes capitalized and sometimes not—to emphasize the gradual dissolution of the individual's ego, to suggest the necessity for unity in the community for which he strives. Capitalization, in a similar way, sometimes connotes pride in his use of "BLACK." At other times, he uses derogatory puns, such as when "U.S." becomes "u ass." His models are street language, urban speech patterns, jazz improvisation, the narrative form of the toast, and the general inventiveness of an oral tradition that belongs wholly to black culture.

DON'T CRY, SCREAM

These early poems continue to develop both thematically and technically in Madhubuti's next two books, *Don't Cry, Scream* and *We Walk the Way of the New World*, in which he began to outline his revolutionary program. Mosher suggests that these works are consciously much less antiwhite and much more problack in their sociopolitical commitment. Madhubuti's artistic commitment fused completely with his politics; as he says in the preface to *Don't Cry, Scream*, "there is *no* neutral blackart." Black poetry is seen as "culture building" rather than as a tool to criticize either white society or blacks who seek assimilation. In this programmatic work, the hate, bitterness, and invective of the earlier two books give way to music, humor, and a gentler insistence on change. The poems are more consciously crafted than previously, but they do not compromise their essentially urgent political fervor.

In perhaps the most widely anthologized poem by Madhubuti, "But He Was Cool or: he even stopped for green lights," he humorously undermines the stance of black radicals who are far more concerned with the appearance of being a revolutionary than with a real commitment to working for change in the black community. His satire here is more implicit than explicit, for the reader views the "supercool/ ultrablack" radical in "a double-natural" hairstyle and "dashikis [that] were tailor made." His imported beads are "triplehip," and he introduces himself "in swahili" while saying "good-by in yoruba." Madhubuti then becomes more explicit in his satire by dividing and modifying "intelligent" to read "ill tel li gent," but he quickly moves back to implication by a rapidly delivered "bop" hyperbole that describes the radical as "cool cool ultracool/ . . ./ cool so cool cold cool/ . . . him was air conditioned cool" and concludes that he was "so cool him nicknamed refrigerator." The dissonance of the last word with the "ice box cool" earlier in the delivery clashes not only in sound, but also in economic and political connotation. This radical is so busy acting the role of a revolutionary that he has been seduced by the very goals of Western culture that Madhubuti is rejecting: money, power, and sex. By his superficial use of gestures, the "radical" has taken himself even further away from an awareness of the real needs in the black community. In the aftermath of riots in "detroit, newark, [and] chicago," the would-be revolutionary must still be informed that "to be black/ is/ to be/ very-hot." Despite the humor, music, and wordplay in one of Madhubuti's most consciously and carefully "aesthetic" poems, the message is still primarily political. Although the poem does react to the shallowness of the radical, it is worth noting that the poem is no longer essentially reactive in its tone; by the very act of informing the radical of his ignorance in the closure of the poem, the implication is established that even this caricature has the possibility of redemption in Madhubuti's version of Black Nationalism.

Throughout *Don't Cry, Scream*, Madhubuti begins to embrace a wider range of sensibilities in the black community while continuing to denounce those who would betray the needs of black people. In "Black Sketches," he describes Republican Senator Ed Brooke from Massachusetts (then a self-proclaimed liberal advocate of civil rights) as "slashing/ his wrist/ because somebody/ called him/ black," and portrays the conservative (relative to Madhubuti) Roy Wilkins as the token figure on the television show, "the mod squad." He is relentless in his attack on black leaders who work within mainstream politics. In another poem, however, "Blackrunners/ blackmen or run into blackness,"

Madhubuti celebrates the Olympic medal winners Tommie Smith and John Carlos for their Black Power salutes in 1968 during the awards ceremony. One could hardly describe their gesture as revolutionary, but Madhubuti accepts and praises their symbolic act as a sign of solidarity with his own sense of revolutionary change. In other poems, he is equally open to the role of black women, intellectuals, and Vietnam veterans. By the final poem of the volume, he is even willing to concede that the "negroes" whom he has denounced in earlier work may also be receptive to his political message. In "A Message All Blackpeople Can Dig (& a few negroes too)," Madhubuti announces that "the real-people" must "move together/ hands on weapons & families" in order to bring new meanings "to/ . . ./ the blackness,/ to US." While not exactly greeting antagonists with open arms (the parenthetical shift to the lower case in the title is quite intentional), his emphasis has changed from the coarse invective found in *Think Black* to a moral, political force that proceeds in "a righteous direction." Not even whites are specifically attacked here; the enemy is now perceived as "the whi-timind," attitudes and actions from "unpeople" who perpetuate racism and oppression. The message, in short, is now much closer to black humanim than it ever has been before: "blackpeople/ are moving, moving to return this earth into the hands of/ human beings."

WE WALK THE WAY OF THE NEW WORLD

The seeds for a revolutionary humanism planted at the close of *Don't Cry, Scream* blossom in *We Walk the Way of the New World*. The flowers are armed to be sure, but in signaling this change, the author's introduction, "Louder but Softer," proclaims that the "cultural nihilism" of the 1960's must give way to the "New World of black consciousness" in which education and self-definition (in the context of the community) will create not noisy, pseudorevolutionaries but self-confident leaders who pursue "real" skills—"doctors, lawyers, teachers, historians, writers"—for ensuring the survival and development of African American culture. Madhubuti's scope and purpose in this book is no less committed than it has been before, but it is far more embracing, compassionate, and visionary. His concern is the establishment of "an ongoing process aimed at an ultimate definition of our being." The tone of urgency ("We're talking about our children, a survival of a people") remains constant and clear, but its directions have moved completely "from negative to positive." While the ideas are not new in *We Walk the Way of the New World*, they do form Madhubuti's most consciously articulated and poetically designed program: Of the three sections that shape the book, "Black Woman Poems," "African Poems," and "New World Poems," he says, "Each part is a part of the other: Blackwoman is African and Africa is Blackwoman and they both represent the *New World*." What is new in the fourth volume, then, is the degree of structural unity and, to a certain extent, a greater clarity in describing the specific meaning of *Nguzo Saba*, a black value system: "design yr own neighborhoods/ . . . teach yr own children/ . . . but/ build yr own loop/ . . ./ feed yr own people/ . . ./ [and] protect yr own communities."

The unifying metaphor for the book is the pilgrimage into the New World. Arming the heroic, Everyman figure "blackman" (unnamed because he is potentially any black man in the service of community rather than in pursuit of individual, egotistical goals) with a knowledge of the contrasts between black women who are positive role-models (with their love tied inextricably to black consciousness) and black women who aspire to imitate white middle-class, suburban women, Madhubuti then distinguishes the values of precolonial Africa from those that have become "contaminated" by Western industrialization. Here his emphasis is on rural communalism, loving family life, and conserving natural resources. By the final section, "blackman" has ceased to function as a depersonalized hero and is embodied in the individuality (having derived such from the community) of real black men, women, and children. This section largely recapitulates the themes and messages of earlier work, but it does so in an affirmative tone of self-asserted action within *kawaida*, African reason and tradition. In the long apocalyptic poem "For Black People," Madhubuti dramatically represents a movement of the entire race from a capitalistic state of self-defeating inactivity to a socialistic economy in which mutual love and respect result in an ecologically sound, peacefully shared world of all races (although the "few whi-te communities/ . . . were closely watched"). The movement of the poem, symphonic in its structure, is, in fact, the culmination of Madhubuti's sociopolitical growth and artistic vision to this point.

BOOK OF LIFE

With *Book of Life*, Madhubuti introduces little new thought, but his ideas are expressed in a much more reserved political tone and poetic structure. His role is that of the visionary prophet, the wise sage offering advice to the young children who must inevitably carry on the struggle to build the New World that he has described. Indeed, the book's cover shows a photograph of his own son in the center of a star, and the volume is dedicated to him "and his sons, and their sons." Throughout the book, photographs of Madhubuti sitting or fishing with his son testify to his affirmation of the future. His introduction still affirms "black world unity" and looks to *kawaida* as the source of this new African frame of reference, but only six new poems speak explicitly to the political dimensions of his vision. The second section, captioned after the title of the book, is composed of ninety-two meditations that echo Laozi's *Dao De Jing* (c. third century B.C.E.). The language is simple but profound; the tone is quiet but urgent; the intended audience seems to be his son, but the community overhears him; the poetics are nearly devoid of device from any cultural context, but the force of the didacticism is sincere and genuine. Madhubuti, thinking of black poets who talk "about going to the Bahamas to write the next book," denounces those "poets [who] have become the traitors." It may well be that his sense of betrayal by black artists whom he had expected to assist him in his struggle for the New World and his own growing quietism combined to bring an end to his poetry—at least since the 1973 publication of this work. He seems to have followed his own proverb in *Book of Life*: "best teachers/ seldom teach/ they be and do."

Madhubuti demonstrated an astonishingly rapid growth in his poetry and thought—in only six years. With that sort of energy and commitment, it is not surprising that he should do what he has asked of others, shunning the success of the "traitors": to be and do whatever is necessary for the building of the New World. For Madhubuti, that necessity has meant a turning away from publishing poetry and a turning toward the education of the future generation. One might quite easily dismiss Madhubuti as a dreamer or a madman, but then one would need to recall such visionaries as William Blake, who was dismissed too much too soon.

EARTHQUAKES AND SUNRISE MISSIONS AND
KILLING MEMORY, SEEKING ANCESTORS

In the 1980's the growth in Madhubuti's poetry is clearly evident. A sizable portion of his later poems teach through the impact of artful language, rather than sounding merely teacherly. In Madhubuti's two poetry collections of the 1980's, *Earthquakes and Sunrise Missions: Poetry and Essays of Black Renewal, 1973-1983* and *Killing Memory, Seeking Ancestors*, represent some of his strongest writing as he trusts that his keen observation will yield a bold enough political statement.

For example, in "The Shape of Things to Come," written about an earthquake in Naples, Italy, he observes: "quicker than one can pronounce free enterprise/ like well-oiled rumors or elastic lawyers smelling money/ plastic coffins appear and are sold/ at dusk behind the vatican on the white market./ in Italy in the christian month of eighty/ in the bottom of unimaginable catastrophe/ the profit motive endures as children replenish the earth/ in wretched abundance."

Poems from these volumes, such as "Abortion," "Winterman," "The Changing Seasons of Life," "White on Black Crime," and "Killing Memory" all reflect his increased technical control and subtle political commentary. Poems collected here also show that ideologically, Madhubuti no longer continues to fight all the old battles. Christianity gets a break now, as do some white individuals. He has not, however, wavered in his fundamental commitment to black liberation and in his belief that cultural awareness can ignite and help sustain progressive political struggle. The love in him and for his mission has not diminished. If anything, it has grown.

HEARTLOVE

Ten years after the publication of his previous volume of poetry, Madhubuti produced *Heartlove*, an elegant collection drawn solely from Madhubuti's poetry and prose and designed to capture and celebrate the essence of love in marriage, family meditations, caring, commitment, and friendships. Acting as a poetic script for the cast of a wedding—minister, bride and groom, the maid of honor, and the best man—Madhubuti counsels, "rise with the wisdom of grandmothers, rise understanding that creation is ongoing, immensely appealing and acceptable to fools and geniuses, and those of us in between."

Each poem offers words of encouragement and advice to new couples or words of tribute to the lives that have influenced Madhubuti's. From "Wedding Poems" to "Quality of Love" to "Extended Families," *Heartlove* addresses crucial questions about building partnerships and the struggle to preserve community.

OTHER MAJOR WORKS

NONFICTION: *Dynamite Voices: Black Poets of the 1960's*, 1971; *From Plan to Planet, Life Studies: The Need for Afrikan Minds and Institutions*, 1973; *Enemies: The Clash of Races*, 1978; *Black Men: Obsolete, Single, Dangerous?*, 1990; *Claiming Earth: Race, Rage, Rape, Redemption—Blacks Seeking a Culture of Enlightened Empowerment*, 1994; *Tough Notes: A Healing Call for Creating Exceptional Black Men, Affirmations, Meditations, Readings, and Strategies*, 2002; *YellowBlack: The First Twenty-one Years of a Poet's Life, a Memoir*, 2005.

EDITED TEXTS: *To Gwen with Love: An Anthology Dedicated to Gwendolyn Brooks*, 1971 (with Francis Ward and Patricia L. Brown); *Say That the River Turns: The Impact of Gwendolyn Brooks*, 1987; *Confusion by Any Other Name: Essays Exploring the Negative Impact of "The Blackman's Guide to Understanding the Blackwoman,"* 1990; *Why L.A. Happened: Implications of the '92 Los Angeles Rebellion*, 1993; *Black Books Bulletin: The Challenge of the Twenty-first Century*, 1995; *Million Man March, Day of Absence: A Commemorative Anthology—Speeches, Commentary, Photography, Poetry, Illustrations, Documents*, 1996 (with Maulana Karenga); *Releasing the Spirit: A Collection of Literary Works from "Gallery Thirty-seven,"* 1998 (with Gwendolyn Mitchell); *Describe the Moment: A Collection of Literary Works from "Gallery Thirty-seven,"* 2000 (with Mitchell).

MISCELLANEOUS: *Earthquakes and Sunrise Missions: Poetry and Essays of Black Renewal, 1973-1983*, 1984.

BIBLIOGRAPHY

Gayle, Addison, Jr. *The Black Aesthetic.* Garden City, N.Y.: Doubleday, 1971. A well-indexed book that discusses Madhubuti in the context of the "new" black poetry of the 1960's. Includes one of Madhubuti's essays on that topic, along with a brief biography.

Hooper, Lita. *Art of Work: The Art and Life of Haki R. Madhubuti.* Chicago: Third World Press, 2007. This biography of Madhubuti looks at both his literary and political life, examining his roles as political activist, writer, educator, and husband.

Jennings, Regina. *Malcolm X and the Poetics of Haki Madhubuti.* Jefferson, N.C.: McFarland, 2006. Looks at the works of Malcolm X and Madhubuti in creating an image for African Americans and defining what it means to be black.

Madhubuti, Haki R. "Hard Words and Clear Songs: The Writing of Black Poetry." In *Tapping Potential: English Language Arts for the Black Learner*, edited by Charlotte K. Brooks et al. Urbana, Ill.: Black Caucus of the National Council of Teachers of English, 1985. Madhubuti outlines some of his poetic philosophy. He explains why he writes, as a poet, and as an African American. Helpful to understanding Madhubuti's outlook.

_____. "Interview with Haki Madhubuti." Interview. In *Heroism in the New Black Poetry: Introductions and Interviews*, edited by D. H. Melhem. Lexington: University Press of Kentucky, 1990. An illuminating discussion of Madhubuti's artistic and political aims.

Mosher, Marlene. *New Directions from Don L. Lee*. Hicksville, N.Y.: Exposition Press, 1975. Mosher provides criticism and interpretation of Madhubuti's important writing up to the mid-1970's. Includes a bibliography and an index.

Randall, Dudley. "Broadside Press: A Personal Chronicle." In *The Black Seventies*, edited by Floyd B. Barbour. Boston: Porter Sargent, 1970. A poet and editor, Randall clarifies the important relationship between Madhubuti's career and the rise of independent black presses in the 1960's. An essay by Madhubuti also appears in the collection.

Thompson, Julius E. "The Public Response to Haki R. Madhubuti, 1968-1988." *Literary Griot: International Journal of Black Expressive Cultural Studies* 4, nos. 1/2 (Spring/Summer, 1992): 16-37. A study of the critical treatment and public response to the works of Madhubuti.

Michael Loudon
Updated by Sarah Hilbert

JEAN TOOMER

Born: Washington, D.C.; December 26, 1894
Died: Doylestown, Pennsylvania; March 30, 1967

PRINCIPAL POETRY
"Banking Coal," 1922
"Blue Meridian," 1936
The Collected Poems of Jean Toomer, 1988

OTHER LITERARY FORMS

Most of the work of Jean Toomer (TEW-muhr) was in genres other than poetry. His one published volume of creative writing, *Cane* (1923), contains only fifteen poems, mostly short, and fourteen pieces that appear to be in prose. However, they are all informed with the poet's rather than the novelist's sensibility, and some of them are poems in all but line breaks, while all of them use assorted poetic devices either throughout or sporadically.

Toomer published several pieces of fiction after *Cane*, generally quite experimental inasmuch as they lacked plot, often included philosophical meditations, and indeed often worked more like poetry, with impressionistic scenes and descriptions and an emphasis on developing a theme through juxtaposition of sections rather than an overall sequence of action. Among these are "Winter on Earth" (*The Second American Caravan*, 1929), "Mr. Costyve Duditch" (*The Dial*, 1928), and "York Beach" (*New American Caravan*, 1929). The first two were collected in the posthumous volume *The Wayward and the Seeking* (1980), edited by Darwin T. Turner, along with a previously unpublished story from 1930, "Withered Skin of Berries," which is more in the style of *Cane*, though much longer than most of the pieces in that book.

Toomer published one short, fragmentary play during his lifetime, "Balo," in Alain Locke's collection *Plays of Negro Life* (1927), and two of several other plays which he wrote in *The Wayward and the Seeking*.

Nonfiction predominates in Toomer's work, indicating his concerns with philosophical and spiritual goals, as in "Race Problems and Modern Society" (1929), "The Flavor of Man" (1949), and *Essentials: Definitions and Aphorisms* (privately printed in 1931, some of its aphorisms having been printed earlier in *The Dial* and *Crisis*, with many appearing much later in *The Wayward and the Seeking*). These aphorisms are occasionally poetic and certainly worthy of contemplation, but they might be stronger if incorporated into actual poems. Portions of several versions of Toomer's autobiography appear in *The Wayward and the Seeking*. The rest of his many unpublished works, including many poems, remain in the Toomer Collection of the Fisk University Library.

ACHIEVEMENTS

Jean Toomer's *Cane* is one of the most memorable and appealing books in African American literature, conveying a vivid sense of the life of southern blacks around 1920 (though little changed since the time of slavery) and showing clearly the conflicts between the feelings of black people and the desensitizing and spirit-diminishing urban life they found in the North. However, *Cane* is significant not only for its content but also for its innovative form and style. Its combination of prose and verse, stories and poems, produces a unified impression, with poems foreshadowing or commenting on adjacent stories and the stories and sketches exploring a multitude of perspectives on black life, rural and urban.

Toomer's impressionistic style, his seductive but not mechanical rhythms, his brilliant imagery and figurative language, and his manipulation of language to produce a wide range of emotional and literary effects were refreshing to many black writers during and after the Harlem Renaissance of the 1920's. Instead of adhering strictly to traditional European models of form and meter (like that of his major black contemporaries Claude McKay and Countée Cullen) or the literary realism and straightforward narrative style of black fiction to that date, he joined the progression of revolutionary poets and fiction writers who were creating literary modernism, from Walt Whitman on through James Joyce, D. H. Lawrence, Gertrude Stein, Sherwood Anderson, and T. S. Eliot, up to Toomer's friend and contemporary Hart Crane.

Very few of Toomer's other works come even close to the towering achievement of *Cane*, but its poems and poetic prose provided later writers a successful means of evoking the feel of the black experience. A reader can still sense echoes of its style in the evocative prose of novelist Toni Morrison.

BIOGRAPHY

Jean Toomer (born Nathan Eugene Toomer) spent most of his life resisting a specific racial label for himself. His childhood and youth were spent in white or racially mixed middle-class neighborhoods in Washington, and his parents were both light skinned. Jean's father left shortly after his birth and his mother died after remarrying, so that the most potent adult influences on his life were his maternal grandparents, with whom he lived until his twenties. His grandfather, P. B. S. Pinchback, had been elected lieutenant-governor in Reconstruction Louisiana and served as acting governor in 1873. Toomer believed that his victory was helped by his announcement that he had black blood, although Toomer denied knowing whether it was true. One thing is clear: Pinchback had indeed served the Union cause in the "Corps d'Afrique."

Later in life, Toomer denied that he was a Negro—an acceptable statement if one understands his definition of "Negro" as one who identifies solely with the black race, for he, with certainly a great deal of nonblack ancestry, saw himself as not white, either, but "American," a member of a new race which would unify the heretofore conflicting racial groups through a mixture of racial strains. The attainment of such an "American" race remained his goal throughout most of his life after *Cane*.

Toomer's education after high school was varied, from agriculture at the University of Wisconsin to the American College of Physical Training in Chicago. Rather than completing courses toward a formal degree, however, he pursued his own reading in literature and social issues while working at assorted jobs until he decided to devote all his efforts to writing.

The real nudge came in the form of a three-month stint as substitute principal of a school in a small Georgia town in the fall of 1921. He returned to Washington in November with material for a whole book. He published several poems and stories in assorted periodicals the following year and then gathered most of them and many new ones into a carefully structured book called *Cane*, published in 1923 by Boni and Liveright. The book caused a considerable stir among the influential white literati with whom he associated (such as Waldo Frank, Sherwood Anderson, and Hart Crane) and among black writers and intellectuals as well. However, in its two printings (the second in 1927), it sold fewer than a thousand copies.

That same year, Toomer met the Russian mystic George Gurdjieff and embraced his philosophy of higher consciousness. After studying with him in France, Toomer returned to spread his teachings in the United States. A ten-month marriage to a white poet, Margery Latimer, ended with her death in childbirth in 1932. Two years later, he married another white woman, Marjorie Content, and spent the rest of his life with her. This period in Toomer's life was largely devoted to self-improvement for himself and others, as he lectured and continued to write primarily philosophical and spiritually oriented work. He continued to publish some literary works until 1936, when his career came virtually to an end, despite attempts to have other works published. He became a Quaker and maintained no further identity with the black race, dying in 1967 largely forgotten.

ANALYSIS

Jean Toomer was the writer of one book; no matter how often the phrase is used to disparage him, it cannot be denied. Beyond *Cane*, his only other works of value are the long poem "Blue Meridian," a small amount of short fiction, and his autobiographical writings. His plays, most of his other poetry, and his nonfiction are negligible, yet even if he had written only *Cane*, he would always be remembered as a major African American author—and primarily as a poet.

CANE

Cane is an eccentric book, experimental and unclassifiable in its combination of poems and what is technically prose—pieces which are generally developed as short stories (somewhat like those of Anderson or Joyce) but are occasionally "mere" sketches, sometimes prose poems without plot, encompassing no more than a few pages and conveying impressionistically the sense of a person's spirit. Some of the pieces approach drama, with conversation printed like dialogue, setting described as meticulously as for a stage designer, and action presented in the present tense.

Whether prose, drama, or verse, all are imbued with a poet's sensibility: precise depiction of details using all the senses vividly, a rhythmic quality without slavish adherence to metrics, a sensitivity to words, phrasing, variations of theme, a fine ear for sound, and a polished sense of organic structure. Few books, whether prose or verse, have less of the prosaic than this one, which can put readers in an almost unabated state of intensity and exaltation, drawing them in by language, sound, rhythm, and form.

Toomer's purpose in this work is to embody what he sees as the dying folk spirit of the South by depicting the lives of its people and re-creating their feelings through language and rhythm. *Cane* achieves a vivid sense of the sensuality of its women, the alternating anguish and joy of life in the South, the toughness and beauty of the land of Georgia. These themes appear primarily in the first third of the book; the second third moves into the city in the North, where blacks from the South have difficulty fitting into the white-dominated social patterns while retaining roots in the South; in the final third, Ralph Kabnis, a northern black man, comes South and the focus is on his conflict with the South, looking ahead to William Faulkner's *Absalom, Absalom!* (1936) and Quentin Compson's climatic cry "I don't hate the South!" Throughout the book, Toomer shows both attraction to the South and a sense of holding back from it—on the part of a narrator in the first third, of Kabnis in the last third, and of assorted northern-based characters in the middle third, who are losing touch with their black roots. The book, however, is hardly a glorification of the way of life of southern blacks: Kabnis notes that things are not so bad as the North thinks; yet the South still hosts an occasional lynching, as Toomer several times reminds his readers. Still, Toomer appreciates a vitality in southern blacks that disappears when they are removed from the land, a process that Toomer views as unfortunately inevitable in the modern world.

To create this sense of vitality and closeness to the land and the natural world, Toomer uses a vast array of references to nature—the pines, the cane fields, the sky at dusk, the red soil—as images themselves, as similes or metaphors in connection with his characters, or as recurring leitmotifs in the operatic development of his sketches. He uses rhythm and repetition to engage the reader in the immediacy of these sensory experiences. A close analysis of one of his pieces—"Karintha," the opening sketch in *Cane*—will illustrate Toomer's typical methods.

"KARINTHA"

Like other pieces in the book, "Karintha" opens with an epigraph, a songlike refrain of four lines that recurs throughout the sketch as a unifying device. The first of four paragraphs of varying lengths then introduces Karintha as a child, summing her up in the first sentence, which is poetically accretive rather than prosaically structured; the final adjective cluster echoes words from the epigraph's refrain. Two sentences in parallel construction follow, dealing with the actions the old men and the young men take with her, followed by two sentences in response to these, describing their respective feelings about her. The final sentence sums up the paragraph and "this interest of the male," with a metaphoric interpretation of it and a note of foreboding.

The second paragraph re-creates her girlhood in terms of concrete actions and images: visual (color, shape, light), auditory (sounds of feet, voice, silence), kinetic (running, wind), and tactile (stoning the cows, touching the earth). It sums up her sexual nature as well and ends with two sentences referring to the wishes of the old and young men from the first paragraph, regarding Karintha as she matures. Before Karintha is shown as a woman, the refrain of the epigraph is repeated, the first three lines each being cut by a few words. The new rhythm creates a pace appropriately faster than the wondering, more meditative earlier version.

The third paragraph makes assorted references to the subject matter and phrasing of earlier paragraphs. Repetitions of actual sentences and phrases and of sentence structure (in a series of short sentences showing what young men do for Karintha) evoke the sense of poetry, as does the second half of the paragraph, which, through indirection, reveals Karintha's murder of her infant. The birth is presented as a kind of emotionless miracle unconnected with Karintha herself, while the scene is given sensory richness. Juxtaposed, after ellipses, is the description of a nearby sawmill, its smoldering sawdust pile, and the heaviness of the smoke after Karintha's return. Ending this paragraph is a short song that someone makes up about smoke rising to "take my soul to Jesus," an unconsciously appropriate elegy for the unwanted baby.

The final paragraph begins as the third did, "Karintha is a woman," and then echoes the last sentence of the first paragraph: "Men do not know that the soul of her was a growing thing ripened too soon." Toomer then suggests her unbreachable remoteness from men; the last sentence recalls the first in this sketch, describing her at twenty in the phrases used to describe her as a child. After a last repetition of her name, followed by ellipses, comes a repetition of the epigraph, followed by an ominous repetition of its last two words, "Goes down," and then more ellipses, hinting at the inevitable descent and defeat of this beautiful, vital creature, brought to maturity too soon through misuse by men.

Though printed as prose, this piece is essentially poetic; the outer details of Karintha's life are merely hinted, but Toomer's poetic prose gives a full sense of Karintha's person and appeal through the precise sensory details of the second paragraph, the recurring patterns of the old and young men's responses to her, and the use of songs as commentary. The echoes and repetitions of images and phrases act as leitmotifs, and Toomer's careful arrangement of them gives the piece a satisfying structure and a strong sense of Karintha's doom, trapped in an unchanging pattern.

FORM, STYLE, AND TONE

Such leitmotifs, along with vivid imagery and sentence patterns that are short, repeated, and often fragmentary, are used throughout the prose pieces of *Cane* in place of rhyme and meter and line division to produce the quality of poetry. Indeed, many of these pieces (including "Rhobert," "Calling Jesus," "Seventh Street") must be read, like "Karintha," more as poetry than as fiction.

In the pieces clearly printed as poetry, Toomer is less experimental. Many of his poems use orthodox rhyme schemes and meters that a Henry Wadsworth Longfellow or James Russell Lowell would approve. However, scarce as the poems in *Cane* are, they cover a variety of forms that few single books of poetry display. "Song of the Son," for example, is skillfully rhymed, beautifully evoking in five stanzas of flowing iambic pentameter the southern music that the poet is trying to capture in literature—as he says in this poem, before it vanishes. There are poems of rhymed couplets and brief pieces such as the Imagists might produce. There is a "Cotton Song," such as the work songs that slaves or free but poor farmhands might sing. There is much free verse, notably in "Harvest Song." Toomer's choices are not arbitrary; they suit the moods and subjects of their respective poems, conveying the spectrum of feelings that the writer wishes to present, from joy and exaltation to bitterness and despair.

Toomer also varies style and tone, as well as form, to suit theme and mood. Grim and laconic irony flavors "Conversion," as the African succumbs to "a white-faced sardonic god." "Georgia Dusk" offers lush images both of southern life and of the African past (a recurring motif throughout the book). "Portrait in Georgia," with its short free-verse lines, reads like a catalog of bodily parts, such as an auctioneer would have prepared. Each is described through images of southern white violence: "lyncher's rope," "fagots," "scars," "blisters," "the ash of black flesh after flame." This poem makes no explicit statement, but the juxtaposition of human parts with these images, presented so simply and concisely, evokes a subtle sense of horror and sets up an appropriately ominous mood for the following story, "Blood-Burning Moon," which ends with an actual lynching. However attractive may be the Georgia of pines, red soil, sweet-smelling cane, and beauteous dusks, Toomer insists on reminding his reader of the dangers there as well, even without explicit condemnation of the bigoted whites or the oppressive social system. Toomer works by indirection, but without diminished effect.

"HARVEST SONG"

A similarly strong but quite different effect is achieved in "Harvest Song," which presents a field worker suffering at the end of a long day from chill, hunger, thirst, and fatigue. Each poetic "line" is made up of one or more sentences and takes up between one and five lines of print on the page. These sentences are generally short, simple statements that the speaker can barely utter, and they are often repeated, emphasizing his basic human needs, which remain unsatisfied. Toomer's words may not be those that the worker would actually use, but they mirror his thoughts closely, just as the prose pieces of *Cane* give a clear sense of their characters' minds and lives without using their actual language. The simple sentences and their repetition give an accurate sense of the worker's numbness. The poem's last long line (five sentences) is a more exalted outburst, though still despairing: The harvester beats his soft palms against the stubble in his field, causing himself pain that takes away his awareness of hunger, as the last sentence makes shockingly clear. "Harvest Song" indeed! The speaker hardly feels like singing with his throat parched from thirst; and what he harvests for himself means only more pain. Through the use of first-person narration and a simple style, Toomer evokes not pity for the poor worker, not an external look as in Edwin Markham's "The Man with the Hoe," but rather an empathy from within, allowing the reader to participate fully in the experience.

SPIRITUAL AND PHILOSOPHICAL BELIEFS

Too often, unfortunately, Toomer's later poetry drops the effective devices used in *Cane* and becomes didactic, explicitly philosophical, lacking *Cane*'s brilliantly realized images of concrete reality or its sharp, often startling metaphors. Toomer was mightily inspired by his few months in Georgia, and his sojourn even affected his interpretations of his own more familiar Washington and New York life; but after he had said what he had to say about the South, and the North in relation to the South, he seems to have exhausted his inspiration, except for his more "universal" themes, with only a little sense of poetry left, to be used in "Blue Meridian" and his stories "Winter on Earth" and "Withered Skin of Berries." The latter story returned Toomer to the lyrical style and poetic sense of structure of the *Cane* stories, but for the most part, Toomer preferred to ignore stylistic and literary matters and chose to express his spiritual and philosophical beliefs, largely influenced by Gurdjieff's teachings, urging a regeneration of humanity that would eliminate the differences imposed by racial and other categories and bring people closer to God, one another, and the natural world.

"BLUE MERIDIAN"

This is the point that Toomer makes explicitly in his last major work, the long poem "Blue Meridian," first published in full in *New American Caravan* (1936) after a selection from an earlier version had appeared in *Adelphi* and *Pagany*. A further revised version is printed in Langston Hughes and Arna Bontemps's anthology *The Poetry of the Negro, 1746-1949* (1949), which places more emphasis on God and more clearly reveals Toomer's notion of the transformed America. A few of the more minor revisions are for the better. This is the version published in *The Wayward and the Seeking*, with some incidental changes.

"Blue Meridian" follows a structure much like that of Walt Whitman's longer poems, such as "Passage to India" or "Crossing Brooklyn Ferry," with recurring phrases or stanzas, often significantly altered. While it is not divided into individual sections, as T. S. Eliot's *The Waste Land* (1922) and Hart Crane's *The Bridge* (1930) are—nor does it use the range of poetic forms of which Eliot and Crane availed themselves—it nevertheless follows those poems in being an examination and criticism of the twentieth century world, achieving a multifaceted view by varying tone and form.

Written largely in a hortatory, exalted style in an effort to invoke Toomer's higher spiritual goals for a better world and unified humankind, "Blue Meridian" explores the past and current conditions of America. The European, African, and "red" races are presented in appropriate images—even stereotypes—each being shown as incomplete. Toomer's goal, as in much of his prose, is to achieve a new race beyond individual racial identities, a "universal human being" to be called the "blue meridian," the highest stage of development beyond white and black, beyond divisions of East and West, of religion, race, class, sex, and occupational classification, and transcending the materialism of a commercial culture and the private concerns of individuals. The message is not so different from Whitman's, except for greater criticism of modern business and the insistence on the mingling of the races.

DETRACTIONS OF LATER WORK

Racial themes and the black experience are missing from Toomer's later poems—and even some of his earlier ones, such as "Banking Coal" (*Crisis*, 1922). He was living with a white wife, quite isolated from the African American literary world, or from any literary world at all. Certainly one should not say that a black writer (even one with so little black ancestry as Toomer) should write only on black themes, but any writer should write out of direct experience; too much of Toomer's poetry aside from *Cane* is vague and didactic, too intentionally "universal," too generally spiritualized, and essentially prosaic, like his aphorisms, which lack the bite of Ralph Waldo Emerson's.

Unfortunately, Toomer's vocabulary in this later poetry—including "Blue Meridian"—too often emulates that of Whitman at his most inflated moments, even when Toomer has a true poetic idea, as in "The Lost Dancer," which opens: "Spatial depths of being survive/ The birth to death recurrences. . . ." It is not so much the Latinate vocabulary, which Toomer's great contemporaries Crane and Wallace Stevens also used, but rather that, while they made much of the orotund, sensual sounds and suggestiveness of Latinate words, Toomer's word choices are flat and vague, words made familiar through bombastic social-science jargon. Whereas the *Cane* poems stand out particularly for the vitality of their imagery, the apt metaphors and similes in "Face" and "Portrait in Georgia," the richness of language and sensory detail in "Song of the Son" and "Georgia Dusk," and the harshness of the concrete nouns, verbs, and adjectives in "Harvest Song," images in the later poetry are greatly minimized. Here Toomer abandons the exalted Romantic eloquence of "Song of the Son" and the verbal and emotional starkness of "Harvest Song" in favor of making philosophical statements.

At his best, Toomer was a brilliant artist in words, a sensitive portrayer of the life he lived and observed, as well as a sincere and concerned member of the human race. *Cane* will forever keep his name alive and arouse an interest in his other work, however inferior most of it has turned out to be. The musical quality of his best poetry and prose will be admired, not for its mere beauty but for its aptness to its subjects: the beauty and appeal as well as the tragedy of the life of the South.

OTHER MAJOR WORKS

SHORT FICTION: "Mr. Costyve Duditch," 1928; "York Beach," 1929.

PLAY: *Balo*, pb. 1927.

NONFICTION: "Race Problems and Modern Society," 1929; "Winter on Earth," 1929; *Essentials: Definitions and Aphorisms*, 1931; "The Flavor of Man," 1949; *Jean Toomer: Selected Essays and Literary Criticism*, 1996 (Robert B. Jones, editor); *The Letters of Jean Toomer, 1919-1924*, 2006 (Mark Whalan, editor).

MISCELLANEOUS: *Cane*, 1923 (prose and poetry); *The Wayward and the Seeking*, 1980 (prose and poetry; Darwin T. Turner, editor); *A Jean Toomer Reader: Selected Unpublished Writings*, 1993 (Frederik L. Rusch, editor).

BIBLIOGRAPHY

Byrd, Rudolph. *Jean Toomer's Years with Gurdjieff: Portrait of an Artist, 1923-1936.* Athens: University of Georgia Press, 1990. A good introduction to Toomer's years of studying Orientalism and the mystical philosophy of George Gurdjieff. It indicates that, although Toomer was an African American writer, his concerns were primarily spiritual and philosophical rather than social and ethnic. It is a fascinating account of one part of Toomer's life.

Fabre, Geneviève, and Michel Feith, eds. *Jean Toomer and the Harlem Renaissance.* New Brunswick, N.J.: Rutgers University Press, 2001. A collection of essays that reexamine Toomer, placing the novelist among his contemporaries in America and in Europe.

Ford, Karen Jackson. *Split-Gut Song: Jean Toomer and the Poetics of Modernity.* Tuscaloosa: University of Alabama Press, 2005. A study of Toomer's poetics, concentrating on *Cane* but also describing the poet's later life.

Grant, Nathan. *Masculinist Impulses: Toomer, Hurston, Black Writing, and Modernity.* Columbia: University of Missouri Press, 2004. Grant compares and contrasts the works of Toomer and Zora Neale Hurston, looking at the ideas of masculinity and modernism.

Griffin, John Chandler. *Biography of American Author Jean Toomer, 1894-1967.* Lewiston, N.Y.: Edwin Mellen Press, 2002. The author traces Toomer's life from its beginnings to his work on *Cane*, to his meeting with Gurdjieff, and to the decline in his later years.

Kerman, Cynthia. *The Lives of Jean Toomer: A Hunger for Wholeness*. Baton Rouge: Louisiana State University Press, 1988. This book gives an account of the various stages of Toomer's life and his attempts to find spiritual guidance and revelation throughout his lifetime. An interesting account of a fascinating life.

Scruggs, Charles, and Lee VanDemarr. *Jean Toomer and the Terrors of American History*. Philadelphia: University of Pennsylvania Press, 1998. Provides critical evaluation of *Cane* and other Toomer works. Includes bibliographical references and an index.

Taylor, Paul Beekman. *Shadows of Heaven*. York Beach, Maine: S. Weiser, 1998. Examines the lives and works of Toomer, George Gurdjieff, and A. R. Orage.

Vetter, Lara. *Modernist Writings and Religio-scientific Discourse: H. D., Loy, and Toomer*. New York: Palgrave Macmillan, 2010. Vetter examines Toomer, H. D., and Mina Loy in terms of how their writings reflect modernism, science, and spirituality.

Scott Giantvalley

ALICE WALKER

Born: Eatonton, Georgia; February 9, 1944

OTHER LITERARY FORMS

Although Alice Walker's poetry is cherished by her admirers, she is primarily known as a fiction writer. The novel *The Color Purple* (1982), generally regarded as her masterpiece, achieved both popular and critical success, winning the Pulitzer Prize and the National Book Award. The Steven Spielberg film of the same name, for which Walker acted as consultant, reached an immense international audience.

Other Walker fiction has received less attention. Her first novel, *The Third Life of Grange Copeland* (1970), depicts violence and family dysfunction among people psychologically maimed by racism. *Meridian* (1976) mirrors the Civil Rights movement, of which the youthful Walker was actively a part. Later novels, *The Temple of My Familiar* (1989), *Possessing the Secret of Joy* (1992), and *By the Light of My Father's Smile* (1998) have employed narrative as little more than a vehicle for ideas on racial and sexual exploitation, abuse of animals and the earth, and New Age spirituality. *In Love and Trouble: Stories of Black Women* (1973) and *You Can't Keep a Good Woman Down* (1981) revealed Walker to be one of the finest of late twentieth century American short-story writers. She also has written an occasional children's book (*To Hell with Dying*, 1988, is particularly notable) and several collections of essays (*In Search of Our Mothers' Gardens: Womanist Prose*, 1983, is the most lyrical) that present impassioned pleas for the causes Walker espouses.

ACHIEVEMENTS

At numerous colleges, as a teacher and writer-in-residence, Alice Walker established herself as a mentor, particularly to young African American women. Her crusades became international. To alert the world to the problem of female circumcision in Africa, she collaborated with an Anglo-Indian filmmaker on a book and film. She has been a voice for artistic freedom, defending her own controversial writings and those of others, such as Salman Rushdie. In her writings and later open lifestyle, she affirmed lesbian and bisexual experience. However, the accomplishment in which she took the most pride was her resurrection of the reputation of Zora Neale Hurston, a germinal African American anthropologist and novelist, whose books had gone out of print.

Walker won the Rosenthal Award of the National Institute of Arts and Letters for *In Love and Trouble* and received a Charles Merrill writing fellowship, a National Endowment for the Arts award, and a Guggenheim Fellowship. Her second book of poetry, *Revolutionary Petunias, and Other Poems*, received the Lillian Smith Award and was nominated for a National Book Award. Her highest acclaim came with the novel *The Color Purple*, for which she won the National Book Award and the 1983 Pulitzer Prize. She received the Fred Cody Award for lifetime achievement in 1990. Walker was inducted into the California Hall of Fame in 2006.

BIOGRAPHY

Alice Malsenior Walker was the youngest of eight children born to a Georgia sharecropper and his wife. Her father earned about three hundred dollars per year, while her mother, the stronger figure, supplemented the family income by working as a maid. Walker herself was a bright, confident child until an accident at age eight blinded her in one eye and temporarily marred her beauty. At this time, she established what was to become a lifelong pattern of savoring solitude and making the most of adversity. She started reading and writing poetry.

Because of her partial blindness and her outstanding high school record, Walker qualified for a special scholarship offered to disabled students by Spelman College, the prestigious black women's college in Atlanta. When she matriculated there in 1961, her neighbors raised the bus fare of seventy-five dollars to get her to Atlanta.

As a Spelman student, Walker was "moved to wakefulness" by the emerging Civil Rights movement. She took part in demonstrations downtown, which brought her into conflict with the conservative administration of the school. Finding the rules generally too restrictive and refreshed with her new consciousness, she secured a scholarship at Sarah Lawrence College in Bronxville, New York. She then felt closer to the real action that was changing the country. At Sarah Lawrence College, she came under the influence of the poet Muriel Rukeyser, who recognized her talent and arranged for her first publications. She also took a summer off for a trip to her "spiritual home," Africa. She returned depressed and pregnant, contemplated suicide for a time, but instead underwent an abortion and poured her emotions into poetry.

After graduation, Walker worked for a time in the New York City Welfare Department before returning to the South to write, teach, and promote voter registration. She married Melvyn Leventhal, a white Jew, and worked with him on desegregation legal cases and Head Start programs. Their child, Rebecca, was born during this highly productive period. By the time the marriage ended in 1976, Walker was already becoming recognized as a writer, though she did not become internationally famous until after the publication of *The Color Purple*.

Walker continued to write during the 1980's and 1990's, though never again achieving the acclaim or the notoriety that *The Color Purple* brought her. Critics complained of her stridency, the factual inaccuracies in her writings, and her tendency to turn her works of fiction into polemics. Many African Americans felt that her writings cast black society in a grim light. Walker moved to California and lived for several years with Robert Allen, the editor of *Black Scholar*. Times had changed; the motto was no longer "black and white together": marriages between Jews and African Americans were out, and black-black relationships were in.

Walker also became more alert to the problems women of color faced throughout the world. Taking a female partner, she decided to devote her time and talents to celebrating women and rectifying wrongs committed against them. In March of 2003, Walker was arrested for protesting the Iraq War. In 2009, Walker visited Gaza to promote peace and friendlier relations between Egypt and Israel. Walker has always encouraged awareness of important issues in her writing, but she has attracted attention to issues such as problems in the black culture, violence against women, and the ravages of war by personally participating in or protesting events about which she feels passionately.

ANALYSIS

Alice Walker writes free verse, employing concrete images. She resorts to few of the conceits, the extended metaphors, the Latinate language, and other common conventions of poetry. Readers frequently say that her verses hardly seem like poetry at all; they resemble the conversation of a highly articulate, observant woman. Although her poetry often seems like prose, her fiction is highly poetic. The thoughts of Miss Celie, the first-person narrator of *The Color Purple*, would not have been out of place in a book of poetry. Boundaries between prose and poetry are minimal in the work of Walker. Her verse, like her prose, is always rhythmic; if she rhymes or alliterates, it seems to be by accident. The poetry appears so effortless that its precision, its choice of exact image or word to convey the nuance the poet wishes, is not immediately evident. Only close scrutiny reveals the skill with which this highly lettered poet has assimilated her influences, chiefly E. E. Cummings, Emily Dickinson, Robert Graves, Japanese haiku, Li Bo, Ovid, Zen epigrams, and William Carlos Williams.

Walker's poetry is personal and generally didactic, generated by events in her life, causes she has advocated, and injustices over which she has agonized. The reader feels that it is the message that counts, before realizing that the medium is part of the message. Several of her poems echo traumatic events in her own life, such as her abortion. She remembers the words her mother uttered over the casket of her father, and she makes a poem of them. Other poems recall ambivalent emotions of childhood: Sunday school lessons which, even then, were filled with discrepancies. Some poems deal with the creative process itself: She calls herself a medium through whom the Old Ones, formerly mute, find their voice at last.

Some readers are surprised to discover that Walker's poems are both mystical and socially revolutionary, one moment exuberant and the next reeking with despair. Her mysticism is tied to reverence for the earth, a sense of unity with all living creatures, a bond of sisterhood with women throughout the world, and a joyous celebration of the female principle in the divine. On the other hand, she may lament that injustice reigns in society: Poor black people toil so that white men may savor the jewels that adorn heads of state.

ONCE

Walker's first collection of poetry, *Once*, communicates her youthful impressions of Africa and her state of mind during her early travels there and the melancholy and thoughts of death and suicide she felt on her return to United States, where racism persisted. Perhaps the epigram from French philosopher Albert Camus, which prefaces the book, expresses its mood best: "Misery kept me from believing that all was well under the sun, and the sun taught me that history wasn't everything."

The title poem of the collection contains several loosely connected scenes of injustice in the American South, small black children run down by vans because "they were in the way," Jewish Civil Rights workers who cannot be cremated because their remains cannot be found, and finally a black child waving an American flag, but from "the very/ *tips*/ of her/ fingers," an image perhaps of irony or perhaps of hope. There are meditations on white lovers—blond, Teutonic, golden—who dare kiss this poet who is "brown-er/ Than a jew." There are memories of black churches, where her mother shouts, her father snores, and she feels uncomfortable.

The most striking poem is certainly "African Images," an assortment of vignettes from the ancestral homeland: shy gazelles, the bluish peaks of Mount Kenya, the sound of elephants trumpeting, and rain forests with red orchids. However, even when viewed in the idealism of youth, Africa is not total paradise. The leg of a slain elephant is fashioned into an umbrella holder in a shop; a rhinoceros is killed so that its horn may be made into an aphrodisiac.

REVOLUTIONARY PETUNIAS, AND OTHER POEMS

Revolutionary Petunias, and Other Poems is divided into two parts. The first is titled "In These Dissenting Times . . . Surrounding Ground and Autobiography." She proposes to write "of the old men I knew/ And the young men/ I loved/ And of the gold toothed women/ Mighty of arm/ Who dragged us all/ To church." She writes also "To acknowledge our ancestors" with the awareness that "we did not make/ ourselves, that the line stretches/ all the way back, perhaps, to God; or/ to Gods." She recalls her bap-

tism "dunked . . . in the creek," with "gooey . . . rotting leaves,/ a greenish mold float-
ing." She was a slight figure, "All in white./ With God's mud ruining my snowy/ socks
and his bullfrog spoors/ gluing up my face."

The last half of the collection, "Revolutionary Petunias . . . the Living Through," begins with yet another epigram from Camus, reminding the reader that there will come a
time when revolutions, though not made by beauty, will discover the need for beauty.
The poems, especially those referred to as "Crucifixions," become more anguished,
more angered. Walker becomes skeptical of the doctrine of nonviolence, hinting that the
time for more direct action may have come. The tone of the last poems in the collection
may be expressed best by the opening lines to the verse Walker called "Rage." "In me, "
she wrote, "there is a rage to defy/ the order of the stars/ despite their pretty patterns."

GOOD NIGHT, WILLIE LEE, I'LL SEE YOU IN THE MORNING

Good Night, Willie Lee, I'll See You in the Morning expands on earlier themes and
further exploits personal and family experiences for lessons in living. The title poem is
perhaps the most moving and characteristic of the collection. Walker shared it again on
May 22, 1995, in a commencement day speech delivered at Spelman College. As a lesson in forgiveness, she recalled the words her mother, who had much to endure and
much to forgive, uttered above her father's casket. Her last words to the man with whom
she had lived for so many years, beside whom she had labored in the fields, and with
whom she had raised so many children were, "Good night, Willie Lee, I'll see you in the
morning." This gentle instinctive act of her mother taught Walker the enduring lesson
that "the healing of all our wounds is forgiveness/ that permits a promise/ of our return/
at the end."

HORSES MAKE A LANDSCAPE LOOK MORE BEAUTIFUL

Horses Make a Landscape Look More Beautiful took its title from words of Lame
Deer, an Indian seer who contemplated the gifts of the white man—chiefly whiskey and
horses—and found the beauty of horses almost made her forget the whiskey. This
thought establishes the tone of the collection. These are movement poems, but as always, they remain intensely personal and frequently elegiac. The poet seems herself to
speak:

> I am the woman
> with the blessed
> dark skin
> I am the woman
> with teeth repaired
> I am the woman
> with the healing eye
> the ear that hears.

There is also lamentation for lost love:

> When I no longer have your heart
> I will not request your body
> your presence
> or even your polite conversation.
> I will go away to a far country
> separated from you by the sea
> —on which I cannot walk—
> and refrain even from sending
> letters
> describing my pain.

HER BLUE BODY EVERYTHING WE KNOW

Her Blue Body Everything We Know contains a selection of poems written between 1965 and 1990, along with a few new verses and revealing commentary. This collection includes poems from *Once*; *Revolutionary Petunias, and Other Poems*; *Good Night, Willie Lee, I'll See You in the Morning*; and *Horses Make a Landscape Look More Beautiful*. Walker provides readers with insights on the art of poetry (in poems such as "How Poems Are Made: A Discredited View" and "I Said to Poetry"). In her introduction to the final section of the collection, Walker relates how she once felt jealous of how musicians connect with their work and seem to be one with it, but that during career as a writer, she has learned that poets share a similar relationship with their poetry. Walker, a woman of passion, shows how her personal beliefs about Africa (in the first section of this collection, "African Images: Glimpses from a Tiger's Back"), multiracial relationships (in the poem "Johann"), and the pangs of love (in poems such as "Did This Happen to Your Mother? Did Your Sister Throw Up a Lot?") are intricately intertwined and evident in her poetic creations.

Walker calls the final section "We Have a Beautiful Mother: Previously Uncollected Poems." The poems in this section, including "Some Things I Like About My Triple Bloods," "If There Was Any Justice," "We Have a Map of the World," and "Telling," are deeply personal and challenge readers to think about boundaries between cultures, countries, and hearts.

ABSOLUTE TRUST IN THE GOODNESS OF THE EARTH

In the preface to *Absolute Trust in the Goodness of the Earth*, Walker confides that she thought that she had reached the end of her career as a poet and was at peace with this, but after the terrorist attacks of September, 11, 2001, on the United States, Walker found herself writing poems regularly. After the attacks, Walker feared imminent war, and her poems in this book reflect that anxiety, including pieces such as "Thousands of Feet Below You," "Not Children," and "Why War Is Never a Good Idea." The narrator of "Thousands of Feet Below You" mentions a boy, running away from the bombs of war, who eventually is shredded to pieces in a violent explosion. Walker shares similar feelings about the concept of war in "Not Children," in which she refers to war as a cowardly act and an event that the world can do without. The title of "Why War Is Never a Good Idea" is self-explanatory, the subtitle of which ("A Picture Poem for Children Blinded by War") emphasizes Walker's stance on the issue.

Walker also continuously challenges readers to think about race relations in the United States, and how they might be improved. For example, "Patriot" encourages readers to respect all Americans, no matter what their country of origin is (she mentions Middle Eastern men, American Indian men, and African women, in particular), because these people all combine to make and define the United States. "Projection" encourages readers to look beyond the stereotypes associated with certain ethnicities (such as Indians, Germans, and Arabs) and remember that, inside each person, exists an innocent child.

In the preface to *Absolute Trust in the Goodness of the Earth*, Walker also shares her interest in and admiration for the environment and plants in particular. These feelings about the natural world are represented clearly in the title of this collection, which praises the earth for its beauty and righteousness. Walker, like many writers, associates nature with an inherent sense of peace. Natural imagery abounds in this collection, appearing in poems such as "Even When I Walked Away," "Red Petals Sticking Out," "Inside My Rooms," and "The Tree." Walker's plant and flower images remind readers of her belief that humankind is deeply rooted in and connected to the earth.

A POEM TRAVELED DOWN MY ARM

In the introduction to *A Poem Traveled Down My Arm*, Walker explains that her publisher sent her blank pages to autograph; these pages would later be bound into copies of *Absolute Trust in the Goodness of the Earth* to save Walker time at forthcoming book signings. Tired of signing her own name so many times, Walker says that she suddenly started drawing little sketches on the pieces of paper. Soon, she was scrambling to keep up with writing down poems that sprang to mind, inspired by the images she had drawn. Walker feels this collection is strange when compared with her others, especially because she thought she was done writing poetry a few years earlier. Instead, she published two collections of poetry in a single year.

The poems in *A Poem Traveled Down My Arm* typically hover around ten words each. These succinct poetic creations address topics prevalent in the rest of Walker's canon, including love, peace, nature, and war. The untitled poems function almost like a series of proverbs, offering her readers advice about living a healthy spiritual life while respecting Earth and all of humanity.

OTHER MAJOR WORKS

LONG FICTION: *The Third Life of Grange Copeland*, 1970; *Meridian*, 1976; *The Color Purple*, 1982; *The Temple of My Familiar*, 1989; *Possessing the Secret of Joy*, 1992; *By the Light of My Father's Smile*, 1998; *Now Is the Time to Open Your Heart*, 2004.

SHORT FICTION: *In Love and Trouble: Stories of Black Women*, 1973; *You Can't Keep a Good Woman Down*, 1981; *The Complete Stories*, 1994; *Alice Walker Banned*, 1996 (stories and commentary).

NONFICTION: *In Search of Our Mothers' Gardens: Womanist Prose*, 1983; *Living by the Word: Selected Writings, 1973-1987*, 1988; *Warrior Marks: Female Genital Mutilation and the Sexual Blinding of Women*, 1993 (with Pratibha Parmar); *The Same River Twice: Honoring the Difficult*, 1996; *Anything We Love Can Be Saved: A Writer's Activism*, 1997; *The Way Forward Is with a Broken Heart*, 2000; *Sent by Earth: A Message from the Grandmother Spirit After the Attacks on the World Trade Center and Pentagon*, 2001; *We Are the Ones We Have Been Waiting For: Light in a Time of Darkness*, 2006; *The World Has Changed: Conversations with Alice Walker*, 2010 (Rudolph P. Byrd, editor).

CHILDREN'S LITERATURE: *Langston Hughes: American Poet*, 1974; *To Hell with Dying*, 1988; *Finding the Green Stone*, 1991; *There Is a Flower at the Tip of My Nose Smelling Me*, 2006; *Why War Is Never a Good Idea*, 2007.

EDITED TEXT: *I Love Myself When I Am Laughing . . . and Then Again When I Am Looking Mean and Impressive: A Zora Neale Hurston Reader*, 1979.

BIBLIOGRAPHY

Bates, Gerri. *Alice Walker: A Critical Companion*. Westport, Conn.: Greenwood Press, 2005. A well-crafted biography that discusses Walker's major works, tracing the themes of her novels to her life.

Bloom, Harold, ed. *Alice Walker*. New York: Chelsea House, 1989. An important collection of critical essays examining the fiction, poetry, and essays of Walker from a variety of perspectives. The fourteen essays, including Bloom's brief introduction, are arranged chronologically. Contains useful discussions of her first three novels, brief analyses of individual short stories, poems, and essays, and assessments of Walker's social and political views in connection with her works and other African American female authors. Chronology and bibliography.

Bloxham, Laura J. "Alice (Malsenior) Walker." In *Contemporary Fiction Writers of the South*, edited by Joseph M. Flora and Robert Bain. Westport, Conn.: Greenwood Press, 1993. A general introduction to Walker's "womanist" themes of oppression of black women and change through affirmation of self. Provides a brief summary and critique of previous criticism of Walker's work.

Gates, Henry Louis, Jr., and K. A. Appiah, eds. *Alice Walker: Critical Perspectives Past and Present.* New York: Amistad, 1993. Contains reviews of Walker's first five novels and critical analyses of several of her works of short and long fiction. Also includes two interviews with Walker, a chronology of her works, and an extensive bibliography of essays and texts.

Gentry, Tony. *Alice Walker.* New York: Chelsea House, 1993. Examines the life and work of Walker. Includes bibliographical references and index.

Lauret, Maria. *Alice Walker.* New York: St. Martin's Press, 2000. Provocative discussions of Walker's ideas on politics, race, feminism, and literary theory. Of special interest is the exploration of Walker's literary debt to Zora Neale Hurston, Virginia Woolf, and even Bessie Smith.

Simcikova, Karla. *To Live Fully, Here and Now: The Healing Vision in the Works of Alice Walker.* Lanham, Md.: Lexington Books, 2007. Simcikova focuses on Walker's spirituality, her relationship with nature, and how these beliefs and connections present themselves in her oeuvre of work.

Smith, Lindsey Claire. "Alice Walker's Eco-'Warriors.'" In *Indians, Environment, and Identity on the Borders of American Literature: From Faulkner and Morrison to Walker and Silko.* New York: Palgrave Macmillan, 2008. Smith analyzes boundaries delineating cultural, geographical, and racial differences in Walker's canon.

Walker, Rebecca. *Black, White, and Jewish: Autobiography of a Shifting Self.* New York: Riverhead, 2001. A self-indulgent but nevertheless insightful memoir by Alice Walker's daughter, Rebecca Walker. She describes herself as "a movement child," growing up torn between two families, two races, and two traditions, always in the shadow of an increasingly famous and absorbed mother.

White, Evelyn C. *Alice Walker: A Life.* New York: Norton, 2004. The life and accomplishments of Walker are chronicled in this biography through interviews with Walker, her family, and friends.

Allene Phy-Olsen
Updated by Karley K. Adney

PHILLIS WHEATLEY

Born: West Coast of Africa (possibly the Senegal-Gambia region); 1753(?)
Died: Boston, Massachusetts; December 5, 1784

PRINCIPAL POETRY
Poems on Various Subjects, Religious and Moral, 1773
The Poems of Phillis Wheatley, 1966, 1989 (Julian D. Mason, Jr., editor)

OTHER LITERARY FORMS

Phillis Wheatley's cultivation of the letter as a literary form is attested by her inclusion of the titles of several letters in each of her proposals for future volumes subsequent to the publication of her *Poems on Various Subjects, Religious and Moral* (1773). Regrettably, none of these proposals provoked enough response to secure publication of any new volumes. Scholars continue to discover both poems and letters that Wheatley names in these proposals. The letters mentioned in them are addressed to such noted persons as William Legge, second earl of Dartmouth; Selina Hastings, countess of Huntingdon; Benjamin Rush; and George Washington. They display a graceful style and articulate some of Wheatley's strongest protestations in support of the cause of American independence and in condemnation of Christian hypocrisy regarding slavery.

ACHIEVEMENTS

From the time of Phillis Wheatley's first published piece to the present day, controversy has surrounded the life and work of America's first black poet and only its second published woman poet, after Anne Bradstreet. Few poets of any age have been so scornfully maligned, so passionately defended, so fervently celebrated, and so patronizingly tolerated. However, during the years of her young adulthood, Wheatley was the toast of England and the colonies. For years before she attempted to find a Boston publisher for her poems, she had published numerous elegies commemorating the deaths of many of the city's most prominent citizens. In 1770, she wrote her most famous and most often-reprinted elegy, on the death of "the voice of the Great Awakening," George Whitefield, chaplain to the countess of Huntingdon, who was one of the leading benefactors of the Methodist evangelical movement in England and the colonies.

Not finding Boston to be in sympathy with her 1772 proposal for a volume, Wheatley found substantial support the following year in the countess of Huntingdon, whose interest had been stirred by the young poet's noble tribute to her chaplain. Subsequently, Wheatley was sent to London, ostensibly for her health; this trip curiously accords, however, with the very weeks that her book was being printed. It is likely that she proofread the galleys herself. At any rate, she was much sought after among the intellec-

Phillis Wheatley
(Library of Congress)

tual, literary set of London, and Sir Brook Watson, who was to become Lord Mayor of London within a year, presented her with a copy of John Milton's *Paradise Lost* (1667, 1674) in folio. The earl of Dartmouth, who was at the time secretary of state for the colonies and president of the board of Trade and Foreign Plantations, gave her a copy of Tobias Smollett's *Don Quixote* (1755), a translation of Miguel de Cervantes's *El ingenioso hidalgo don Quixote de la Mancha* (1605, 1615; *The History of the Valorous and Wittie Knight-Errant, Don Quixote of the Mancha*, 1612-1620; better known as *Don Quixote de la Mancha*). Benjamin Franklin, to whom she would later inscribe her second book of poetry (never published), has even recorded that, while in London briefly, he called on Wheatley to see whether "there were any service I could do her."

In the opening pages of her 1773 volume appears a letter of authentication of Wheatley's authorship, which is signed by still another of the signatories of the Declaration of Independence, John Hancock. Added to the list of attesters are other outstanding Bostonians, including Thomas Hutchinson, then governor of Massachusetts, and James Bowdoin, one of the founders of Bowdoin College. Later, during the early months of the American Revolution, Wheatley wrote a poem in praise of General Washington, "To His Excellency General Washington." As a result, she received an invitation to visit the general at his headquarters, and her poem was published by Tom Paine in *The Pennsyl-*

vania Magazine. John Paul Jones, who also appreciated Wheatley's celebration of freedom, even asked one of his officers to secure him a copy of her *Poems on Various Subjects, Religious and Moral.*

Nevertheless, she did not continue to enjoy such fame. A country ravaged by war has little time, finally, for poetry, and Wheatley regrettably, perhaps tragically, faced the rejection of two more proposals for a volume of new poems. Thwarted by the vicissitudes of war and poverty, Wheatley died from complications resulting from childbirth. Even so, her poetry has survived and is now considered to be among the best of its period produced in America or in England. It is just beginning to be recognized that, contrary to the opinion of those who would dispose of Wheatley as a mere imitator, she produced sophisticated, original poems whose creative theories of the imagination and the sublime anticipate the Romantic movement.

BIOGRAPHY

The known details of Phillis Wheatley's life are few. According to her master, John Wheatley of Boston, she "was brought from Africa to America in the Year 1761, between Seven and Eight Years of Age [sic]." Her parents were apparently sun-worshipers, for she is supposed to have recalled to her white captors that she remembered seeing her mother pouring out water to the sun every morning. If such be the case, it would help to explain why the sun is predominant as an image in her poetry.

Her life with the Wheatleys, John and Susanna and their two children, the twins Mary and Nathaniel, was probably not too demanding for one whose disposition toward asthma (brought on or no doubt exacerbated by the horrible "middle passage") greatly weakened her. The Wheatleys' son attended Harvard, so it is likely that Nathaniel served as the eager young girl's Latin tutor. At any rate, it is certain that Wheatley knew Latin well; her translation of the Niobe episode from Ovid's *Metamorphoses* (c. 8 C.E.; English translation, 1567), book 6, displays a learned knowledge and appreciation of the Latin original. Wheatley's classical learning is evident throughout her poetry, which is thick with allusions to ancient historical and mythological figures.

The turning point of Wheatley's career, not only as an author but also as a human being, came when her *Poems on Various Subjects, Religious and Moral* was published in London in 1773. After she returned from England, having been recalled because of Susanna Wheatley's worsening illness, she was manumitted sometime during September, 1773. It is probable that Wheatley was freed because of the severe censure that some English reviewers of her *Poems on Various Subjects, Religious and Moral* had directed at the owners of a learned author who "still remained a slave." At this very point, however, the poet's fortunes began a slow decline. In 1778, at the height of the war and after the deaths of both John and Susanna Wheatley, she married John Peters, a black man of some learning who failed to rescue the poet from poverty.

Wheatley died alone and unattended in a hovel somewhere in the back streets of the

Boston slums in 1784, truly an ignominious end for one who had enjoyed such favor. She was preceded in death by two of her children, as well as by the third, to whom she had just given birth. She was at most only thirty-one years old. Given Wheatley's vision of the world "Oppress'd with woes, a painful endless train," it should not be surprising that her most frequently adopted poetic form is the elegy, in which she always celebrates death as the achievement of ultimate freedom—suggesting the thanatos-eros (desire for death) motif of Romanticism.

ANALYSIS

Beginning in the 1970's, Phillis Wheatley began to receive the attention she deserves. George McMichael and others, editors of the influential two-volume *Anthology of American Literature* (1974, 1980), observe that she and Philip Freneau were "the most important poets" of America's Revolutionary War era. To be sure, one of the major subjects of her poetry is the American struggle for independence. Temporal freedom is not her only subject, however; she is also much concerned with the quest for spiritual freedom. Consequently, the elegy, in which she celebrates the Christian rewards of eternal life and absolute freedom after death, is her favorite poetic form. In addition, she delights in describing God's creation of nature's splendors and sometimes appears to enjoy the beauties of nature for their own sake and not simply as acts of God's providence. It is in "On Imagination," however, that Wheatley waxes most eloquent; in this poem, perhaps her most important single work, she articulates a theory of the imagination that strikingly anticipates that of Samuel Taylor Coleridge. Indeed, Wheatley's affinities with Romanticism, which run throughout her poetry, may come to be seen as her surest claim to a place in literary history.

Such an approach to this early American poet contradicts the widespread critical view that Wheatley was a highly derivative poet, inextricably mired in the neoclassical tradition. Her preference for the heroic couplet, one of the hallmarks of neoclassicism, has deceived many into immediately classifying her as neoclassical. One must recall, however, that Lord Byron also had a passion for the couplet. Surely, then, one must not be satisfied with a cursory glance at Wheatley's adoption of the heroic couplet; one must go on to explore the content of her poetry.

POLITICAL POEMS

Her political poems document major incidents of the American struggle for independence. In 1768, she wrote "To the King's Most Excellent Majesty on His Repealing the American Stamp Act." When it appeared, much revised, in *Poems on Various Subjects, Religious and Moral*, the poet diplomatically deleted the last two lines of the original, which read, "When wars came on [against George] the proudest rebel fled/ God thunder'd fury on their guilty head." By that time, the threat of the King's retaliation did not seem so forbidding nor the injustice of rebellion against him so grave.

"America," a poem probably written about the same time but published more than two hundred years later, admonishes Britain to treat "americus," the British child, with more deference. According to the poem, the child, now a growing seat of "Liberty," is no mere adorer of an overwhelming "Majesty," but has acquired strength of his own: "Fearing his strength which she [Britain] undoubted knew/ She laid some taxes on her darling son." Recognizing her mistake, "great Britannia" promised to lift the burden, but the promise proved only "seeming Sympathy and Love." Now the Child "weeps afresh to feel this Iron chain." The urge to draw an analogy here between the poem's "Iron chain" and Wheatley's own predicament is irresistible; while America longs for its own independence, Wheatley no doubt yearns for hers.

The year 1770 marked the beginning of armed resistance against Britain. Wheatley chronicles such resistance in two poems, the second of which is now lost. The first, "On the Death of Mr. Snider Murder'd by Richardson," appeared initially along with "America." The poem tells how Ebenezer Richardson, an informer on American traders involved in circumventing British taxation, found his home surrounded on the evening of February 22, 1770, by an angry mob of colonial sympathizers. Much alarmed, Richardson emerged from his house armed with a musket and fired indiscriminately into the mob, killing the eleven- or twelve-year-old son of Snider, a poor German colonist. Wheatley calls young Christopher Snider, of whose death Richardson was later found guilty in a trial by jury, "the first martyr for the common good," rather than those men killed less than two weeks later in the Boston Massacre. The poem's fine closing couplet suggests that even those not in sympathy with the quest for freedom can grasp the nobility of that quest and are made indignant by its sacrifice: "With Secret rage fair freedom's foes beneath/ See in thy corse ev'n Majesty in Death."

Wheatley does not, however, ignore the Boston Massacre. In a proposal for a volume which was to have been published in Boston in 1772, she lists, among twenty-seven titles of poems (the 1773 volume had thirty-nine), "On the Affray in King Street, on the Evening of the 5th of March." This title, naming the time and place of the massacre, suggests that the poet probably celebrated the martyrdom of Crispus Attucks, the first black to lose his life in the American struggle, along with the deaths of two whites. Regrettably, the poem has not yet been recovered. Even so, the title alone confirms Wheatley's continued recording of America's struggle for freedom. This concern shifted in tone from obedient praise for the British regime to supplicatory admonition and then to guarded defiance. Since she finally found a publisher not in Boston but in London, she prudently omitted "America" and the poems about Snider and the Boston Massacre from her 1773 volume.

She chose to include, however, a poem dedicated to the earl of Dartmouth, who was appointed secretary of state for the colonies in August, 1772. In this poem, "To the Right Honourable William, Earl of Dartmouth, His Majesty's Principal Secretary of State for North America," she gives the earl extravagant praise as one who will lay to rest "hatred faction." She knew of the earl's reputation as a humanitarian through the London contacts of her mistress, Susanna. When the earl proved to support oppressive British policies, the poet's expectations were not realized; within four years of the poem's date, America had declared its independence. Since her optimism was undaunted by foreknowledge, Wheatley wrote a poem that was even more laudatory than "To The King's Most Excellent Majesty on His Repealing the American Stamp Act." Perhaps she was not totally convinced, however; the poem contains some unusually bold passages for a colonist who is also both a woman and a slave.

For example, she remarks that, with Dartmouth's secretaryship, America need no longer "dread the iron chain,/ Which wanton *Tyranny* with lawless hand/ Had made, and with it meant t'enslave the land." Once again Wheatley uses the slave metaphor of the iron chain. Quite clearly she also accuses the Crown of "wanton *Tyranny*," which it had wielded illegally and with the basest of motives—to reduce the colonies to the inhuman condition of slave states. Here rebellious defiance, no longer guarded, is unmistakable; the tone matches that of the Declaration of Independence. It is a mystery how these lines could have gone unnoticed in the London reviews, all of them positive, of her 1773 volume. Perhaps the reviewers were too bedazzled by the "improbability" that a black woman could produce such a volume to take the content of her poetry seriously.

In this poem, Wheatley also presents a rare autobiographical portrait describing the manner in which she was taken from her native Africa. The manuscript version of this passage is more spontaneous and direct than the more formally correct one printed in the 1773 volume and thus is closer to the poet's true feelings. It was "Seeming cruel fate" that snatched her "from Afric's fancy'd happy seat." Fate here is only apparently cruel, since her capture has enabled her to become a Christian; the young poet's piety resounds throughout her poetry and letters. Her days in her native land were, nevertheless, happy ones, and her abduction at the hands of ruthless slavers doubtless left behind inconsolable parents. Such a bitter memory of the circumstances of her abduction fully qualifies her to "deplore the day/ When Britons weep beneath Tyrannic sway"; the later version reads: "And can I then but pray/ Others may never feel tyrannic sway?" Besides toning down the diction, this passage alters her statement to a question and replaces "Britons" with the neutral "others." The question might suggest uncertainty, but it more probably reflects the author's polite deportment toward a London audience. Since, in the earlier version, she believed Dartmouth to be sympathetic with her cause, she had no reason to exercise deference toward him; she thought she could be frank. The shift from "Britons" to "others" provokes a more compelling explanation. In the fall of 1772, Wheatley could still think of herself as a British subject. Later, however, after rejoicing that the earl's administration had given way to restive disillusionment, perhaps the poet was less certain about her citizenship.

Three years after the publication of her 1773 volume, Wheatley unabashedly celebrated the opposition to the "tyrannic sway" of Britain in "To His Excellency General

Washington," newly appointed commander in chief of the Continental Army; the war of ideas had become one of arms. In this piece, which is more a paean to freedom than a eulogy to Washington, she describes freedom as "divinely fair,/ Olive and laurel bind her golden hair"; yet "She flashes dreadful in refulgent arms." The poet accents this image of martial glory with an epic simile, comparing the American forces to the power of the fierce king of the winds:

> As when Eolus heaven's fair face deforms,
> Enwrapp'd in tempest and a night of storms;
> Astonish'd ocean feels the wild uproar,
> The refluent surges beat the sounding shore.

For the young poet, America is now "The land of freedom's heaven-defended race!" While the eyes of the world's nations are fixed "on the scales,/ For in their hopes Columbia's arm prevails," the poet records Britain's regret over her loss: "Ah! cruel blindness to Columbia's state!/ Lament thy thirst of boundless power too late." The temper of this couplet is in keeping with Wheatley's earlier attitudes toward oppression. The piece closes as the poet urges Washington to pursue his objective with the knowledge that virtue is on his side. If he allows the fair goddess Freedom to be his guide, Washington will surely emerge not only as the leader of a victorious army but also as the head of the newly established state.

In Wheatley's last political poem, "freedom's heaven-defended race" has won its battle. Written in 1784 within a year after the Treaty of Paris, "Liberty and Peace" is a demonstrative celebration of American independence. British tyranny, the agent of American oppression, has now been taught to fear "americus" her child, "And newborn *Rome* shall give *Britannia* Law." Wheatley concludes this piece with two pleasing couplets in praise of America, whose future is assured by heaven's approval:

> Auspicious Heaven shall fill with favoring Gales,
> Where e'er *Columbia* spreads her swelling Sails:
> To every Realm shall *Peace* her Charms display,
> And Heavenly *Freedom* spread her golden Ray.

Personified as Peace and Freedom, Columbia (America) will act as a world emissary, an emanating force like the rays of the sun. In this last couplet, Wheatley has captured, perhaps for the first time in poetry, America's ideal mission to the rest of the world.

The fact that Wheatley so energetically proclaims America's success in the political arena certainly attests her sympathies—not with the neoclassic obsession never to challenge the established order nor to breach the rules of political and social decorum—but with the Romantic notion that a people who find themselves unable to accept a present, unsatisfactory government have the right to change that government, even if such a change can be accomplished only through armed revolt. The American Revolution against Britain was the first successful such revolt and was one of the sparks of the French Revolution. Wheatley's steadfast literary participation in the American Revolution clearly aligns her with such politically active English Romantic poets as Percy Bysshe Shelley and Lord Byron.

THE ELEGIES

In her elegies, on the other hand, Wheatley displays her devotion to spiritual freedom. As do her political poems, her elegies exalt specific occasions, the deaths of people usually known to her within the social and religious community of the poet's Old South Congregational Church of Boston. As do her poems on political events, however, her elegies exceed the boundaries of occasional verse. The early, but most famous of her elegies, "On the Death of the Rev. Mr. George Whitefield, 1770," both illustrates the general structure in which she cast all seventeen of her extant elegies and indicates her recurring ideological concerns.

Wheatley's elegies conform for the most part to the Puritan funeral elegy. They include two major divisions: First comes the portrait, in which the poet pictures the life of the subject; then follows the exhortation, encouraging the reader to seek the heavenly rewards gained by the subject in death. The portrait usually comprises three biographical steps: vocation or conversion; sanctification, or evidence of good works; and glorification, or joyous treatment of the deceased's reception into heaven. Wheatley's elegy on Whitefield surprisingly opens with the glorification of the Great Awakener, already in heaven and occupying his "immortal throne." She celebrates the minister's conversion or vocation in an alliterative line as "The greatest gift that ev'n a God can give." Of course, she writes many lines describing the good works of a man wholly devoted to the winning of souls during the seven visits he made to America during and after the period of the Great Awakening.

Whitefield died in Newburyport, Massachusetts, on September 30, 1770, having left Boston only a week or so before, where he had apparently lodged with the Wheatley family. Indeed, the young poet of sixteen or seventeen appears to recollect from personal experience when she observes that the minister "long'd to see *America* excel" and "charg'd its youth that ev'ry grace divine/ Should with full lustre in their conduct shine." She also seizes this opportunity to proclaim to the world Whitefield's assertion that even Africans would find Jesus of Nazareth an "*Impartial Saviour.*" The poem closes with a ten-line exhortation to the living to aspire toward Whitefield's example: "Let ev'ry heart to this bright vision rise."

As one can see, Wheatley's elegies are not sad affairs; quite to the contrary, they enact joyful occasions after which deceased believers may hope to unite, as she states in "On the Death of the Rev. Dr. Sewell, 1769," with "Great God, incomprehensible, unknown/ By sense." Although people's senses may limit their firsthand acquaintance with God, these same senses do enable them to learn about God, especially about God's works in nature. The poem in the extant Wheatley canon that most pointedly addresses God's works in nature is "Thoughts on the Works of Providence." This poem of 131 lines opens with a 10-line invocation to the "Celestial muse," resembling Milton's heavenly muse of *Paradise Lost.*

Identifying God as the force behind planetary movement, she writes, "Ador'd [is] the God that whirls surrounding spheres" which rotate ceaselessly about "the monarch of the earth and skies." From this sublime image she moves to yet another: "'Let there be light,' he said: from his profound/ Old chaos heard and trembled at the sound." It should not go unremarked that Wheatley could, indeed, find much in nature to foster her belief, but little in the mundane world of ordinary humans to sustain her spiritually. The frequency of nature imagery but the relative lack of scenes drawn from human society (with the exception of her political poems, and even these are occasions for abstract departures into the investigation of political ideologies) probably reflects the poet's insecurity and uncertainty about a world which first made her a slave and then gave her, at best, only second-class citizenship.

In "An Hymn to the Morning," one of her most lyrical poems, Wheatley interprets the morn (recall her mother's morning ritual of pouring out water to the rising sun) as the source of poetic afflatus or inspiration. The speaker of the poem, Wheatley herself, first perceives the light of the rising sun as a reflection in the eye of one of the "feather'd race." After she hears the song of the bird that welcomes the day, she turns to find the source of melody and sees the bird "Dart the bright eye, and shake the painted plume." Here the poet captures with great precision the bird's rapid eye movement. The bird, archetypal symbol of poetic song, has received the dawn's warm rays that stimulate him to sing. When the poet turns to discover the source of melody, however, what she sees first is not Aurora, the dawning sun, but Aurora the stimulus of song reflected within the "bright eye" of the bird.

In the next stanza, the poet identifies the dawn as the ultimate source of poetic inspiration when she remarks that the sun has awakened Calliope, here the personification of inspiration, while her sisters, the other Muses, "fan the pleasing fire" of the stimulus to create. Hence both the song of the bird and the light reflected in its eye have instructed her to acknowledge the source of the bird's melody; for she aspires to sing with the same pleasing fire that animates the song of the bird. Like many of the Romantics who followed her, Wheatley perceives nature both as a means to know ultimate freedom and as an inspiration to create, to make art.

It is in her superlative poem, "On Imagination," however, that Wheatley most forcefully brings both aspirations, to know God and to create fine poetry, into clear focus. To the young black poet, the imagination was sufficiently important to demand from her pen a fifty-three-line poem. The piece opens with this four-line apostrophe:

> Thy various works, imperial queen, we see,
> How bright their forms! how deck'd with pomp by thee!
> Thy wond'rous acts in beauteous order stand,
> And all attest how potent is thine hand.

Clearly, Wheatley's imagination is a regal presence in full control of her poetic world, a world in which her "wond'rous acts" of creation stand in harmony, capturing a "beauteous order." These acts themselves testify to the queen's creative power. Following a four-line invocation to the Muse, however, the poet distinguishes the imagination from its subordinate fancy:

> Now, here, now there, the roving Fancy flies;
> Till some lov'd object strikes her wand'ring eyes,
> Whose silken fetters all the senses bind,
> And soft captivity involves the mind.

Unlike the controlled, harmonious imagination, the subordinate fancy flies about here and there, searching for some appropriate and desired object worthy of setting into motion the creative powers of her superior.

FANCY AND MEMORY

In "Thoughts on the Works of Providence," the poet describes the psychology of sleep in similar fashion. Having entered the world of dreams, the mind discovers a realm where "ideas range/ Licentious and unbounded o'er the plains/ Where Fancy's queen in giddy triumph reigns." Wheatley maintains that in sleep the imagination, once again "Fancy's queen," creates worlds that lack the "beauteous order" of the poet sitting before a writing desk; nevertheless, these dreamworlds provoke memorable images. In "On Recollection," Wheatley describes the memory as the repository on which the mind draws to create its dreams. What may be "long-forgotten," the memory "calls from night" and "plays before the fancy's sight." By analogy, Wheatley maintains, the memory provides the poet "ample treasure" from her "secret stores" to create poetry: "in her pomp of images display'd,/ To the high-raptur'd poet gives her aid." "On Recollection" asserts a strong affinity between the poet's memory, analogous to the world of dreams, and the fancy, the associative faculty subordinate to the imagination. Recollection for Wheatley functions as the poet's storehouse of images, while the fancy channels the force of the imagination through its associative powers. Both the memory and the fancy, then, serve the imagination.

Wheatley's description of fancy and memory departs markedly from what eighteenth century aestheticians, including John Locke and Joseph Addison, generally understood as the imagination. The faculty of mind that they termed "imagination" Wheatley relegates to recollection (memory) and fancy. Her description of recollection and fancy closely parallels Coleridge's in the famous thirteenth chapter of *Biographia*

Literaria (1817), where he states that fancy "is indeed no other than a mode of Memory emancipated from the order of time and space." Wheatley's identification of the fancy as roving "Now here, now there" whose movement is analogous to the dream state, where "ideas range/ Licentious and unbounded," certainly frees it from the limits of time and space. Coleridge further limits the fancy to the capacity of choice. "But equally with the ordinary memory," he insists, "the Fancy must receive all its materials ready made from the law of association." Like Coleridge's, Wheatley's fancy exercises choice by association as it finally settles on "some lov'd object."

If fancy and memory are the imagination's subordinates, then how does the imagination function in the poet's creative process? Following her description of fancy in "On Imagination," Wheatley details the role the imagination plays in her poetry. According to her, the power of the imagination enables her to soar "through air to find the bright abode,/ Th' empyreal palace of the thund'ring God." The central focus of her poetry remains contemplation of God. Foreshadowing William Wordsworth's "winds that will be howling at all hours," Wheatley exclaims that on the wings of the imagination she "can surpass the wind/ And leave the rolling universe behind." In the realm of the imagination, the poet can "with new worlds amaze th' unbounded soul."

Immediately following this arresting line, Wheatley illustrates in a ten-line stanza the power of the imagination to create new worlds. Even though winter and the "frozen deeps" prevail in the real world, the imagination can take one out of unpleasant reality and build a pleasant, mythic world of fragrant flowers and verdant groves where "Fair Flora" spreads "her fragrant reign," where Sylvanus crowns the forest with leaves, and where "Show'rs may descend, and dews their gems disclose,/ And nectar sparkle on the blooming rose." Such is the power of imagination to promote poetic creation and to release one from an unsatisfactory world. Unfortunately, like reality's painful intrusion on the delicate, unsustainable song of John Keats's immortal bird, gelid winter and its severe "northern tempests damp the rising fire," cut short the indulgence of her poetic world, and lamentably force Wheatley to end her short-lived lyric: "Cease then, my song, cease the unequal lay." Her lyric must end because no poet can indefinitely sustain a mythic world.

In her use of the imagination to create "new worlds," Wheatley's departure from eighteenth century theories of this faculty is radical and once again points toward Coleridge. Although she does not distinguish between "primary" and "secondary" imagination as he does, Wheatley nevertheless constructs a theory which approaches his "secondary" imagination. According to Coleridge, the secondary imagination, which attends the creative faculty, intensifies the primary imagination common to all people. Coleridge describes how the secondary imagination operates in this well-known passage: "It dissolves, diffuses, dissipates, in order to recreate;/ or where this process is rendered impossible, yet still at all/ events it struggles to idealize and to unify." In spite of the fact that Wheatley's attempt to dissolve, diffuse, and dissipate is assuredly more modest than Coleridge's "swift half-intermitted burst" in "Kubla Khan," she does, nevertheless, like the apocalyptic Romantics, idealize, unify, and shape a mythopoeic world. Proceeding in a systematic fashion, she first constructs a theory of mental faculty that, when assisted by the associative fancy, builds, out of an act of the mind, a new world that does indeed stand in "beauteous order." This faculty, which she identifies as the imagination, she uses as a tool to achieve freedom, however momentary.

Wheatley was, then, an innovator who used the imagination as a means to transcend an unacceptable present and even to construct "new worlds [to] amaze the unbounded soul"; this practice, along with her celebration of death, her loyalty to the American struggle for political independence, and her consistent praise of nature, places her firmly in that flow of thought that culminated in nineteenth century Romanticism. Her diction may strike a modern audience as occasionally "got up" and stiff, and her reliance on the heroic couplet may appear outdated and worn, but the content of her poetry is innovative, refreshing, and even, for her times, revolutionary. She wrote during the pre-Revolutionary and Revolutionary War eras in America, when little poetry of great merit was produced. Wheatley, laboring under the disadvantages of being not only a black slave but also a woman, nevertheless did find the time to depict that political struggle for freedom and to trace her personal battle for release. If one looks beyond the limitations of her sincere if dogmatic piety and her frequent dependence on what Wordsworth called poetic diction, one is sure to discover in her works a fine mind engaged in creating some of the best early American poetry.

OTHER MAJOR WORKS

MISCELLANEOUS: *Memoir and Poems of Phillis Wheatley: A Native African and a Slave*, 1833; *The Collected Works of Phillis Wheatley*, 1988 (John Shields, editor).

BIBLIOGRAPHY

Cook, William W., and James Tatum. *African American Writers and Classical Tradition*. Chicago: University of Chicago Press, 2010. Examines the relationship of African American writers, beginning with Wheatley, to Greek and Roman classics.

Engberg, Kathrynn Seidler. *The Right to Write: The Literary Politics of Anne Bradstreet and Phillis Wheatley*. Lanham, Md.: University Press of America, 2010. Examines the first two published women poets of the United States and the problems and challenges they faced.

Gates, Henry Louis, Jr. *The Trials of Phillis Wheatley: America's First Black Poet and Her Encounters with the Founding Fathers*. 2003. Reprint. New York: Basic Civitas Books, 2010. A biography of Wheatley that examines her life and works, including Thomas Jefferson's harsh critique of her work and her lack of popularity among African Americans.

Hayden, Lucy K. *"Poems on Various Subjects, Religious and Moral."* In *Masterplots II: African American Literature*, edited by Tyrone Williams. Rev. ed. Pasadena, Calif.: Salem Press, 2009. Examines this work in detail, looking at themes and meanings and the critical context.

Morton, Gerald W. *Phillis Wheatley: Slave and Poet*. Baltimore: PublishAmerica, 2008. A biography that looks at Wheatley's life and writings.

Robinson, William H. *Phillis Wheatley and Her Writings*. New York: Garland, 1984. A fine introduction to Wheatley, by an eminent Wheatley scholar. Presents a brief biography, the text of all the poems and surviving letters (several in facsimile) with an analysis, nine appendixes providing background information, bibliography, and index.

Shields, John C. *Phillis Wheatley and the Romantics*. Knoxville: University of Tennessee Press, 2010. Looks at the poetry of Wheatley and how it influenced the Romantics who followed her.

_____. *Phillis Wheatley's Poetics of Liberation: Backgrounds and Contexts*. Knoxville: University of Tennessee Press, 2008. Examines how evaluation of Wheatley's poetry has changed over the years.

John C. Shields

CHECKLIST FOR EXPLICATING A POEM

I. THE INITIAL READINGS

A. Before reading the poem, the reader should:
  1. Notice its form and length.
  2. Consider the title, determining, if possible, whether it might function as an allusion, symbol, or poetic image.
  3. Notice the date of composition or publication, and identify the general era of the poet.

B. The poem should be read intuitively and emotionally and be allowed to "happen" as much as possible.

C. In order to establish the rhythmic flow, the poem should be reread. A note should be made as to where the irregular spots (if any) are located.

II. EXPLICATING THE POEM

A. *Dramatic situation.* Studying the poem line by line helps the reader discover the dramatic situation. All elements of the dramatic situation are interrelated and should be viewed as reflecting and affecting one another. The dramatic situation serves a particular function in the poem, adding realism, surrealism, or absurdity; drawing attention to certain parts of the poem; and changing to reinforce other aspects of the poem. All points should be considered. The following questions are particularly helpful to ask in determining dramatic situation:
  1. What, if any, is the narrative action in the poem?
  2. How many personae appear in the poem? What part do they take in the action?
  3. What is the relationship between characters?
  4. What is the setting (time and location) of the poem?

B. *Point of view.* An understanding of the poem's point of view is a major step toward comprehending the poet's intended meaning. The reader should ask:
  1. Who is the speaker? Is he or she addressing someone else or the reader?
  2. Is the narrator able to understand or see everything happening to him or her, or does the reader know things that the narrator does not?
  3. Is the narrator reliable?
  4. Do point of view and dramatic situation seem consistent? If not, the inconsistencies may provide clues to the poem's meaning.

C. *Images and metaphors.* Images and metaphors are often the most intricately crafted vehicles of the poem for relaying the poet's message. Realizing that the images and metaphors work in harmony with the dramatic situation and point of view will help the reader to see the poem as a whole, rather than as disassociated elements.

1. The reader should identify the concrete images (that is, those that are formed from objects that can be touched, smelled, seen, felt, or tasted). Is the image projected by the poet consistent with the physical object?
2. If the image is abstract, or so different from natural imagery that it cannot be associated with a real object, then what are the properties of the image?
3. To what extent is the reader asked to form his or her own images?
4. Is any image repeated in the poem? If so, how has it been changed? Is there a controlling image?
5. Are any images compared to each other? Do they reinforce one another?
6. Is there any difference between the way the reader perceives the image and the way the narrator sees it?
7. What seems to be the narrator's or persona's attitude toward the image?

D. *Words.* Every substantial word in a poem may have more than one intended meaning, as used by the author. Because of this, the reader should look up many of these words in the dictionary and:

1. Note all definitions that have the slightest connection with the poem.
2. Note any changes in syntactical patterns in the poem.
3. In particular, note those words that could possibly function as symbols or allusions, and refer to any appropriate sources for further information.

E. *Meter, rhyme, structure, and tone.* In scanning the poem, all elements of prosody should be noted by the reader. These elements are often used by a poet to manipulate the reader's emotions, and therefore they should be examined closely to arrive at the poet's specific intention.

1. Does the basic meter follow a traditional pattern such as those found in nursery rhymes or folk songs?
2. Are there any variations in the base meter? Such changes or substitutions are important thematically and should be identified.
3. Are the rhyme schemes traditional or innovative, and what might their form mean to the poem?
4. What devices has the poet used to create sound patterns (such as assonance and alliteration)?
5. Is the stanza form a traditional or innovative one?
6. If the poem is composed of verse paragraphs rather than stanzas, how do they affect the progression of the poem?

7. After examining the above elements, is the resultant tone of the poem casual or formal, pleasant, harsh, emotional, authoritative?

F. *Historical context.* The reader should attempt to place the poem into historical context, checking on events at the time of composition. Archaic language, expressions, images, or symbols should also be looked up.

G. *Themes and motifs.* By seeing the poem as a composite of emotion, intellect, craftsmanship, and tradition, the reader should be able to determine the themes and motifs (smaller recurring ideas) presented in the work. He or she should ask the following questions to help pinpoint these main ideas:
1. Is the poet trying to advocate social, moral, or religious change?
2. Does the poet seem sure of his or her position?
3. Does the poem appeal primarily to the emotions, to the intellect, or to both?
4. Is the poem relying on any particular devices for effect (such as imagery, allusion, paradox, hyperbole, or irony)?

BIBLIOGRAPHY

GENERAL REFERENCE SOURCES

BIOGRAPHICAL SOURCES

Baughman, Ronald, ed. *American Poets*. Vol. 3 in *Contemporary Authors: Bibliographical Series*. Detroit: Gale Research, 1986.

Conte, Joseph, ed. *American Poets Since World War II: Fourth Series*. Dictionary of Literary Biography 165. Detroit: Gale Research, 1996.

_____. *American Poets Since World War II: Fifth Series*. Dictionary of Literary Biography 169. Detroit: Gale Research, 1996.

_____. *American Poets Since World War II: Sixth Series*. Dictionary of Literary Biography 193. Detroit: Gale Research, 1998.

Greiner, Donald J., ed. *American Poets Since World War II*. Dictionary of Literary Biography 5. Detroit: Gale Research, 1980.

Gwynn, R. S., ed. *American Poets Since World War II: Second Series*. Dictionary of Literary Biography 105. Detroit: Gale Research, 1991.

_____. *American Poets Since World War II: Third Series*. Dictionary of Literary Biography 120. Detroit: Gale Research, 1992.

Quartermain, Peter, ed. *American Poets, 1880-1945: First Series*. Dictionary of Literary Biography 45. Detroit: Gale Research, 1986.

_____. *American Poets, 1880-1945: Second Series*. Dictionary of Literary Biography 48. Detroit: Gale Research, 1986.

_____. *American Poets, 1880-1945: Third Series*. Dictionary of Literary Biography 54. Detroit: Gale Research, 1987.

CRITICISM

Alexander, Harriet Semmes, comp. *American and British Poetry: A Guide to the Criticism, 1925-1978*. Manchester, England: Manchester University Press, 1984.

_____. *American and British Poetry: A Guide to the Criticism, 1979-1990*. 2 vols. Athens, Ohio: Swallow Press, 1995.

Annual Bibliography of English Language and Literature. Cambridge, England: Modern Humanities Research Association, 1920-   .

Brooks, Cleanth, and Robert Penn Warren. *Understanding Poetry*. 4th ed. Reprint. Fort Worth, Tex.: Heinle & Heinle, 2003.

Childs, Peter. *The Twentieth Century in Poetry: A Critical Survey*. New York: Routledge, 1999.

Cline, Gloria Stark, and Jeffrey A. Baker. *An Index to Criticism of British and American Poetry*. Metuchen, N.J.: Scarecrow Press, 1973.

Contemporary Literary Criticism. Detroit: Gale Research, 1973- .

Day, Gary. *Literary Criticism: A New History.* Edinburgh, Scotland: Edinburgh University Press, 2008.

Guide to American Poetry Explication. Reference Publication in Literature. 2 vols. Boston: G. K. Hall, 1989.

Jason, Philip K., ed. *Masterplots II: Poetry Series, Revised Edition.* 8 vols. Pasadena, Calif.: Salem Press, 2002.

Kuntz, Joseph M., and Nancy C. Martinez. *Poetry Explication: A Checklist of Interpretation Since 1925 of British and American Poems Past and Present.* 3d ed. Boston: Hall, 1980.

Lodge, David, and Nigel Wood. *Modern Criticism and Theory.* 3d ed. New York: Longman, 2008.

Magill, Frank N., ed. *Magill's Bibliography of Literary Criticism.* 4 vols. Englewood Cliffs, N.J.: Salem Press, 1979.

MLA International Bibliography. New York: Modern Language Association of America, 1922- .

Roberts, Neil, ed. *A Companion to Twentieth-Century Poetry.* Malden, Mass.: Blackwell Publishers, 2001.

Twentieth-Century Literary Criticism. Detroit: Gale Research, 1978- .

Walcutt, Charles Child, and J. Edwin Whitesell, eds. *Modern Poetry.* Vol. 1 in *The Explicator Cyclopedia.* Chicago: Quadrangle Books, 1968.

DICTIONARIES, HISTORIES, AND HANDBOOKS

Carey, Gary, and Mary Ellen Snodgrass. *A Multicultural Dictionary of Literary Terms.* Jefferson, N.C.: McFarland, 1999.

Deutsch, Babette. *Poetry Handbook: A Dictionary of Terms.* 4th ed. New York: Funk & Wagnalls, 1974.

Draper, Ronald P. *An Introduction to Twentieth-Century Poetry in English.* New York: St. Martin's Press, 1999.

Drury, John. *The Poetry Dictionary.* Cincinnati, Ohio: Story Press, 1995.

Gingerich, Martin E. *Contemporary Poetry in America and England, 1950-1975: A Guide to Information Sources.* American Literature, English Literature, and World Literatures in English: An Information Guide Series 41. Detroit: Gale Research, 1983.

Hamilton, Ian, ed. *The Oxford Companion to Twentieth-Century Poetry in English.* New York: Oxford University Press, 1994.

Kamp, Jim, ed. *Reference Guide to American Literature.* 3d ed. Detroit: St. James Press, 1994.

Lennard, John. *The Poetry Handbook: A Guide to Reading Poetry for Pleasure and Practical Criticism.* New York: Oxford University Press, 1996.

Matterson, Stephen, and Darryl Jones. *Studying Poetry*. New York: Oxford University Press, 2000.

Packard, William. *The Poet's Dictionary: A Handbook of Prosody and Poetic Devices*. New York: Harper & Row, 1989.

Parini, Jay, ed. *The Columbia History of American Poetry*. New York: Columbia University Press, 1993.

Perkins, David. *From the 1890's to the High Modernist Mode*. Vol. 1 in *A History of Modern Poetry*. Cambridge, Mass.: Belknap-Harvard University Press, 1976.

_____. *Modernism and After*. Vol. 2 in *A History of Modern Poetry*. 2 vols. Cambridge, Mass.: Belknap-Harvard University Press, 1987.

Perkins, George, Barbara Perkins, and Phillip Leininger, eds. *Benét's Reader's Encyclopedia of American Literature*. New York: HarperCollins, 1991.

Preminger, Alex, et al., eds. *The New Princeton Encyclopedia of Poetry and Poetics*. 3d rev. ed. Princeton, N.J.: Princeton University Press, 1993.

Shucard, Alan. *American Poetry: The Puritans Through Walt Whitman*. Twayne's Critical History of Poetry Series. Boston: Twayne, 1988.

Waggoner, Hyatt H. *American Poets from the Puritans to the Present*. Rev. ed. Baton Rouge: Louisiana University Press, 1984.

INDEXES OF PRIMARY WORKS

American Poetry Index: An Author, Title, and Subject Guide to Poetry by Americans in Single-Author Collections. Great Neck, N.Y.: Granger, 1983-1988.

Annual Index to Poetry in Periodicals. Great Neck, N.Y.: Poetry Index Press, 1985-1988.

Caskey, Jefferson D., comp. *Index to Poetry in Popular Periodicals, 1955-1959*. Westport, Conn.: Greenwood Press, 1984.

Frankovich, Nicholas, ed. *The Columbia Granger's Index to Poetry in Anthologies*. 11th ed. New York: Columbia University Press, 1997.

_____. *The Columbia Granger's Index to Poetry in Collected and Selected Works*. New York: Columbia University Press, 1997.

Guy, Patricia. *A Women's Poetry Index*. Phoenix, Ariz.: Oryx Press, 1985.

Hazen, Edith P., ed. *Columbia Granger's Index to Poetry*. 10th ed. New York: Columbia University Press, 1994.

Hoffman, Herbert H., and Rita Ludwig Hoffman, comps. *International Index to Recorded Poetry*. New York: H. W. Wilson, 1983.

Index of American Periodical Verse. Lanham, Md.: Scarecrow, 1971.

Index to Poetry in Periodicals: American Poetic Renaissance, 1915-1919: An Index of Poets and Poems Published in American Magazines and Newspapers. Great Neck, N.Y.: Granger, 1981.

Index to Poetry in Periodicals, 1920-1924: An Index of Poets and Poems Published in American Magazines and Newspapers. Great Neck, N.Y.: Granger, 1983.

Index to Poetry in Periodicals, 1925-1992: An Index of Poets and Poems Published in American Magazines and Newspapers. Great Neck, N.Y.: Granger, 1984.

Marcan, Peter. *Poetry Themes: A Bibliographical Index to Subject Anthologies and Related Criticisms in the English Language, 1875-1975.* Hamden, Conn.: Linnet Books, 1977.

Poem Finder. Great Neck, N.Y.: Roth, 2000.

Poetry Index Annual: A Title, Author, First Line, Keyword, and Subject Index to Poetry in Anthologies. Great Neck, N.Y.: Poetry Index, 1982-   .

POETICS, POETIC FORMS, AND GENRES

Attridge, Derek. *Poetic Rhythm: An Introduction.* New York: Cambridge University Press, 1995.

Fussell, Paul. *Poetic Meter and Poetic Form.* Rev. ed. New York: McGraw-Hill, 1979.

Hollander, John. *Rhyme's Reason.* 3d ed. New Haven, Conn.: Yale University Press, 2001.

Malof, Joseph. *A Manual of English Meters.* Bloomington: Indiana University Press, 1970.

Padgett, Ron, ed. *The Teachers and Writers Handbook of Poetic Forms.* 2d ed. New York: Teachers & Writers Collaborative, 2000.

Pinsky, Robert. *The Sounds of Poetry: A Brief Guide.* New York: Farrar, Straus and Giroux, 1998.

Preminger, Alex, and T. V. F. Brogan, eds. *New Princeton Encyclopedia of Poetry and Poetics.* 3d ed. Princeton, N.J.: Princeton University Press, 1993.

Shapiro, Karl, and Robert Beum. *A Prosody Handbook.* New York: Harper, 1965.

Turco, Lewis. *The New Book of Forms: A Handbook of Poetics.* Hanover, N.H.: University Press of New England, 1986.

Williams, Miller. *Patterns of Poetry: An Encyclopedia of Forms.* Baton Rouge: Louisiana State University Press, 1986.

AFRICAN AMERICAN POETRY

BIOGRAPHICAL SOURCES

Harris, Trudier, ed. *Afro-American Writers Before the Harlem Renaissance.* Dictionary of Literary Biography 50. Detroit: Gale Research, 1986.

_____. *Afro-American Writers from the Harlem Renaissance to 1940.* Dictionary of Literary Biography 51. Detroit: Gale Research, 1987.

Harris, Trudier, and Thadious M. Davis, eds. *Afro-American Poets Since 1955.* Dictionary of Literary Biography 41. Detroit: Gale Research, 1985.

INDEXES OF PRIMARY WORKS

Chapman, Dorothy Hilton, comp. *Index to Black Poetry.* Boston, G. K. Hall, 1974.

_____. *Index to Poetry by Black American Women.* Bibliographies and Indexes in Afro-American and African Studies 15. New York: Greenwood Press, 1986.

Frankovich, Nicholas, and David Larzelere, eds. *The Columbia Granger's Index to African-American Poetry.* New York: Columbia University Press, 1999.

DICTIONARIES, HISTORIES, AND HANDBOOKS

French, William P., et al. *Afro-American Poetry and Drama, 1760-1975: A Guide to Information Sources.* American Literature, English Literature, and World Literatures in English: An Information Guide Series 17. Detroit: Gale Research, 1979.

Lee, Valerie, ed. *The Prentice Hall Anthology of African American Women's Literature.* Upper Saddle River, N.J.: Pearson Prentice Hall, 2006.

Major, Clarence, ed. *The Garden Thrives: Twentieth Century African-American Poetry.* New York: HarperPerennial, 1996.

Rampersad, Arnold, and Hilary Herbold, eds. *The Oxford Anthology of African-American Poetry.* New York: Oxford University Press, 2005.

Sherman, Joan R. *Invisible Poets: Afro-Americans of the Nineteenth Century.* 2d ed. Urbana: University of Illinois Press, 1989.

Wagner, Jean, and Kenneth Douglas, trans. *Black Poets of the United States: From Paul Laurence Dunbar to Langston Hughes.* Urbana: University of Illinois Press, 1973.

Maura Ives

Updated by Tracy Irons-Georges

GUIDE TO ONLINE RESOURCES

The following sites were visited by the editors of Salem Press in 2010. Because URLs frequently change, the accuracy of these addresses cannot be guaranteed; however, long-standing sites, such as those of colleges and universities, national organizations, and government agencies, generally maintain links when their sites are moved.

Academy of American Poets
http://www.poets.org

The mission of the Academy of American Poets is to "support American poets at all stages of their careers and to foster the appreciation of contemporary poetry." The academy's comprehensive Web site features information on poetic schools and movements; a Poetic Forms Database; an Online Poetry Classroom, with educator and teaching resources; an index of poets and poems; essays and interviews; general Web resources; links for further study; and more.

The Cambridge History of English and American Literature
http://www.bartleby.com/cambridge

This site provides an exhaustive examination of the development of all forms of literature in Great Britain and the United States. The multivolume set on which this site is based was published in 1907-1921 but remains a relevant, classic work. It offers "a wide selection of writing on orators, humorists, poets, newspaper columnists, religious leaders, economists, Native Americans, song writers, and even non-English writing, such as Yiddish and Creole."

A Celebration of Women Writers
http://digital.library.upenn.edu/women

This site is an extensive compendium on the contributions of women writers throughout history. The "Local Editions by Authors" and "Local Editions by Category" pages include access to electronic texts of the works of numerous writers. Users can also access biographical and bibliographical information by browsing lists arranged by writers' names, countries of origin, ethnicities, and the centuries in which they lived.

LiteraryHistory.com
http://www.literaryhistory.com

This site is an excellent source of academic, scholarly, and critical literature about eighteenth, nineteenth, and twentieth century American and English writers. It provides numerous pages about specific eras and genres, including individual pages for eighteenth, nineteenth, and twentieth century literature and for African American and postcolonial literatures. These pages contain alphabetical lists of authors that link to articles, reviews, overviews, excerpts of works, teaching guides, podcasts, and other materials.

The Modern Word: Authors of the Libyrinth
http://www.themodernword.com/authors.html

The Modern Word site, although somewhat haphazard in its organization, provides a great deal of critical information about writers. The "Authors of the Libyrinth" page is very useful, linking author names to essays about them and other resources. The section of the page headed "The Scriptorium" presents "an index of pages featuring writers who have pushed the edges of their medium, combining literary talent with a sense of experimentation to produce some remarkable works of modern literature."

Outline of American Literature
http://www.america.gov/publications/books/outline-of-american-literature.html

This page of the America.gov site provides access to an electronic version of the ten-chapter volume *Outline of American Literature*, a historical overview of poetry and prose from colonial times to the present published by the Bureau of International Information Programs of the U.S. Department of State.

Poetry Foundation
http://www.poetryfoundation.org

The Poetry Foundation, publisher of *Poetry* magazine, is an independent literary organization. Its Web site offers links to essays; news; events; online poetry resources, such as blogs, organizations, publications, and references and research; a glossary of literary terms; and a Learning Lab that includes poem guides and essays on poetics.

Representative Poetry Online
http://rpo.library.utoronto.ca

This award-winning resource site, maintained by Ian Lancashire of the Department of English at the University of Toronto in Canada, has several thousand English-language poems by hundreds of poets. The collection is searchable by poet's name, title of work, first line of a poem, and keyword. The site also includes a time line, a glossary, essays, an extensive bibliography, and countless links organized by country and by subject.

Voice of the Shuttle
http://vos.ucsb.edu

One of the most complete and authoritative places for online information about literature, Voice of the Shuttle is maintained by professors and students in the English Department at the University of California, Santa Barbara. The site provides countless links to electronic books, academic journals, literary association Web sites, sites created by university professors, and many other resources.

Voices from the Gaps
http://voices.cla.umn.edu/

Voices from the Gaps is a site of the English Department at the University of Minnesota, dedicated to providing resources on the study of women artists of color, including writers. The site features a comprehensive index searchable by name, and it provides biographical information on each writer or artist and other resources for further study.

ELECTRONIC DATABASES

Electronic databases usually do not have their own URLs. Instead, public, college, and university libraries subscribe to these databases, provide links to them on their Web sites, and make them available to library card holders or other specified patrons. Readers can visit library Web sites or ask reference librarians to check on availability.

Literary Reference Center

EBSCO's Literary Reference Center (LRC) is a comprehensive full-text database designed primarily to help high school and undergraduate students in English and the humanities with homework and research assignments about literature. The database contains massive amounts of information from reference works, books, literary journals, and other materials, including more than 31,000 plot summaries, synopses, and overviews of literary works; almost 100,000 essays and articles of literary criticism; about 140,000 author biographies; more than 605,000 book reviews; and more than 5,200 author interviews. It also contains the entire contents of Salem Press's MagillOnLiterature Plus. Users can retrieve information by browsing a list of authors' names or titles of literary works; they can also use an advanced search engine to access information by numerous categories, including author name, gender, cultural identity, national identity, and the years in which he or she lived, or by literary title, character, locale, genre, and publication date. The Literary Reference Center also features a literary-historical time line, an encyclopedia of literature, and a glossary of literary terms.

MagillOnLiterature Plus

MagillOnLiterature Plus is a comprehensive, integrated literature database produced by Salem Press and available on the EBSCOhost platform. The database contains the full text of essays in Salem's many literature-related reference works, including *Masterplots*, *Cyclopedia of World Authors*, *Cyclopedia of Literary Characters*, *Cyclopedia of Literary Places*, *Critical Survey of Poetry*, *Critical Survey of Long Fiction*, *Critical Survey of Short Fiction*, *World Philosophers and Their Works*, *Magill's Literary Annual*, and *Magill's Book Reviews*. Among its contents are articles on more than 35,000 literary works and more than 8,500 poets, writers, dramatists, essayists, and philosophers; more than 1,000 images; and a glossary of more than 1,300 literary terms. The biographical essays include lists of authors' works and secondary bibliographies, and hundreds of overview essays examine and discuss literary genres, time periods, and national literatures.

Rebecca Kuzins; updated by Desiree Dreeuws

CATEGORY INDEX

SUBJECT INDEX